The Economics of Irving Fisher

The Economics of Irving Fisher

Reviewing the Scientific Work of a
Great Economist

Edited by

Hans-E. Loef

University of Siegen, Germany

and

Hans G. Monissen

University of Würzburg, Germany

Edward Elgar
Cheltenham, UK • Northampton, MA, USA

Published by
Edward Elgar Publishing Limited
Glensanda House
Montpellier Parade
Cheltenham
Glos GL50 1UA
UK

Edward Elgar Publishing, Inc.
6 Market Street
Northampton
Massachusetts 01060
USA

A catalogue record for this book
is available from the British Library

Library of Congress Cataloguing in Publication Data

The economics of Irving Fisher: reviewing the scientific work of a
   great economist / edited by Hans-E. Loef and Hans G. Monissen.
      A collection of 14 papers presented at a conference of the Irving
   -Fisher-Gesellschaft held May 22–24, 1997, Königstein, Germany, in
   commemoration of the 50th anniversary of Fisher's death, with the
   addition of some reprints of non-conference papers.
      Includes bibliographical references and index.
      1. Fisher, Irving, 1867–1947. 2. Economists—United States—
   Congresses. 3. Macroeconomics—Congresses. 4. Economics—
   Statistical methods—Congresses. 5. Econometrics—Congresses.
   I. Fisher, Irving, 1867–1947. II. Loef, Hans-Edi. III. Monissen,
   Hans G.
   HB119.F5E27 1999
   330.1—dc21   98–50845
                                                                    CIP

ISBN 1 84064 037 5

Printed and bound in Great Britain by
Biddles Ltd, Guildford and King's Lynn

Contents

List of Figures

List of Tables

List of Contributors

Volbert Alexander is Professor of Economics at the University of Gießen, Germany.

William J. Barber is Emeritus Professor of Economics at Wesleyan University, Middletown, CN, USA.

Dr. János Barta is *Assistent* at the Institute for Operations Research and Mathematical Methods, University of Zürich, Switzerland.

Dr. Udo Broll is *Privatdozent* in the Department of Economics at the University of München, Germany.

Volker Caspari is Professor of Economics at the University of Darmstadt, Germany.

John S. Chipman is Regents' Professor of Economics at the University of Minnesota, MN, USA.

Robert W. Dimand is Professor of Economics at Brock University, St. Catharines, Canada.

Horst Entorf is Professor of Econometrics at the University of Würzburg, Germany.

Dr. Clemens Fuest is *Assistent* at the Staatswirtschaftliches Institut, University of München, Germany.

Andreas Gintschel is a Ph.D. student at the University of Rochester; NY, USA.

Thomas M. Humphrey is Vice President and Economist at the Federal Reserve Bank of Richmond, VA, USA.

Jan A. Kregel is Professor of Economics at the University of Bologna, Italy.

Hans-E. Loef is Professor of Economics at the University of Siegen, Germany.

Hellmuth Milde is Professor of Business Administration at the University of Trier, Germany.

Hans G. Monissen is Professor of Economics at the University of Würzburg, Germany.

Christian Scheer is Professor of Public Finance at the University of Hamburg, Germany.

Bertram Schefold is Professor of Economics, University of Frankfurt, Germany.

Norbert Schulz is Professor of Economics, University of Würzburg, Germany.

Dr. Ulrich Schwalbe is *Privatdozent* in the Department of Economics at the University of Mannheim, Germany.

Frank G. Steindl is Regents' Professor of Economics and Ardmore Professor of Business Administration at the Oklahoma State University, Stillwater, OK, USA.

Preface

This volume on *The Economics of Irving Fisher: Reviewing the Scientific Work of a Great Economist* compiles 14 invited papers – not including three related comments – presented at the conference of the Irving-Fisher-Gesellschaft in commemoration of the scholar whose name the society bears on the occasion of the 50th anniversary of his death. The fortunate circumstance that William J. Barber was able to participate in the conference was sufficient reason to relieve the editors of the burden of offering their own summary evaluation of the life and works of Irving Fisher. With the permission of Pickering and Chatto Publishers Ltd., London, they made the wise decision to reprint William J. Barber's 'Irving Fisher (1867-1947): Career Highlights and Formative Influences' the introductory article to *The Works of Irving Fisher* which he published as the main editor.* A planned paper with the aim of demonstrating the particular importance of Irving Fisher for the development of modern business administration became the victim of special circumstances. Therefore, the editors decided to include an additional paper by Andreas Gintschel – a young Ph.D. student at the University of Rochester – as a partial compensation. The paper bears the title 'Beyond Fisher's NPV? Much Ado About Nothing!'. Robert W. Dimand contributed two papers to the present volume: one piece was written for the conference, another one on 'Irving Fisher's Debt Deflation Theory of Great Depressions' is included as a reprint. As in the case of William Barber, Robert Dimand's unrivaled familiarity with the works of Irving Fisher was taken into account. A competing duplication of the subject was considered to be a second-best solution.

An indispensable condition for organizing an international conference is the provision of adequate funding: The editors would like to express their sincere gratitude to the board of directors and especially to Professor Christian Seidel of the Dresdner Bank AG. In addition to generous financial support the Dresdner Bank provided the intellectually stimulating atmosphere of its guesthouse in Königstein. The editors are also grateful to their friend and colleague Volbert Alexander who did more than just establish contacts to our sponsors.

Bettina Monissen first worked as an efficient conference secretary. In addition, without her commitment and motivation the present volume would not have been presented. It was with particular diligence and patience that she prepared the camera ready copies for Edward Elgar.

* The fourteen volumes of Fisher's *Works* are listed on page 18 of William J. Barber's article. Pickering and Chatto made it possible to present these 14 volumes at the conference to a deeply impressed group of international scholars.

Hans-E. Loef
Hans G. Monissen

The Irving-Fisher-Gesellschaft (IFG)

The Irving-Fisher-Gesellschaft e.V. – Gesellschaft für Geld- und Währungs-fragen was founded in 1989 in Frankfurt/Main on the initiative of Hans Cohrssen who alongside the editors of this volume was among the founding members of the society. During the formative years of the IFG he served as its secretary.

It was Hans Cohrssen, then 84 years old, who urged his young co-members to discuss not only more arcane monetary-theory and monetary-policy issues but to also institutionalize a forum to address broader economic and political problems of the day. This clearly reflects the influence of his mentor: Hans Cohrssen was associated with Irving Fisher from 1937 to 1942. Irving Fisher recorded his association with Hans Cohrssen in a certificate informing us that

he has been the most valuable assistant I have ever had

and continued

at a time of uncertainty such as the present, with drastic business regulation and dislocated production consequent upon foreign events, and possibly impending in-flation, a man of his ability and experience should prove particularly valuable.

The founding members thought that these historical circumstances together with the society's explicit commitment to monetary stability would justify the fact that the society bears Irving Fisher's name.*

Hans Cohrssen died on January 10, 1997 at the age of 92, four months be-fore Fisher's anniversary conference took place, an event which he consid-ered a culmination of his own economic endeavors. On behalf of all members the editors would like to take the opportunity to acknowledge his efforts in founding and promoting the ideas and purposes of the IFG. The by-laws of the society preserve Hans Cohrssen's timeless influence:

The purpose of the Irving-Fisher-Gesellschaft is to study and disseminate informa-tion on monetary relationships in the economy and their effects upon the wellbeing of the individual and the welfare of the society.

An orderly, stable national and international monetary system is the basic prerequisite for a free and legitimate economic and social order. Without such monetary order, the coordination of economic forces cannot be realized. Obvious consequences here include monetary instability, disorder in public finances, suboptimal credit structures, and national and international debt problems. Even more grave, though less evident, are repercussions varying from unemployment, misallocation of economic resources to political and social instability.

Research and dissemination of information on these relationships and their consequences for human welfare is a prime educational task. Topics include the basic requirements for a suitable monetary order and its practical implementation. There is a need for the wide distribution of easily understood information on the principles of a proper monetary order.

The Irving-Fisher-Gesellschaft contributes towards the development and adoption of a suitable monetary order by initiating and supporting scientific research and organizing conferences on monetary issues.

From 1990 onwards the IFG has organized five major conferences: Problems discussed and analyzed among others have focused on sound money and central bank independence, monetary problems of countries in transition, and monetary policy with the European Central Bank. The conference in 1997 was exclusively dedicated to *The Works of Irving Fisher*. The proceedings of this conference are compiled in this volume.

---

* Speaking for the founding members we have to admit that we were unaware of the fact that in 1946 Irving Fisher originated a foundation bearing his name: Cf. 'An Address on the Fisher Foundation' by Irving Fisher, September 11, 1946, reproduced in Fisher's *Works* (see page 18 of this volume), Volume 1, pp. 22-37.

Hans-E. Loef
Hans G. Monissen

Introduction

In trying to provide an integrated structure to the volume the editors organized the contributions into seven parts summarizing Irving Fisher's special fields of research and his associated publications in economics. Part One highlights his economic endeavors during his career, relying on published documents as well as on valuable information contained in letters and related material. The next three parts (Two to Four) are devoted to Irving Fisher's works on macroeconomics and related policy recommendations, while the last three parts (Five to Seven) deal with his research in statistics and econometrics, his famous work on the theory of income, interest, and capital, as well as his 'microeconomic' investigations summarized under the heading 'Value, Prices, and Financial Assets'. Even though this classification may appear rather arbitrary or *ad hoc*, the editors thought that this would be an appropriate procedure to reconstruct the works of our great economist.

It seems – possibly induced by the proposed classification – that Fisher's economic endeavors are temporarily and thematically disparate or disconnected. This, however, would do Fisher an injustice. In his 'An Address on the Irving Fisher Foundation' Fisher wrote on September 11, 1946:

> It will be noticed that in the field of economics – and even more in other fields – my endeavors to contribute anything new to economic science have been confined to monograph-writing, each monograph being a little brick, as it were, in the great structure of human knowledge. Probably this fact has given many the impression that my work has consisted of totally disconnected items. This, however, is scarcely a correct impression. On the contrary there are, in almost all cases, close relationships between the monographs.

The central theme of Irving Fisher's writings in economic science is the problem of what he called 'the betterment of the masses' which he sees not primarily as one of distribution but mainly as one of production. Therefore, the following chapters with their emphasis on special aspects of the general economic problem should be treated as an attempt to pay tribute to the immense work and efforts of Irving Fisher in making general economics a genuine science on the basis of a strong commitment to economic welfare.

Since there are many as well as excellent biographies about Irving Fisher we decided against including a new one in this volume which could have only replicated and reiterated what others have already said. As mentioned in the *Preface* the editors decided to include the reprint of a paper by William J. Barber from Fisher's *Works*. Barber describes Fisher's development into an internationally recognized scientist and policy adviser where the personal circumstances of Fisher's life form the background of his academic career. In doing so, Barber not only relies on Fisher's main scientific publications but also on letters Fisher wrote to various persons. In Chapter 2 William J. Barber reports about his work in evaluating the papers Fisher wrote during his lifetime, including articles in professional and popular periodicals, letters to editors, newspaper columns, and Fisher's less readily available personal correspondence, most of which is housed in the Manuscripts and Archives Collections of Yale University.

Chapter 3 on 'Irving Fisher's Monetary Macroeconomics' by Robert W. Dimand is the first of two papers which are especially concerned with Fisher's contributions to macroeconomics and the quantity theory (Part Two). Dimand argues that, in historical perspective, Fisher can now be recognized as one of the most fruitful innovators in the development of theoretical and empirical monetary macroeconomics. This chapter focuses on Fisher's reformulating the quantity theory of money and presenting his monetary theory of economic fluctuations as it is outlined in his *The Purchasing Power of Money*. The book's contribution is examined, with particular references to its influence on Fisher's later work and on subsequent developments in macroeconomics.

The second paper with special emphasis on the quantity theory of money appears as Chapter 4. Thomas M. Humphrey investigates the interpretations of the quantity theory of money by Irving Fisher and Knut Wicksell. Despite their differing interpretations of the quantity theory, both Fisher and Wicksell used it to argue that the monetary authority possesses the power to stabilize the price level. According to them, the authority stabilizes prices by adjusting its direct operating instrument – whether gold content of the dollar, monetary base, or central bank interest rate – in response to price level deviations from target. Fisher and Wicksell maintained that the stock of monetary purchasing power is the crucial intermediate variable through which instrument adjustment influences prices.

The first main sections of Chapter 5 of Part Three are a natural extension of the previously discussed monetary macroeconomics in Fisher's work. Hans-E. Loef and Hans G. Monissen describe four important phases in Fisher's life as a monetary reformer and crusader. These four episodes were supported by Fisher's theoretical investigations in monetary problems and his special concern about stabilizing the purchasing power of money. In the second part of the chapter the authors develop a simple monetary model which contains Fisher's essential quantity theoretic insights. In its steady-state or equilibrium solution the model exhibits the well-known quantity theoretic results and shows that money is both neutral and super-neutral with respect to real variables. By applying appropriate monetary policy rules, the monetary authorities, during the more important transition periods where both neutrality propositions do not apply, would be able to stabilize the purchasing power of money as well as avoiding fluctuations in economic activity.

Even though Fisher did not spend much effort on discussing fiscal policy matters in general, his proposals with respect to taxation are still taken into consideration in the modern theory of optimal taxation. Clemens Fuest in Chapter 6 discusses Irving Fisher's contribution to the debate on income versus consumption taxation. He gives a survey of the main arguments which play a role in the modern debate on this issue and emphasizes the importance of Irving Fisher's contribution to the subject. Departing from a summary of Fisher's proposals for a reform of the classical income tax system, efficiency and equity aspects of the consumption versus income tax controversy are discussed. Implications of international economic integration, practical solution schemes and problems of switching from an income tax system to a consumption tax system are taken into consideration as well.

While Volbert Alexander provides a supplementary note to Chapter 5, Christian Scheer discusses the modern interpretation of a constructive income taxation by Clemens Fuest in a comment to Chapter 6.

The foregoing chapters (3 to 5) outlined Fisher's monetary macroeconomics and policy proposals, as they are rooted in the quantity theory tradition. However, the Great Depression with its worldwide, and Fisher's personal, financial disaster changed his emphasis with respect to the cause of economic fluctuations and depressions in particular. In Chapter 7 of Part Four Robert W. Dimand shows that Fisher in his *Booms and Depressions* and 'The Debt-Deflation Theory of Great Depressions' went beyond his earlier analysis of the so-called business cycle as a 'dance of the dollar', to try to explain why a deep and lasting depression could sometimes occur. Fisher argued that unanticipated increases in the real value of inside debt is not neutral, as increased risk of bankruptcy undermines confidence, causing a scramble for liquidity that further increases the real value of the debt and depresses spending. A model of Fisher's debt-deflation theory is suggested, drawing on works by James Tobin.

In the same vein Frank G. Steindl argues in Chapter 8 of the same Part Four that Fisher, remarkably, revised his views about the causes of depressions and the necessary policy proposals for the remedy. This change of emphasis led Fisher to an interpretation of the Great Depression and a proposed solution which contrasted fundamentally with that for which the pre-depression Fisher would have crusaded. While in his quantity theoretic phase Fisher accepted the notion of an exogenously determined supply of money which in turn influenced prices and in the short-run real activity, in the after-depression phase, for him, money was now endogenously determined with the slide in prices and output resulting from attempts to reduce an exogenously given state of general over-indebtedness. Besides stamp script Fisher proposed reflation as the necessary monetary policy actions as a remedy.

Part Five of the volume, consisting of three chapters, concentrates on aspects of statistics, econometrics, and index numbers in Irving Fisher's work. In Chapter 9 John S. Chipman examines three of Fisher's contributions to economic statistics and econometrics. First, Fisher's 1892 formulation of the measurement of marginal utility is examined critically, as well as his improved 1927 formulation; it is shown that had he made full use of his assumptions, he would have concluded that the optimal income tax was proportional rather than progressive. Second, Chipman argues that Fisher's 1913 method of testing the quantity theory of money failed to conform to his 'factor reversal test' or 'total value criterion', and thus consisted in comparing a Paasche with a Laspeyres price index. Third, Fisher's series of studies from 1923 to 1937 deriving a close statistical relationship between trade, employment, and interest rates (as dependent variables) and a distributed lag of past inflation rates (as independent variable) – a kind of 'acceleration principle' – could have been used to predict the Great Depression.

A special piece of empirical work in Fisher's writings was later identified as a forerunner of the so-called 'Phillips-Curve'. Horst Entorf replicates Fisher's search for a statistical relation between employment and price changes using data for the United States and Germany, 1960-1995. Using Fisher's method and the recent data it is shown in Chapter 10 that Fisher's correlation method of analyzing the relationship is still valid. However, Entorf in his investigation is not able to confirm the lead of price changes over employment, as Fisher did. Instead, the author finds that shocks to labor demand anticipate price instability in the countries and period under his investigation.

Chapter 11 by János Barta highlights Irving Fisher's contributions to index number theory from the perspective of a mathematician. He recalls that Fisher is a pioneer in mathematical statistics and shows some of his main achievements in the domain of price index theory. The well-known price indices of Laspeyres, Paasche and Fisher are presented in a mathematical framework. Furthermore the Divisia indices and their specialization by Arthur Vogt are introduced. Fisher's two great reversal tests, the time reversal test and the factor reversal test, are discussed in a subsection. Fisher also introduced the idea of antitheses of price indices, which, many years later, led to the discovery of astonishing mathematical properties in price index theory. The need of a rigorous definition of price indices induced the search for a suitable axioms system. This question resulted in many answers, but no definitive and universally accepted solution. Some of the most recent contributions to the axiomatics of price index theory are discussed by Barta in this chapter.

The title of Chapter 12 written by Bertram Schefold is a compound of Fisher's main contributions to the theory of capital, income, and interest, namely his *The Nature of Capital and Income* and his *The Rate of Interest*. After a short discussion of *The Nature of Capital and Income* in a sub-section with reference to Fisher's book of the same title the author turns to the conceptual foundations of Fisher's theory of interest. In essence Schefold compares Fisher's interpretations of interest rates with those of Böhm-Bawerk. He considers their contributions to special problems of the theory of capital: the productivity of a system determining an upper limit for the rate of interest and the period of production used to specify the actual rate. Turning to Fisher's *Appreciation and Interest* the distinction of own-rates of interest, money-rates of interest and the real-rates of interest becomes crucial. Fisher's distinction between the productivity or investment opportunity side and the subjective or 'impatience' side of the determination of interest rates is taken up by Schefold in a sub-section entitled 'Intertemporal and Long Period Equilibrium' where tribute is paid to Fisher's *The Theory of Interest*. In a comment on Schefold Volker Caspari discusses further the relation between intertemporal and long-period equilibrium and that between the money-rate and the own-rates of interest.

Additional elaboration on Fisher's contributions to the theory of capital, income, and interest are provided by Jan A. Kregel in Chapter 13. He considers Fisher as one of the founders of the financial macroeconomics approach and as part of a group of economists which included Hayek, Böhm-Bawerk, Schumpeter, Wicksell, Hawtrey, Robertson and Keynes. It is the comparison of Fisher's contributions to the theory of financial macroeconomics and Keynes' theory of investment and output which constitutes the main part of this chapter.

The last Part of this volume might be seen as more on the microeconomic level of Fisher's work on value, prices, and financial assets than the foregoing two chapters.

Chapter 14 discusses Irving Fisher's doctoral dissertation *Mathematical Investigations in the Theory of Value and Prices* which contains important contributions to general equilibrium theory as well as to consumer and utility theory. Ulrich Schwalbe shows that, in contrast to what is claimed in the literature, Fisher's definition of an exchange economy does not constitute a general equilibrium system, and his model of a production economy is formally equivalent to an exchange economy. To illustrate an equilibrium graphically, Fisher developed a device which is known as the 'net trade diagram'. This concept has recently been rediscovered as an alternative to the well-known Edgeworth box. In a comment to Schwalbe Norbert Schulz deplores the fact that Fisher's work has disappeared from the history of general equilibrium theory. He stresses the important point that his formulation of general equilibrium uses only information on marginal utilities.

The last two chapters are concerned with special aspects of financial assets. Udo Broll and Hellmuth Milde examine in Chapter 15 the investment and hedging decision of a risk-averse decision maker, where the output prices and financial returns are assumed to be uncertain. They confirm the Fisher separation theorem and the full-double hedge theorem.

Andreas Gintschel in Chapter 16 analyzes the application of the net present value criterion which has already been derived by Irving Fisher in his capital theory considerations for a world of uncertainty. While the recently popularized real-options approach to analyzing investment projects is sometimes propagated as superior to the net present value analysis Gintschel rejects this claim since it relies on an erroneous calculation of expected cash-flows. By means of a simple example, he demonstrates the general fact that net present value, state pricing, and the real-options approach are consistent.

Hans-E. Loef
Hans G. Monissen

PART ONE:
IRVING FISHER'S WORKS
AND CORRESPONDENCE

1. Irving Fisher (1867-1947): Career Highlights and Formative Influences*

William J. Barber

Most members of the generation of American economists who came to professional maturity in the last two decades of the nineteenth century approached their discipline with a conditioning acquired from post-graduate study in Germany. Those who shared that experience were prominent in the formation of the American Economic Association in 1885 – among them, Richard T. Ely, John Bates Clark, Henry Carter Adams, and Edwin R.A. Seligman.

Irving Fisher was a significant exception. All of his formal academic training – from his undergraduate work through the completion of his Ph.D. in 1891 – took place on American soil and at a single institution, Yale University. Unlike most of his contemporaries, he was innocent of direct exposure to the doctrines of the 'German Historical School', which spurned abstract theorizing and urged the intervention of the state to improve economic life. Fisher's career path was molded by distinctly different intellectual influences. His early work in mathematics – the subject of his undergraduate concentration – predisposed him in favor of abstract reasoning and persuaded him that mathematical tools were essential if the discipline of economics were to acquire genuine scientific standing. In addition, he felt the impact of the teachings of Yale's William Graham Sumner, the nation's most prominent 'Social Darwinist'. Preaching the virtues of unbridled *laissez-faire*, Sumner was the *bête noire* of the German-educated 'Young Turks' who organized themselves as the American Economic Association. Though Fisher was to distance himself from Sumner's views on the futility of social reforms, he nonetheless hailed Sumner as 'the inspirer'.

On the occasion of his seventh-fifth birthday, Fisher reminisced as follows about the early phases of his intellectual development:

> I entered economics from the side of mathematics ... . (W)hen a mathematics teacher got me started in the beauties of mathematics, I suddenly, and thereafter rapidly, took an enthusiastic interest in the subject, which lasted through preparatory school and college and into Graduate School at Yale, where I was preparing to be a teacher of mathematics. It was there that I came in contact with J.

Willard Gibbs, the greatest mind which I have ever met in my life, except Einstein, and probably the greatest mathematical and scientific mind which Yale has ever produced ... . Up to this time the only economics I had ever taken was an elementary course under Professor [Arthur T.] Hadley when I was an undergraduate. Later he and I were colleagues and life-long friends before and after he became President of Yale ... . But before I really became his colleague, and while I was still studying for a mathematical education, I took a course under Sumner. Billy Sumner, as we called him, was perhaps the most picturesque figure in American economics, and, in his day, the leading economist.

I took his courses, however, not because I ever expected to enter economics, but because I wanted to meet such a personality before leaving Yale. The more I saw of him, the more I wanted to get his point of view, so that when the time came to select my thesis, I found that I had devoted nearly half of my time to his courses. I went to him and told him that I was perplexed as to what to choose for a doctor's thesis, since half of my time had been outside of my field of mathematics and instead in his field of economics. He said 'Why don't you write on mathematical economics?' I replied 'I have never heard of such a subject'. He said 'That is because I myself have never studied it enough to use it, but I can put you on to the literature.' The result was that I became fascinated with Cournot, with Walras, and with Jevons, not to mention Auspitz and Lieben, joint authors of a book called *Untersuchungen über die Theorie des Preises* [1889], a book which I studied perhaps more thoroughly than any other, though it has had few readers (Transcript of a talk by Irving Fisher to the Economics Department of Harvard University on the 75th anniversary of his birth, Cambridge, MA, February 27, 1942, Yale University Archives).

This was the route Fisher traveled to the preparation of *Mathematical Investigations in the Theory of Value and Prices* (1892), a work which the first American Nobel Laureate in Economics – Paul Samuelson – has characterized as the 'greatest doctoral dissertation in economics ever written'.

1 YALE AS A LAUNCHING PAD

When viewed against the backdrop of his personal circumstances at the time, Fisher's accomplishments as a student at Yale can be seen to be all the more remarkable. His father, a Congregational clergyman, had died of tuberculosis only two months before Irving Fisher enrolled as a freshman. Primary responsibility for the support of the Fisher household (which included his widowed mother and a younger brother) fell to the seventeen-year old Irving. In the ensuing years, he managed to keep the family afloat financially with fees earned from tutoring and with prize monies awarded in recognition of his academic distinctions.

More than most of his classmates, Fisher had an incentive to excel in student competitions. Even if no cash awards had been at stake, there can be little doubt that he would still have displayed a determination to succeed. Throughout his undergraduate years, his major competitor was Henry L. Stimson, a fellow member of the Yale class of 1888. Fisher bested Stimson by becoming the class valedictorian, but had to settle for being runner-up to him in the prestigious oratorical competitions. Stimson went on to a distinguished public career, serving as Secretary of War (1911-1913), as Secretary of State (1929-1933), and as Secretary of War (1940-1945). The paths of the two men crossed frequently during their mature years. An element of friendly rivalry in their relationship was to persist.

When he completed his doctoral studies in 1891, Fisher's career trajectory appeared to be the standard one for an academic mathematician. Though he had decided to write a dissertation in mathematical economics, mathematics was still his primary disciplinary loyalty. His appointment as an instructor in Yale's Department of Mathematics in 1891 – and his promotion to an assistant professorship a year later – seemed to follow naturally. The first phase in his transition to economics was profoundly affected by a happy change in his personal situation in 1893, when he married Margaret Hazard, the daughter of a wealthy manufacturer of woolen textiles. (Fisher was often to declare that, for his part, this union was a case of 'love at first sight'.) As a wedding gift, Fisher's father-in-law underwrote a year-long trip to Europe for the young couple.

This *Wanderjahr* enabled Fisher to feel the pulse of what was going on in European economics and it provided him with opportunities to meet a number of the discipline's luminaries as well. He was not impressed by his exposure to German economics. Writing to his mother from Berlin in November 1893, he observed:

> Yesterday I tried another course in Economics and was quite disgusted. I guess Prof. Sumner is right in thinking ill of German economics. The *Germans* however fancy themselves quite ahead of the rest of the world in this as in other branches (Fisher to Ella Wescott Fisher, November 5, 1893, emphasis in original).

His contacts with economists interested in applying mathematical techniques were quite another matter. He noted with satisfaction, as he informed a close friend from high-school days, 'my little book [*Mathematical Investigations*] had really made a small path before me. It was at least a letter introduction to a great many people' (Fisher to William Greenleaf Eliot, March 25, 1894). In Rome, he made the acquaintance of Pantaleoni and, in Lausanne, he met Pareto and Walras. His visit to Vienna included sessions with Menger, Böhm-Bawerk, and Lieben. 'All of these men' [in the Viennese contingent], he reported, 'knew my name, tho none of them are mathematical economists ... . Menger was very cordial and had me to lunch with him.' He added that Menger believes that the immediate work in economics of clearing up ideas is to be done by himself and his school, but later – say thirty years from now – the mathematical method will come in for the 'finishment' of the science. He does not impress one as the German Profs. do, as eaten up with conceit ... (Fisher to Ella Wescott Fisher, January 28, 1894).[1]

A significant milestone in Fisher's professional reorientation was a by-product of his contact with Francis Y. Edgeworth, Professor of Political Economy in the University of Oxford and the editor of the *Economic Journal*. Edgeworth was familiar with the published version of Fisher's Ph.D. dissertation and invited him to prepare a paper in which the hydrostatic model developed therein would be applied in the analysis of a real-world problem. The resulting essay – 'The Mechanics of Bimetallism' ([1894] 1997, Volume 1) – was initially presented at the meeting of the Economics Section of the British Association for the Advancement of Science in 1894. This exercise marked Fisher's initial engagement with a hotly disputed issue of economic policy. At the time it was written, he acknowledged that he had little acquaintance with the economic literature on bimetallism.

A shift in Fisher's departmental affiliation at Yale – from the Department of Mathematics to the Department of Political Economy – was formally accomplished in mid-1895. He welcomed this reassignment, writing at the time that

I am delighted with the opportunity to be in touch with human life so directly and shall find no lack of opportunity to use my mathematical training. This had been my one regret about the mathematical life – its lack of direct contact with the living age (Fisher to William Greenleaf Eliot, July 29,1895).

Reflecting on this episode in his life nearly a half century later, he enlarged on this theme:

I was beginning to feel that, while I loved pure mathematics and could get more intellectual pleasure from working in that field than I could in the more empirical field of economics, it was a sort of selfish indulgence like chess-playing or spending one's time with crossword puzzles, while the great work of the world was needing to be done. Perhaps there was born in me the yearning of a reformer, since my father was a preacher (Transcript of a talk by Irving Fisher to the Economics Department of Harvard University, February 27, 1942).

The monograph entitled *Appreciation and Interest* ([1896] 1997, Volume 1, part C) was Fisher's first substantial contribution from his base in a Department of Political Economy. This analysis clearly bears the imprint of the moment in American history at which it was written. The timing of its publication coincided with the populist campaign for the Presidency of William Jennings Bryan whose battle cry was 'free coinage of silver' at a silver-gold ratio of 16:1. When drafting this document, Fisher informed a correspondent that he was

> working on an essay which will either be a long article or a short book on bimetallism *against* its expediency or necessity ... . I never was so morally aroused I think as against the 'silver craze' (Fisher to William Greenleaf Eliot, July 29, 1895, emphasis in original).

Fisher's findings in this work struck a responsive chord among champions of 'sound money' in the controversies of the 1890s. They were also received appreciatively in Britain.[2] In the 1930s – when Fisher was championing some heterodox monetary interventions – he expressed regret that, in his youthful exuberance, he had not been more sympathetic to the objectives of the bimetallists in the 1890s.

In 1896 and 1897, Fisher also began to lay the groundwork for a fresh conceptualization of the nature of capital, a topic that was to be a central preoccupation for the remainder of his career.[3] Along the way, he treated – in embryonic form – a number of additional themes that were to become his stock in trade: among them, the quantity theory of money, a distinction between savings and income, and the importance of the rate of interest. These analytic enterprises, however, were interrupted by personal tragedy. In the summer of 1898 – shortly after his elevation to full professorship at Yale – Fisher was informed that he had contracted tuberculosis, the disease that had claimed his father's life some fourteen years earlier.

2   THE BATTLE AGAINST TUBERCULOSIS AND ITS IMPACT ON THE CAREER TRAJECTORY

Fisher's successful battle against tuberculosis led him to re-order his priorities. The recovery process itself took three years – first, at Saranac Lake in the Adirondacks, subsequently at Colorado Springs and Santa Barbara, California. Even though he resumed teaching at Yale on a part-time basis in the autumn of 1901, it was another three years before he regained full strength. He was often to remark that six years of his life had effectively been wasted and that it was thus all the more important that he operate at peak efficiency in order to make up for the 'waste spaces'. In a self-assessment prepared in the mid-1920s, Fisher wrote:

> My illness and the enforced idleness for several years, during which I had much occasion to think of the vital problems of life and death, greatly changed my point of view from that of an academic student of supply and demand as a mathematical

problem to that of partaker in public movements for the betterment of mankind. While I have never given up my narrow specialty of mathematical economics I have added to that central interest a keen interest in the world around me (extract from copy prepared in February 1925 for 'Political Economists in Autobiographies').[4]

In view of his own experience, it is hardly surprising that Fisher elected to engage intensely in advancing the cause of improved health. His activity in this field focused, in the first instance, on inquiries into the impact of various types of diet on physical well-being. Fisher's approach to these questions was influenced in some measure by the doctrines espoused by Dr. John Harvey Kellogg, Director of a Sanitarium at Battle Creek, Michigan and the entrepreneur of the breakfast cereals that bore his name.[5] Fisher did not identify completely with Kellogg's conception of 'biologic living' (which called for vegetarianism without compromise). But he was inspired to conduct experiments with Yale students to investigate the influence of 'flesh eating' on endurance. His findings – reported in the *Yale Medical Journal* in 1907 – indicated that the 'flesh-abstainers' dominated the 'flesh-eaters' in physical performance. Fisher took these results to heart in his own practice of dietary discipline, exercise, and teetotalism. Health concerns also stimulated his inventive faculties: he created a mechanical device to aid in determining dietary 'balance' and he invented a tent for the outdoor treatment of tuberculosis patients.[6]

The attention Fisher gave to this dimension of his interests obviously competed for time with his work as a professional economist. He nonetheless insisted on the complementarity of his various activities. After all, his approach to 'causes' was consistently informed by his background as an economist. The task of bettering the human condition, as he saw it, always reduced to one of maximizing efficiency and eliminating waste. Though presumably he could have done more in economics had he allocated less energy to human uplift, still the work he produced in economics in 1906 and 1907 was formidable indeed. *The Nature of Capital and Income* and *The Rate of Interest* stand as monumental analytic achievements (see Fisher, 1997, Volumes 2 and 3). If events had taken a different turn in late 1906, it is at least conceivable that *The Rate of Interest* might have been his final contribution to the theoretical literature of economics. He was then an active candidate for the post of Secretary of the Smithsonian Institution in Washington, a position which attracted him because it seemed to be a base from which the direction of the nation's scientific research could be shaped. His ego was bruised a bit when he was passed over for this appointment. But as he wrote to his Yale classmate, Henry L. Stimson, on receipt of this news:

Tho I should have been quite content to have tried my hand, and should always have been discontented if I had not allowed my name to be considered, I am not all displeased at the result (Fisher to Henry L. Stimson, December 5, 1906).

Fisher's participation in the health movement took another turn in early 1907 when he organized a Committee of One Hundred (under the sponsorship of the American Association for the Advancement of Science) to lobby for the creation of a National Department of Health. In this role, Fisher's public visibility was considerably enhanced: he was thus well positioned to receive a governmental assignment that came his way in 1908. He was invited to survey issues facing the nation on the health front as part of the work of the National Conservation Commission, created by President Theodore Roosevelt. The study he prepared – entitled *National Vitality, Its Wastes and Conservation* (1909) – foreshadowed much of his subsequent work in this field (for the message of this document, see Fisher, 1997, Volume 13, Chapter II). The data presented in this document laid the foundations, for example, for the Life Extension Institute (which he co-founded in 1914). This Institute served multiple purposes: it sought to demonstrate that it would be a paying proposition for life insurance companies to finance annual physical examinations for their policy-holders and that self-interested employers should provide the same service to their employees. In addition, the Life Extension Institute sponsored the preparation of a guide-book for healthy living which Fisher put together with the assistance of a co-author. *How to Live: Rules for Healthful Living Based on Modern Science* was originally published in 1915; the twenty-first edition appeared in 1946 (see Fisher, 1997, Volume 13, Chapter III).

Concurrent with these activities, Fisher maintained an active scholarly program in economics. Monetary analysis was his primary professional preoccupation in the years immediately preceding the outbreak of war in Europe in 1914. *The Purchasing Power of Money*, which appeared in 1911, broke fresh ground in its treatment of the quantity theory of money. The contents of that work brought a kind of symmetry to his writings as a social reformer and as an economist. In the early days of his career, he had attacked the enthusiasts for 'doing something' which led to recommendations for policy before their implications had been exhaustively studied.[7] By 1911, Fisher had moved beyond that view. He then maintained that *The Purchasing Power of Money* would be incomplete if it were published only as a technical analysis of a problem: completeness required that remedies be proposed as well. As he then informed Edwin W. Kemmerer, Princeton's monetary expert, his remedy – a 'compensated dollar' of varying gold content but constant purchasing power – was inserted in the text at the last minute because he could not be satisfied with a book on a problem if it failed to point toward a solution (see the discussion of this point in Fisher, 1997, Volume 4). This attitude stayed with him the rest of his life. In the 1930s, his insistence on the urgency of 'quick fix' solutions generated frictions between Fisher and other professional economists (see, for example, Fisher, 1997, Volume 14, especially Chapters III, IV, and VII).

3   CRUSADING IN WAR AND PEACE

Fisher's activism was unabated during the First World War. The guns of August 1914 had sounded for only a fortnight when he called for a novel approach to the world's governance – the creation of a 'league for peace' with an international police force at its command. This proposal grew out of an idea he had first presented to the Yale Political Science Club in 1890 (see Fisher, 1997, Volume 13, Chapter VI). In 1915, Fisher was a charter member of a group of citizens mobilized to persuade the nation's leaders to support a 'League to Enforce Peace' and he was gratified when President Woodrow Wilson incorporated this idea into his 'Fourteen Points' for a peace settlement.

The war added to the list of causes Fisher was prepared to campaign for. Though he had earlier taken a strong personal position with regard to the dangers he associated with consumption of alcoholic beverages, he argued in 1916 that the national interest demanded suppression of their production and organized a 'Committee of Sixty' – with himself as its president – to lobby for national prohibition (see Fisher, 1997, Volume 13, Chapter IV). In addition – believing as he did that the genetically fittest in the belligerent nations would be disproportionately cut down by war – he devoted more time to the eugenics movement (see Fisher, 1997, Volume 13, Chapter V). He presided over the affairs of two other organizations during years of war. From his platform as President of the American Association for Labor Legislation, he called upon state governments to recognize the social and economic benefits that would accrue from enactment of compulsory health insurance (see Fisher, 1997, Volume 13, Chapter III). In 1917 and 1918 – from his office as President of the American Economic Association – he created expert committees to study economic problems arising from the war. He hoped that the AEA's Committee on *The Purchasing Power of Money in Relation to the War* would both enlighten the public on the necessities of war-time stabilization and fertilize the soil for his own scheme for stabilizing the dollar (see the Editorial Introduction to Fisher, 1997, Volume 6).

In November 1919, tragedy visited the Fisher household – and it was one that Fisher construed as a legacy of war. At the age of 24, his eldest daughter, Margaret, died. She had suffered a nervous breakdown some eighteen months earlier when the man to whom she had become engaged was expected to depart for France. Fisher found this loss extraordinarily difficult to accept: Margaret, his favorite child, had been much more responsive to her father's health teachings than had her sister, Carol, or her brother, Irving Norton. Fisher dedicated his book, *League or War?*, published in 1923, as follows: 'To the Memory of My Daughter Margaret – One of the Many Million Radiant Young Souls Torn from This Earth by the World War.'

4   ACTIVITIES IN THE 1920s

During the decade of the 1920s, Fisher continued to pursue old interests, but also added new ones. In these years, he spent a fair amount of his time on the road. Meanwhile he cut back considerably on his activities at Yale. He taught only one term a year – and usually a single course – and he played no role in the regular routines of faculty governance. Even when in New Haven, he spent most of his working time with his office staff at the family residence.

In the Presidential campaign of 1920, Fisher acquired added stature as a public figure. The over-riding issue at this time, as he saw matters, was America's membership in the League of Nations. He attended the political conventions of the two major national parties and interviewed personally their nominees for the Presidency – Warren G. Harding (for the Republicans) and James Cox (for the Democrats). Persuaded that a Democratic victory offered the best prospects for U.S. membership in the League, he formed an organization styled as the 'Pro-League Independents' to campaign for the election of Cox and his Vice-Presidential running mate, Franklin D. Roosevelt. Under the auspices of this organization, Fisher toured the country in the late summer and early autumn of 1920 and made scores of speeches on behalf of the Democratic ticket. Though dismayed by the electoral success of the Republicans, Fisher's support for this cause did not flag. His book *League or War?*, published in 1923, was intended to persuade doubters that American membership in the League was imperative and that the isolationist mood of the country should be cast aside (for the essentials of the substantive argument of this work, see Fisher, 1997, Volume 13, Chapter V). In the Presidential campaign of 1924, he again spoke in support of the Democratic ticket, headed by John W. Davis.

One of Fisher's crusades took a different twist. The ratification of the Eighteenth Amendment to the U.S. Constitution made prohibition the law of the land. He was already prominently identified as a champion of prohibition of the production and consumption of alcoholic beverages as a war-time measure, and he clearly favored the same course in peace-time. Debate over prohibition did not disappear from the national agenda, however, when it did become national policy in 1920. Attention was instead redirected to the effectiveness (or otherwise) of the enforcement of this legislation and to the desirability (or otherwise) of repealing the Constitutional amendment authorizing it. Fisher placed himself at the forefront of the strict-enforcement and anti-repeal lobby and was the author (or co-author) of three book-length studies arguing this point of view: *Prohibition at Its Worst* (1926); *Prohibition Still at Its Worst* (assisted by H. Bruce Brougham, 1928); and *The 'Noble Experiment'* (assisted by H. Bruce Brougham, 1930. Details of the arguments Fisher deployed in defense of Prohibition are to be found in Fisher, 1997, Volume 13, Chapter IV). In the 1920s, Fisher remained loyal to another of his causes – eugenics. He served successively as President of the Eugenics Research Association, Chairman of the Eugenics Committee of the United States of America (an organization that was the creature of the International Eugenics Committee), and as the first President of the American Eugenics Society, founded in 1926. From these posts, he urged that American immigration policies be informed by the insights of this new 'science' (Fisher's views on these topics are reported in Fisher, 1997, Volume 13, Chapter V). He also wrapped up the affairs of the Committee of One Hundred – dating from the unsuccessful campaign to create a National Department of Health that was launched in 1907 – and arranged to have its residual assets re-assigned to support eugenics.

Fisher's professional work as an economist took a back seat to his other activities in the 1920s, but it was certainly not crowded out altogether. His *The Making of Index Numbers* – which appeared in 1922 – was a bravura technical performance (see Fisher, 1997, Volume 7). He also enriched economic literature with analyses of 'so-called' business cycles – and of the way they might be tamed – that he published as articles in professional journals. Impressive originality was on display in these works: for example, in his pioneering use of distributed lags and in his anticipation of a relationship that a later generation of macro-economists would recognize under the label of the 'Phillips Curve' (in this connection, see the materials collected in Fisher, 1997, Volume 8).

The Fisher of this period, however, was much less interested in developing analytic insights for their own sake than he was in guiding policy-makers. The management of monetary policy became his central focus, and he insisted that stabilization of the general price level should be its target. He had long been interested in that topic. But, in the 1920s, there was a perceptible modulation in his thinking about the vital importance of reaching that objective. His earlier writings had emphasized the evils of distributive injustices arising from variations in price levels which distorted the relative positions of creditors and debtors. He was now to stress instead the unfortunate consequences of changing price levels for the volumes of production and employment. But, as he argued with some passion, serious disturbances to the economy's performance did not have to be tolerated. Monetary policy, conducted in accordance with his prescriptions, would forestall them (Fisher's monetary thinking in the 1920s is on exhibit in Fisher, 1997, Volumes 6 and 8).

When disseminating his message on economic stabilization, Fisher made use of a variety of techniques. In 1921, he was a prime mover in the formation of the Stable Money League, an organization designed to shape public opinion and to lobby legislators. He appeared with some frequency before Congressional Committees in support of legislation that would charge the Federal Reserve System to make stabilization of the general price level its primary responsibility and oblige the central bank to achieve it (Samples of his Congressional testimony on the management of monetary policy may be found in Fisher, 1997, Volumes 6 and 8). When the opportunity presented itself, he would put his case directly before leading statesmen – and, on one occasion, before a foreign dictator (see the Editorial Postcript to Fisher, 1997, Volume 8 for an account of his audience with Mussolini in September 1927). After 1923 – when he founded the Index Number Institute – he could also speak to members of the public through a syndicated weekly newspaper column. His calculations of index numbers reflecting the economy's recent performance, as well as his commentary on current events, were reported therein. At its peak, the Index Number Institute's weekly report reached a potential readership of about seven million people.

The Index Number Institute was a business venture which he operated from his own home. Fisher regarded its work largely as an educational service from which he made little or no money. Another of his ventures, however, turned out to be fabulously profitable. In 1913, he had patented a unique filing device which he called the Index Visible (a photograph of this invention is reproduced in the Appendix to Fisher, 1997, Volume 13). Though he had only limited success in attracting financial supporters, he proceeded to arrange for the manufacture of the Index Visible at a plant in New Haven. For a number of years, it was a struggling operation. But Fisher's fortunes changed dramatically in 1925 when his firm was merged with Rand-Kardex (shortly to become Remington-Rand) in exchange for a handsome block of stock and a position for Fisher on the corporation's board of directors. Fisher rejoiced at this turn of events. In a letter to his son, he described his state of mind:

> (H)aving paid my own way and supported others going through college and then entering a profession which scarcely pays a living wage, I have felt ever since I married, despite all Mother's sweet wishes that 'all mine shall be thine' and despite every effort to be sensible about it, that I was not enjoying our joint income as I would if I contributed a larger part of it.
>
> That feeling, as much as anything, was the reason I turned to inventing as a chance to make money. I felt it would be foolish and quixotic to go into business or

try to make money by work and so sacrifice the professional work, ambitions and usefulness to gratify what seemed even to me to be a foolish but irrepressible whim. Inventing offered the one chance I saw of making money without a great sacrifice of time.

And at last my dream has come true and I am happy on that score.

The money itself is not needed greatly for added personal comforts and neither Mother nor I want it for swelling around. So it is dedicated primarily to the causes in which Mother and I are interested. So I'm getting double satisfaction. For there is nothing more satisfying than having a part in an enterprise greater and longer than one's own life. This added income will enable me to further the four chief causes which we have at heart, the abolition of war, disease, degeneracy, and instability of money (Fisher to Irving Norton Fisher, June 17, 1925).[8]

Fisher found his newly acquired affluence to be agreeable. He was also persuaded that conditions of 'new era' prosperity were propitious for a further strengthening of his financial position. Accordingly, he was eager to add to his portfolio of common stocks and placed himself in some exposed positions in order to do so. At this time, his confidence in the soundness of the American economy was complete.

Multiple claims on his energies in these years notwithstanding, Fisher still managed to produce a major theoretical treatise. *The Theory of Interest* – published in 1930 – remains among the foremost treatments of its topic and is appropriately regarded as among the landmarks of economic analysis in the twentieth century. Fisher had embarked on this project as a clarification – and modest revision – of *The Rate of Interest* of 1907. The final product was much more than that. His latter-day discussion of 'investment opportunities' and their impact on the determination of interest rates reflected the temper of the time at which it was written. Fisher's 'new era' optimism was clearly in evidence in his references to the manner in which the accelerated tempo of invention in the America of the 1920s magnified opportunities for productive investment (see Fisher, 1997, Volume 9).

5   DEPRESSION AND ITS CONSEQUENCES, BOTH PERSONAL AND PROFESSIONAL

Fisher was caught totally off-guard by the events of the early 1930s. He had expected that the disturbances on the stock market that had begun in October 1929 would be a minor affair, which would pose no threat to the fundamental vitality of the American economy. The tone of his commentary continued to be upbeat throughout 1930 (see the documents assembled in the Editorial Introduction to Fisher, 1997, Volume 10 and in Volume 14, Chapter I). He was certainly not quick to grasp the magnitude of his misjudgment about the flow of economic events. In late 1932 – when addressing the American Statistical Association as its president – he offered a confession of sorts:

> It is well that we face these failures and that, when we fail, we confess it with due humility. I confess it. It is true that in September, 1929, I publicly stated my belief that we were 'then at the top of the stock market' and that there would be a recession, this forecast being largely on the strength of the elaborate correlation work of Karl Karsten [a new Haven-based statistician]. And this proved true. But unfortunately I also stated my belief that the recession would be slight and short; and this proved untrue. I can see that my failure was due to insufficient knowledge of both kinds, scientific and historical. I did not then know certain scientific laws and I did not know, as well as I should, the historical background of conditions. For instance, I had counted on the continuance of the open market policy of Benjamin Strong of the Federal Reserve Bank of New York, not knowing that these had largely died with Governor Strong the year before. As to the laws governing depressions, I did not then know, what since I have learned and embodied in my book, *Booms and Depressions* [1932], the important role of over-indebtedness and its tendency to break down the price level through distress selling, contraction of deposit currency, and slackening of its velocity. Had I had these two sorts of knowledge in 1929, even to the modest extent which I can now claim to have them, that is, if I had had more correct and complete historical information on the one hand, and more correct and complete knowledge of some of the scientific laws involved on the other, my failure to predict this economic eclipse would at least have been lessened (Fisher, 1933, pp. 9-10).[9]

It was noteworthy that Fisher continued to search for silver linings amidst the storm clouds. His rethinking of where he had gone wrong had indeed generated innovative insights in the form of his 'Debt-Deflation Theory of Great Depressions'. This line of analysis – which was to be the *Leitmotiv* of his subsequent commentary on the depression – appeared to offer a persuasive explanation of what had happened and to point toward a prescription that would restore economic health. 'Reflation' of the price level to relieve the burden of indebtedness was the appropriate remedy and it should be achieved through monetary manipulations. With respect to economic policy, Fisher was to develop a number of ingenious variations on these themes.[10]

Fisher also suggested that something hopeful could be salvaged from the wreckage of depression in the form of lasting improvement in the character of scientific investigation in economics. It had long been his dream to build an international organization to bring economists interested in linking economic theory with mathematics and statistics into closer collaboration. Circumstances of the early 1930s permitted this dream to became a reality. The presence at Yale of Ragnar Frisch of the University of Oslo in 1930 made it easier for three who shared the dream – Fisher, Frisch, and C.F. Roos – to lay the groundwork for the formation of an Econometric Society. But the depression also had something to do with its realization. As Fisher explained this point in December 1932:

> It was because practically all the would-be economic forecasters have for the last four years failed dismally to tell the business man what to expect that a business man, Mr. Alfred Cowles, III, has stepped forward to finance the Econometric Society in the hope that out of it might grow scientific prediction (Fisher, 1933, p. 9).

Fisher always spoke with pride about his role in the formation of the Econometric Society and he became the Society's first president.

Fisher's miscalculation about the fate of the American economy in the early 1930s was not just a professional embarrassment: it also meant that his personal fortune was battered. He managed to stave off personal bankruptcy only because he borrowed heavily from his wife's unmarried sister. (These loans he was never able to repay and his sister-in-law forgave them in her will.) To raise cash in 1931, he sold his New Haven residence to Yale with the understanding that he and his wife could remain there as life tenants. In 1933, he resorted to another expedient, which he explained in a letter to Henry L. Stimson:

> Being, like so many others today, short of cash and long of stock, I am forced to sell some of the latter. My liquid assets having been almost exhausted, I am now offering to sell at $ 5.00 a share to people I know, and who know me, 5 per cent or 10 per cent of my 220,000 shares in 'Sonotone' [a maker of hearing aids], an unlisted company with only a few shareholders, I being second largest.
>
> So, if you have any money to invest, I want it! Incidentally (!) you will probably be getting the best investment of your life. If you are interested, I'll write you details.
>
> I have decided to donate to Yale one-fifth of all I get from selling to classmates, so as to help the '88 fund for next Commencement, to which otherwise I could not subscribe much if at all (Fisher to Henry L. Stimson, March 14, 1933).[11]

In the early days of President Franklin D. Roosevelt's 'New Deal', Fisher spent a substantial amount of time in Washington – and he was quite single-minded about why he was there. His purpose was to persuade policy-makers to engineer recovery through 'reflation' of the general price level. Roosevelt's commitment to experimentation – and his skeptical attitude toward 'orthodox' academic economics – provided some house-room for Fisher's style of monetary thinking. But Fisher never held any official appointment, nor was he ever a member of the President's inner circle. It was not for want of trying. He bombarded the White House with memoranda and, on a number of occasions, he had face-to-face conferences with Roosevelt. His recommendations were politely received and, typically, politely ignored. Nevertheless, Fisher liked to think of himself as a member of Roosevelt's 'Brains Trust' (see Fisher's voluminous correspondence with Roosevelt contained in Fisher, 1997, Volume 14) .

For a time in 1934, Fisher flirted with the thought of entering the political arena in his own right. He was then entertaining the possibility of competing for the Democratic nomination for a Senate seat from Connecticut. He was well aware, however, that he would need formidable assistance from persons in high places if anything were to come of that. He could hardly claim a track record as a party loyalist: though he had voted for Wilson in 1912 and 1916 and supported the Democratic Presidential candidates in 1920 and 1924, it was no secret that he had voted for Hoover in 1928 and 1932. He nonetheless solicited Roosevelt's backing for a Senatorial bid as a Democrat in 1934 – but it was not forthcoming. The President, however, did honor Fisher's request to allow *Stable Money: A History of the Movement* (which appeared in 1934) to be dedicated to him (see the exchange of correspondence on these points in Fisher, 1997, Volume 14).

Though Fisher frequently felt frustrated when his policy recommendations went unheeded, he still managed to sustain his reformist zeal. The substantive content of his messages, however, mutated over time. During the depression years, there was consistency in his insistence that monetary policy should be conducted to 'reflate' the general price level to a pre-depression target (say, its altitude in 1926) and that it should thereafter be stabilized. But he shifted his views on the types of reforms needed for the longer-term. At one stage, he assigned primary emphasis to legislation requiring the Federal Reserve to carry out his program. By mid-1934, however, he had concluded that that step would no longer be sufficient. Economic stability would be endangered, he then maintained, so long as the commercial banks had the capacity to create 'check-book money' by extending loans or to destroy 'check-book money' by calling them in or by failing to renew them (see Fisher, 1997, Volume 11). Nothing short of legislation to eliminate fractional-reserve commercial banking would do. This doctrine of '100% Money' was not original with Fisher. But from the date he embraced it until the day of his death, he made it a central part of his mission (see the documentation of his campaigning for this 'Program for Monetary Reform' in Fisher, 1997, Volumes 11 and 14).

In 1937, Fisher became a vigorous advocate of a fundamental reform in the tax system. He then called for what amounted to a consumption tax – with exemption of savings from taxation and with the elimination of taxes on capital gains. This program, though not enacted, received a serious hearing in the U.S. Treasury in 1942. In the context of war-time fiscal management, there was some overlap at the practical level between Fisher's recommendations and those emanating from a new breed of American Keynesians. The intellectual foundations for their respective recommendations, however, were totally different. Fisher's analysis could be traced back to *The Nature of Capital and Income* (1906) in which he had excluded savings from his definition of income. This was totally distinct from a Keynesian approach to aggregate demand management. Indeed a late twentieth century reader of Fisher's statement of his case for tax reform may find its affinity with some arguments of the 1980s on repeal of the capital gains tax and reform of income taxation to be arresting (see Fisher, 1997, Volume 12).

6   THE FINAL YEARS

In the early 1940s, Fisher's pace slackened a bit, though he remained remarkably active for a person of his years. His days were darkened by the death – in January 1940 – of his beloved wife. He had also suffered a personal blow some months earlier when he had been obliged to petition the Treasurer of Yale to cancel the notes he had given to the University in lieu of rental payments. Yale agreed to this cancellation. When requesting relief from his obligations, Fisher noted that – 'with the exception of a few years' – he had returned all of his salary to Yale.

> I subscribed (anonymously) $100,000 to the Yale Endowment Fund. After paying in about a third of this amount, as I remember, I was compelled to postpone further payments because of the effects on my affairs of the depression (Fisher to George Parmly Day, Treasurer of Yale University, May 29, 1939).

Fisher continued to offer unsolicited advice to economic policy-makers. The receptivity of Roosevelt's White House to his ideas, however, was not enhanced by Fisher's support for Republican Presidential candidates in the elections of 1940 and 1944: as a matter of principle, he maintained that no President should serve more than two terms. He was dismayed when Roosevelt did not respond to his request that he be appointed as a special adviser on methods to combat inflation in war-time (see Fisher to President Roosevelt, December 28, 1942 in Fisher, 1997, Volume 14, Chapter 5). He was also free with advice on other matters, among them techniques to improve the physical fitness of the armed forces. Henry L. Stimson, as Secretary of War, did not take up Fisher's proposal that he be given an assignment as a 'special assistant to recommend methods of improving endurance' (Fisher to Henry L. Stimson, May 12, 1942).

Even in his late seventies, Fisher sustained his enthusiasm for mobilizing economists (and others) to influence public opinion. In 1944, for example, he served as the Honorary Chairman of an organization styled as 'Citizens, Inc.', the mission of which was to enlighten the citizenry on the virtues of the

American system of free enterprise.[12] As World War II drew to a close, he renewed his call to members of the American Economic Association to join him in endorsing the 'Program for Monetary Reform' based on '100% money'. As is abundantly apparent in his post-war correspondence with professional colleagues, he was out of sympathy with the drift of the profession toward Keynesianism and with the fiscal orientation in governmental thinking that was embedded in the Employment Act of 1946 (see Fisher, 1997, Volume 14, Chapter VII). Septuagenarianism, however, was not the problem. Even after he had reached that status, he was able to produce novelties of his own: note his inventions of a portable chair and of an icosahedral map (which are on display in the Appendix to Fisher, 1997, Volume 13). And he remained intellectually active with a research program – uncompleted when he died – investigating the velocity of monetary circulation.

In the final year of his life, Fisher entertained high hopes for accomplishments to be achieved later by an Irving Fisher Foundation[13]. His confidence in the funding pledged by one Warren Hunter was badly misplaced: Hunter soon thereafter disappeared from sight as a fugitive from the law.

On the occasion of his eightieth birthday, Fisher was honored by a dinner to celebrate him at the Yale Club in New York City. This was a last appearance in public. An inoperable cancer took his life on April 29, 1947.

NOTES

*   This article was originally published in *The Works of Irving Fisher*, (Fisher, 1997) and is reprinted by permission of Pickering and Chatto Publishers Ltd., London.
    Detailed accounts of Fisher's life are available in Irving Norton Fisher, 1956; and Robert Loring Allen, 1993.

1   Subsequently, Fisher was to write appreciations of most of the economists he encountered during his European tour.

2   For example, Professor Alfred Marshall of the University of Cambridge paid tribute to Fisher's contribution when testifying before a Parliamentary Committee on Indian Currency. See Marshall, 'Minutes of Evidence before the Committee Appointed to Inquire into the Indian Currency,' January 11, 1899; as reproduced in J.M. Keynes (ed.), 1926, pp. 271-273.

3   The pertinent early articles are reproduced in Fisher, 1997, Volume 1, part D.

4   The volume for which this material was written was published in 1929 by Felix Meiner.

5   Fisher first met Kellogg in 1904. Writing to his wife about his trip to Battle Creek, he observed:
      I am on a quest not like Ponce de Leon for the fountain of youth but for ideas which may help us to lengthen and to enjoy youth and the spirit of youth (Fisher to Margaret Hazard Fisher, December 27, 1904).

6   These inventions are on display in the Appendix to Fisher, 1997, Volume 13. It is worth noting that these were not Fisher's first inventions. He received his first patent when a Yale

freshman for a device to improve the performance of the piano, but it failed to find commercial application.

7   In 1895, for example, he wrote as follows to his friend, Will Eliot:

... I feel most earnestly the truth of this idea: that social science is very immature and that it will be a long time before it reaches the 'therapeutic' stage, that the efforts of philanthropists to treat of therapeutics too soon, both delays the solid progress of the humbler preliminary stages of the anatomy and physiology of society and is more likely to lead to evil than good ... (Fisher to Will Eliot, July 29, 1895).

8   A decade later he reported:

I have spent about a million dollars on prospects of health (including the alcohol problem and world peace and eugenics) and economic reforms, especially the stable money movement (Fisher to Henry L. Stimson, July 4, 1935).

9   This was delivered as the Presidential Address to the Association on December 29, 1932.

10 See Fisher, 1997, Volume 10 and his memoranda on economic policy appropriate for depression-fighting contained in Fisher, 1997, Volume 14.

11 Two months later Fisher reminded Stimson of this proposition (to which the latter had not responded) and added:

I have sold most of the stock necessary for the present and may soon raise the price, so that if you are shifting from bonds to stocks and want to consider one of the best investment opportunities now is the time (Fisher to Stimson, June 22, 1933).

12 For details of this venture, see Fisher, 1997, Volume 13, Chapter VII.

13 For his vision for that enterprise – described in his own words – see Fisher, 1997, Volume 1.

REFERENCES

Allen, R.L. (1993), *Irving Fisher: A Biography,* Cambridge, MA, Blackwell.

Auspitz, R. and Lieben, R. (1889), *Untersuchungen über die Theorie des Preises*, Leipzig, Duncker and Humblot.

Barber, W.J. (ed.), assisted by R.W. Dimand and K. Foster, consulting editor J. Tobin, (1997), *The Works of Irving Fisher*, London, Pickering and Chatto:

Volume 1: *The Early Professional Works.*

Volume 2: *The Nature of Capital and Income.*

Volume 3: *The Rate of Interest.*

Volume 4: *The Purchasing Power of Money.*

Volume 5: *Elementary Principles of Economics.*

Volume 6: *Stabilizing the Dollar.*

Volume 7: *The Making of Index Numbers.*

Volume 8: *The Money Illusion and Related Writings.*

Volume 9: *The Theory of Interest.*

Volume 10: *Booms and Depressions and Related Writings.*

Volume 11: *100% Money.*

Volume 12: *Contributions to the Theory and Practice of Public Finance.*

Volume 13: *A Crusader for Social Causes.*

Volume 14: *Correspondence and other Commentary on Economic Policy 1930-1947.*

Fisher, I. (1892), *Mathematical Investigations in the Theory of Value and Prices*, in *Transactions of the Connecticut Academy*, **9**, 1-124. Reprinted New Haven, Yale University Press, 1925. Facsimile reprint, New York, A.M. Kelley, 1961.

Fisher, I. (1894), 'The Mechanics of Bimetallism', *Economic Journal*, **4**, 1-11.

Fisher, I. (1896), *Appreciation and Interest*, Publication of the American Economic

Association, Third Series, Vol. XI, No. 4, New York. Published for the American Economic Association by Macmillan. Facsimile reprint, bound with *Mathematical Investigations in the Theory of Value and Prices*, New York, A.M. Kelley, 1961.

Fisher, I. (1906), *The Nature of Capital and Income*, New York, Macmillan. Facsimile reprint, Düsseldorf, Verlag Wirtschaft und Finanzen GmbH, 1992.

Fisher, I. (1907), *The Rate of Interest*, New York, Macmillan. Facsimile reprint, Düsseldorf, Verlag Wirtschaft und Finanzen GmbH, 1994.

Fisher, I. (1909), *Report on National Vitality, Its Wastes and Conservation*, (for T. Roosevelt's National Conservation Commission), Senate Document No. 676, 60th Cong., 2nd Session, Vol. III, Government Printing Office, July.

Fisher, I., assisted by H.G. Brown (1911), *The Purchasing Power of Money*, New York, Macmillan.

Fisher, I. (1913), 'A compensated dollar', *Quarterly Journal of Economics*, **27**, 213-235, 385-397.

Fisher, I., assisted by E.L. Fisk (1915), *How to Live: Rules for Healthful Living Based on Modern Science*, New York, Funk and Wagnalls, 21st ed. with H. Emerson, New York, Funk and Wagnalls, 1946.

Fisher, I. (1922), *The Making of Index Numbers*, Boston and New York, Houghton Mifflin, 2nd ed. 1923, 3rd ed., 1927.

Fisher, I. (1923), *League or War?*, New York, Harper and Brothers.

Fisher, I. (1925), extract from copy prepared in February 1925 for 'Political Economists in Autobiographies'. The volume for which this material was written was published in 1929: Fisher, I. 'Irving Fisher' in F. Meiner (ed.).

Fisher, I. (1926), *Prohibition at Its Worst*, New York, Macmillan.

Fisher, I., assisted by H.B. Brougham (1928), *Prohibition Still at Its Worst,* New York, Alcohol Information Commission.

Fisher, I., assisted by H.B. Brougham (1930), *The 'Noble Experiment'*, (revision of *Prohibition Still at Its Worst*), New York, Alcohol Information Service.

Fisher, I. (1930), *The Theory of Interest*, New York, Macmillan. Reprinted in I. Fisher, 1997, Volume 9.

Fisher, I. (1932), *Booms and Depressions. Some First Principles*, New York, Adelphi. Reprinted in I. Fisher, 1997, Volume 10.

Fisher, I. (1933), 'Statistics in the Service of Economics', *Journal of the American Statistical Association*, **28**, 1-13.

Fisher, I. (1933), ' The debt-deflation theory of great depressions', *Econometrica*, **1**, 337-357. Reprinted in I. Fisher, 1997, Volume 10.

Fisher, I., assisted by H.R.L. Cohrssen (1934), *Stable Money: A History of the Movement*, New York, Adelphi.

Fisher, I. (1997), cf. W.J. Barber, 1997.

Fisher, I.N. (1956), *My Father Irving Fisher*, New York, Comet Press Books.

Marshall, A. (1899), 'Minutes of evidence before the committee appointed to inquire into the Indian currency,' in J.M. Keynes (ed.), *Official Papers by Alfred Marshall*, London, 1926, Macmillan, 271-273.

Meiner, F. (ed.) (1929), *Volkswirtschaftslehre in Selbstdarstellungen*, Bd. II, Leipzig, Germany.

Samuelson, P. (1967), 'Irving Fisher and the theory of capital', in W. Fellner (ed.), *Ten Economic Studies in the Tradition of Irving Fisher*, New York, J. Wiley and Sons, 17-38.

2.   On Working with Irving Fisher's Papers

William J. Barber

My title is inspired by the one that Hans Cohrssen assigned to a delightful essay entitled 'Working for Irving Fisher' that appeared in the *Cato Journal* several years back. I deeply regret that Hans Cohrssen is not with us on this occasion. I had greatly looked forward to making his acquaintance and to learning more about what it was like to experience life with Fisher at first hand.

My exposure to Fisher is entirely at second hand – that is, through the paper trail that he left behind. And a bulky trail it is. His prolific output of publications – books, articles in professional and popular periodicals, letters to editors, syndicated newspaper columns – is accessible to all within reach of a research library of world-class standing. The most important of these documents are also collected in the fourteen-volume Pickering and Chatto edition of his *Works*. The agenda of this conference speaks to the continuing capacity of his published writings to stimulate learned discussion.

I should like to offer some comments on attributes of his legacy that are less readily visible. I refer to the Fisher revealed in his personal correspondence, most of which is housed in the Manuscripts and Archives Collections of Yale University. As a survivor of total immersion in those documents, I can testify that working with Irving Fisher's papers provides intriguing insights into his life and endeavors.

First let me report that those who inspect Fisher's archives in search of dramatic and hitherto unsuspected revelations will be disappointed. There are no major surprises here. After all, the highlights of his career, for the most part, are common-property knowledge. His pioneering contributions to general equilibrium theory, to the theory of capital and interest, and to monetary theory and policy are certainly well established. Most economists who know anything at all about Fisher are also aware that he was among the most colorful figures of all time in our profession – especially by virtue of his passionate crusading for causes (which included advocacy of improved health, prohibition of alcohol and tobacco, eugenics, and international organizations to promote world peace). In the United States at least, most first-year students of economics learn about Fisher's disastrous misreading of the stock market in 1929.

Details of these familiar features of his interests and activities are abundantly recorded in his papers. Perhaps, however, the most significant rewards from a study of Fisher's correspondence lie elsewhere. In my judgment, they are to be found – in the first instance – in what their cumulative impact tells us about his conception of scientific professionals and their social responsibilities; secondly, in the supplementary light they throw on his professional and personal reactions to the shocks of the Great Depression; and, thirdly, in the windows they open on Fisher's relationships with fellow economists. Altogether, these findings enrich our knowledge of Fisher as an economist and as a person, as well as our grasp of 'the state of the art' in his lifetime. In addition, they can contribute to improving our understanding of why his economic messages were received as they were by contemporaries and by later generations of economists.

1   ARTICULATING THE SOCIAL RESPONSIBILITIES OF SCIENTIFIC PROFESSIONALS

One who works with Fisher's papers cannot fail to be impressed by the intensity of his core convictions with regard to the social responsibilities of scientific professionals. Part of his attitude is conveyed in a letter written to a close friend in mid-1895 when his departmental affiliation at Yale was shifted from mathematics to political economy:

> I am delighted with the opportunity to be in touch with human life so directly and shall find no lack of opportunity to use my mathematical training. This had been my one regret about the mathematical life – its lack of direct contact with the living age (Fisher to William Greenleaf Eliot, July 29, 1895).

Reminiscing about this phase in his life nearly a half-century later, he expanded on this theme:

> I was beginning to feel that, while I loved pure mathematics and could get more intellectual pleasure from working in that field than I could in the more empirical field of economics, it was sort of a selfish indulgence like chess-playing or spending one's time with crossword puzzles while the great work of the world was needing to be done. Perhaps there was born in me the yearning of a reformer since my father was a preacher (Fisher, Transcript of a talk to the Economics Department of Harvard University, February 27, 1942).

Though he often spoke with pride about his contribution to positioning economics on solid mathematical foundations, one can surmise that Fisher would be less than totally pleased with the character of some of the mathematical economics being produced fifty years after his death.

Throughout his mature career, Fisher was uncompromising in his insistence that the purpose of economic analysis was to generate insights to uplift the human condition. The attitude he struck in *The Purchasing Power of Money* – which appeared in 1911 – exemplifies this point. That work began as an analytic study of the quantity theory and he might well have brought it to closure solely as a scholarly treatise on the conditions under which changes in the quantity of money generated proportionate variations in the price level. But Fisher was not content to offer just an analytic explanation for fluctuations in the purchasing power of money. Convinced as he was that monetary instability produced distributive injustices by distorting the relative positions of creditors and debtors, he felt obliged to suggest a corrective, which took the form of his recommendation for a 'compensated dollar' – i.e., one with constant purchasing power but with varying gold content. As the book was approaching completion, he reported his reasoning in a letter to Edwin W. Kemmerer, writing that he had 'restrained [himself]from putting in [his] remedy until the last moment' and that he would have 'felt so dissatisfied having written a book on the problem' if he had failed to advance a solution (Fisher to Edwin W. Kemmerer, January 11, 1911). It should be noted that Fisher had not always held the view articulated here. In his first years as a professional economist, his correspondence indicates a negative attitude toward those who rushed to judgment with appeals to 'do something' to fix problems. What was needed instead, he then argued, was patient, detached analysis to solidify the theoretical foundations upon which informed policies could be built. He abandoned that position following his recovery from a potentially fatal bout with tuberculosis. The post-TB Fisher became the impatient reformer who insisted on 'action now'.

The actions that Fisher called for over the rest of his career, it must be emphasized, were not restricted to economic improvements as narrowly construed. Writing to his son in 1925, he ranked the 'four chief causes ... [he] had at heart' in the following order: 'the abolition of war, disease, degeneracy, and instability of money' (Fisher to Irving Norton Fisher, June 17, 1925). Whatever the crusade – world peace, health and life extension, prohibition, eugenics, or stable money – Fisher took on the challenge with missionary zeal. In each instance, however, his approach reflected his background as an economist. Whatever the subject at hand – from the management of the nation's health to the management of its monetary affairs – his perspective consistently focused on promoting efficiency and suppressing waste. Some commentators have suggested that there is a disjunction between his work as an economist and his activism as a lobbyist for social causes. Fisher himself would have rejected that assessment completely. In his self-image, his crusades for social causes and his efforts to develop economic science as a tool for betterment were inseparable parts of his being.

An additional dimension of Fisher's conception of the obligations of scientific professionals calls for comment. Just as he had insisted that the diagnosis of problems should be accompanied by proposals for solutions, he also maintained that the scientist was honor-bound to disseminate results in ways to insure that they had social impact. He set out this point of view in 1913 in a letter to Charles B. Davenport, a geneticist who directed the Eugenics Research Office:

> Formerly I used to dislike the very word 'propaganda' and the idea still more. Now I have come to believe that 'science can justify itself to the world only by being harnessed up to the world' ... and it seems to me that every practical man, whether his tastes are naturally academic or scientific, or otherwise, must recognize the need of some machinery for harnessing up scientific work .... And on the other hand when propaganda gets started it still needs to be guided by some sort of connection with the scientific fountainhead. (Fisher to Charles B. Davenport, December 18, 1913.)

In that spirit, Fisher could be the prime mover in organizing the Stable Money League as well as the Committee of One Hundred (in support of the creation of a Federal Department of Health), the Committee of Sixty (in support of national prohibition), and the pro-League of Nations Independents. There was also a symmetry in the organizational style he deployed in the creation of the Eugenics Society and the Life Extension Institute, on the one hand, and in the creation of the Econometric Society, on the other.

In short, Fisher was quite unambiguous when asserting that the scientific professional's proper role was to improve the world by engaging it head-on. And he certainly practiced what he preached.

2 PROFESSIONAL AND PERSONAL REACTIONS TO THE GREAT DEPRESSION

Let me turn now to the topic of Fisher's professional and personal reactions to the Great Depression. Not surprisingly, these matters are richly documented in his correspondence. The events of the 1930s presented formidable challenges for Fisher as an economic theorist, as an economic policy advocate, and as a stock market participant.

Fisher had been totally unprepared for this crisis. The depth of his confidence in the permanence of 'new era' prosperity was abundantly on display, for example, in an address – unpublished until 1997 – he delivered to a meeting of bankers in Washington, D.C. on October 23, 1929. Even though some volatility was already in evidence on the New York Stock Exchange, Fisher's remarks on this occasion amounted to one of the classic statements of 'new era' optimism. Faith in a bright future for the American economy was well grounded, he argued, for a number of fundamental reasons: among them, corporate sponsorship of scientific research that accelerated the flow of inventions; the emergence of 'investment trusts' – known nowadays as mutual funds – that imposed efficiency-disciplines on corporate managements; the effects of Prohibition on raising the productivity of the labor force and on reducing worker absenteeism. In addition, the general price level had been remarkably stable for the preceding half-decade or so. Within the framework of the model he had developed in the 1920s, this state of affairs would appear to augur well for continued macro-economic stability.

Archival papers of the early 1930s testify to his struggle to come to grips with what had happened. The realities of those years, it should be noted, presented Fisher with more than analytic perplexities. There was a decided urgency as well about his own financial circumstances: he was spared the humiliation of declaring personal bankruptcy only because he was able to borrow heavily from a wealthy sister-in-law. (Incidentally, he was never able to repay these loans.) By late 1932, Fisher could offer an account of why his prognostications in the late 1920s had been so drastically wrong:

> I did not then know certain scientific laws and I did not know, as well as I should, the historical background of conditions .... As to the laws governing depressions, I did not then know, what since I have learned and embodied in my book *Booms and Depressions*, the important role of over-indebtedness and its tendency to break down the price level through distress selling, contraction of deposit currency, and slackening of its velocity (1933a, pp. 9-10).

When he made these remarks, Fisher was convinced that his newly-conceived 'debt-deflation theory of Great Depressions' explained the catastrophe that had befallen the American economy. In correspondence with Ragnar Frisch, editor of *Econometrica* (the journal in which this line of analysis was published in article form), Fisher made clear that he regarded the 'debt-deflation theory' as his 'chief practical contribution to economic science' and that 'the sooner economic telescopes are pointed in these new directions the sooner we can expect to avoid great depressions in the future' (Fisher to Frisch, September 4, 1933).

In Fisher's judgment, the most arresting finding of the 'debt-deflation theory' was that deflation had no inherent self-correcting properties, but simply generated more deflation. Bankruptcies and shrinking profits led to reductions in output and employment. These circumstances bred pessimism, hoarding, and a further slowdown in the velocity of monetary circulation. The remedy, however, was implicit in the diagnosis: 'reflating the price level up to the average level at which outstanding debts were contracted by existing debtors and assumed by existing creditors, and then maintaining that level unchanged' (Fisher, 1933b, p. 346). Debt burdens would thereby be relieved. Debtors would then have more discretionary income available for spending on goods and services, and the resulting resurgence in purchasing power would reinvigorate production and employment.

For the next several years Fisher poured virtually all of his extraordinary energies into getting this message out. And he was encouraged to think that his recommendations for a 'reflationary' economic program might get a sympathetic hearing at the highest levels of government following Franklin D. Roosevelt's electoral success in the Presidential campaign of 1932. (The fact that he had voted for Hoover – largely on grounds that Hoover had run on the 'dry' side of the Prohibition issue – did not deter Fisher from bombarding Roosevelt with a monumental flow of unsolicited advice.) As the archival documents reveal, Fisher was inclined to exaggerate his own importance in Presidential decision-making. Nevertheless, Roosevelt did act on one of the points on Fisher's policy agenda when embarking on the program to raise the price of gold by nearly 70 percent between October 1933 and January 1934. On the other hand, Fisher was totally opposed to the technique of price-raising through supply restriction, as practiced in the farm programs introduced in the early days of the New Deal. As he noted in a letter to his son, a fundamental confusion seemed to have clouded the President's thinking.

> It's all a strange mixture. I am much against the restriction of acreage but much in favor of inflation. Apparently FDR thinks of them as similar – merely two ways of raising prices! But one changes the monetary unit to restore it to normal while the other spells scarce food and clothing when many are starving or half-naked. (Fisher to Irving Norton Fisher, August 15, 1933.)

While he applauded the attempt to raise the general price level through the gold purchase program, he was disappointed when the President abandoned this strategy before exhausting his legal authority to elevate the gold price. In addition, Fisher maintained that this policy initiative would have been much more effective if an additional bit of his counsel had been heeded. He had proposed that the nominal 'gold profit' – the increment in the official value of the Treasury's gold stock – be monetized. The quantity of the circulating medium could be substantially enlarged, he pointed out, if this 'gold profit' were used to back a new currency issue to be known as 'yellowbacks' (so styled to distinguish them from 'greenbacks'). If holders of maturing government debt, for example, were paid out in 'yellowbacks', the money supply would instantly be increased, with an impact on the 'reflationary' program that could only be positive. This recommendation fell on deaf ears.

Fisher fared no better with some of his other efforts to persuade the government to act on his thinking. At least he succeeded, however, in convincing Roosevelt that a proposal to issue 'stamped money' merited serious consideration. This scheme – which called upon government to issue a special series of dollar bills that would depreciate in value by 2 cents each week unless a 2 cent stamp were affixed to them – was not original with Fisher. Hans Cohrssen had brought it to his attention and Cohrssen, in turn, had picked it up from Gesell. As initially formulated, 'stamped money' was designed as an attack on the hoarding of currency – after all, holders of 'stamp-scrip' had an obvious incentive to move it before its value shrank. The velocity of monetary circulation would thereby be stimulated. Fisher fully embraced this feature of the proposal, but maintained that it had a further positive recommendation. At the end of the year, he observed, the government would have collected $1.04 in stamp revenues per dollar of 'stamp-scrip'. These proceeds would enable the special currency issue to be retired and still yield a 'surplus' that could be allocated to the relief of the unemployed. Fisher's strenuous lobbying for this program went unrewarded at the national level. Nevertheless, he still pressed for its adoption by municipal governments, as his correspondence with the Mayor of New Haven, Connecticut establishes.

Study of Fisher's papers, it should be emphasized, throws arresting light on his style of policy advocacy as well as on its substance. It is clear that he believed that the challenge of winning converts to his positions was not simply a matter of persuading officialdom of their intrinsic merits. He understood that valuable points could also be carried when he introduced arguments designed to demolish other approaches to policy then competing for official favor. He never wavered in his view that prospects for the economy's recovery hinged almost exclusively on 'reflation' achieved through monetary measures. But he was well aware that an alternative approach to macro-economic stimulation – namely, a 'massive' (in the usage of the time) program of spending on public works – had attracted an influential following. This strategy, in Fisher's judgment, was totally misguided. As an employment-creating device, it would fail dismally. Given the magnitudes involved, the task of creating worthwhile public sector jobs to absorb the unemployed was un-doable and the mere attempt to address the problem in this way would generate unacceptable economic inefficiencies. But, even if a public works program could pass a test of feasibility, he held that it would still be a mistake. Fisher insisted that it would be far better for government to assist in supporting re-employment in the private sector. Toward that end, he urged the Federal government to extend interest-free loans to those private employers who agreed to enlarge their payrolls. Ideally, the government should finance this lending through the creation of new money. This in itself would be a plus for the 'reflationary' program that was needed to make the job-creation effort successful.

The inside story of Fisher's distaste for public works spending – even when financed by new money – comes through in correspondence in which he recorded his reactions to a presentation in June 1934 by John Maynard Keynes to a group of economists meeting in New York. Keynes then set out his case for 'loan expenditures' on public works, supplementing it with an explication of the concept of the 'multiplier'. When reporting this event to his wife, Fisher wrote (to Margaret Hazard Fisher, June 7, 1934):

> His paper was interesting but to me – and I think to everyone else – rather obscure and unconvincing. He was very skillful in answering questions but seemed to get nowhere.

Aware that Keynes had already put this argument before Roosevelt, Fisher took it upon himself to instruct the President on what he should absorb from Keynes's message:

> I had a long talk with J. Maynard Keynes and find myself in substantial agreement with him, but it should be noted that:
> (1) 'loan expenditure' is really a *monetary* measure involving added (govern-ment) deposits and their use as purchasing power;
> (2) the quickest, cheapest and most beneficial loan expenditure is, it seems to me, ... to lend to all those going concerns a year or more old, who want it a dollar and a half per day per employee added to payroll for one hundred consecutive days;
> (3) public works make the slowest, dearest, and usually least beneficial form. It will require something of a wrench later to get millions of workers out of jobs under government into their normal jobs in industry. Under the plan I propose, most would be re-employed in their normal jobs to start with (Fisher to Roosevelt, June 11, 1934, emphasis in original).

As one might expect, the overwhelming bulk of Fisher's letters to Roosevelt are concerned with economic policy issues at the forefront of contemporary debate. But there were some exceptions. Fisher, for example, was not above advising Roosevelt on how to treat a common cold. When doing so, he begged to be excused for 'venturing to write you on so personal a subject' and added that he did so 'on the principle that our President's health and efficiency are of a public concern' (Fisher to Roosevelt, October 27, 1943). Fisher was also free with advice to the President on the qualifications of candidates for vacancies on the Federal Reserve Board. On at least two occasions, he recommended Hans Cohrssen for a high public appointment. In June 1940, he drew Roosevelt's attention to Cohrssen's qualifications to serve with the Commissioner of Price Stabilization who was then charged to counter inflationary pressures arising from the American defense build-up. Fisher (to Roosevelt, June 19, 1940) wrote to the President as follows:

> H.C. is familiar with our domestic monetary and banking problems and understands them unusually well. ... I can speak with conviction of his high integrity and his brilliant mind; for he has been associated with me for the past eight years. You may

remember that he was co-author with me of the book 'Stable Money' which I
dedicated to you.

A comment is also in order about Fisher's reaction to the impact of the Great
Depression on his personal affairs. With the collapse of the stock market, he
experienced financial adversity in full measure. If the embarrassment of his
dependence on the charity of his wife's sister were not enough, it was
compounded by his inability to cover the rentals he contracted to pay after
selling his house to Yale University. He absorbed these blows with an
extraordinary, if unrealistic, resilience. Even in his later years, he continued to
believe that his capacity as an inventor would ultimately enable him to
discharge his financial obligations. After all, his Index Visible filing system –
sold to what became Remington Rand in 1925 – had made him a wealthy
man, permitting him to pour substantial funding into his various causes and to
cut back on time allocated to academic activities at Yale.

3   RELATIONSHIPS WITH PROFESSIONAL
CONTEMPORARIES

Let us now reflect a bit on aspects of what the archives can tell us about
Fisher's relationships with his professional contemporaries. There is an
abundance of materials bearing on these matters which has been generated by
his leadership role in various professional organizations: e.g., as President of
the American Economic Association, the American Statistical Association,
the American Association for Labor Legislation, and as a founding member
of the Econometric Society. His contacts with fellow economists were further
multiplied by his work in attempting to recruit them to join him in lobbying
organizations such as the Stable Money League and the Committee for the
Nation (which promoted the 'reflationary' program in the early 1930s).
Immediately before and immediately after World War II, he was in contact
with virtually every member of the American Economic Association urging
endorsement of a 'Program of Monetary Reform' that called for legislation to
reorganize the American commercial banking system around the principle of
'100% reserves' behind demand deposits.

Fisher's papers contain a fair amount of evidence indicating that his
influence on professional colleagues was less than it might have been because
of attributes of his personal style. When preparing each of his major
economic treatises for publication, he made it a standard practice to circulate
drafts of the manuscript among fellow economists. Seldom did the comments
he received have much impact on the final text. But Fisher's invitation did

provide commentators with an opportunity to speak directly, should they choose to do so. One such instance is illuminating – the reaction of Edwin R.A. Seligman of Columbia University to the manuscript of *Booms and Depressions*. Observing that he was being 'entirely frank', Seligman wrote that he feared that Fisher was 'incurring the danger of being classed with the horde of panacea-mongers' and that the work, as he read it, was 'meant primarily for the general public'. And he added (Edwin R.A. Seligman to Fisher, April 27, 1932.):

> Now so far as the general public is concerned, you are known chiefly for three doctrines.
> 1) That common stocks are a better and safer investment than bonds and that the level of stock values in 1929 was not an exaggerated one.
> 2) That stabilization of money can best be secured by changing the content of the gold dollar without any regard for what is done in other countries and for its effect on international exchange.
> 3) That prohibition has spelled economic progress because of alleged steadiness of the workman – without any regard for the vast economic and fiscal sacrifices involved ... . None of the above doctrines is shared by the overwhelming majority of your economic colleagues, yet I find repeated allusions to those broad and in my opinion unfounded generalizations in your book.

Seligman was not alone in his assessment. Even in Fisher's own faculty at Yale, there were far more skeptics than sympathizers. His local reputation was largely that of a crank with a weakness for promoting unconventional causes.

But even when the objective of the crusade was an economic reform, Fisher's promotional enthusiasms cost him some potential allies. The campaign to promote '100% reserves' is a case in point. Fisher had picked up this plan from a group of economists at the University of Chicago, headed by Henry C. Simons, and for several years they worked in tandem. By 1937, Simons had distanced himself from Fisher's style of advocacy. Indeed there are some indications that Simons had come to regard Fisher's more ambitious claims for '100% money' to be something of an embarrassment. In Simons's judgment, Fisher had gone too far in the direction of premature popularization. What was needed instead was further technical analysis to fine-tune the proposed reform and it should be subjected to expert criticism. Nonetheless, Fisher persisted in his attempt to rally the membership of the American Economic Association to march behind this banner. This exercise was put 'on hold' during World War II, but it resumed in 1945 when Fisher sent copies of 'A Program for Monetary Reform' to AEA members asking them to register their approval in writing. He was disappointed by the response and concluded that the capacity of economists to influence the shaping of sound legislation was compromised by the 'tendency for each economist to insist on stressing his own very minor reservations', rather than 'emphasiz[ing] fundamental points on which agreement is possible'.

Fisher's correspondence in the last decade of his life amply documents his lack of sympathy for the new fiscal orientation toward policy-making that was coming into official and professional favor. He was not well informed about the analytic properties of the arguments making up the 'Keynesian revolution'. It appears that he never read *The General Theory*, despite his personal contacts with Keynes over the years. In light of these findings, it is easier to understand why Fisher's work should have been regarded as out-of-step with the times in the era when the momentum of the profession was being driven by Keynesianism. His fate during the heyday of the Keynesian ascendancy has had a further consequence: it has meant that some of the most creative of his intellectual achievements were overlooked and literally had to be rediscovered. From the vantage point of the 1990s – when the Keynesian era no longer shines with its earlier lustre – Fisher's contributions to the architecture of the 'pillars and arches' of modern economics (to borrow Schumpeter's phrase) can be more readily appreciated. We should be grateful as well for his work as a popularizer. More so than any other single economist, Fisher has been responsible for raising the consciousness of the public to the hazards of monetary instability.

Fifty years after his death, it is altogether appropriate that we extend honors that were largely denied him in the last decade and a half of his life. It is now clear that his analytic powers have contributed much more to the shaping of economics as we know it today than most of his contemporaries in the 1930s and 1940s would have thought possible.

REFERENCES

Cohrssen, Hans (1991), 'Working for Irving Fisher', *Cato Journal*, **10**, 825-833.

Fisher, I., assisted by H.G. Brown (1911), *The Purchasing Power of Money*, New York, Macmillan.

Fisher, I. (1933a),'Statistics in the service of economics', *Journal of the American Statistical Association*, **28**, 1-13.

Fisher, I. (1933b) 'The debt-deflation theory of great depressions', *Econometrica*, **1**, 337-357. Reprinted in I. Fisher, 1997, Volume 10.

PART TWO:
MACROECONOMICS AND
THE QUANTITY THEORY

3. Irving Fisher's Monetary Macroeconomics

Robert W. Dimand

[I]sn't Irving Fisher the quintessential quantity theorist if there ever was one and yet, after 'inventing' the famous equation of exchange $MV = PT$ in 1911, did he or did he not spend the rest of his life as a monetary economist ringing new changes on 'the dance of the dollar', a short-run theory of the decidedly non-neutral role of money in the business cycle? – Mark Blaug, introduction to Blaug *et al.* (1995, p. 3).

1 INTRODUCTION

Irving Fisher's multifaceted work on *The Purchasing Power of Money: Its Determination and Relation to Credit, Interest and Crises* (assisted by Harry Gunnison Brown, [1911] 1913; 1997, Volume 4) stands as a towering achievement of neoclassical monetary economics and as a landmark in the development of modern macroeconomics. Together with his earlier books on capital and interest, Fisher's monetary treatise established him as the most cited author in English-language economics journals in the period 1886-1925 (Stigler and Friedland, 1979). Firmly rooted in the long tradition of the quantity theory of money, *The Purchasing Power of Money* restated the quantity theory proposition that the long-run effect of an exogenous change in the money supply is a proportional change in prices, not lasting changes in real variables, and defended the quantity theory both against inflationists and against such hard-money critics of the quantity theory as J. Laurence Laughlin. The book was, however, far more than a mere restatement and defense of an existing theory. Fisher extended the equation of exchange, as formulated by earlier writers such as Simon Newcomb (to whom Fisher dedicated the book), to allow for differing velocities of circulation of currency and bank deposits, and for the influence of book credit (Dimand, 1997b). Fisher's systematic approach to attempting statistical verification (Chapters XI and XII) represented an integration of theory and empiricism on a level far beyond that attempted by, for instance, Price (1896) or Kemmerer (1907). Fisher's efforts at statistical verification of the quantity theory and his compensated dollar plan for monetary reform led him to important studies on the best formula for an index of purchasing power (Chapter

35

X and its appendix), providing a foundation for *The Making of Index Numbers* ([1922a] 1927; 1997, Volume 7).

Chapter IV, on 'Disturbance of Equation [of Exchange] and of Purchasing Power during Transition Periods', presented Fisher's (and Brown's) monetary theory of economic fluctuations, arguing for monetary disturbance as the driving force underlying short-run fluctuations in economic activity and real interest. Fisher's subsequent articles on fluctuations elaborated and applied the theory presented in Chapter IV (cf. Patinkin, 1972, Dimand, 1993a, Pavanelli, 1996), until the challenge of explaining the Great Depression of the early 1930s led Fisher to introduce his debt-deflation theory of depressions (Fisher, 1997, Volume 10; Dimand, 1994a). The rate of interest linked Fisher's major theoretical works: *Appreciation and Interest* (1896) decomposed nominal interest into real interest and expected inflation, *The Rate of Interest* (1907) and *The Theory of Interest* (1930) showed how impatience (time preference) and opportunity to invest (expected rate of return over costs) determine real interest in equilibrium, and *The Purchasing Power of Money* explained price level changes, with imperfectly-anticipated price changes causing real interest to vary in transition periods. The Keynesian Revolution and the efforts of Chicago monetarists to trace their approach to a thinly-documented Chicago oral tradition of monetary theory combined with Fisher's much-publicized stock market debacle, his many eccentric crusades (a 13-month calendar, a new world map projection, Prohibition) and the structure of *The Purchasing Power of Money*, causing Fisher's monetary macroeconomics to be neglected for several decades. In recent years Fisher has been increasingly recognized as a crucial figure in the development of modern macroeconomics, both for specific analytical contributions or anticipations (the Phillips curve, the P-star model, distributed lags, adaptive expectations, the intertemporal consumption diagram, marginal efficiency of capital, reswitching, chain-weighted index numbers, indexed bonds) and more broadly for his influence on monetarism (the quantity theory, a policy rule), Keynesian economics (see Kregel, 1988; de Boyer, 1988; Dimand, 1995), and Post Keynesian economics (debt-deflation, taken up by Hyman Minsky).

2   CONTEXT AND PURPOSE

Although the history of the quantity theory of money stretches back to the Salamanca school and to Jean Bodin in the sixteenth century, with short-run non-neutrality incorporated by Hume in 1752, to a surprising extent *The Purchasing Power of Money* lacked competitors as a definitive restatement and reformulation of the quantity theory. David Laidler (1991) identified *The*

Golden Age of the Quantity Theory as the era from the 1870s to the First World War, with Fisher, Alfred Marshall and Knut Wicksell as the central figures. Wicksell's brilliantly innovative analysis of cumulative inflation or deflation in a pure credit economy, the foundation of the Stockholm School of macroeconomics, was a specialized variant of the quantity theory, and was little known outside Scandinavia and Germany until the 1930s. The octogenarian Marshall finally presented his monetary economics, long influential in Cambridge teaching, to the public in *Money, Credit and Commerce* (1923), based on his official evidence from earlier decades and on manuscripts from as far back as the 1870s, while his evidence scattered in the reports of official inquiries on monetary issues was not widely circulated outside Cambridge before Keynes's edition of Marshall's *Official Papers* in 1926. *The Economist* (January 6, 1912) predicted that 'As very little of an authoritative nature has been written in this country on this question, outside the covers of formidable Blue Books, Professor Fisher's book should be widely read.' Fisher (1896, p. 79) credited Marshall with distinguishing real and nominal interest, and later quoted Marshall on fluctuations resulting from slow adjustment of interest rates to price changes (Fisher, with Brown, [1911] 1913, pp. 71-72). Marshall's evidence to the Indian Currency Committee in 1899 stressed the importance of Fisher's *Appreciation and Interest*, a definitive monograph on a topic Marshall had previously treated in passing.

Even at Cambridge, home of an oral tradition presenting the quantity theory in terms of cash balances rather than velocity of circulation, *The Purchasing Power of Money* was quickly accepted as the leading published account of monetary theory. Keynes (1971-1989, XII, pp. 700, 702, 760-764, 771) used the book's material on inductive verification of the quantity theory and on factors influencing the velocity of circulation in his elementary and advanced lectures on money from 1912 to 1914. In a December 1913 talk to the Political Economy Club in London, 'How Far Are Bankers Responsible for the Alternations of Crisis and Depression?', Keynes (1971-1989, XIII, p. 2) referred to 'The most ordinary theory of the way in which banking considerations come in, chiefly associated perhaps with the name of Professor Irving Fisher.' The Cambridge Manual of Science and Literature on *The Theory of Money* paid tribute to 'the brilliant analysis of Professor Irving Fisher' (Barker 1913, p. 69) and stated that 'Indeed the portion of this book dealing with 'velocity of circulation' is practically a *précis* of the corresponding chapters of Professor Irving Fisher's book, *The Purchasing Power of Money*' (Barker 1913, p. vi). Fisher was the only author cited (for *The Rate of Interest* and the compensated dollar) in Hawtrey's *Good and Bad Trade* (1913, pp. 44n, 256-259). Professor S.J. Chapman of Manchester University, who had studied with Marshall at Cambridge, entitled his review of *The Purchasing Power of Money* in the *Manchester Guardian* 'A Masterpiece in Economics' and wrote in the *Journal of the Royal Statistical Society* (LXXIV, June 1911): 'In the opinion of the reviewer, this book is a magnificent achievement' (as Fisher's publishers noted in their advertising, Fisher 1997, Volume 5, pp. 576, 578).

The long delay in Marshall's publication of a volume on money contributed to the reception of *The Purchasing Power of Money* as an authoritative restatement of the quantity theory, deflecting attention from its more distinctive monetary theory of fluctuations. The context of American monetary controversy also contributed to this. Fisher wrote in the preface to the first edition of *The Purchasing Power of Money* ([1911] 1913, p. viii) that

> since the 'quantity theory' has become the subject of political dispute, it has lost prestige and has even come to be regarded by many as an exploded fallacy. The attempts by promoters of unsound money to make an improper use of the quantity theory – as in the first Bryan campaign – led many sound money men to the utter repudiation of the quantity theory. The consequence has been that, especially in America, the quantity theory needs to be reintroduced into general knowledge.

Nearly a quarter century of declining prices once called 'The Great Depression' (see Saul, 1969) sparked populist, bimetallist efforts to increase the money supply by adding silver to the monetary base of gold. Perhaps a million copies were circulated of William H. Harvey's 1894 bimetallic tract, *Coin's Financial School* (see Richard Hofstadter's introduction to the 1963 reissue). The bimetallists argued that an increase in the quantity of money would lead to a proportional increase in prices. In contrast to orthodox quantity theorists such as Kemmerer and Fisher, the bimetallists held that raising the price level would provide a lasting stimulus to real economic activity. The Klondike and South African gold discoveries, together with the cyanide process for extracting grade from lower-grade ores, increased the money supply and undermined the bimetallic crusade after 1896, but William Jennings Bryan, the bimetallic standard-bearer of 1896, was again the Democratic nominee for President in 1908, while Fisher was writing *The Purchasing Power of Money*. Proposals for monetary and banking reform abounded in the wake of the financial crisis of 1907, leading to the creation of the Federal Reserve System in 1913.

Harvey (1894) used a 'Professor Laughlin' as the sound-money butt in a debate with the fictional Coin. J. Laurence Laughlin, founding head of the Economics Department at the University of Chicago, took up the populist challenge as an opponent of the quantity theory denying both the exogeneity of the money supply and any monetary explanation of agricultural distress, and engaged Harvey in a real public debate in May 1895 (Skaggs, 1995, p. 4). Quantity theorists from Fisher to Friedman recognized that gold mining responds to the price of gold and that international gold flows under fixed exchange rates make national money supplies endogenous, but emphasized such exogenous monetary shocks as discoveries of ore bodies or invention of the cyanide process. Like von Mises ([1912] 1935), Laughlin distrusted aggregative reasoning in terms of the price level (as in the equation of exchange), preferring to avoid index number problems by dealing with individual prices. While Fisher wished a monetary reform to establish an elastic currency that would stabilize the price level, Laughlin's concept of an elastic currency was one that would accomodate the needs of trade, a real-bills view that influenced the Federal Reserve System in its first decade.

Three of Laughlin's students, Sara McLean Hardy (1895), Wesley C. Mitchell (1896) and H. Parker Willis (1896), published empirical articles in Laughlin's *Journal of Political Economy* denying that changes in the quantity of money could explain observed American price level movements (a position that Mitchell later qualified). The University of Chicago was then no stronghold of the quantity theory of money; the *Journal of Political Economy* did not even review *The Purchasing Power of Money*. A defence of the quantity theory by General Francis Amasa Walker, President of MIT and founding president of the American Economic Association and American Statistical Association, was no more congenial to Fisher, for Walker (1895) presented the quantity theory as an irrefutable tautology, not requiring verification (see Skaggs, 1995).

Fisher wrote *The Purchasing Power of Money* to redeem the quantity theory of money from the inflationism of the bimetallists and from those who reduced the theory to a tautological equation of exchange, and to defend it against such sound money advocates as Laughlin who denied exogenous changes in the quantity of money as the principal determinant of price level movements. This led Fisher to emphasize statistical verification of the long-run quantity theory proposition that (taking the determinants of demand for real money balances as given) price level changes reflect changes in the money supply, which have no lasting effect on real output. The short-run non-neutrality of money, Fisher's theory in Chapter IV of economic fluctuations as 'a dance of the dollar' (as he termed it in 1923), was kept backstage, neither encouraging the inflationists nor offending the sound money advocates. 'Why was it,' asked Joseph Schumpeter (1948, p. 234)

> that friends and foes of *The Purchasing Power of Money* saw nothing in it but another presentation, statistically glorified, of the oldest of old quantity theories – that is, a monument of an obsolescent theory that was to become obsolete before long? The answer is simple: because Fisher said so himself – already in the Preface and then repeatedly at various strategic points.

Chapters I to III presented the equation of exchange and the argument that in the long-run a change in the money supply leads to 'an exactly proportional change in the general level of prices'. Chapters IX and X discussed the appropriate index number for the price level, and Chapters XI and XII statistical verification of the theory. In between, noted Schumpeter (1948, pp. 234-235), Fisher shoved all his really valuable insights mercilessly into chapters IV, V, VI, and disposed of them semi-contemptuously as mere disturbances that occur during 'transition periods' when indeed the quantity theory is 'not strictly true'.

Thus, for example, Edwin Dean failed to remark the short-run non-neutrality of money in Fisher, even though he reprinted extensive extracts from Chapters II, III and VIII of *The Purchasing Power of Money* in *The Controversy Over the Quantity Theory of Money* (Dean, 1965, pp. 10-28), using Chapter VIII to show that Fisher's quantity theory was not as mechanical as the earlier chapters might suggest. Lawrence Ritter (1963, p. 82) cited *The Purchasing Power of Money* as evidence that according to the pre-Keynesian quantity theory an increase in the money supply, even in a period of substantial unemployment, would only cause a proportionate change in the price level. Even Keynes, reviewing *The Purchasing Power of Money* in the *Economic Journal*, neglected Chapter IV to focus instead on index numbers, which had been the subject of Keynes's Adam Smith Prize essay. The context in which Fisher wrote *The Purchasing Power of Money* led him to confine his monetary theory of fluctuations in middle chapters (especially Chapter IV), where too often it was overlooked.

3   THE EQUATION OF EXCHANGE AND VERIFICATION OF THE QUANTITY THEORY

Fisher (1897, p. 517) adapted his equation of exchange from Simon Newcomb's 'equation of societary circulation' (Newcomb, 1885, p. 346), extending it to allow differing velocities of circulation for currency and bank deposits. This step had been taken by Sir John Lubbock in his 1840 pamphlet *On Currency* (Humphrey, 1984; Henderson, 1986), but this was unknown to Fisher. Although Fisher dedicated *The Purchasing Power of Money* 'To the Memory of Simon Newcomb, Great Scientist, Inspiring Friend, Pioneer in the Study of "Societary Circulation" ', he did not discover until late 1914 that Newcomb (1879) had anticipated his compensated dollar plan for stabilizing the purchasing power of the dollar (Fisher, 1997, Volume 4, p. 576). Fisher went beyond Lubbock in extending the equation of exchange to allow for the use of book credit (trade credit) in payments, so that $PT = E + E' + E'' - E'''$, where $E (= MV)$ represents payments in cash, $E' = (M'V')$ payments by cheque, E'' creation of book credit and time loans, and E''' extinguishment of such credit (see Dimand, 1997b). However, in his appendix on the 'Effect of Time Credit on Equation of Exchange' ([1911] 1913, pp. 370-371), Fisher jumped from stating that if E'' and E''' were equal, nonbank credit would not affect the price level, to asserting without further argument that since E'' and E''' are approximately equal, nonbank credit does not affect the price level.

Newcomb (1885, p. 346) wrote the equation of societary circulation as $VR = KP$, where V was the volume of currency, R its average rapidity of circulation, K the number of real transactions, and P the price level. Arguing that changes in the volume of currency would have no lasting effect on R or K, Newcomb held that a change in the volume of currency would change the price level in the same proportion. In Fisher's notation, Newcomb's equation became $MV = PT$, with M for the quantity of money, V its velocity of circulation, P the price level, and T an index of the volume of real transactions (with PT being the sum across markets of pQ, price times quantity in each market). Without a method for independently measuring the velocity circulation, the equation would become simply a tautology, defining V as PT/M, devoid of testable implications. Fisher's extension of the equation to include bank deposits subject to cheque (M') as well as currency (M), $MV + M'V' = PT$, would not even define the velocities V and V'. The equation of exchange might serve as a convenient framework for arranging one's thoughts, but some independent constraint on the value of velocity was needed to move from the equation to a quantity of money theory of the purchasing power of money. Fisher's analysis of velocity of circulation was crucial to his formulation of a meaningful theory susceptible to statistical verification (see Dimand, forthcoming).

Fisher made use of two investigations into velocity in the United States undertaken by David Kinley of the University of Illinois, together with studies of European data by Pierre des Essars (1895) and Adolphe Landry (1905). For the Comptroller of the Currency in 1896 and the National Monetary Commission in 1909, Kinley (1910) measured bank deposits and the volume of transactions settled by cheque on July 1, 1896, and March 16, 1909. This provided Fisher with figures for $E' = M'V'$ (the volume of payments by cheque) and of V' on two dates (subject to adjustment because more payments would fall on the first on a month than on a mid-month date). Fisher interpolated figures for the intervening years. Bank records of deposits and withdrawals could also provide information about the volume of payments, given some hypothesis about how often a dollar was likely to be used in payment between withdrawal and redeposit. Fisher ([1911] 1913, p. 287) argued

(1) that in actual fact much money circulates out of bank only once, as in the hypothetical case just mentioned; (2) that when it is paid for wages, it usually circulates twice; and (3) that only rarely does it circulate three or more times before completing its circuit back to the banks.

Taking wages as a proxy for spending by nondepositors, Fisher ([1911] 1913, p. 475, his emphasis) concluded that '*money deposits plus wages, divided by money in circulation* will always afford a good barometer of the velocity of circulation'. He assumed that book credit or bills of exchange would usually be used only once, even though a bill of exchange can change hands several times in payment. In addition to working with aggregate data, Fisher ([1911] 1913, p. 379) also persuaded 113 Yale undergraduates, a professor, a librarian and a stenographer (the only woman in the sample) to record their daily cash spending and their cash balances at start and end of each day for a month, obtaining not only an average velocity of 66 per year but also evidence that velocity increased with increasing expenditure (which is consistent with the square root rules of the Allais-Baumol-Tobin inventory approach to the transactions demand for money and Edgeworth's 1888 model of optimal bank reserves). (Another data point is available: John Maynard Keynes (1971-89, XII, p. 763) quoted this finding of Fisher's in notes for a lecture, then went on, '[In] my own case velocity is about 34 I should guess. What is yours?')

As David Laidler (1991, pp. 81-82) remarks, Fisher's

> use of bank clearing data to get at deposit velocities involved a plausible enough approach to the problem, and his actual construction of the series presents an early and important example of the use of benchmarking and interpolation in the construction of a time series. However, Fisher's estimates of currency's velocities were derived from the volume of wage payments and of withdrawals and deposits of currency with banks, by way of essentially unsupported assumptions about the frequency with which currency turned over between appearing in wage packets and being redeposited at the bank. They are a good deal less convincing.

Having obtained time series for money, velocity and transactions, Fisher used the equation of exchange to calculate the price level as $(MV + M'V')/T$, and compared this computed price series P^* with the observations for P. In Fisher's view, the quantity theory of money would be verified if P and P^* were closely correlated and the gap between P and P^* predicted changes in P, so that P would converge to P^*. His procedure anticipated the Federal Reserve Board's P-Star model, which received extensive newspaper coverage in 1989. The P-Star model predicts that inflation will rise, fall, or stay unchanged as actual prices (P) are below, above, or at their equilibrium level (P^*), respectively. Thomas Humphrey (1989) found verbal anticipations of this approach as early as Hume and Thornton (but not Ricardo or Wheatley, who assumed P always equal to P^*) and a clear statement in *The Purchasing Power of Money*. Since Fisher took the steady state rate of inflation to be zero, he discussed changes in the price level where the later Federal Reserve model considered changes in the inflation rate.

The dates of Kinley's estimates were important for Fisher's attempted statistical verification of the quantity theory. Kemmerer (1907) had claimed that visual comparison of two series, graphed from the restoration of gold convertibility in 1879 to 1901, showed a close fit between the actual price level and that implied by a constant-velocity equation of exchange. Warren Persons of Harvard, in a review of Kemmerer's book, reported the correlation between the two series over 1879-1901 as only 0.23 (Humphrey, 1973). Fisher found a much closer fit, a correlation of 0.97 between P and P^* for 1896-1909, the only years for which he had values for all elements of his version of the equation of exchange. First differencing to remove trend only lowered the correlation to 0.62 between proportional first differences of P and P^*. Fisher concluded that the quantity theory was empirically verified, but his result was partly an artifact of the sample period for which he could obtain data. It happened that 1896, the year of Kinley's first estimates, marked the end of a period of falling prices and the start of rising prices. Fisher thus failed to discover the difference between pre-1896 velocities under falling prices and post-1896 velocities under rising prices, an empirical finding that could have pointed to an insight into the determination of the velocity of circulation.

Fisher ([1911] 1913, p. 79) classified causes affecting V or V' under three headings: habits of the individual (with regard to thrift and hoarding, use of book credit, and use of cheques), systems of payments in the community, and general causes (density of population, rapidity of transportation). Under systems of payment, Fisher held that increased frequency, regularity, or synchronization of receipts and disbursements would raise velocity of circulation. Fisher's argument that increased regularity in the payments pattern increases velocity is the concept underlying models of precautionary demand for cash balances. The Allais-Baumol-Tobin inventory approach shares Fisher's position that cash balances are held because payments and receipts are not synchronized. Fisher saw velocity as primarily determined by exogenous factors, but not in general constant over time, and varying procyclically in transition periods.

Fisher's list of factors influencing velocity missed transactions costs and the opportunity cost of holding money. Fisher ([1911] 1913, pp. 86-87) came close to recognizing the latter influence when considering the case where

> the individual is willing and able to borrow in order to meet his tax or other special expense, repaying the loan later at his convenience. This is one of the ways in which banking, as already explained, through loans and deposits, serves the convenience of the public and increases the velocity of circulation of money and deposits.

However, the author of *The Rate of Interest* did not take the next step of mentioning that the interest rate could affect willingness to take such loans, even though Fisher (1897, p. 518n) had remarked that the interest rate would affect velocity. Keynes, in *A Tract on Monetary Reform* in 1923 (1971-1989, IV), noted the decline in real money balances during the German hyperinflation as a social cost of inflation, and Eleanor Lansing Dulles (1929) cited expected inflation among the psychological determinants of velocity of circulation. McCallum and Goodfriend (1988, p. 20, based on their *New Palgrave* article) credit Fisher's *Theory of Interest* (1930, p. 216; 1997, Volume 9) with the first correct statement of the marginal opportunity cost of holding money. Since Fisher worked with velocity of circulation rather than a money demand function, it was left to Keynes to formally write money demand (liquidity preference) as a function of income and the interest rate in *The General Theory* in 1936 (1971-1989, p. VII, cf. Patinkin, 1990).

Although Fisher recognized that M' had grown relative to M over time (and that M' grew relative to M during booms), he sometimes jumped from arguing that 'by convenience a rough ratio is fixed between M and M' ' to assuming this ratio to be fixed:

> It further follows that any change in M, the quantity of money normally in circulation, requiring as it normally does a proportional change in M', the volume of bank deposits subject to check, will result in an exactly proportional change in the general level of prices except, of course, so far as this effect be interfered with by concomitant changes in the V's or the Q's ([1911] 1913, p. 52).

Don Patinkin (1993) pointed out that Fisher's compensated dollar plan for stabilizing prices concentrated on M, even though the more general version of Fisher's quantity theory crucially involved M' as well.

4   THE DANCE OF THE DOLLAR

Having established to his satisfaction that, after allowing for trends in the work to be performed by money, changes in money supply determined changes in the price level, Fisher then used changes in the price level to explain short-run fluctuations in real interest and output. Chapter IV of *The Purchasing Power of Money*, innocuously entitled 'Disturbance of Equation [of Exchange] and of Purchasing Power during Transition Periods,' was in fact an argument that the so-called business cycle was really a 'dance of the dollar', in the words of the titles of two later Fisher articles (Fisher, 1923, 1925). At the time Fisher wrote, theories of economic fluctuations as truly periodic cycles, perhaps caused by cyclical phenomena in nature, were widespread – in the 1920s centres of such research ranged from Wesley Mitchell's National Bureau of Economic Research in New York to N.D. Kondrate'ev's Conjuncture Institute in Moscow. Herbert Stanley Jevons, who held chairs of economics successively in Cardiff, Allahabad and Rangoon, continued into the 1930s to expound the sunspot theory of the trade cycle developed by his father, William Stanley Jevons. In the decade after *The Purchasing Power of Money* was published, Henry Ludwell Moore of Columbia University and Sir William Beveridge, director of the London School of Economics from 1919, attributed economic fluctuations to rainfall cycles. Fisher, like Hawtrey (1913), argued instead that apparent cycles represented responses to monetary shocks. Unlike Hawtrey, Fisher (1923, 1925, 1926) undertook systematic statistical investigations in support of his theory that imperfectly anticipated price changes, caused by monetary shocks, were behind fluctuations in output, employment and real interest. In the course of seeking statistical support for the theory he and Brown had advanced in Chapter IV of *The Purchasing Power of Money*, Fisher pioneered the use of distributed lags. One of his papers, 'A Statistical Relation between Unemployment and Price Changes' (1926), was reprinted in 1973 under the appropriate heading 'I discovered the Phillips Curve – Irving Fisher.'

Fisher wrote in Chapter IV that

> the chief object of this chapter is to show that the peculiar behavior of the rate of interest during transition periods is largely responsible for the crises and depressions in which price movements end.

When prices are rising, 'The rate of interest rises, but not sufficiently,' and when prices are falling, 'The rate of interest falls, but not sufficiently' (Fisher, with Brown [1911] 1913, pp. 56, 60, 68). The problem is what Fisher later named 'the money illusion' (the title of his 1928 book, reprinted Fisher 1997, Volume 8).

> [W]e are so accustomed in our business dealings to consider money as the one thing stable, – to think of a 'dollar as a dollar' regardless of the passage of time, that we reluctantly yield to this process of readjustment, thus rendering it very slow and imperfect. ... This inadequacy and tardiness of adjustment are fostered, moreover, by law and custom, which arbitrarily tend to keep down the rate of interest [when prices are rising]. ... If there were a better appreciation of the meaning of changes in the price level and an endeavor to balance these changes by adjustment in the rate of interest, the oscillations might be very greatly mitigated. ...On this point Marshall well says: 'The cause of alternating periods of inflation and depression of commercial activity ... is intimately connected with those variations in the real rate of interest which are caused by changes in the purchasing power of money' (Fisher with Brown, [1911] 1913, pp. 57-58, 71-72, cf. Marshall and Marshall, 1879, pp. 150-157).

Fisher (with Brown, [1911] 1913, pp. 61-63) made clear in Chapter IV that during transition periods, monetary changes would affect 'the Q's (or in other words T)' as well as prices: 'Trade (the Q's) will be stimulated by the easy terms for loans. This effect is always observed during rising prices.' Prices, as well as the nominal interest rate, adjust sluggishly:

> The first cause of the unhealthy increase in trade lies in the fact that prices, like interest, lag behind their full adjustment and have to be pushed up, so to speak, when the original impetus came from an increase in money. The surplus money is first expended at nearly the old price level, but its continued expenditure gradually raises prices. In the meantime, the volume of purchases will be somewhat greater than it would have been had prices risen more promptly.

Fisher explained how output could be increased in the transition period, in ways that he did not believe could last permanently:

although the gains of the enterpriser-borrower may exert a psychological stimulus on trade, though a few unemployed may be employed, and some others in a few lines induced to work overtime, and although there may be some additional buying and selling which is speculative, yet almost the entire effect of an increase of deposits must be seen in a change of prices. Normally the entire effect would so express itself, but transitionally there will be also some increase in the Q's.

In the chapter on purchasing power during transition periods in his *Elementary Principles of Economics*, Fisher ([1912] 1997, p. 223) noted as a disturbance caused by an increase in M that 'In particular, trade (the Q's) will be stimulated by the stimulation of loans. New constructions of buildings, etc., are entered upon.'

These statements about quantity changes in transition periods appear to me inconsistent with the statement by David Laidler (1996, p. 48 n1), 'Note that the cycle described in Fisher (1911) is a cycle in the price level. (On this matter see Laidler 1991, pp. 93-95). It was only after World War I that Fisher began to consider fluctuations in real variables.' In *The Golden Age of the Quantity Theory*, Laidler (1991, p. 95) granted that 'Fisher did recognize that quantities of goods produced might expand a little during the boom, and contract during the downswing.' Chapter IV of *The Purchasing Power of Money* does not provide a formal model of the determination of real output and employment, beyond citing sluggish adjustments of interest and prices as the channel transmitting nominal shocks to real activity, but then neither do Fisher's justly celebrated articles of the 1920s correlating output and employment with distributed lags of price level changes (Fisher, 1923, 1925, 1926). Fisher phrased his recognition of how output would be increased (a few of the unemployed hired, some workers induced to supply more hours) to avoid undue emphasis on the transitional effects (lest easy-money populists be encouraged), but he was quite clear that real output and employment would be affected by monetary shocks during transitional periods.

While this account by Fisher of how price changes affect real output in transition periods stressed that such non-neutrality of money is temporary, a phenomenon of transition periods, earlier in the same chapter he had stated that the 'permanent or ultimate effects follow after a new equilibrium is established, – if indeed, such a condition as equilibrium may be said ever to be established' ([1911] 1913, p. 56). In his unpublished 1909-1910 lectures on 'Principles of Economic Science,' Fisher stated that 'The temporary effects are just as important as, and perhaps more [than], the permanent effects. [They] become very serious if the rise in prices culminates in a crisis' (quoted by Pavanelli 1996, p. 2n). In *The Purchasing Power of Money* ([1911] 1913, p. 70) Fisher argued that

In most cases the time occupied by the swing of the commercial pendulum to and fro is about ten years. While the pendulum is continually seeking a stable position, practically there is almost always some occurrence to prevent perfect equilibrium. Oscillations are set up which, though tending to be self-corrective, are continually perpetuated by fresh disturbances.

While singling out changes in the quantity of money as an especially common source of such disturbance, Fisher also recognized harvest fluctuations, invention and 'a shock to business confidence (affecting enterprise, loans, and deposits)' as possible shocks (cf. Patinkin, 1972, pp. 5-10). He did not, however, investigate further either shocks to business confidence, which could change M' even without any shock to M, or the Schumpeterian theme of invention.

Although the short-run non-neutrality of money was relegated to Chapter IV on transition periods, it was the justification for Fisher's concluding chapter, Chapter XIII on 'The Problem of Making Purchasing Power More Stable.' Fisher's later work in monetary economics was motivated by this belief that imperfectly anticipated and understood price changes caused economic fluctuations. He campaigned tirelessly to educate the public against money illusion, promoted indexed bonds whose interest rate would automatically adjust to inflation (Fisher, 1997, Volume 8, pp. 336-339), and proposed his compensated dollar policy rule to stabilize the price level (by varying the gold content of the dollar to offset observed changes in a price index). Each of these efforts depended on knowing the purchasing power of money, so Fisher also developed his test approach to determining the best index number formula (Chapter X and its appendix in *The Purchasing Power of Money*, followed by *The Making of Index Numbers*, 1922a, in Fisher, 1997, Volume 7) and founded his Index Number Institute, which issued weekly price indices accompanied by a weekly explanatory article by Fisher. Fisher published empirical articles on the equation of exchange in the *American Economic Review* each year from 1910 to 1919, and on his weekly wholesale price index in the *Journal of the American Statistical Association* each year from 1923 to 1930 (except for 1929). As Patinkin (1972, p. 10) remarked,

over his lifetime, Irving Fisher devoted far more attention to the problem of the 'transition period' – and to his proposal for a 'stable dollar' that was designed to smooth out the fluctuations of this period – than to his famous long-run proposition about the proportionate relationship between the quantity of money and the price level.

5 EMPIRICAL PROBLEMS OF FISHER'S THEORY OF FLUCTUATIONS

Ironically, given that Fisher presented his monetary theory of economic fluctuations as an alternative to cyclical explanations, David Hendry and Mary Morgan (1995, p. 47) report that

> The Durbin-Watson statistic for our nearest approximation to his model [Fisher 1923] is less than 0.2, and even fitting a twelfth-order autoregressive error did not whiten the residuals completely. Such autoregressive residuals are at odds with his claim that they showed no cyclical tendencies.

The leading contemporary critique of Chapter IV of *The Purchasing Power of Money* was by Minnie Throop England, whose work on credit had been favorably reviewed by Fisher in the *Yale Review* and cited in *The Purchasing Power of Money* (see Dimand, 1994b). In the preface to the second edition, Fisher (1913, p. xiii) reported that

> I have endeavored to avoid disturbing the plates of the first edition more than was absolutely necessary. Otherwise I should have been glad to incorporate some changes to make use of some valuable but general criticisms. In particular I should have liked to modify somewhat the statement of the theory of crises in chapter IV and in chapter XI to make use of the helpful criticism of Miss Minnie Throop England, of the University of Nebraska, in *The Quarterly Journal of Economics*, November, 1912; also to meet a criticism of Mr. Keynes' to the effect that, while my book shows *that* the changes in the quantity of money do affect the price level, it does not show *how* they do so.

Fisher directed attention to his *Elementary Principles of Economics* (1912, pp. 242-247) for the issue raised by Keynes, but he never responded to England.

England (1912) praised Fisher for offering a definite explanation of booms and crises: booms occur when nominal interest rates rise insufficiently in response to rising prices, and end in crises when nominal interest has adjusted fully, restoring real interest to its normal level. However, 'examination of five crises in Germany and six in England does not bring to light any uniform tendency for interest as a cost of production to lag behind prices' as shown in four tables of data (England, 1912, p. 97). She found that 'sometimes a crisis occurs even tho virtual [i.e. real] interest rates are abnormally low, as in 1873 in Germany and England, or in 1900 in the latter country' and that

> prosperity may continue for several years after virtual interest rates are high, as in the crisis of 1883 in England. ... It looks as if it could more properly be said that the rapid rise of virtual interest rates was due to the stoppage of prosperity, than that the check to prosperity comes from the rise of virtual interest rates (England, 1912, pp. 103-104).

England (1912, p. 101) attributed the empirical weakness of Fisher's theory to arbitrariness in its construction:

> it would be as fitting to substitute for interest in sequence 2 of Professor Fisher any other one of the elements that go to make up the cost of production as to leave interest to fill that place alone. We could as well say (1) prices rise, (2) the cost of raw materials rises but not as much as the prices of finished products, hence profits are large, and (3) enterprisers are encouraged by large profits to expand their loans, and so on; or we could say (1) prices rise, (2) wages rise, but not so much as prices, hence profits are large, – and so on.

She also objected that the relative movements of interest and prices in transition periods cannot be understood without considering the fluctuating demand for credit for promotion and speculation, a theme of her promotion theory of crises (England, 1912, p. 98; Dimand, 1994b).

6   HARRY GUNNISON BROWN'S CONTRIBUTION

Fisher never had at Yale a group of devoted students or close research associates comparable to the Cambridge circus around Keynes or to Wesley Mitchell's National Bureau of Economic Research. His senior colleagues at Yale had little understanding of his scientific work. *The Purchasing Power of Money* is the only one of Fisher's major works whose title page is shared. Harry Gunnison Brown completed a Ph.D. dissertation on 'Some Phases of Railroad Combination' under Fisher's direction in 1909 (one of only six that Fisher ever supervised), and remained at Yale as an instructor until he joined the University of Missouri in 1915. His first publication, on railroad combination, appeared in the *Yale Review* (of which Fisher was an editor) in 1907, while Brown was still a student (Ryan, 1987, p. 4). After finishing his thesis on railroads, Brown worked closely with Fisher on monetary economics as long as he remained at Yale, but other influences on Brown grew stronger after he moved to the University of Missouri (where Thorstein Veblen then taught). Brown became closely identified with the single tax movement inspired by Henry George, and wrote mostly on public finance (Ryan, 1987, passim). Although Frank Steindl (1993, 1995) has considered Brown as comprising, together with Fisher and James Harvey Rogers, a 'Yale school' with a monetary interpretation of the Great Depression, this rests on a single essay in a student magazine (Brown, 1933), whereas his central message to the economics profession and public was embodied in a long series of single-tax books and articles. Brown's other monetary publication after 1911 (apart from monetary chapters in his principles textbook) was a 1940 *American Economic Review* critique of Fisher's proposal for a 100% reserve requirement on bank deposits (see Dimand, 1993b).

In the preface to the first edition of *The Purchasing Power of Money*, Fisher ([1911] 1913, p. xi) wrote that

> There are two persons to whom I am more indebted than to any others. These are my brother, Mr. Herbert W. Fisher, and my colleague, Dr. Harry G. Brown. To my brother my thanks are due for a most searching criticism of the whole book from the standpoint of pedagogical exposition, and to Mr. Brown for general criticism and suggestions as well as for detailed work throughout. In recognition of Mr. Brown's assistance, I have placed his name on the title-page.

As Christopher Ryan (1987, p. 38) notes, Brown's exact role is impossible to determine. Some indication is provided by Fisher's references to Brown's publications. In Chapter X, on 'The Best Form of Index Numbers', Fisher ([1911] 1913, p. 252n), arguing that an index number intended as a standard for deferred payments must be based on a broad selection of goods, remarked that

> The argument of the remainder of this section is substantially the same as that in a paper by Harry G. Brown, in the *Quarterly Journal of Economics*, August 1909, entitled 'A Problem in Deferred Payments and the Tabular Standard'.

Fisher ([1911] 1913, p. 470n) referred to a discussion of asymmetry of price dispersion in Brown's review of a book by Wesley Mitchell (Brown, 1909a). Fisher ([1911] 1913, p. 37n) drew the reader's attention to Brown (1910b) for an account of banks as an intermediary between borrowers and lenders, whose activity would tend to lower the interest rate by increasing the supply of credit.

Most importantly, a footnote in Chapter IV ([1911] 1913, p. 65n) states that 'A part of the theory of crises here presented is similarly explained in a paper by Harry G. Brown, *Yale Review*, August, 1910, entitled "Typical Commercial Crises versus a Money Panic" '. In Chapter XI on statistical verification, Fisher ([1911] 1913, p. 269n) also cited Brown (1910a) for a comparison of the crisis of 1893 with typical crises. Brown (1910a) emphasized lagging adjustment of nominal interest to unanticipated price changes, causing alternating prosperity and depression even with a sound banking system. With an unsound banking system, a loss of confidence could precipitate a money panic. Low real interest stimulates credit expansion, reducing the reserve/deposit ratio and leaving the banking system open to a money panic (with a rapid rise in nominal interest rates) when expansion ends. Brown drew on Fisher's *Rate of Interest* (1907) and on an article by Wicksell (which was cited in *The Purchasing Power of Money*, [1911] 1913, pp. 59, 60). A later principles text by Brown dropped Fisher's emphasis on lagging adjustment of nominal interest as the main explanation of crises (Ryan, 1987, pp. 40-41), but the analysis of Chapter IV remained central to Fisher's later work on the so-called business cycle as largely a dance of the dollar.

7 FISHER'S LEGACY IN MACROECONOMICS

Irving Fisher's monetary macroeconomics suffered an extended period of neglect beginning in the 1930s. Fisher's spectacular misprediction of stock prices in 1929 hurt his public reputation (and devastated his personal finances): 'in the Crash [Fisher] lost between eight and ten million dollars. This was a sizable sum, even for an economics professor' (Galbraith, 1977, p. 192). His monetary theory of economic fluctuations did not provide a formal model of the determination of output and employment, and so did not satisfy the strongly-felt demand for a theory of unemployment in the Great Depression. Keynes's *General Theory* created a new agenda and vocabulary for macroeconomics, compared to which Fisher's quantity theory seemed old-fashioned, even though Keynes (1971-1989, XIV, p. 203n) wrote in 1937 that 'I find, looking back, that is was Professor Irving Fisher who was the great-grandparent who first influenced me strongly towards regarding money as a "real" factor'. Fisher's use of velocity of circulation rather than a money demand function obscured the links between his monetary macroeconomics and the Chicago-based revival of the quantity theory of money. In the five essays in *Studies in the Quantity Theory of Money* (Friedman, 1956), the only references to Fisher were by Richard Selden to Fisher's efforts at measurement of velocity. Instead, Friedman and his students emphasized a Chicago oral tradition in monetary theory. However, Don Patinkin, himself a Chicago Ph.D., questioned Friedman's account of such a thinly-documented oral tradition (see the articles collected in Patinkin, 1981). Thomas Humphrey (1971) presented evidence that several characteristic doctrines of modern Chicago monetary thought originated not with Friedman's mentors, but with equation of exchange quantity theorists outside Chicago (such as Carl Snyder), whose work 'has its roots in and emanates from the earlier Fisherian tradition'.

Fisher's ambitious statistical verification of the quantity theory of money and later of the monetary theory of economic fluctuations encountered empirical problems. His close correlation between actual and predicted price levels depended on the accident that he could not obtain data series for all the elements of his version of the equation of exchange before 1896, and the model and data set that he used to show that fluctuations are a dance of the dollar, not reflecting true underlying cycles, in fact had cyclical residuals. To empirical monetary macroeconomics, Fisher contributed distributed lags, his 'ideal index' formula (adopted by the US Commerce Department in 1995), and the first correlation estimate of a Phillips Curve relationship in 1926 (Jan Tinbergen provided the first regression estimate of it ten years later). Modern theoretical macroeconomics displays even stronger connections to Fisher. His two-period diagram for optimal intertemporal consumption (Fisher, 1907, p. 409) is the basis for the life-cycle and permanent income theories of consumption. Fisher's expected rate of return over costs was stated by Keynes to be the same as Keynes's marginal efficiency of capital (but see Dimand, 1995, for Keynes's reservations in his lectures). Although it was Keynes, not Fisher, who wrote money demand as an explicit function of income and interest, McCallum and Goodfriend (1988) credit Fisher (1930, p. 216) with the first unambiguous and correct statement of the marginal opportunity cost of holding money.

Fisher was an early advocate of a monetary policy rule (other than the fixed exchange rate of the gold standard), rather than discretion. Scott Sumner (1990) has identified Fisher's compensated dollar as a close forerunner of the Black-Fama-Hall proposed monetary system, in which the government defines the unit of account in terms of a comprehensive basket of commodities. Fisher's correlations between the interest rate and a distributed lag of past inflation, given his decomposition of nominal interest into real interest and expected inflation, was a pioneering application of adaptive expectations. Another work in the quantity theory tradition, Keynes's *Tract on Monetary Reform* (1923, 1971-1989, IV), contributed inflation as a tax on holding money, reduced demand for real money balances as a cost of inflation, and the nominal interest differential between two countries as the forward premium or discount between their currencies (Dimand, 1988, Chapter 1).

Like Friedman and Schwartz (1963), Fisher attributed the severity of the Great Depression to the contraction of the money supply, emphasizing the effect on Federal Reserve policy-making of the death of Benjamin Strong (Cargill, 1992; Steindl, 1993, 1995). Fisher (1936, p. 104) held that

> one cause towers above all others, the collapse of our deposit currency. The depression was a money famine – a famine, not of pocket-book money but of check-book money, the money, or so-called money, recorded on the stubs of our check-books, our deposits subject to check. ... Moreover in 1929 all money circulated faster than in 1933 when people were hoarding.

The rising reserve/deposit and currency/deposit ratios of the early 1930s could be explained by Fisher's debt-deflation theory of depressions (Fisher, 1933), a contribution made by Fisher after he had lost his audience and one which long remained outside the mainstream of macroeconomics. Given high levels of inside debt with fixed nominal values, an unanticipated price decline starts a scramble for liquidity that further deflates asset and commodity prices, increasing the real value of inside debt, which raises risk premia and transfers purchasing power from debtors to creditors (with lower propensities to spend). Such a Fisher effect on inside debt can more than offset the Pigou-Haberler real balance effect on outside money, affecting the stability of full-employment equilibrium (Tobin, 1980, pp. 9-18). Fisher's debt-deflation theory long figured in Post Keynesian economics through Hyman Minsky's work on fragility of the financial system, and has more recently been taken up by Ben Bernanke and

Mervyn King in more mainstream literature (see Minsky, 1986; Kindleberger, 1989; Dimand, 1994a).

The extent of Fisher's anticipations of later monetary macroeconomics is only gradually being fully appreciated. The role of monetary standards in the interwar transmission of business cycles has been studied in recent years (without reference to Fisher) by Ehsan Choudhri and Levis Kochin, James Hamilton, Peter Temin, and Barry Eichengreen. In 1933, the International Statistical Institute asked Fisher to undertake a study, published in the Institute's *Bulletin* in 1935 as 'Are Booms and Depressions Transmitted Internationally through Monetary Standards?' (Fisher, 1935). This article is yet noticed in the literature only by a paragraph by Giovanni Pavanelli (1996, p. 25), who recognized it as 'a pathbreaking paper'. Fisher's comparative of study price level and output of twenty-seven countries, grouped by monetary standard, led him to conclude that those outside the gold standard or which left gold earlier had more stable prices and better output performance. This supported Fisher's preference for domestic price level stabilization over fixed exchange rates (in contrast to the support of the gold standard by his fellow quantity theorist, Kemmerer). Fisher's papers at meetings of the International Statistical Institute in the 1930s are a remarkable testimony to the fertility, and what in retrospect seems the modernity, of his thought at a time when he seemed to have been passed by in macroeconomics: the debt-deflation theory at the 1933 meeting in Mexico City, monetary standards and international transmission of depressions in 1935, and a short-cut method for estimating distributed lags (the Fisher lag, with arithmetically declining weights) in 1937.

James Tobin (1985, pp. 36-37) concluded that Fisher's

> insights contain the makings of a theory of the determination of economic activity, prices, and interest rates in short and medium runs. Moreover, in his neo-classical writings on capital and interest Fisher had laid the basis for the investment and saving equations central to modern macroeconomic models. Had Fisher pulled these strands together into a coherent theory, he could have been an American Keynes.

Fisher never pulled the strands of his economics together in a grand synthesis. His monetary economics, from his 1896 monograph on real and nominal interest through *The Purchasing Power of Money*'s Chapter IV on transition periods to his writings on index numbers, economic fluctuations as a dance of the dollar, and money illusion, was united by a concern with the consequences of imperfectly-expected monetary shocks (cf. Dimand, 1997a). He did not, however, set his monetary economics in the context of either his capital theory or the general equilibrium analysis of his doctoral dissertation. His fervent desire to improve the world sometimes led to policy recommendations that did less than justice to his theory (see Patinkin, 1993, on the compensated dollar). In the 1936 Cowles Commission lecture quoted in the paragraph before last, Fisher endorsed raising reserve requirements to eliminate the inflationary menace posed by excess reserves as a step toward his 100% money plan that would insulate the medium of exchange against the hazards of financial intermediation: the Federal Reserve's doubling of reserve requirements combined with a fiscal contraction to produce the sharp recession of 1937-38. Fisher's stock debacle provoked public glee at the discomfiture of a supposed financial expert; in contrast, few noticed when a retired economics professor died as the richest man in the world (Lambert, 1993). Above all, Fisher did not deal with the macroeconomic coordination problem that Keynes and Hayek tackled in very different ways in the 1930s. He offered no theory of how a collapse in nominal income and spending led to mass unemployment in the 1930s, for he did not add an analysis of the labor market to his monetary economics. Because of this lack, and amid the wreckage of his reputation and his finances by his misjudgement of stock prices, Fisher found little contemporary audience for his debt-deflation theory of depressions, his explanation of the spending collapse. Even his monetary theory of economic fluctuations was neglected as introductory textbooks attached his name to a constant-velocity, constant-output quantity theory. With historical perspective, however, Fisher can now be recognized among the most fruitful builders of modern macroeconomics, a giant figure in the development of both theoretical and empirical monetary macroeconomics. He can also be recognized as a monetary economist whose work embodied strong tensions: between the quest for theoretical understanding and for immediate policy relevance, between the long-run neutrality of money and the short-run dance of the dollar, between neoclassical equilibrium economics and the possibly unstable financial system illuminated by the debt-deflation process.

REFERENCES

Barber, W.J. (ed.), assisted by R.W. Dimand and K. Foster, consulting editor J. Tobin (1997), *The Works of Irving Fisher*, London, Pickering and Chatto:
Volume 1: *The Early Professional Works.*
Volume 2: *The Nature of Capital and Income.*
Volume 3: *The Rate of Interest.*
Volume 4: *The Purchasing Power of Money.*
Volume 5: *Elementary Principles of Economics.*
Volume 6: *Stabilizing the Dollar.*
Volume 7: *The Making of Index Numbers.*
Volume 8: *The Money Illusion and Related Writings.*
Volume 9: *The Theory of Interest.*
Volume 10: *Booms and Depressions and Related Writings.*
Volume 11: *100% Money.*
Volume 12: *Contributions to the Theory and Practice of Public Finance.*
Volume 13: *A Crusader for Social Causes.*
Volume 14: *Correspondence and other Commentary on Economic Policy 1930-1947.*

Barker, D.A (1913), *The Theory of Money*, Cambridge, Cambridge University Press, The Cambridge Manuals of Science and Literature.

Blaug, M., Eltis, W., O'Brien, D., Patinkin, D., Skidelsky, R. and Wood, G.E. (1995), *The Quantity Theory of Money from Locke to Keynes and Friedman*, Aldershot, UK, and Brookfield, VT, Edward Elgar.

Boyer, J. de (1988), 'Irving Fisher, great-grandparent of the 'General Theory': Un Commentaire', *Cahiers d'Economie Politique*, **14-15**, 69-73.

Brown, H.G. (1909a), Review of *Gold, Prices, and Wages under the Greenback Standard* by Wesley Mitchell, *Yale Review*, **18**, 99-101.

Brown, H.G. (1909b), 'A problem in deferred payments and the tabular standard', *Quarterly Journal of Economics*, **23**, 714-718.

Brown, H.G. (1910a), 'Typical commercial crises versus a money panic', *Yale Review* **19**, 168-176.

Brown, H.G. (1910b), 'Commercial banking and the rate of interest', *Quarterly Journal of Economics* **24**, 743-749.

Brown, H.G. (1933), 'Sense and nonsense in dealing with the depression', *Beta Gamma Sigma Exchange*, (Spring), 97-107.

Cargill, T.F. (1992), 'Miscellany: Irving Fisher comments on Benjamin Strong and the Federal Reserve in the 1930s', *Journal of Political Economy*, **100**, 1273-1277.

Dean, E. (ed.) (1965), *The Controversy Over the Quantity Theory of Money*, Boston, D.C. Heath.

Dimand, R.W. (1988), *The Origins of the Keynesian Revolution*, Aldershot, UK, Edward Elgar, and Stanford, CA, Stanford University Press.

Dimand, R.W. (1993a), 'The dance of the dollar: Irving Fisher's monetary theory of economic fluctuations', *History of Economics Review*, **20**, 161-172.

Dimand, R.W. (1993b), '100% money: Irving Fisher and monetary reform in the 1930s', *History of Economic Ideas* **1**, 59-76.

Dimand, R.W. (1994a), 'Irving Fisher's debt-deflation theory of great depressions', *Review of Social Economy*, **52**, (Spring), 92-107. Revised as Chapter 7 below.

Dimand, R.W. (1994b), 'Minnie Throop England on crises and cycles: a neglected early macroeconomist', presented to History of Economics Society annual meeting, Babson College.

Dimand, R.W. (1995), 'Irving Fisher, J.M. Keynes and the transition to modern macroeconomics', in A.F. Cottrell and M.S. Lawlor (eds), *New Perspectives on Keynes, annual supplement to History of Political Economy*, **27**, 247-266.

Dimand, R.W. (1997a), 'Irving Fisher and modern macroeconomics', *American Economic Review, Papers and Proceedings*, **87**, 440-442.

Dimand, R.W. (1997b), 'The role of credit in Fisher's monetary economics', in A. Cohen, H. Hagemann and J. Smithin (eds), *Money, Financial Institutions and Macroeconomics*, Boston, Kluwer Academic, 101-108.

Dimand, R.W. (forthcoming), 'Fisher and the inconstant velocity of circulation', forthcoming in proceedings of 1996 colloquium of l'Association Charles Gide pour l'Etude de la Pensée Economique, A. Lapidus and O. Hamouda (eds).

Dulles, E.L. (1929), *The French Franc, 1914-1928*, New York, Macmillan.

England, M.T. (1912), 'Fisher's theory of crises: a criticism', *Quarterly Journal of Economics*, **27**, 95-106.

Essars, P. des (1895), 'La Vitesse de la Circulation de la Monnaie', *La Journal de la Société de Statistique de Paris*, **36**, 143-151.

Fisher, I. (1896), 'Appreciation and interest', *American Economic Association Publications* 3rd series, **11**. Reprinted in I. Fisher, 1997, Volume 1.

Fisher, I. (1897), 'The role of capital in economic theory', *Economic Journal, 7*, 511-537. Reprinted in I. Fisher, 1997, Volume 1.

Fisher, I. (1907), *The Rate of Interest, Its Nature, Determination and Relation to Economic Phenomena*, New York, Macmillan. Reprinted in I. Fisher, 1997, Volume 3.

Fisher, I., assisted by H.G. Brown ([1911] 1913) *The Purchasing Power of Money: Its Determination and Relation to Credit, Interest and Crises*, 2nd ed. New York, Macmillan. Reprinted in I. Fisher, 1997, Volume 4.

Fisher, I. (1912), *Elementary Principles of Economics*, New York, Macmillan. Reprinted in I. Fisher, 1997, Volume 5.

Fisher, I. (1923), 'The business cycle largely a "dance of the dollar" ' *Journal of the American Statistical Association* **18**, 1024-1028. Reprinted in I. Fisher, 1997, Volume 8.

Fisher, I. (1925), 'Our unstable dollar and the so-called business cycle', *Journal of the American Statistical Association,* **20**, 179-202. Reprinted in I. Fisher, 1997, Volume 8.

Fisher, I. (1926), 'A statistical relation between unemployment and price changes', *International Labour Review* **13**, 785-792. Reprinted as 'Lost and found: I discovered the Phillips curve – Irving Fisher', *Journal of Political Economy,* **81,** 496-502, and in I. Fisher, 1997, Volume 8.

Fisher, I. (1930), *The Theory of Interest As Determined by Impatience to Spend Income and Opportunity to Invest It*, New York, Macmillan. Reprinted in I. Fisher, 1997, Volume 9.

Fisher, I. (1933), 'The debt-deflation theory of great depressions', *Econometrica,* **1,** 337-357. Reprinted in I. Fisher, 1997, Volume 10. (Also in *Review of the International Statistical Institute,* **1,** 1934, 48-65.)

Fisher, I. (1935), 'Are booms and depressions transmitted internationally through monetary standards?' *Bulletin de l'Institut International de Statistique,* **28,** 1-29.

Fisher, I. (1936), 'Abstracts of public lectures: the depression, its causes and cures', *Abstracts of Papers Presented at the Research Conference on Economics and Statistics Held by the Cowles Commission for Research in Economics*, Colorado College Publication, General Series No. 208, Study Series, No. 21, Colorado Springs, CO, Colorado College, 104-107.

Fisher, I. (1937), 'Note on a short-cut method for calculating distributed lags', *Bulletin de l'Institut International de Statistique,* **29,** 323-328. Reprinted in I. Fisher, 1997, Volume 8.

Fisher, I. (1997), cf. W.J. Barber, 1997.

Friedman, M. (ed.) (1956), *Studies in the Quantity Theory of Money*, Chicago, University of Chicago Press.

Friedman, M. and Schwartz, A.J. (1963), *A Monetary History of the United States 1867-1960* Princeton, NJ, Princeton University Press for the National Bureau of Economic Research.

Galbraith, J.K. (1977), *The Age of Uncertainty*, Boston, Houghton Mifflin.

Hardy, S.McL. (1895), 'The quantity theory of money and prices, 1860-1891', *Journal of Political Economy,* **3,** 145-168.

Harvey, W.H. ([1894] 1963), *Coin's Financial School*. Reprinted with introduction by R. Hofstadter, Cambridge, MA, Harvard University Press (John Harvard Library edition).

Hawtrey, R.G. (1913), *Good and Bad Trade*, London, Constable. Reprinted (with 1962 foreword) New York, A.M. Kelley, 1970.

Henderson, J.P. (1986), 'Sir John William Lubbock's *On Currency* – "an interesting book by a still more interesting man" ', *History of Political Economy,* **18**, 383-404.

Hendry, D.F. and Morgan, M.S. (1995), 'Introduction' to Hendry and Morgan (eds), *The Foundations of Econometric Analysis*, Cambridge, Cambridge University Press, 1-84.

Humphrey, T.M. (1971), 'Role of Non-Chicago Economists in the Evolution of the Quantity Theory in America 1930-1950', *Southern Economic Journal,* **38**, 12-18.

Humphrey, T.M. (1973), 'Empirical Tests of the Quantity Theory of Money in the United States, 1900-1930', *History of Political Economy,* **5**, 285-316.

Humphrey, T.M. (1984), 'Algebraic quantity equations before Fisher and Pigou', *Federal Reserve Bank of Richmond Economic Review,* **70**. As reprinted in Humphrey, *Essays on Inflation,* 5th ed., Richmond, VA, Federal Reserve Bank of Richmond, 1986, 278-287.

Humphrey, T.M. (1989), 'Precursors of the P-star model', *Federal Reserve Bank of Richmond Economic Review,* **75**, 3-9.

Kemmerer, E.W. (1907), *Money and Credit Instruments in their Relation to General Prices*, New York, Henry Holt and Co. Reprinted New York and London, Garland Publishing, 1983.

Keynes, J.M. (1971-1989), *Collected Writings*, 30 vols., D.E. Moggridge and E.A.G. Robinson (eds), London, Macmillan, and New York, Cambridge University Press, for the Royal Economic Society.

Kindleberger, C.P. (1989), *Manias, Panics, and Crashes*, revised ed., New York, Basic Books.

Kinley, D. (1910), *The Use of Credit Instruments in Payments in the United States,* Washington, DC, National Monetary Commission, 61st Congress, 2nd session, Document No. 399.

Kregel, J. (1988), 'Irving Fisher, great-grandparent of the *General Theory*: money, rate of return over cost and efficiency of capital', *Cahiers d'Economie Politique,* **14-15**, 59-68.

Laidler, D. (1991), *The Golden Age of the Quantity Theory*, Princeton, NJ, Princeton University Press.

Laidler, D. (1996), 'American macroeconomics between world war I and the depression', Department of Economics, University of Western Ontario, Research Report 9606.

Lambert, B. (1993), 'Taikichiro Mori, Tokyo developer rated as richest man, dies at 88', *New York Times,* January 31.

Landry, A. (1905), 'La Rapidité de la Circulation Monétaire', *Revue d'Economie Politique,* **19**, 156-174.

Marshall, A. and Marshall, M.P. (1879), *Economics of Industry*, London, Macmillan. Reprinted with introduction by Denis O'Brien, Bristol, Thoemmes Press, 1994.

Marshall, A. (1923), *Money, Credit and Commerce,* London, Macmillan.

Marshall, A. (1926), *Official Papers*, J.M. Keynes (ed.), London, Macmillan for the Royal Economic Society.

McCallum, B.T. and Goodfriend, M.S. (1988), 'Theoretical analysis of the demand for money', *Federal Reserve Bank of Richmond Economic Review,* **74**, 16-24.

Minsky, H.P. (1986), *Stabilizing an Unstable Economy*, New Haven, CT, Yale University Press.

Mises, L. von ([1912] 1935), *The Theory of Money and Credit*, trans. H.E. Batson from 2nd German ed. of 1924, London, Jonathan Cape.

Mitchell, W.C. (1896), 'The quantity theory of the value of money', *Journal of Political Economy,* **4**, 139-165.

Newcomb, S. (1879), 'The standard of value', *North American Review,* **124**, 234-237.

Newcomb, S. (1885), *Principles of Political Economy*, New York, Harper.

Patinkin, D. (1972), 'On the short-run non-neutrality of money in the quantity theory', *Banca Nazionale del Lavoro Quarterly Review*, No. **100**, 3-22.

Patinkin, D. (1981), *Essays On and In the Chicago Tradition*, Durham, NC, Duke University Press.

Patinkin, D. (1990), *Irving Fisher, the Cambridge School and the Quantity Theory*, Seoul, Korea Development Institute, Distinguished Lecturer Program Report Series, no. 90-01.

Patinkin, D. (1993), 'Irving Fisher and his compensated dollar plan', *Federal Reserve Bank of Richmond Economic Quarterly*, **79**, 1-33.

Pavenelli, G. (1996), 'Non-neutrality of money and business cycles in Irving Fisher's work', Quaderni del Dipartimento di Scienze Economiche e Finanziarie 'G. Prato', Facolta di Economia, Universita degli Studi di Torino, Quaderno n. **29**.

Price, L.L. (1896), *Money and Its Relation to Prices*, London. Reprinted New York and London, Garland Publishing.

Ritter, L.S. (1963), 'The role of money in Keynesian theory', in D. Carson (ed.), *Banking and Monetary Studies*, Chicago, Irwin, 134-150. Reprinted in J. Lindauer (ed.), *Macroeconomic Readings*, New York, Free Press, 1968, 79-88.

Ryan, C.K. (1987), *Harry Gunnison Brown, Economist*, Boulder, CO, and London, Westview Press.

Saul, S.B. (1969), *The Myth of the Great Depression 1873-1896*, London, Macmillan for the Economic History Society.

Schumpeter, J.A. (1948), 'Irving Fisher's econometrics', *Econometrica*, **16**. As reprinted in Schumpeter, *Ten Great Economists*, New York, Oxford University Press, 1965.

Skaggs, N.T. (1995), 'The methodological roots of J. Laurence Laughlin's anti-quantity theory of money and prices', *Journal of the History of Economic Thought*, **17**, 1-20.

Steindl, F.G. (1993), 'Yale and the monetary interpretation of the great depression', *Quarterly Review of Economics and Finance*, **33**, 305-323.

Steindl, F.G. (1995), *Monetary Interpretations of the Great Depression*, Ann Arbor, MI, University of Michigan Press.

Stigler, G.J. and Friedland, C. (1979), 'The pattern of citations practices in economics', *History of Political Economy*, **11**, 1-20.

Sumner, S. (1990), 'The forerunners of "new monetary economics" proposals to stabilize the unit of account', *Journal of Money, Credit, and Banking*, **22**, 109-118.

Tobin, J. (1980), *Asset Accumulation and Economic Activity*, Chicago, University of Chicago Press.

Tobin, J. (1985), 'Neoclassical theory in America: J.B. Clark and Fisher', *American Economic Review*, **75**, 28-38.

Walker, F.A. (1895), 'The quantity theory of money', *Quarterly Journal of Economics* **9**, 372-379.

Willis, H.P. (1896), 'Credit devices of the quantity theory', *Journal of Political Economy*, **4**, 281-308.

4. Irving Fisher and Knut Wicksell: Different Interpretations of the Quantity Theory?

Thomas M. Humphrey

The quantity theory of money, dating back at least to the mid-sixteenth-century Spanish Scholastic writers of the Salamanca School, is one of the oldest theories in economics. Modern students know it as the proposition stating that an exogenously given one-time change in the stock of money has no lasting effect on real variables but leads ultimately to a proportionate change in the money price of goods. More simply, it declares that, all else being equal, money's value or purchasing power varies inversely with its quantity.

There is nothing mysterious about the quantity theory. Classical and neoclassical economists never tired of stressing that it is but an application of the ordinary theory of demand and supply to money. Demand-and-supply theory, of course, predicts that a good's equilibrium value, or market price, will fall as the good becomes more abundant relative to the demand for it. In the same way, the quantity theory predicts that an increase in the nominal supply of money will, given the real demand for it, lower the value of each unit of money in terms of the goods it commands. Since the inverse of the general price level measures money's value in terms of goods, general prices must rise.

In the late nineteenth and early twentieth centuries, two versions of the theory competed. One, advanced by the American economist Irving Fisher (1867-1947), treated the theory as a complete and self-contained explanation of the price level. The other, propounded by the Swedish economist Knut Wicksell (1851-1926), saw it as part of a broader model in which the difference, or spread, between market and natural rates of interest jointly determine bank money and price level changes.

The contrasts between the two approaches could hardly have been more pronounced. Fisher's version was consistently quantity theoretic throughout and indeed focused explicitly on the received classical propositions of neutrality, equiproportionality, money-to-price causality, and independence of money supply and demand. By contrast, Wicksell's version contained certain elements seemingly at odds with the theory. These included (1) a real shock explanation of monetary and price movements, (2) the complete absence of money (currency) in the hypothetical extreme case of a pure credit economy, and (3) the identity between deposit supply and demand at all price levels in that same pure credit case rendering prices indeterminate.

Despite these anomalies, Wicksell was able to derive from his analysis essentially the same conclusion Fisher reached. Both concluded that the monetary authority bears the ultimate responsibility for price level stability, a responsibility it fulfills either by determining some nominal variable – such as dollar price of gold, monetary base, bank reserves – under its control or by adjusting its lending rate in response to price level deviations from target.

The story of how Fisher and Wicksell reached identical policy conclusions from seemingly distinct models is instructive. It reveals that models appearing to be substantially different may be only superficially so. In the case of Fisher and Wicksell, it reveals that their models may not have been as dissimilar as often thought. Indeed, the alleged non-quantity-theory elements in Wicksell's work prove, upon careful examination, to be entirely consistent with the theory. In an effort to document these assertions and to establish Wicksell's position in the front rank of neoclassical quantity theorists with Fisher, the paragraphs below identify the two men's contributions to the theory and show how their policy conclusions derived from it.

1   FISHER'S VERSION OF THE QUANTITY THEORY

In his 1911 book *The Purchasing Power of Money*, Fisher gave the quantity theory, as inherited from his classical and pre-classical predecessors, its definitive modern formulation. In so doing, he accomplished two tasks. First, he expressed the theory rigorously in a form amenable to empirical measurement and verification. Indeed, he himself fitted the theory with statistical data series, many of them of his own construction, to demonstrate its predictive accuracy.

Second, he spelled out explicitly what was often merely implicit in the work of John Locke, David Hume, Richard Cantillon, David Ricardo, John Wheatley, and other early quantity theorists, namely the five interrelated propositions absolutely central to the theory. These referred to (1) equiproportionality of money and prices, (2) money-to-price causality, (3) short-run non-neutrality and long-run neutrality of money, (4) independence of money supply and demand, and (5) relative-price/absolute-price dichotomy attributing relative price movements to real causes and absolute price movements to monetary causes in a stationary fully employed economy.[1]

Fisher enunciated these propositions with the aid of the equation of exchange $P = (MV + M'V') / T$, which he attributed to Simon Newcomb even though Joseph Lang, Karl Rau, John Lubbock, and E. Levasseur had formulated it even earlier. Here P is the price level, M is the stock of hard or metallic money consisting of gold coin and convertible bank notes, V is the turnover velocity of circulation of that stock, M' is the stock of bank money consisting of demand deposits transferable by check, V' is its turnover velocity, and T is the physical volume of trade. Fisher's assumption that metallic money divides in fixed proportions between currency and bank reserves and that reserves are a fixed fraction of deposits allowed him to treat checkbook money as a constant multiple c of hard money. His assumption allows one to simplify his expression to $P = MV^* / T$, where $V^* = V + cV'$.

Of the equation's components, Fisher ([1911] 1963, p. 155) assumed that, in long-run equilibrium, the volume of trade is determined at its full-capacity level by real forces including the quantity and quality of the labor force, the size of the capital stock, and the level of technology. Save for transition adjustment periods in which the variables interact, these real forces and so the level of trade itself are independent of the other variables in the equation. Likewise, institutions and habits determine aggregate velocity, whose magnitude is fixed by the underlying velocity turnover rates of individual cashholders, each of whom has adjusted his turnover to suit his convenience (Fisher [1911] 1963, p. 152). Like the volume of trade, velocity is independent of the other variables in the equation of exchange. And with trade and velocity independent of each other and of everything else in the equation, it follows that equilibrium changes in the price level must be due to changes in the money stock.

1.1 Classical Propositions

All the fundamental classical quantity theory propositions follow from Fisher's demonstration. Regarding proportionality, he writes that 'a change in the quantity of money must normally cause a proportional change in the price level' ([1911] 1963, p. 157). For, with trade and velocity independent of the money stock and fixed at their long-run equilibrium levels, it follows that a doubling of the money stock will double the price level.

Fisher realized, of course, that proportionality holds only for the ceteris paribus thought experiment in which trade and velocity are provisionally held fixed. In actual historical time, however, trade and velocity undergo secular changes of their own independent of the money stock. In that case, proportionality refers to the *partial* effect of money on prices. To this partial effect must be added the parallel effects of coincidental changes in velocity and trade (see Niehans, 1990, p. 277). The sum of these separate effects shows the influence of all on the price level. Thus if M, V^*, and T evolve secularly at the percentage rates of change denoted by the lowercase letters m, v^*, and t, respectively, then the price level P evolves at the percentage rate $p = m+v^*-t$. Fisher ([1911] 1963, pp. 246-247) himself expressed the matter precisely when he declared that the history of the price level is a history of the race between increases in the money stock and increases in the volume of trade.

Fisher was equally adamant on the neutrality of money other than during transition adjustment periods. Regarding long-run neutrality, he says that 'An inflation of the currency cannot increase the product of ... business' since the latter 'depends on natural resources and technical conditions, not on the quantity of money' ([1911] 1963, p. 155). In short, trade's long-run independence of money in the equation of exchange means that money cannot permanently influence real activity.

Money can, however, influence real activity temporarily. Indeed, the classical proposition regarding the short-run non-neutrality of money posits that very point. Fisher ([1911] 1963, pp. 58-72), in his theory of the cycle, attributes such non-neutrality to delays in the revision of lenders' inflation expectations and the resulting sluggish adjustment of nominal interest rates. A monetary shock sets prices rising. Rising prices generate inflation expectations among business borrowers whose perceptions of current and likely future price changes are superior to those of lenders. These inflationary expectations engender corresponding expectations of higher business profits. Sluggish nominal loan rates, however, fail to rise enough to offset these rising expectations. Consequently, real loan rates fall. Spurred by the fall in real rates, business borrowers increase their real expenditure on factor inputs. Employment and output rise. Eventually, nominal loan rates catch up with and surpass business profit (and inflation) expectations. Real rates rise thereby precipitating a downturn.[2]

As for the proposition of unidirectional money-to-price causality, Fisher established it in two ways. First, he denied that causation, under the gold standard then prevailing, could possibly run in the reverse direction from prices to money ([1911] 1963, pp. 169-171). To demonstrate as much, he supposed prices miraculously to double, the other variables in the exchange equation initially remaining unchanged. Far from inducing an accommodating expansion in the money stock, the price increase would, in an open trading economy, actually prompt that stock to contract. The stock would contract as the price increase, by rendering domestic goods expensive in relation to foreign ones, engendered a trade balance deficit and a resulting external drain of monetary gold. The upshot is that the price increase would not cause a supporting rise in the money stock as reverse causation implies. Nor for that matter could the price increase spawn validating changes in the other variables of the exchange equation. The independence of those variables with respect to the price level rules out this possibility. In short, the price level is 'the one absolutely passive element in the equation' (Fisher, [1911] 1963, p. 172). Its movements are the result, not the cause, of prior changes in the quantity of money per unit of trade.

Alternatively, Fisher demonstrates M-to-P causality by showing that no variables in the exchange equation can intervene to absorb permanently the impact of a change in M and thus prevent the force of that impact from being transmitted to P. No compensating changes in trade will occur to blunt M's impact since the two variables are independent in long-run equilibrium. Nor will M exhaust its effect in reducing velocity permanently. For cashholders have already established velocity at its desired level, a level independent of M.

Instead, Fisher ([1911] 1963, pp. 153-154) argued that money will transmit its full effect to prices through the following cash-balance adjustment mechanism. Let the money stock double from M to $2M$, the price level initially remaining unchanged. With prices and trade given, actual velocity $V^* = PT/2M$ falls to one-half the level cashholders desire it to be, or PT/M. In an effort to restore actual velocity to its desired level, cashholders will increase their rate of spending. The increased spending will, because trade is fixed at its full-capacity level, put upward pressure on prices. Prices will continue to rise until actual and desired velocities are the same $(V^* = 2PT/2M = PT/M)$. At this point, prices will have doubled equiproportionally with money.

The remaining classical propositions follow directly from Fisher's analysis. Regarding the relative-price/absolute-price dichotomy, he denied that real factors change the absolute price level in a stationary, fully-employed economy. In particular, he insisted that price level changes cannot be caused by cost-push forces emanating from trade-union militancy, business-firm monopoly power, commodity shortages, and the like ([1911] 1963, pp. 179-180).[3] Such forces, he says, drive relative prices, not absolute ones. In other words, given the money stock, velocity, and trade, real shock-induced changes in some relative prices produce compensating changes in others, leaving the absolute price level unchanged. Real shocks, if they are to affect absolute prices as well as relative ones, must somehow also cause changes in M, V^*, or T. Fisher saw little reason to expect them to do so. And even if they did, their effect would always be so small as to be swamped by exogenous changes in money.

Finally, with respect to independence of money supply and demand, Fisher attempts to establish it by arguing that the money stock owes its determination to 'influences outside the equation of exchange,' that is, to influences other than the trade-to-velocity ratio T / V^* $(= M / P)$ which constitutes the public's real demand for money ([1911] 1963, p. 90). For a closed gold-standard economy, these outside influences include the rate of gold production as influenced by new gold discoveries and technological innovations, both of which temporarily lower the metal's production cost below its market value and so give a profit boost to mining. For open economies operating on the gold standard, additional external influences include foreign price levels. These, when high or low relative to the domestic price level, induce specie flows through the balance of payments. Such specie flows in turn raise or lower the domestic money stock and through it the domestic price level. From the viewpoint of the open domestic economy, money-stock changes are predetermined exogenously by the height of the foreign price level. These money-stock changes then endogenously affect domestic prices. As Fisher put it ([1911] 1963, p. 172),

> the price level outside of New York City ... affects the price level in New York City only *via* changes in the money in New York City. Within New York City it is the money which influences the price level, and not the price level which influences the money.

Today, of course, we would say that an open economy's money stock is endogenously determined by the requirement that domestic price levels move in step with foreign ones to maintain equilibrium in the balance of payments (see Friedman and Schwartz, 1991, p. 42). But Fisher, by contrast, argued that the open economy's money stock is determined exogenously by the *given* state of the balance of payments resulting from the *given* foreign (relative to domestic) price level.

We will see in Section 4 below, however, that he did correctly apply the exogeneity, or independence, proposition to so-called compensated dollar and inconvertible paper standard regimes. He recognized that, in such regimes, the policy authority governs money exogenously either through control of the gold weight of the dollar or through the high-powered monetary base consisting of the authority's own liabilities. Through these instruments, the authority renders the money stock independent of money demand.

2   WICKSELL'S INTERPRETATION OF THE QUANTITY THEORY

Knut Wicksell's perception of the classical quantity theory, as expounded in his 1898 *Interest and Prices* and Volume 2 of his 1906 *Lectures on Political Economy,* was less comprehensive than Fisher's. Wicksell understood the theory to mean only the proposition that prices are proportional to hard money, or metallic currency, in long-run equilibrium. This proportional relationship was, he believed, established through the operation of a real balance effect. In his view, cashholders had a well-developed demand for a constant stock of real cash balances. This demand together with the given nominal money supply ensured price level determinacy.

Thus a random shock to the price level that temporarily raised it above its equilibrium level would, by making actual real balances smaller than desired, induce cashholders either to cut their expenditure on or to increase their sales of goods in an effort to restore the desired level of real balances. The resulting excess supply of goods on the market would put downward pressure on prices until they reestablished their initial proportional relationship to the unchanged money stock, thus restoring real balances to equilibrium. In Wicksell's own words ([1898] 1965, pp. 39-40):

> suppose that for some reason or other commodity prices rise while the stock of money remains unchanged, ... The cash balances will gradually appear to be *too small in relation to the new level of prices.* ... I therefore seek to enlarge my balance. This can only be done ... through a *reduction* in my *demand* for goods and services, or through an *increase* in the *supply* of my own commodity ... or through both together. The same is true of all other owners and consumers of commodities. But in fact nobody will succeed in realizing the object at which each is aiming – to increase his cash balance; for the sum of individual cash balances is limited by the amount of the available stock of money, or rather is identical with it. On the other hand, the universal reduction in demand and increase in supply of commodities will necessarily bring about a continuous fall in all prices. This can only cease when prices have fallen to the level at which the cash balances are regarded as *adequate,* [that is, when] prices ... have fallen to their original level.

This same stability condition, Wicksell noted, ensured that a decrease in the money stock would, by rendering real balances smaller than desired, induce a proportional fall in spending, and therefore prices, to restore real balances to their desired level. For Wicksell, then, the classical quantity theory implied money stock and price level proportionality achieved through real balance effects.

2.1 Pure Cash Economy

Wicksell found the theory to be perfectly valid for hypothetical pure cash economies in which no banks exist to issue checkable deposits, all transactions being mediated entirely by gold currency. In such economies, a demand for a fixed quantity of real gold balances ensures that prices move proportionally to money in long-run equilibrium. Thus newly discovered gold in a closed economy will, at initially unchanged prices, make real balances larger than desired. Cashholders will spend the excess, thereby putting upward pressure on prices which rise proportionally to the increased monetary gold stock.

In an open trading economy, cashholders' adjustments will induce equilibrating real balance effects abroad as well as at home. For let all goods worldwide be tradeables – exportables and importables – whose prices are, by the law of one price, kept everywhere the same by the operation of commodity arbitrage. Then the increased home expenditure on these goods, induced by the gold discovery and resulting excess cash balance, will raise prices abroad thus eroding real balances there. In an effort to rebuild their balances, foreigners cut their spending on and increase their offer of tradeables. The resulting trade surplus is financed by a specie inflow that restores foreign real balances to their desired level. Real balance effects operate to establish proportionality between money and prices throughout the world (see Myhrman, 1991, pp. 269-270).

2.2 Mixed Cash-Credit Economy

To Wicksell, however, the classical quantity theory, applying as it did to pure cash economies, seemed much too narrow and antiquated. It omitted banks and the deposit liabilities they issue by way of loan. It therefore could account neither for the influence of checking deposits on the price level, nor for how both variables move from one equilibrium level to another. Nor for that matter could it account for the forces inducing their movement. To overcome these deficiencies, Wicksell sought to supplement the quantity theory with a description of the mechanism through which monetary equilibrium is disturbed and subsequently restored in mixed cash-credit, or currency-deposit, economies. Thus was born his celebrated analysis of the cumulative process (see Jonung, 1979, pp. 166-167; Laidler, 1991, pp. 135-139; Leijonhufvud, 1981, pp. 151-160; and Patinkin, 1965, pp. 587-597).

That analysis attributes deposit and price level movements to discrepancies between two interest rates. One, the market or money rate, is the rate banks charge on loans and pay on deposits. The other is the natural or equilibrium rate that equates desired saving with intended investment at full employment and that also corresponds to the expected marginal yield or internal rate of return on newly created units of physical capital. Or, equivalently, it is the rate that equates aggregate demand for real output with the available supply.

When the loan rate lies below the natural rate such that the cost of capital is less than capital's expected rate of return, planned investment will exceed planned saving. Entrepreneur investors seeking to finance new capital projects will wish to borrow more from banks than savers deposit there. Since banks accommodate these extra loan demands by creating checking deposits, a deposit expansion occurs. This expansion, by underwriting the excess *desired* aggregate demand implicit in the investment-saving gap, transforms it into excess *effective* aggregate demand that spills over into the commodity market to put upward pressure on prices. In so doing, the deposit expansion produces a persistent and cumulative rise in prices for as long as the interest differential lasts.

Now Wicksell argued that, in mixed cash-credit economies using currency and bank deposits convertible into currency, the rate differential would quickly vanish. The public's demand for real cash balances ensures as much. For let cashholders transact a certain portion of their real payments in currency. Then a rise in prices stemming from the rate differential necessitates additional currency to satisfy that real transaction demand. The ensuing public conversion of deposits into currency and the resulting drain on bank reserves induces banks to raise their loan rates until they (loan rates) equal the natural rate. This last step stems the reserve drain and also brings the price rise to a halt. If banks, because they initially possessed excess reserves, were willing to let reserves run down a bit, then prices would stabilize at the new, higher level. But if banks possessed no excess reserves and so had to restore reserves to their initial level following the price rise, then they (banks) would continue to raise the market rate above the natural rate until prices returned to their pre-existing level. Either way, a quantity theory element in the form of the public's demand for currency works to anchor the price level in the mixed cash-credit economy. Nominal determinacy prevails in that economy as it did in the pure cash economy.

2.3 Cumulative Process Model

Expressed symbolically and condensed into a simple algebraic model, Wicksell's cumulative process can be put through its paces to reveal the exact workings of its constituent quantity theory elements. Since these elements have provoked so much controversy in the Wicksell literature, it is important to specify precisely how Wicksell used them.[4] Assume with Wicksell that all saving is deposited with banks, that all investment is bank-financed, that banks lend solely to finance investment, and that full employment prevails such that shifts in aggregate demand affect prices but not real output. Then his model reduces to the following equations linking the variables investment I, saving S (both planned, or ex ante, magnitudes), loan rate i, natural rate r, loan demand L_D, loan supply L_S, excess aggregate demand E, change in the stock of checkable deposits dD / dt, price level change dP / dt, and market-rate change di / dt.

The first equation says that planned investment exceeds saving when the loan rate of interest falls below its natural equilibrium level (the level that equilibrates saving and investment):

$$I - S = a(r - i), \tag{4.1}$$

where the coefficient a relates the investment-saving gap to the interest differential that creates it.

The second equation states that the excess of investment over saving equals the additional checkable deposits newly created to finance it:

$$dD / dt = I - S. \tag{4.2}$$

In other words, since banks create new checkable deposits by way of loan, deposit expansion occurs when banks lend to investors more than they (banks) receive from savers. Thus equation (4.2) admits of the following derivation. Denote the investment demand for loans as $L_D = I(i)$, where $I(i)$ is the schedule relating desired investment spending to the loan rate of interest. Similarly, denote loan supply as the sum of saving plus new deposits created by banks in accommodating loan demands. In short, $L_S = S(i) + dD / dt$. Equating loan demand and supply and solving for the resulting gap between investment and saving yields equation (4.2).

The third equation says that the new deposits, being spent immediately, spill over into the commodity market to underwrite the excess aggregate demand for goods E implied by the gap between investment and saving:

$$dD / dt = E. \tag{4.3}$$

The fourth equation says that this excess aggregate demand bids up prices, which rise in proportion to the excess demand:

$$dP / dt = bE, \tag{4.4}$$

where the coefficient b is the factor of proportionality between price level changes and excess demand.

Substituting equations (4.1), (4.2), and (4.3) into (4.4), and (4.1) into (4.2), one obtains

$$dP / dt = ab(r - i) \tag{4.5}$$

and

$$dD / dt = a(r - i) \tag{4.6}$$

which together state that price inflation and the deposit growth that underlies it stem from the discrepancy between the natural and market rates of interest.

Finally, since bankers must at some point raise their loan rates to protect their gold reserves from inflation-induced cash drains into hand-to-hand circulation, one last equation

$$di / dt = gdP / dt \tag{4.7}$$

closes the model. This equation says that bankers, having worked off excess reserves, now raise their rates in proportion to the rate of price change (g being the factor of proportionality). The equation ensures that the loan rate eventually converges to its natural equilibrium level, as can be seen by substituting equation (4.5) into the above formula to obtain

$$di / dt = gab(r - i). \tag{4.8}$$

Solving this equation for the time path of the loan rate i yields

$$i(t) = (i_0 - r)e^{-gabt} + r, \tag{4.9}$$

where t is time, e is the base of the natural logarithm system, i_0 is the initial disequilibrium level of the loan rate, and r is the given natural rate. With the passage of time, the first term on the right-hand side vanishes and the loan rate converges to the natural rate. At this point, monetary equilibrium is restored. Saving equals investment, excess demand disappears, deposit expansion ceases, and prices stabilize at their new, higher level.[5]

3 WAS WICKSELL A QUANTITY THEORIST?

At first glance the preceding model, especially equation (4.5), appears to attribute price level changes directly to the interest rate differential rather than to monetary causes. This point is sometimes cited as evidence that Wicksell was not a quantity theorist (see Greidanus, 1932, p. 83, and Adarkar, 1935, p. 27, as cited in Marget, 1938, pp. 183, 187). But it is patently obvious that the model is perfectly consistent with the quantity theory when monetary shocks generate the rate differential. Under these conditions the differential and the resulting price movements clearly have a monetary origin.

Indeed, Wicksell himself described how a monetary impulse would trigger the cumulative process consistent with the classical quantity theory. Assuming the monetary impulse took the form of a gold inflow from abroad, he noted that the new gold ordinarily would be deposited in banks. So deposited, the gold would augment bank reserves beyond the level banks desired to hold. The resulting pressure of excess reserves would, he argued, induce banks to lower their loan rate below the natural rate, thus precipitating the cumulative rise in the volume of bank lending, bank money (deposits) and prices. Under these conditions, one could confidently attribute changes in both the stock of deposits and the price level to preceding changes in the monetary gold stock.

Having recognized potential monetary origins of the cumulative process as a theoretical possibility, however, Wicksell rejected this possibility on empirical grounds. His study of nineteenth-century British prices and interest rates had convinced him that the cumulative process typically originated not in monetary shocks to the loan rate but rather in real shocks to the natural rate. His consequent stress on real shocks in the form of wars, technological progress, innovations, and the like has spurred some scholars to ask: if real shocks predominate over monetary shocks in generating the rate differential, doesn't it follow that the resulting price level movements are real rather than monetary phenomena, contrary to the quantity theory?

In answering this question in the affirmative, these scholars imply that Wicksell may have done more to subvert the theory than to support it. Thus Lars Jonung states (1979, p. 179; see also Cagan, 1965, p. 253, and Laidler, 1997, p. 5):

> Wicksell's approach emphasizes nonmonetary developments, that is 'real' factors, as the principal sources of price changes. Although the monetary sector has a central position in the transmission mechanism from 'real' developments to changes in prices, there is a tendency to ignore monetary factors in a theory that assumes that movements in the real rate are the driving force behind deflations and inflations. It is thus easy to end up with a theory of the price level that relates the behavior of prices directly to variables that influence the real rate, such as changes in the flow of innovations and technological improvements. Here Wicksell's theory has much in common with the Schumpeterian 'longwave explanation,' which associates price level changes with the introduction of new production techniques, which implies that non-monetary factors are the causes behind long-run changes in prices.

What such interpretations overlook, however, is that Wicksell himself always saw his cumulative process model as embodying the quantity theory and being entirely consistent with it. His model was to him nothing less than a full-scale extension of the theory to account for the influence of bank deposits on the price level. In particular, his equations (4.3) and (4.4) upon substitution reduce to $dP / dt = b(dD / dt)$. In so doing, they reveal that a price level change could never occur without the accompanying change in the supply of deposits to support it.

In short, real shocks and the resulting rate differential alone could never sustain price level changes. Instead, something else is required to translate shocks into commodity price inflation. Something, in other words, must finance the excess demand for goods that keeps prices rising. That something is deposit expansion. Without it, excess demand and price increases could never occur and the cumulative process would be abortive. The upshot is that

Wicksell thought the key factor underlying and permitting price movements was deposit expansion, not real shocks and rate differentials.

Of the few commentators who underscore this point, none are more emphatic than Charles Rist and Arthur Marget. Rist ([1938] 1966, p. 300) likens Wicksell to Voltaire's sorcerer, whose incantations could kill a herd of cattle if accompanied by a lethal dose of arsenic. In Wicksell's case, the arsenic – the true cause – was an elastic supply of deposits. The incantations took the form of rate differentials. Similarly, Marget (1938, p. 183) cites 'abundant passages in Wicksell's writings which show that he did think of the "plentiful creation of money" (that is, bank-credit, or the M' of our equation) as being the crucial link in the [cumulative] process'. In short, changes in the stock of deposits were to Wicksell the one absolutely necessary and sufficient condition for price level movements.

3.1 Critique of Tooke's Interest Cost-Push Theory

Nowhere did Wicksell express this view more forcefully than in his famous critique of Thomas Tooke (Wicksell [1898] 1965, pp. 99-100, and [1906] 1978, pp. 180-187). Tooke, author of the celebrated *History of Prices* and leader of the English Banking School, had disputed, indeed scorned, the quantity theoretic doctrines of the rival Currency School. In opposition to those doctrines, Tooke, in his 1844 (1959) volume *An Inquiry into the Currency Principle*, argued that price level changes stem from cost-push forces originating in the real economy rather than from disturbances originating in the monetary sector. In particular, he argued that interest rate increases, by raising the cost of doing business, would raise general prices as the increased costs were passed on to buyers. The resulting price inflation, Tooke implied, would occur even in the face of a constant money stock.

Wicksell, however, maintained that such price level increases could never occur unless underwritten by expansion of that stock. According to him, it is deposit growth stemming from a two-rate differential, and not interest cost-push per se, that constitutes the necessary condition for general prices to rise. Without the accommodating monetary growth, the interest cost-push forces would, he insisted, exhaust themselves in changing relative, not absolute, prices ([1906] 1978, p. 180). The prices of interest-intensive goods would rise relative to the prices of non-interest-intensive ones. But the general price level would remain unchanged. For if the money stock were constant and banks possessed no excess reserves, any rise in the natural rate would force bankers to engineer a matching rise in the loan rate to protect their reserves from cash drains into hand-to-hand circulation. The two rates would remain equal and prices would stay constant. Only if banks initially possessed excess

reserves could a positive shock to the natural rate permanently raise the equilibrium price level. And even here the price increase is attributable to the
monetary factor – the excess reserve – that permits it to occur. All of which is
consistent with the quantity theory and confirms Wicksell's adherence to it.

3.2 Pure Credit Economy

To summarize, Wicksell had shown that the quantity theory applies perfectly
to the pure cash economy. He had then shown that, when augmented to account for the influence of deposit-financed demand on prices, it applies to
mixed cash-credit economies as well. In both cases, he had established that a
real currency demand together with an independent nominal currency supply
are sufficient to pin down the price level. Seeking to extend the theory to its
logical limit, he next applied it to the hypothetical extreme case of a pure
credit economy in which no currency exists and all transactions are settled by
transfers of deposits on the books of banks. Here he showed that the theory
fails to hold in the absence of central bank intervention.

According to him, it fails to hold in the first place because the pure credit
economy employs no currency to which the theory can apply. With currency
absent, no demand for and supply of it exists to determine the price level. Nor
can deposit demand and supply be relied upon to determine the price level.
For, in the pure credit economy, the two deposit variables are identical to
each other at all price levels. Being identical, they cannot exhibit demand-
supply independence as price determinacy requires. Wicksell explains
([1898] 1965, pp. 110-111):

> in our ideal [pure credit] state every payment ... is accomplished by means of
> cheques or *giro* facilities. It is then no longer possible to refer to the supply of
> money as an independent magnitude, differing from the demand for money. No
> matter what amount of money may be demanded from the banks, that is the amount
> which they are in a position to lend ... The banks have merely to enter a figure in
> the borrower's account to represent a credit granted or a deposit created. When a
> cheque is then drawn and subsequently presented to the banks, they credit the
> amount of the owner of the cheque with a deposit of the appropriate amount (or re-
> duce his debit by that amount). The 'supply of money' is thus furnished by the de-
> mand itself. ... It follows that ... the banks can raise the general level of prices to
> any desired height.

In other words, since banks automatically accommodate all loan demands via
deposit creation, it follows that borrower demand for deposits and bank supply of those deposits must be one and the same. With deposit supply identical
to demand at all prices, there is no unique equilibrium price level or deposit
quantity. Rather, there is an infinity of price-quantity equilibria. The price

level, in other words, is indeterminate. Wicksell's cumulative process model applied to the pure credit economy cannot determine it.

Instead, his credit economy model specifies the rate of rise of the price level dP / dt (see Leijonhufvud, 1997, p. 8). Starting from some historically given position, this rise can continue indefinitely as long as a natural-rate/market-rate disparity persists, that is, as long as banks are under no reserve pressure to raise their rates. Since no currency demand exists to drain reserves in the pure credit economy, banks need hold no reserves other than central bank credit. And even this form of reserve is unnecessary in a banking system – Wicksell's 'ideal' system – composed of a single central bank with branches in every town and hamlet (see Uhr, 1960, p. 222). As a central bank, the ideal bank need hold no credit reserves with itself. Moreover, as a monopoly institution, the ideal bank can lose no reserves through the clearing-house to other banks (of which there are none) and so need hold no reserves whatsoever. The result is a system totally devoid of reserve constraints to anchor nominal variables. In such a system, deposit supply possesses potentially unlimited elasticity. Consequently prices, in addition to being indeterminate, theoretically can rise (or fall) forever.

Wicksell insisted, however, that it was up to the central bank to impose nominal determinacy in this case. The central bank could do so through control of the market rate. By adjusting the rate when prices threaten to rise or fall, the bank could close and reverse the rate differential. In so doing, the bank could maintain prices and the supporting volume of deposits at fixed, determinate levels. Here the central bank's obligation to impose price determinacy replaces the missing reserve constraint to force equilibrating rate adjustment. Nominal determinacy is preserved, consistent with the quantity theory. In this way, Wicksell ensures that at least one element of the theory survives even in the pure credit case.

4   POLICY REFORM PROPOSALS

The preceding remarks contend that Wicksell was, commentators' views to the contrary notwithstanding, every bit as much a quantity theorist as Fisher. Evidence reveals that he, like Fisher, understood and indeed enriched the theory's postulates.

But there is a simpler way to prove he and Fisher saw things much the same as far as the quantity theory was concerned. That way is to compare the policy views of the two. One can employ a simple litmus test: a person essentially is a quantity theorist if he believes the monetary authority can stabilize the price level through control, direct or indirect, of the stock of money or nominal purchasing power. Both Fisher and Wicksell pass this test with flying colors.

Both advocated price level stability, albeit for different reasons. Fisher thought such stability would smooth, if not eliminate completely, the business cycle. In so doing, it would alleviate the overuse (stress, strain, exhaustion) of labor and capital resources endured in business booms and the loss of output and employment suffered during depressions. By contrast, Wicksell thought price stability would stop the arbitrary and unjust redistribution of income and wealth that unanticipated inflation and deflation produce. In this way, it would prevent the loss in aggregate social welfare that occurs, because of diminishing marginal utility of income, when unanticipated price movements transfer real income from losers to gainers.

Both also advocated that price stability be achieved through feedback policy rules. In this connection, both devoted their best efforts to devising effective rules. Each writer proposed rules directing the monetary authority to adjust its policy instrument in corrective response to price level deviations from target. Such instrument adjustment would in turn produce a corresponding adjustment in the money stock. This latter adjustment would act to stabilize prices. The money stock was of key importance here. Only by operating through it could instrument adjustment stabilize prices.

In Fisher's famous compensated dollar plan, the policy instrument is the gold content of the dollar, or official dollar price of gold (see Patinkin, 1993). The monetary authority adjusts this price in response to price level deviations from target. Since the price level, or dollar price of goods, is by definition the dollar price of gold times the world gold price of goods, the authority must offset movements in the gold price of goods with compensating adjustments in the dollar price of gold so as to keep the general price level constant.

Fisher made it clear, however, that his compensated dollar plan would operate on the price level through the money stock. It would do so by changing both the physical amount and the nominal valuation of the nation's stock of monetary gold. Thus when world gold inflation was raising the dollar price of goods, the American policy authority would lower the official buying and selling price of gold. Industry and the arts, finding gold less expensive, would therefore demand more of it. Consequently, part of the nation's gold stock would be diverted from monetary to nonmonetary uses (see Lawrence, 1928, p. 432). The resulting shrinkage in the stock of monetary gold would lower the price level. In addition, the reduced official price of gold, by producing a corresponding reduction in the nominal value of physical gold reserves, would lessen the nominal volume of paper money issuable against such backing (see Patinkin, 1993, p. 16). This reduced nominal issue too would put downward pressure on prices. In sum, whether through physical reduction or nominal revaluation, the monetary gold stock would shrink and so too would the quantity of money and level of prices it could support.

Later on, in the mid-1930s, Fisher (1935, p. 97) proposed another policy rule. It had the central bank adjusting, via open market operations, the monetary base in response to price deviations from target. In this case, the price level was the goal variable, the monetary base was the instrument, and the money stock was the intermediate variable. To minimize slippage between the base instrument and the money stock, Fisher advocated a system of 100 percent-required reserves behind deposit money.

Although Wicksell's preferred policy instrument differed from Fisher's, his activist feedback rule followed exactly the same pattern as Fisher's. The authority would adjust its policy instrument, namely its lending rate, in response to price deviations from target. In Wicksell's own words (1919, p. 183, cited in Jonung, 1979, p. 168),

> the Riksbank's tool to keep the price level ... constant is to be found exclusively in its interest rate policy, such that the Riksbank has to increase its rates as soon as the price level shows a tendency to rise and lower them, as soon as it shows a tendency to fall.

Such rate adjustments would in turn produce corresponding corrective movements in the money stock. These latter movements then would stabilize prices.[6] Together, these propositions constitute what Howard S. Ellis, in his classic *German Monetary Theory: 1905-1933,* called Wicksell's 'central theorem,' namely the theorem 'that bank rate controls the price-level through its effect on the amount of available purchasing power' (Ellis, 1934, p. 304).

Thus if prices were rising, the central bank would raise the bank rate. The rise in the bank rate would close the gap between it and the natural rate. The closing of the gap would eliminate the differential between the investment demand for and saving supply of loanable funds. The elimination of that differential would arrest growth in the stock of deposits and bring price rises to a halt. Further raising of the bank rate would cause deflationary monetary contraction, thereby reversing the preceding inflationary price movement and restoring prices to target. Here is a classic quantity theoretic prescription for achieving price stability through monetary means. It is proof positive that Wicksell, like Fisher, was a bona fide quantity theorist.

5 CONCLUSION

What then remains of the alleged difference between Fisher's and Wicksell's interpretation of the quantity theory? Not much, in this observer's opinion.

Any existing difference seems superficial rather than substantive, more semantic than real. And it virtually vanishes once their policy reform proposals are taken into account.

Commentators typically claim that interest rates are the key to Wicksell's analysis, whereas for Fisher the money stock is pivotal. They likewise claim that real shocks initiate the inflationary process in Wicksell's model, whereas monetary shocks do so in Fisher's. True enough. But these distinctions largely lose force when one realizes that both men saw changes in the stock of monetary purchasing power consisting of bank deposits and currency as the one absolutely indispensable and potentially controllable factor responsible for price level changes. Moreover, both regarded this stock as the crucial intermediate variable connecting policy instruments to price targets. Finally, both concluded that the monetary authority bears the ultimate responsibility for monetary and price level stability, a responsibility it discharges by giving some nominal variable under its control a stable, determinate value. In so doing, both enunciated the principle of nominal determinacy, the sine qua non of the quantity theory. These similarities would seem to outweigh any differences.

One reads Fisher and Wicksell today not so much to note the contrasts in their analytical models as to appreciate the brilliant, prescient, and imaginative ways they applied the quantity theory. In arguing for price stability achievable through monetary means, both were adherents of monetary policy in the classical quantity theory tradition. Their two treatments are complementary rather than competitive.

NOTES

1   For a discussion of these classical propositions, see Blaug (1995) and Patinkin (1995).
2   As we will see, such nonneutralities are absent from Wicksell's work. Adhering as he did to a real theory of the cycle, he denied that business fluctuations stem from monetary shocks (see Leijonhufvud, 1997). Such shocks in his view leave the economy always at full employment. Consequently, he held that neutrality of money prevailed in the short-run as well as the long.
3   In his 1920 book *Stabilizing the Dollar*, Fisher listed 41 frequently cited nonmonetary causes of inflation and noted that 'while some of them are important factors in raising particular prices, none of them ... has been important in raising the general scale of prices' (p. 11). To him 'no explanation of a general rise in prices is sufficient which merely explains one price in terms of another price' (p. 14).
4   For similar attempts to model algebraically the cumulative process see Brems (1986), Eagly (1974), Frisch (1952), Laidler (1975), Niehans (1990), and Uhr (1960).
5   Of course if there were no excess reserves to begin with, prices would have to stabilize at their pre-existing level. Bankers, having no excess reserves to lose, would adjust their loan rates either to forestall all reserve drains or to reverse (annul) drains that had already occurred. Either way, prices would stabilize at their initial level.
6   Uhr (1991, p. 94) notes that Wicksell believed that the application of his rule would prevent

the price level from varying more than three percentage points above or below its target or base-year level.

REFERENCES

Adarkar, B.P. (1935), *The Theory of Monetary Policy*, London, P.S. King and Son.

Blaug, M. (1995), 'Why is the quantity theory of money the oldest surviving theory in economics?', in M. Blaug (ed.), *The Quantity Theory of Money from Locke to Keynes and Friedman*, Aldershot, UK, Edward Elgar.

Brems, H. (1986), *Pioneering Economic Theory, 1680-1980*, Baltimore, Johns Hopkins University Press.

Cagan, P. 1965, *Determinants and Effects of Changes in the Stock of Money, 1875-1960*, New York, Columbia University Press.

Eagly, R. (1974), *The Structure of Classical Economic Theory*, New York, Oxford University Press.

Ellis, H.S. (1934), *German Monetary Theory: 1905-1933*, Cambridge, MA, Harvard University Press.

Fisher, I. (1911), *The Purchasing Power of Money: Its Determination and Relation to Credit, Interest, and Crises*, New York, Macmillan. Reprinted, New York, 1963, A.M. Kelley.

Fisher, I. (1920), *Stabilizing the Dollar*, New York, Macmillan.

Fisher, I. (1935), *100% Money*, New York, Adelphi.

Friedman, M. and. Schwartz A.J. (1991), 'Alternative approaches to analyzing economic data', *American Economic Review*, **81**, 39-49.

Frisch, R. (1952), 'Frisch on Wicksell,' in H.W. Spiegel (ed.), *The Development of Economic Thought, Great Economists in Perspective*, New York, J.Wiley.

Greidanus, T. (1932), *The Value of Money*, London, P.S. King and Son.

Jonung, L. (1979), 'Knut Wicksell and Gustav Cassel on secular movements in prices', *Journal of Money, Credit, and Banking*, **11**, 165-181.

Laidler, D. (1975), 'On Wicksell's Theory of Price Level Dynamics', in his *Essays on Money and Inflation*, Chicago, University of Chicago Press.

Laidler, D. (1991), *The Golden Age of the Quantity Theory: The Development of Neoclassical Monetary Economics, 1870-1914*, Princeton, Princeton University Press.

Laidler, D. (1997), 'The Wicksell Connection, the Quantity Theory and Keynes', Unpublished paper.

Lawrence, J.S. (1928), *Stabilization of Prices: A Critical Study of the Various Plans Proposed for Stabilization*, New York, Macmillan.

Leijonhufvud, A. (1981), 'The Wicksell Connection: Variations on a Theme', in his *Information and Coordination: Essays in Macroeconomic Theory*, New York, Oxford University Press.

Leijonhufvud, A. (1997), 'The Wicksellian Heritage', Unpublished Discussion Paper No. 5, Universita Degli Studi di Trento-Dipartimento di Economia.

Marget, A.W. (1938), *The Theory of Prices: A Re-examination of the Central Problems of Monetary Theory*, Vol. 1, New York, Prentice-Hall.

Myhrman, J. (1991), 'The Monetary Economics of the Stockholm School', in L. Jonung (ed.), *The Stockholm School of Economics Revisited*, Cambridge,

Cambridge University Press.

Niehans, J. (1990), *A History of Economic Theory: Classic Contributions, 1720-1980*, Baltimore, Johns Hopkins University Press.

Patinkin, D. (1965), *Money, Interest, and Prices*, 2d ed. New York, Harper & Row,

Patinkin, D. (1993), 'Irving Fisher and His Compensated Dollar Plan', *Federal Reserve Bank of Richmond Economic Quarterly*, **79**, 1-33.

Patinkin, D. (1995), 'Concluding comments on the quantity theory', in M. Blaug (ed.), *The Quantity Theory of Money from Locke to Keynes and Friedman*, Aldershot, UK, Edward Elgar.

Rist, C. (1966), *History of Monetary and Credit Theory from John Low to the Present Day*, 1938, translated by J. Degras, 1940, reprinted, New York, A.M. Kelley.

Tooke, T. (1844), *An Inquiry into the Currency Principle*. Reprinted, London, The London School of Economics and Political Science, 1959.

Uhr, C.G. (1960), *Economic Doctrines of Knut Wicksell*, Berkeley, University of California Press.

Uhr, C.G. (1991), 'Knut Wicksell, Neoclassicist and Iconoclast', in B. Sandelin (ed.), *The History of Swedish Economic Thought*, London and New York, Routledge.

Wicksell, K. (1898), *Interest and Prices*, translated by R.E Kahn, London, Macmillan, 1936. Reprinted, New York, A.M. Kelley, 1965.

Wicksell, K. (1906), *Lectures on Political Economy*, Vol.2, *Money*, translated by E. Classen, edited by L. Robbins, London, Routledge and C. Kegan Paul, 1935. Reprinted, New York, A.M. Kelley, 1978.

Wicksell, K. (1919), 'Riksbanken och privatbankerna. Forslag till reform av det svenska penningoch kreditvasendet', [The Riksbank and the commercial banks. A proposal to a reform of the Swedish monetary and credit system]. *Ekonomisk Tidskrift*, **2**, 177-188.

PART THREE:
MONETARY POLICY,
MONETARY REFORM, AND
CONSTRUCTIVE INCOME TAXATION

5.   Monetary Policy and Monetary Reform: Irving Fisher's Contributions to Monetary Macroeconomics

Hans-E. Loef and Hans G. Monissen[*]

1   INTRODUCTION

Irving Fisher, in a letter to his son Irving Norton Fisher, wrote that he had four chief causes at heart, 'the abolition of war, disease, degeneracy, and instability of money' (quoted in Barber, n.d., p. 1). Among those four causes, only one is of a direct economic source: monetary instability. He did not mention unemployment, real growth or income distribution. 'In fact, an unstable monetary unit breeds radicalism, whether the movements be up or down, deflation or inflation, if it goes far enough. The French had an aphorism "after the printing press, the guillotine" ' (Fisher, [1935a] 1936, p. 218). And in his *Principles* Irving Fisher reminds us that the problem of making the purchasing power of money stable is one of the most serious problems in applied economics (Fisher, [1912] 1918, pp. 256-257). Since money is not neutral during transition periods, changes in the price level tend to change the volume of trade. The idea of monetary induced fluctuations in economic activity is not unique to or even outlined by Irving Fisher in the first place. Ricardo, Marshall and Fisher as representatives of the mainstream classical and neoclassical view 'were seriously concerned that monetary expansion, associated with inappropriate low interest rates, would unduly stimulate the economy, while monetary contraction might precipitate a recession. Price fluctuations were regarded to be accompanied by output fluctuations' (Niehans, 1987, p. 420; cf. also Loef and Monissen, 1998). It follows immediately that in order to eliminate or at least to greatly mitigate the business cycle it is necessary to stabilize the price level (see Patinkin, 1990, p. 12; Patinkin, 1993, p. 4; and Barber, n.d., p. 6). 'Monetary policy, properly conducted, could thus eliminate the phenomenon of the business cycle' (Barber, n.d., p. 6; see also Dimand, 1993a, p. 170; and R.L. Allen, 1993, p. 14). This sounds totally monetaristic – and it is. Patinkin answers his former puzzlement or question why the Chicago School 'did not do justice to

Irving Fisher – despite the fact that long before the Chicago School, Fisher had advocated the policy of stabilizing the price level as a means of mitigating – if not avoiding – cyclical fluctuation' (Patinkin, 1973, p. 456) 20 years later by his interpretation that Irving Fisher has become a follower and the Chicago school a leader on questions of monetary policy (Patinkin, 1993, p. 27). Stabilization of the price level was also proposed by many other quantity theorists as well as Keynes in his quantity theory period (Patinkin, 1993, p. 4, fn 4, and the literature mentioned there; Patinkin, 1972; and Laidler, 1991a; see also Tavlas, 1997).

Fisher's theoretical analyses of monetary fluctuations and the subsequent search and crusade for economic policy recommendations are generally summarized by R.L. Allen (1993, p. 14):

> Fisher saw fluctuations in the price level, inflation and deflation, and their consequences, as the prime economic evils of his time. He wanted to keep prices stable, wishing to avoid both deflation and inflation, and therefore, in his belief, the effects of the business cycle. He promoted among fellow professionals, as well as the public, monetary policy and institutional arrangements that he believed would stabilize prices, and therefore the value of the dollar, by controlling the money supply. The economic theory on which he spent more time than any other was the promotion of economic stabilization through monetary policy. To him economic stabilization meant price stabilization because he believed that movements in production correlated with price movements. He argued that money was the key to price movements. He proposed to alter the organization of the banking system so one part of each existing bank would become an independent institution. It would serve only to warehouse money, keeping all deposits fully available to depositors. Another part, an institution independent of deposit banking, would only borrow from savers in order to lend to investors. The national monetary authority would regulate the supply of money by issuing assets in which this second part of the bank could lend money.

This is the essence of Irving Fisher's monetary reform proposals, especially as outlined in his *100% Money*. In order to reach his goal of stabilizing the purchasing power of money he wrote numerous articles and books, made speeches and wrote letters to representatives and even presidents of the USA. He used different analytical methods and theoretical levels to convince his professional colleagues, congressmen and the general public. For example, in the preface to the first edition of his *100% Money* Fisher encourages laymen to read his whole proposal as summarized in the first 30 pages (Part I) and to skip the more detailed discussions of the other parts because these are 'designed to meet the possible objections of bankers and of technical students of banking' (Fisher, [1935a] 1936, p. xvi).

Fisher's interest in and concern about the problem of stabilizing the purchasing power of money dates back to 1892, as soon as his economic studies began, with his first solution in 1911 in *The Purchasing Power of*

Money (Appendix to Fisher, 1935b; see also R.L. Allen, 1993, p. 261). Besides his famous Ph.D. thesis, *Mathematical Investigations in the Theory of Value and Prices* (1892), one other paper with economic content was published in 1892 which might be considered as Irving Fisher's academic starting career as a monetary theorist.[1] From that time on he wrote and spoke in defense of stabilization of the purchasing power of money. Irving Fisher reports that since that time (until 1935), 'My secretary counts up: 99 addresses, besides 37 letters to the press, and 161 special articles, as well as 9 testimonies at hearings held by government bodies and 12 privately printed circulars, together with 13 books bearing on the subject' (I. Fisher, 1935b, autobiographical appendix).[2]

The first proposals to stabilize the purchasing power of money are based on Fisher's business cycle theories prior to the Great Depression. Since then, however, Fisher changed his views about the severity and origins of booms and depressions. Now over-indebtedness and deflation are of major concern and require appropriate monetary policy actions which lead temporarily to reflation and later on to normal periods of stable prices. One remedy was his proposed 'stamp-scrip-money'. The sub-title of his *100% Money* book stated clearly a second proposal which can prevent depressions: '100% Money. Designed to keep checking banks 100% liquid; to prevent inflation and deflation; largely to cure or prevent depressions; and to wipe out much of the National Debt'.

The present chapter is subdivided into two main parts. Part 1 discusses and describes Irving Fisher as a scientist and crusader in monetary policy and reform. It distinguishes four phases of his monetary proposals, starting with *The Purchasing Power of Money* and the compensated-dollar-plan in 2.1. The emphasis given to open market operations in conducting central bank policies is taken up in section 2.2, while the shift to a new interpretation of severe depressions and possible monetary rescues is discussed in 2.3. Irving Fisher's last period of monetary reform proposals is connected with his 100% money idea (section 2.4). The last sub-section (2.5) of the first part of this chapter is devoted to the question why with respect to practical political imple-mentations these proposals were not successful.

Part 2 tries to formulate a simple monetary macro-model of fluctuations and equilibrium conditions which are fundamentally Fisherian and can be traced back to his various writings in monetary theory and policy. Sub-section 3.1 outlines a quantity theoretic model with adaptive expectations which exhibits money neutrality in the long-run but non-neutrality in transition periods. The following paragraph (3.2) develops optimal monetary policy rules given the economic paradigm of the previous sub-section. It follows in particular that stabilizing the price level automatically stabilizes the economy, i.e. real output fluctuations. The chapter ends with a summary of the findings and concluding remarks.

2   IRVING FISHER: MONETARY POLICY AND MONETARY REFORM

Fisher embodied two roles: one as a scientist and one as a crusader. 'These two roles of Irving Fisher's life cooperated and conflicted with each other to produce a long, varied, and complex life, full of contributions, contradictions' (R.L. Allen, 1993, p. 4). He did not hesitate to spend his own money to finance his crusading campaigns. According to one of his biographers he spent more than $100,000 of his own money promoting the cause of economic stability during his lifetime (R.L. Allen, 1993, p. 15).

Even though R.L. Allen (1993, pp. 2-3) states that Fisher, in the economic field, espoused two principles encompassing three fundamental changes, which were monetary and tax reform by using his commodity-dollar standard, the 100 percent monetary reserve and the idea of taxing consumption, with respect to monetary reform, it is worthwhile distinguishing at least four phases in Irving Fisher's career as a reformer and a crusader.[3]

2.1 Monetary Scientist and Reformer

Phase 1 starts around 1911 and ends around the middle of the 1920s, even though central and fundamental ideas and issues continue to play a role in later episodes as well. The theoretical underpinning is, of course, Irving Fisher's *The Purchasing Power of Money* (first ed., 1911). However, in this important work monetary reforms are hardly mentioned, even though the theoretical argumentations point to the possible stabilizing role of monetary policy in the presence of fluctuating prices and output due to monetary (velocity) disturbances and other sources. Instead of designing specific monetary policy measures or institutional changes he relies on increasing knowledge and information on the part of the public to understand the underlying forces behind the quantity theoretic context.

Irving Fisher ([1911] 1985, p. 347) writes:

> we reviewed the principles determining the purchasing power of money and the practical problems involved. We then considered the possible methods of avoiding the evils of variability in purchasing power. Among these, one of the most feasible

and important was found to be an increase of knowledge, – both specific knowledge of conditions and general knowledge of principles.

And, more important, he continues (Fisher, [1911] 1985, p. 348):

> It was suggested that the first step in this needed reform would be to persuade the public, and especially the business public, to study the problem of monetary stability and to realize that, at present, contracts in money are as truly speculative as the selling of futures, – are, in fact, merely a subdivision of future-selling.
>
> The necessary education once under way, it will then be time to consider schemes for regulating the purchasing power of money in the light of public and economic conditions of the time. All this, however, is in the future. For the present there seems nothing to do but to state the problems and the principles of its solution in the hope that what is now an academic question may, in due course, become a burning issue.

It was only in the second edition of *The Purchasing Power of Money* (1913) that Fisher added an appendix on *Standardizing the Dollar*, describing his plan for stabilizing the price level by means of a composite standard or his famous compensated-dollar-plan.

Fisher in his first years as a scientist had a rather negative attitude towards monetary policy advising;[4] however, this attitude changed a little later (after he recovered from his tuberculosis) and he became the impatient reformer and crusader, for which he is known from then on.

The monetary policy reform he advocated then was his famous compensated-dollar-plan as outlined in Fisher (1913) and Fisher (1920) with numerous smaller contributions, articles, discussions and comments on the same subject (see the relevant literature in Patinkin, 1993; and I.N. Fisher, 1961).

The idea is rather simple. If the relation (see Patinkin, 1993, p. 5)

> dollar price of basket of goods and services = gold price of basket *times* dollar price of gold holds true, then the general price level (the dollar price of basket of goods and services) can be kept stable by appropriately changing the dollar price of gold (that is the gold content of the dollar) by the monetary authority whenever the gold price of the basket changes.

Since this plan operates in the given context of the then prevailing gold-standard it was important for this plan not only to be accepted nationally but also by all the major economic powers of that time, i.e. by all other countries as well (Patinkin, 1995, p. 122).

The compensated-dollar-plan was essentially a commodity-dollar-plan, that is, the purchasing power of money was determined by the value of its gold content. Contrary to this view, in *The Purchasing Power of Money* it is the quantity of money which determines the general price level. But Fisher did not assign a primary role to the quantity of money in his policy proposal.[5] Patinkin (1993, p. 9) replies to this and related puzzles by saying:

that the person who is our present concern is not Irving Fisher the author of the scientific work on The Purchasing Power of Money, but Irving Fisher the deviser of a plan to be 'sold' to the economics profession as well as to the business community and government – and to be 'packaged' accordingly. The quantity theory of money was out of favor in some circles, so the plan should not be explicitly associated with it. The commodity theory of money had influential supporters, so the plan should be presented in language that had the sounds of that theory. The gold standard was sacred, so it should be emphasized that the plan did not involve its abandonment.

2.2 Modern Central Banking

In the middle of the 1920s Irving Fisher changed his mind, when he discovered that the volume of credit is more important than the volume of gold in determining the purchasing power of money. While his compensated-dollar-plan was invented at a time when the Federal Reserve System was just about to shape its status as a central bank, his new ideas concentrated on the ability and importance of the Federal Reserve's conduct of open-market operations. This was, at that time, a new monetary technique. By purchasing and selling government securities the central bank was now able to alter the lending capacity of commercial banks.

Barber (n.d., pp. 5-6) reports about Irving Fisher's activity in the light of his appreciation of the importance of open-market-operations:

> In the version of a price stabilization bill that Fisher supported in 1926, the Federal Reserve's capacity to alter the lending capacity of commercial banks through its open-market operation was identified as the primary instrument of monetary control. When endorsing this view, he noted that 'today it is the volume of credit that determines the purchasing power of the dollar – the price level – more than the volume of gold'. Even so he argued, 'You have got to have your gold control as well as your credit control, if you are going to prevent the terrible evils of inflation and deflation in the future' (Fisher, 1926). He held that the Federal Reserve's stabilizing role might be compromised unless discretionary authority to alter the gold content of the dollar were available.

2.3 Disaster and Rescue

For Irving Fisher the business cycle, that is, fluctuations in economic activity, is a monetary phenomenon. This is true for the general description of fluctuations prior to the Great Depression, as outlined in *The Purchasing Power of Money*, as well as his interpretations of the events after 1929. However, in *Booms and Depressions* the causes of severe depressions are emphasized as being over-indebtedness and deflation as a result of the break-down of the price level by contraction in deposits and reduction in velocities (Fisher, 1932, and 1933a; see also Dimand, 1994). Besides his different analytical and theoretical explanations of economic fluctuations he was sure by now that those depressions could be prevented and cured by appropriate monetary policy measures conducted by the Federal Reserve Bank System.

His practical monetary advice was reflation. Now reflation replaced his long-run theme of stabilization. However, reflation is not inconsistent with a stable purchasing power of money. Reflation does not mean inflation. 'The objective was simply to restore an earlier price level – say that of 1926. Once that had been accomplished, price stabilization would again be the order of the day' (Barber, n.d., p. 9).

The technical monetary procedures to stop deflation and to reflate were mostly known already. It could be done by means of his compensated-dollar-plan using commodity money or by his later approval of open market procedures. Stamped money, an idea of stamp scrip going back to Silvio Gesell, would, he thought, be able to increase velocity again (Fisher, 1933b). Dollar bills would depreciate in value by a particular amount each period (i.e., a week) unless a stamp in the same amount were affixed to them. This would increase velocity and discourage hoarding. The tax proceeds could in addition be used to support the creation of new jobs for the unemployed.

Irving Fisher did not like public works and special fiscal policies to create new employment opportunities. His only recommendation in this respect was the provision of interest-free loans to those employers who agreed to enlarge their payrolls (Barber, n.d., p. 13).[6] Again all these sound very monetaristic. W. Allen (1993, p. 704) summarizes the analyses and policy recommendations as follows:

> In those early days of the Depression, Fisher persistently provided a basic orientation of monetarism in analysis and in policy prescription. 'The chief direct cause of the depression' (letter from Fisher to F.D. Roosevelt in 1936) was the one-third reduction of the money stock between 1929 and 1933, and 'the only sure and rapid recovery is through monetary means' (letter from Fisher to the Secretary of the President, 1934). He provided a stream of detailed proposals: devalue the dollar, most immediately in connection with raising prices generally; pursue aggressive open market operations in order to increase the money stock; provide governmental guarantee of bank deposits; use dated stamp scrip in order to maintain or increase monetary velocity; and, rather outside the realm of monetary policy, subsidize firms that increase their hiring of labor for minimum periods.

2.4 Monetary Policy, Banking Regulation and Currency Commission

Even though Fisher did not give up his compensated-dollar-plan entirely (Patinkin, 1993, p. 23) he advocated a system of monetary control from the middle of 1934 until his death which in essence was intended to stabilize the purchasing power of money by open market operations, velocity control and tightening deposit money and its velocity by a 100% reserve requirement.[7] Again the idea behind the monetary and banking reform is as simple as the proposal itself: divorce the process of issuing money from the general bank business by requiring private banks to back deposits of their customers by 100% central bank money. In Fisher's words ([1935a] 1936, pp. xvii and xviii):

> The essence of the 100% plan is to make money independent of loans; that is, to divorce the process of creating and destroying money from the business of banking. A purely incidental result would be to make banking safer and more profitable; but by far the most important result would be the prevention of great booms and depressions by ending the chronic inflation and deflation which have ever been the great economic curse of mankind and which have sprung largely from banking. And further: I have come to believe that that plan, properly worked out and applied, is incomparably the best proposal ever offered for speedily and permanently solving the problem of depressions; for it would remove the chief cause of both booms and depressions, namely, the instability of demand deposits, tied, as they now are, to bank loans.

In order to ensure the transition from the present less-then-100% reserve system to the new one a Currency Commission should be created (for example an Open-Market committee of the Federal Reserve Board) which would also be responsible for conducting the future issue of the money of the nation 'in accordance with a legal criterion of stabilization ... accomplished by open market operations, that is, buying and selling United States bonds and any other items made eligible, as well as gold and foreign exchange – also by changing the price of gold, silver and foreign exchange' (Fisher, [1935a] 1936, p. 21).

With respect to the Currency Commission the proposal sounds very modern. Open market policy with government securities should be the primary instrument, but exchange rate policy is considered as well. However, the Currency Commission is supposed to be tied to a kind of a monetary rule which ensures purchasing power stabilization.[8] The management of the monetary authority (Currency Commission) would 'increase or decrease the supply of money in order to meet whatever type of stabilization requirement should be prescribed in the law' (Fisher, [1935a] 1936, pp. 25-26). And 'to be most efficient, the Currency Commission should have no other function than the regulation of the value of the dollar' (Fisher, [1935a] 1936, p. 27).

He did foresee the necessity of some discretion in the daily monetary policy operations, however, in a very narrow sense: 'In order to provide needed elasticity some continuous management of the money supply would be necessary, though this management need not require any more discretion than the discretion of a chauffeur who is ordered to drive a definite, prescribed course' (Fisher, [1935a] 1936, p. 24). Even more novel with its relation to modern practices in some countries (e.g. New Zealand) is the proposed technique 'for keeping the members of the National Monetary Authority on course. If the price level deviated from the target norm by as much as ten percent for three consecutive months, its officers would automatically forfeit their jobs' (Barber, n.d., p. 18).

Fisher's 100% money plan was not uniquely created by him. It far antedates the 1930s. W. Allen (1993) starts the historical search with Hume, Ricardo and the Peel Bank Act of 1844. The idea was revived in the 1920s and early 1930s by Fredrick Soddy, a Nobel Laureate in chemistry (W. Allen, 1993, p. 705)[9] and later on by some economists at the University of Chicago, including Director, Douglas, Hart, Knight, Mints, Schultz and Simons.[10]

2.5 Reforms and Success

Even though great parts of Irving Fisher's proposals became well known to the public as well as academics and were incorporated in today's thinking about monetary reforms and strategies, his main goals and tasks were, in general and particularly in political terms, not attained.[11] This is also true for his consumption tax proposal. Especially with respect to the commodity dollar and 100% monetary reserves he failed completely (R.L. Allen, 1993, pp. 5 and 248).[12]

Reasons for these failures might be seen in Fisher himself and in his surroundings. His proposals for monetary policy and reform were largely motivated and accentuated by his nature to be a crusader. Fisher the scientist and analyst was only partly involved. Redundancy and impertinent insistence made the political addresses, congressmen and Presidents, to whom his numerous speeches, pamphlets and letters were directed, deaf.

Patinkin (1990, p. 2) observes:

> Fisher was very much of a pedant: someone who never said anything once what he could say three times. But though this unnecessary repetition may tax the patience of the reader, he would be seriously mistaken to disregard the economic significance of the point in question that Fisher was in each case making.[13]

His personal financial disaster in the Great Depression did not contribute to his reputation of being a good adviser in monetary affairs. However, some contemporary economists might regret that the Fisher-Simons revolution was aborted and this road of monetary reform with its emphasis on stable purchasing power of money and its modern type monetary macroeconomic paradigm was not taken. There was at the time a more challenging, maybe opportunistic, view of the macroeconomic and policy problems which led to the Keynesian Revolution (see Hotson, 1987). And, of course, Keynes found immediately and easily disciples who promoted his rather simple political messages among scholars and politicians. Fisher did not found or leave behind a 'school' of disciples. There was no 'New Haven Circus' to match Keynes's 'Cambridge Circus' as Barber puts it (Barber, n.d., p. 21). But as Niehans (1987, p. 422) remarks correctly, 'Great economists rarely founded schools, and the schools rarely produced great economists'.

3 A SIMPLE FISHERIAN MODEL OF PRICE AND OUTPUT DETERMINATION AND MONETARY POLICY DESIGN

Irving Fisher's monetary policy reform proposals and his political crusades were mostly motivated by his intrinsic belief that stabilizing the purchasing power of money is the primary and most important economic issue. In most parts his proposals were founded on his understanding of how the economy works, especially what determines the fluctuations in economic activity, the so-called business cycle.[14] There was no doubt for him that the origins of the disturbances are monetary. His monetary theory of fluctuations[15] would in modern terms be characterized as monetaristic or perhaps neo-classical. The theoretical basis of monetarism and the theoretical structure of the monetary model of Irving Fisher goes back at least to Hume (Wood, 1995, pp. 101-103, 104; Patinkin, 1995, p. 127; and Laidler, 1991b, p. 291).[16] Irving Fisher and monetarism and their emphasis on sluggish expectation formation, as opposed to what now is commonly employed and termed rational expectations, share the same origin in the quantity theory.[17] A difference between Fisher and monetarism is to be found in their different interpretations of the equation of exchange. For Fisher it is mainly a reduced form of the determination of nominal income while for Friedman it is a money demand function.

Irving Fisher's reforms and crusades could be subdivided into four phases, as was done in the previous sections. The development of the theoretical foundations underlying these proposals can, however, be partitioned into two.

First, the monetary theory of fluctuations in its normal version was set out in *The Purchasing Power of Money* in 1911 and his *Principles* in 1912

(Fisher, [1911] 1985; and Fisher, [1912] 1918). Numerous articles enlarge and deepen the theoretical description of a fluctuating economy, especially his 'The business cycle largely a "dance of the dollar" ' (1923) and his 'Statistical relation between unemployment and price changes' (1926) which was reprinted in 1973 as 'I discovered the Phillips curve'.

Second, after the experience of the Great Depression, Irving Fisher's theoretical concerns shifted to the description and the possible prevention of severe booms and depressions, which he considered mainly the result of debt and deflation (Fisher, 1932 and 1933a; see also Dimand, 1993a).

This section of the chapter deals mainly with Fisher's normal theory of fluctuations and not with his debt-deflation theory, even though in special circumstances the model presented is able to produce severe deflations, however not caused by the debt-problem, which is not modeled.[18]

There are some attempts in the economic literature to outline Fisher's monetary theory of fluctuations. Among them are Dimand (1994), Humphrey (1990, 1992a) and Monissen (1989). The first two, however, in our opinion use rather non-Fisherian elements like a Walras-Keynes-Phillips model (Dimand, 1994, which, however, is designed to model the debt-deflation situation) as in Tobin (1975) or an excess money-demand equation to model price changes (Humphrey, 1990 and 1992a). The present chapter is based on Monissen (1989); it deviates in some respects, however, from the formulations made there.

3.1 A Simple Fisherian Monetary Model

The model consists of four equations which describe prices and output as determined in the output and money markets:

$$m + v = p + y, \tag{5.1}$$

$$y = y^p + \lambda(p - p^e) \text{ for } \lambda > 0, \tag{5.2}$$

$$v = \bar{v} + g(p - p_{-1}); \quad g \geq 0, \tag{5.3}$$

$$p^e = \alpha p_{-1} + (1 - \alpha)p_{-1}^e; \quad 0 < \alpha \leq 1. \tag{5.4}$$

All variables are in natural logarithms, $m =$ nominal money supply, $p =$ price level, $y =$ real output, $y^p =$ potential output, $v =$ velocity, $p^e =$ expected price level, α, λ and γ are parameters with the given restrictions. The lower index -1 indicates the previous period $t-1$. The actual period t is not explicitly designated, i.e. $m = m_t$ applies.

Equation (5.1) states the quantity equation in logarithmic form. It can easily, under certain assumptions, be derived from Fisher's famous version of the quantity equation

$$MV + M'V' = PY \qquad (5.1a)$$

where the variables have the same economic meaning, except for being levels and not their logarithms. M denotes central bank money used by private agents (currency), M' denotes private bank deposits, and V and V' are the appropriate velocities.

Assuming that both velocities are equal $(V = V')$ equation (5.1a) can be written as

$$(M + M')V = PY$$

where by definition of M and M' the sum of the two can be expressed as central and private bank money in private non-bank agents' portfolio; this, of course, is equal to the money definition M_1 in modern terms.[19]

If the ratio $c = M / M'$ is determined by the non-bank agents, and private banks are required to hold a fraction r of deposits M' in central bank's money as required reserves R than the simple money supply process $M_1 = bB$ emerges, where $b = \dfrac{1+c}{r+c}$; and $B = M + R$ is defined as the uses side of the monetary base, assuming the sources side to be completely controlled by the monetary authority. Combining these assumptions the relation

$$M_1V = PY \quad \text{or} \quad bBV = PY \qquad (5.1b)$$

holds. Taking natural logarithms on both sides of (5.1b) equation (5.1) results with m being interpreted as the logarithm of either M_1 or bB. Since M or B are, but M_1 or b are not controllable by the monetary authority, formulation (5.1b) must be considered by designing an appropriate monetary policy rule.

Equation (5.1) is a variant of the quantity equation (on the origin and formulations of the quantity equation see, for example, Humphrey, 1984; Niehans, 1990, p. 277; Laidler, 1991b, p. 291; Marget, [1938-1942] 1966; and Morgan, 1995, p. 20), but not the outcome of the quantity theory (see below). As mentioned before, it is not interpreted as a money demand equation as by Friedman (1956), but rather as a reduced form determining nominal output demanded. Therefore the resulting monetary theory of price and output fluctuations is not the same as in modern monetaristic versions as, for example, the one of Laidler (1976), even though the conclusions with respect to the origin of fluctuations and their possible political remedies are equivalent.

Equation (5.2) determines the real output supplied and looks similar to the famous Lucas-supply equation (Lucas, 1973) or the expectations-augmented

Phillips-curve with an Okun's law relation involved (see Dimand, 1994, p. 102; Dimand, 1993a, pp. 167-168; Laidler, 1991b, pp. 199-300; Tavlas and Aschheim, 1985, p. 295; and R.L. Allen, 1993, p. 182). However, the formulation is originally by Fisher; even so he did not write out the equation in its mathematical form (see Fisher, [1926] 1973). His descriptions in his 1926 article incorporated all the ingredients which constitute what is now known as the Lucas-supply function: Deviations of real output supplied from its normal or potential level y^p are explained by unexpected prices. (On the natural rate hypothesis and Irving Fisher see Dimand, 1994, p. 102.)

Fisher ([1926], p. 785) writes, 'It has likewise been recognized that inflation carries with it a great stimulation to trade and an increase in employment (or decrease in unemployment)'.

And he continues ([1926], p. 787):

The principle underlying this relationship is, of course familiar. It is that when the dollar is losing value, or in other words when the price level is rising, a business man finds his receipts rising as fast, on the average, as the general rise of prices, but not his expenses, because his expenses consist, to a large extent, of things which are contractually fixed, such as interest on bonds; or rent, which may be fixed for five, ten, or ninety-nine years; or salaries, which are often fixed for several years; or wages, which are fixed sometimes, either by contract or custom, for at least a number of months. For this and other reasons, the rise in expenses is slower than the rise in receipts when inflation is in progress and the price level is rising or the dollar falling.[20]

In *The Purchasing Power of Money* Fisher describes the relationship between inflation and the business cycle as the result of the dynamics of interest rate adjustments in the following way (Fisher, [1911] 1985, pp. 58-59):

As prices rise, profits of business men, measured in money, will rise also, even if the costs of business were to rise in the same proportion. ... Of course such a rise of prices would be purely nominal, as it would merely keep pace with the rise in price level. The business man would gain no advantage, for his larger money profits would buy no more than his former smaller money profits bought before. But, as a matter of fact, the business man's profits will rise more than this because the rate of interest he has to pay will not adjust itself immediately. Among his costs is interest, and this cost will not, at first, rise. Thus the profits will rise faster than prices. Consequently, he will find himself making greater profits than usual, and be encouraged to expand his business by increasing his borrowings.

Rutledge (1977, p. 204) summarizes Fisher's emphasis on transition periods and the impact of inflation on real variables:

Fisher's theory of appreciation and interest, as he advised his readers many times, was based on the crucial distinction between periods of full equilibrium and those of transition, or disequilibrium. Fisher explained that in steady state equilibrium, nominal interest will be bid up by exactly the rate of inflation, and real interest will remain unchanged. But the overwhelming impact of inflation during the transition period is on real variables: real interest, real profit, real investment and real income. In fact Fisher argued that the real effects of inflation on interest were the major determinants of booms in business activity.[21]

The relationship between inflation, nominal and real interest rates, credit and business activity is somewhat similar to Knut Wicksell's treatment of the same subject.[22]

Equation (5.3) states that velocity v is a constant $\bar{v}$, determined by exogenous factors, in addition to endogenous forces which are in operation during transition periods. And transition periods are the important economic situation, not the equilibrium ones. It is surprising that Fisher's biographer R.L. Allen turns Fisher's explicit statement about the relative importance of equilibria and disequilibria (transition periods) upside-down (Fisher, [1911] 1985, pp. xiii, 55, especially 71, 72, 165; Fisher, [1912] 1918, Chapter X; and R.L. Allen, 1993, p. 118; see also Patinkin, 1990, pp. 10-13). But even Keynes in his review of Fisher's *The Purchasing Power of Money* neglected Chapter 4 on transition periods which led Fisher, in the preface to the second edition of his work, to explicitly point to his lengthy treatment of this issue in his *Elementary Principles*. The powerful short-run effects of money during transition periods was already noticed by Hume in 1752 and fully articulated by Thornton in 1802 (on this special point see Niehans, 1987, pp. 416-417).

Patinkin (1993, p. 3) is correct in stating:

> Though most of 'The Purchasing Power of Money' (...) is devoted to the long-run proportionality between the quantity of money and the price level, Fisher attached great importance to Chapter 4 of the book on 'transition periods', in which this proportionality did not obtain. ... It is accordingly in this chapter that Fisher develops his theory of 'crisis', or what we now call 'cycles'.[23]

As Morgan (1995, p. 3) points out, Fisher's Purchasing Power of Money 'contains at least four models of money showing considerable variety of form (including visual, analogue, mathematical and methodological) and range of function'. The models she distinguishes are: the accounting-balance model; the connecting-reservoirs model; the model of Boyle's law and the money-circulation model. In the accounting-balance model the equation of exchange is illustrated and discussed in arithmetical, mechanical and algebraic forms (Morgan, 1995, p. 11; and Patinkin, 1990, p. 2). It is the mechanical version which enables Fisher to illustrate the dynamic forces and adjustments during transition periods, which in modern language would be described by means of difference or differential equations.

As Morgan (1995, p. 17) observes:

> The balance introduces a completely new element into the equation of exchange. In the arithmetic example, a simple change in one element necessitates a matching change in one of the other elements to maintain equality. In the mechanical

illustration a similar change in one element creates an oscillation of the arms of the balance as part of the process of coming back into a position of rest. The model here introduces a new element into the discussion of the equation of exchange – a new theory about the behaviour of the economic system in 'transition periods'.

It is somewhat surprising that Fisher the mathematician and author of *Appreciation and Interest* did not make use of difference or differential equations. But as Niehans (1990, p. 375) points out, it was only in the 1920s that economists discovered differential and difference equations, which then became the major tool in business cycle research following Ragnar Frisch's propagation and impulse problems in 1933.[24]

Equation (5.3) incorporates the idea of transition periods outlined above. Fisher made it clear that velocity is far from being constant (Wood, 1995, p. 104; Fisher, [1911] 1985, pp. 55, 63, 64, 320). Moreover, velocity is a function of expected price changes or the expected inflation rate. The positive correlation between velocity and expected inflation seems to be a major assumption in theories following the quantity theoretic tradition, as the Chicago School and the Cambridge approach (see Patinkin, 1969, pp. 50, 51; Laidler, 1991b, pp. 292-293; Tavlas and Aschheim, 1985, p. 295). For Fisher ([1912] 1918, p. 56) it is the discrepancy between nominal and real interest rates which can be approximated by the expected inflation rate, which constitutes the cycle or the fluctuations in economic activity: 'The peculiar behavior of the rate of interest during transition periods is largely responsible for the crises and depressions in which price movements end'. When prices are rising, the nominal interest rate rises but not sufficiently, and when prices are falling, the nominal interest rate falls, but not sufficiently. This insufficient adjustment is attributed to confusions between real and nominal magnitudes (Fisher, [1912] 1918, pp. 60 and 68; Dimand, 1993a, p. 163; and Patinkin, 1993, p. 4). In the end this confusion points to money illusion which he was eager to eliminate by educating the public (Fisher, 1935a, p. 195; Fisher, [1912] 1918, p. 71; Fisher, 1928; see also Dimand, 1993a, pp. 164 and 169; and Patinkin, 1993, p. 27. A short historical note is provided by Niehans, 1987, pp. 418-419).

Expected inflation may well be destabilizing by increasing or decreasing velocity in such a way that the economic system might be far from being stable. 'If velocity is *sufficiently* sensitive to inflation, the latter, once started, can accelerate without limit even in the absence of any monetary expansion' (Laidler, 1991b, p. 292). And Patinkin summarizes (1969, p. 50):

> Thus, if individuals expect prices to rise and earnings to be good, they will dishoard – that is, increase in velocity of circulation. But the crucial point here is that these expectations will be self-justifying: for the very act of dishoarding will cause prices to rise even further, thus leading to further dishoardings, and so on. In this way a 'cumulative process' of expansion is set into operation which 'feeds upon itself'

and which has no 'natural' limit. Conversely, an indefinite 'cumulative' process of hoarding, price declines and depression and further hoarding is set into operation by the expectation that the price level will fall and/or that earnings will be poor. Thus the economic system is essentially unstable.

In equation (5.3) the actual inflation rate ($p - p_{-1}$) is incorporated instead of the expected rate. This can – by referring to equation (5.2) and (5.4) – be justified by assuming a faster rate of reaction in financial markets than in output markets.[25]

The last equation (5.4) constitutes price expectations as they are made by the numerous agents in the output market. It assumes adaptive expectations in the now well known form. Restricting α to one reduces the complexity of the model considerably without losing anything of its major economic content, as will be shown below. Equation (5.4) captures Irving Fisher's ideas about sluggish adjustment in expectations and the observed non-neutrality behavior of actual individuals. Together with the supply function (5.2) it also points to Irving Fisher's innovative calculations of correlations between unemployment or output and distributed lags of changes in the price level.[26]

The monetary macroeconomic model (5.1) to (5.4) in Fisher's tradition of describing economic fluctuations, long-run equilibria and transition periods can easily be solved.[27] Equation (5.5a) is a second-order inhomogeneous linear difference equation in p:

$$p + \frac{(1-\alpha)(\gamma-1)-\lambda+\gamma}{1+\lambda-\gamma} p_{-1} - \frac{(1-\alpha)\gamma}{1+\lambda-\gamma} p_{-2}$$

$$= \frac{1}{1+\lambda-\gamma}\left[m+\bar{v}-y^p-(1-\alpha)(m_{-1}+\bar{v}_{-1}-y^p_{-1})\right] \text{ for } 1+\lambda \neq \gamma. \qquad (5.5a)$$

The corresponding characteristic equation (5.5b) points to a rather complex dynamic behavior of the price level p (and the output level y which can be solved as a similar difference equation out of equations (5.1) to (5.4):

$$q_{1,2} = -\frac{(1-\alpha)(\gamma-1)-\lambda+\gamma}{2(1+\lambda-\gamma)} \pm \sqrt{\frac{(1-\alpha)\gamma}{1+\lambda-\gamma}+\left[\frac{(1-\alpha)(\gamma-1)-\lambda+\gamma}{2(1+\lambda-\gamma)}\right]^2} \qquad (5.5b)$$

where the $q's$ constitute the familiar part in the general homogenous solution to equation (5.5a).

The system (5.5a) exhibits stable and unstable regions as well as cycles and no cycles depending on the values of the parameters involved. As can be easily demonstrated, the parameter γ of equation (5.3) is of crucial importance for the dynamic behavior of the system, whereas parameter α is of minor importance. Assuming, for example, $\gamma = 0$ and $0 < \alpha < 1$, equation

(5.5a) reduces to a first-order difference equation which is always stable since the resulting stability condition $\dfrac{1-\alpha+\lambda}{1+\lambda} < 1$ is fulfilled.

Assuming instead $\alpha = 1$ and $\gamma > 0$ a first-order difference equation emerges as well, however, with a different dynamic behavior as in the former case. This assumption does not essentially eliminate the rich dynamic properties of the system of equations (5.1) to (5.4) and therefore the major economic contents, but reduces the complexity considerably. Therefore, for the rest of the present chapter we assume without much loss of generality the simplified version of the adaptive expectation scheme in equation (5.4) with $\alpha = 1$, that is $p^e = p_{-1}$.

This qualification leads to equation (5.5) instead of equation (5.5a).

$$p - \frac{\lambda-\gamma}{1+\lambda-\gamma} p_{-1} = \frac{1}{1+\lambda-\gamma}\left[m+\bar{v} - y^p\right] \text{ for } 1+\lambda \neq \gamma. \tag{5.5}$$

The steady-state or long-run equilibrium p^* is established when $p = p_{-1} = p^*$ holds true:

$$p^* = m + \bar{v} - y^p. \tag{5.6}$$

Equation (5.6) is the long-run quantity theoretic solution in determining the price level. Thus, equation (5.6) and not equation (5.1) contains all the quantity theoretic elements.[28] Given constant velocity $\bar{v}$ and constant (or exogenously determined) potential real output y^p the price level p^* is uniquely determined by the money supply stock m. As was noted earlier in the text the long-run equilibrium (5.6) is not the typical situation. Changes in the variables on the right-hand side of equation (5.6) throw the system out of equilibrium and lead to the normal situation of transition periods towards a new equilibrium. The transition period with respect to prices is given by the general solution to the first-order difference equation (5.5) in equation (5.7):

$$p = p^* + (p_0 - p^*)\left(\frac{\lambda-\gamma}{1+\lambda-\gamma}\right)^t \tag{5.7}$$

where p^* is the equilibrium value given in equation (5.6) and p_0 is the starting value of p in period $t = 0$. The system will be stable and converges to the equilibrium value p^* continuously, provided the parameter restriction $\lambda > \gamma$ holds true. If $1+\lambda < \gamma$ is given, however, the system will be unstable without cycles. Fluctuations around the equilibrium value p^* result whenever the parameters λ and γ are in the regions $\lambda < \gamma$ and $1+\lambda > \gamma$. The cycles[29] will be damped if in addition $\lambda > \gamma - \frac{1}{2}$ holds true and explosive if $\lambda < \gamma - \frac{1}{2}$. For $\lambda = \gamma - \frac{1}{2}$ the cycles show a constant amplitude. As mentioned before the relation $\gamma = \lambda + 1$ is excluded since in this case the price level p at time t is not determined. For the special case $\lambda = \gamma$ the system will always be in equilibrium. Looking at equations (5.1) to (5.4) with the restriction $\alpha = 1$ it can be seen that a higher output $y > y^p$ as a result of $p > p^e = p_{-1}$ is provided by a higher velocity due to $p > p_{-1}$. In the more general system with $0 < \alpha < 1$ this special case does not emerge, however.

Given any value of λ the system will become unstable whenever γ increases beyond the limits indicated. As was pointed out verbally, extreme hoardings or dishoardings might lead to abnormal velocity movements when γ takes on high values. In these cases severe booms or (perhaps more likely) severe depressions may happen. The initial shocks or impulses in Ragnar Frisch's terms for these developments could be a monetary policy action by changing, for example, the money stock m erratically. A shock in velocity or in permanent output might induce these developments as well.

The monetary model of fluctuations (5.1) to (5.4) can of course be solved for the real output y, too, which in the theory of business cycles is the more familiar approach. The relevant calculations lead to the first-order difference equation (5.8) in y, where again $\alpha = 1$ is assumed:

$$y - \frac{\lambda - \gamma}{1 + \lambda - \gamma} y_{-1} = \frac{1}{1 + \lambda - \gamma} \left[\lambda(\Delta m + \Delta \bar{v}) + y^p - \gamma \Delta y^p \right]; \quad 1 + \lambda \neq \gamma. \qquad (5.8)$$

The usual way to establish the steady states or long-run equilibrium values of real output y^* is to assume $y = y_{-1} = y^*$ and $y^p = y^p_{-1}$ which leads to equation (5.9):

$$y^* = y^p + \lambda(\Delta m + \Delta \bar{v}) \qquad (5.9)$$

Equation (5.9) states that in the long run real output is equal to its potential level and depends on the growth rates of money supply and long-run velocity. It seems as if positive money growth rates can raise long-run equilibrium real output y^* permanently above the potential level y^p. That would mean that although money is neutral in the long-run, as can be seen by equations (5.6) and (5.9) it is not super-neutral according to equation (5.9). Does that mean that Blaug is correct in stating for the whole quantity theory of money, that money is not neutral in both senses in the short run and not super-neutral in the long run? (Cf. Blaug, 1995b, pp. 29-34; and Niehans, 1987, pp. 413, 418-419; but see Patinkin, 1995, pp. 123 and 124; and Patinkin, 1987.)

Blaug (1995b, pp. 29-30, emphasis in original) writes:

This theorem came to be known in the 1930s as 'neutrality of money' (Patinkin, (1987) but it was a familiar quantity-theory proposition all through the nineteenth century long before a memorable name for it had been invented. Alongside this long-run theorem about neutral money ran the notion that money in the short-run was almost certainly non-neutral; here too, the inspiration was Hume (and possibly Richard Cantillon) who had argued, not only that the *level* of output in an economy is invariant to the *level* of the money supply, but also that it can be raised by a positive *rate of change* of the money supply ... . What was called 'neutral money' in the interwar period has come to be known more recently as the vertical long-run Phillips curve or the 'policy ineffectiveness' proposition of the New Classical Macroeconomics. Hume apparently did not believe in the neutrality of money with respect to a sustained rate of change of the money supply; in other words, he denied what is now called 'superneutrality'. Had he expressed himself in modern language, he would have repudiated Friedman's notion of a natural rate of unemployment and insisted on the existence of a trade-off between output and inflation even in the long-run.

Contrary to Blaug's interpretation the present quantity theoretic model does not confirm this view. Equation (5.9) is not the correct long-run steady state description of the economy. In establishing the long-run equilibrium (5.6) with respect to prices it was assumed that $p = p_{-1} = p^*$, that is, $\Delta p = \Delta p^* = 0$. Equation (5.6), however, states that $\Delta p^* = 0$ provided $\Delta m = \Delta \bar{v} = \Delta y^p = 0$ (or, more, generally $\Delta m + \Delta v = \Delta y^p$). But only the assumption $\Delta y^p = 0$ was used in deriving equation (5.9). Therefore, to be consistent with the long-run price behavior, Δm and $\Delta \bar{v}$, too, must equal zero (or, more, generally, $\Delta m = -\Delta \bar{v}$), which leads to equation (5.10) and ensures long-run neutrality and super-neutrality:

$$y = y^* = y^p. \tag{5.10}$$

Of course, during transition periods, money is neither neutral nor super-neutral. And as mentioned before, transition periods are the normal situations.[30]

The general dynamic solution with respect to real output is given by

$$y = y^* + \left(y_0 - y^*\right)\left(\frac{\lambda - \gamma}{1 + \lambda - \gamma}\right)^t \tag{5.11}$$

where the same stability considerations apply as in the case of the price equation (5.7).

3.2 Monetary Policy Design to Ensure Stable Purchasing Power of Money

Equations (5.1) to (5.4) describe Fisher's quantity theory version of the model economy. Monetary policy is supposed to optimize a given objective function subject to the economic structure. A natural version would be for the monetary authority to attain a predetermined but stable price level $\bar{p}$, in which case the objective function

$$L_p = (p - \bar{p})^2 \tag{5.12}$$

should be minimized with respect to the money supply m under the condition of equations (5.1) to (5.4) or equivalently equation (5.5).

The resulting calculations lead to the optimal money supply rule:

$$m^* = y^p - \bar{v} + \bar{p} + (\lambda - \gamma)(\bar{p} - p_{-1}). \tag{5.13}$$

Assuming the target price level $\bar{p}$ to be equal to the equilibrium level p^* it follows that

$$m^* = y^p - \bar{v} + p^* + (\lambda + \gamma)(p^* - p_{-1}). \tag{5.13a}$$

Inserting (5.13a) into (5.5) yields $p = \bar{p} = p^*$.

The first three terms on the right hand side of equation (5.13) or (5.13a) capture the quantity-theory aspects. The last term is needed to eradicate the fluctuations in p and is in accordance with the optimal control theory result that an optimal policy rule should contain as many lags as the underlying structural model of the economy. Using, for example, equation (5.5a) instead of equation (5.5) as the relevant economic model, the resulting equation for the optimal money stock would contain two lags in p instead of only one in equation (5.13).

Even though the monetary authority can stabilize the purchasing power of money by applying equation (5.13) or (5.13a), it should be remembered that m is the natural logarithm of either M_1 or bB. The central bank can by open market operations (Fisher's second phase of monetary reforms) only control B. To completely control M_1, Fisher's last policy recommendation should be applied, that is, 100% money reserves. This change in the banking system leads to a money supply consisting only of base money, $M_1 = B$, or a money multiplier b of one.

It could also be argued that the object of monetary policy is to control the real output y. An optimal output rule could be established by minimizing the objective function

$$L_y = (y - \bar{y})^2 \tag{5.14}$$

with respect to Δm and the structure given in equation (5.8). Since only changes in m influence y (or m and m_{-1}), the policy instrument in this case must be the growth rate of M_1. Assuming the target output level $\bar{y}$ to be equal to the potential output y^p, the optimal $(\Delta m)^*$ is given in equation (5.15) with the usual and similar interpretation as in the optimal price level case.

$$(\Delta m)^* = \Delta y^p - \Delta \bar{v} + \left(\frac{\lambda - \gamma}{\lambda}\right)\left(y_{-1}^p - y_{-1}\right).$$ (5.15)

Inserting equation (5.15) into equation (5.8) it follows of course that $y = y^p$.

It looks as if the monetary authority could follow two alternative monetary rules to stabilize the economy. Fisher, however, was sure that stabilizing the purchasing power of money ensures stabilizing the economy (see the discussion and arguments in sections 1 and 2 above). Therefore, by using the money rule (5.13) or (5.13a), prices or the purchasing power of money not only are stabilized but real output should also be stabilized.

In order to establish the relationship proposed it can easily be demonstrated that both rules (5.13) and (5.15) are equivalent, provided the monetary authority seeks a constant price level target, i.e. $\Delta \bar{p} = 0$.

Differencing equation (5.13) once and assuming $\Delta \bar{p} = \Delta p^* = 0$ it follows that

$$\Delta m^* = \Delta y^p - \Delta \bar{v} - (\lambda - \gamma)\Delta p_{-1}.$$

Using equation (5.2) and (5.4) we get

$$\Delta p_{-1} = \frac{1}{\lambda}\left(y_{-1} - y_{-1}^p\right).$$

Combining both equations equation (5.16) emerges:

$$\Delta m^* = \Delta y^p - \Delta \bar{v} + \frac{\lambda - \gamma}{\lambda}\left(y_{-1}^p - y_{-1}\right).$$ (5.16)

which is equivalent to equation (5.15), i.e. $\Delta m^* = (\Delta m)^*$, the growth rate of the optimal money supply which ensures stable purchasing power is the same as the optimal monetary growth rate which leads to output stabilization given the dynamic context.

4   SUMMARY AND CONCLUSION

Irving Fisher's monetary policy recommendations were motivated by two underlying forces. First, they were backed by an outgrowth of his theoretical investigation in monetary problems in general and his quantity theoretic foundations in particular. Second, among his concerns to relieve society from what he considered major evils of his time, instability of money was the economic problem he ranked highest. Even though both forces supported each other, in some circumstances they seemed to be obstacles to each other as well. Proposing his compensated-dollar-plan, for example, Irving Fisher endorsed the gold standard for political and practical reasons, while his theoretical concern about stabilizing the purchasing power of money was centered around the money stock as outlined in *The Purchasing Power of Money*. His crusades in monetary policy campaigns were sometimes in contrast to his sound and profound theoretical analyses of monetary problems.

The present chapter discusses four episodes or phases of Irving Fisher's monetary policy proposals. The first phase beginning about 1910 and ending in the middle of the 1920s was centered theoretically around his major work on monetary theory, *The Purchasing Power of Money*, and his policy proposals of the compensated-dollar-plan. Even though Irving Fisher did not give up this idea completely, he later changed his views about the design of monetary policy. In his second phase Irving Fisher outlined a rather modern idea of central bank policy conducted by open market operations in selling and buying government bonds. The experience of the Great Depression after 1929 not only changed Irving Fisher's personal financial situation but also his theoretical views about the origins of booms and depressions. While milder business fluctuations are mostly originated by monetary forces behind the money supply and/or velocity behavior, severe booms and depressions are unleashed by over-indebtedness and deflation. In any case, for him, economic fluctuations were a monetary phenomenon. His practical monetary advice in his third phase of monetary policy proposals consequently became reflation to cure deflation, which of course was not inconsistent with his life-long concern with the stable purchasing power of money. His last period of monetary policy reforms started in the middle of the 1930s. The creation of a currency commission as an Open-Market Committee of the Federal Reserve Board represented his institutional design for the conduct of monetary policy to ensure price stability. Monetary policy control was completed by banking reform suggestions which in essence resulted in his 100%-reserve requirement proposal.

In order to combine Irving Fisher's theoretical views about the monetary economy and the monetary origins of business cycles and his policy proposals to keep the purchasing power of money stable, a simple Fisherian Monetary Model is outlined in the second part of this chapter which contains the essential quantity theoretic insights of Irving Fisher. Together with his emphasis on transition periods, non-neutral or non-rational expectations and his early discovery of the relation between inflation and employment in 1926 a simple monetary model of fluctuations emerges which incorporates the long-run steady state properties of the quantity theory and exhibits neutrality and super-neutrality in equilibrium but not in transition periods, which of course, are the normal cases.

Monetary policy is optimally designed by solving a simple objective function which incorporates stable prices with respect to the monetary economy model outlined above. The resulting policy rule ensures stable purchasing power of money and automatically stabilizes the real economy as well. The optimal money supply rule for base money should in Irving Fisher's understanding be completed by his 100%-reserve requirement to assure a complete control of the (M_1)-money stock as well. The optimal money base rule can be seen as a prototype of an activistic policy rule like the recommendations of Friedman (1960, 1968, 1985), McCallum (1985, 1987) or Meltzer (1984, 1985, 1987). Other modern proposals like those, for example, of Hall (1983), Tobin (1983), Taylor (1985) or Barro (1986, 1989) could also be connected with Irving Fisher's work on monetary policy design, which, however, is not taken up, but would be worth including in future investigations.

NOTES

* The authors acknowledge helpful comments by Volbert Alexander, John S. Chipman, Robert W. Dimand and Thomas M. Humphrey.
1 Translation and translator's Note for 'The Geometrical Theory of the Determination of Prices' by Léon Walras. A second paper in 1894 was read to the British Association for Advancement of Science: 'The Mechanics of Bimetalism'. See I.N. Fisher (1961, pp. 2-3).
2 R.L. Allen (1993, p. 129) restricts the period under consideration from 1912 to 1934. See, however, the citation of Fisher on page 261 in R.L. Allen (1993).
3 The following owes much to William I. Barber's unpublished manuscript (Barber, n.d.).
4 Barber states, 'What was needed instead, he then argued, was quiet, detached analysis to strengthen the theoretical foundations upon which informed policies could be built. Premature action would lead to nothing but mischief' (Barber, n.d., p. 2).
5 This oddity was noticed by Schumpeter (1948) and Patinkin (1993). See Barber (n.d., p. 3).
6 On the general discussion about monetary financed fiscal policies in the policy proposals by the Chicago school and before 1933 see Tavlas (1997).
7 On this monetary strategy see especially Fisher ([1935a] 1936); W. Allen (1993); Tolley (1962); Hotson (1987) and Tavlas (1975).
8 Fisher actually discusses several possible outlines for a monetary statute to embody his 100% money plan. Among them are: fixed total money supply, fixed per capita money supply and fixing the purchasing power. Theoretically Fisher preferred a fixed fraction of the per capita income of the country. Fisher ([1935a] 1936, pp. 22-27).
9 Allen writes that Soddy was at Cambridge University, but actually he was professor of chemistry at Oxford (1919-1936) after he worked with the physicist Sir Ernest Rutherford at McGill University, Montreal, and the chemist Sir William Ramsay at University College, London.
10 On the discussion who persuaded whom and who took the lead in this policy proposal see especially Patinkin (1969); W. Allen (1993); Barber (n.d.) and Tavlas (1975).
11 Niehans is skeptical even in this respect when he writes, 'By and large, however, these tracts contributed little of lasting value'. (Niehans, 1990, p. 270).
12 See also Tavlas (1997) on the role of Chicago economists and questions on why the Great Depression happened and what could have been done to avoid it.

13 Later in his article Patinkin writes about Fisher's crusades in monetary affairs: 'Thus, to be quite frank, on this issue, as well as the many others that he espoused at various stages of long lifetime (healthy exercise, vegetarianism, world peace, prohibition), Fisher was a crank'. (Patinkin, 1990, pp. 12-13; on this see also R. Allen, 1993, p. 129).

14 Fisher did not like the description of the ups and downs of economic activity like sine waves, which became popular with the work of Ragnar Frisch (1933).

15 See Fisher ([1911] 1985, pp. 66 and 70); Fisher (1923); Fisher (1925); Dimand (1993a, pp. 167, 168, 170); Dimand (1994, p. 96); Laidler (1991b, pp. 300-301); Morgan (1995, pp. 24-25); R.L. Allen (1993, pp. 111, 116, 181); Patinkin (1993, pp. 3-4); Tavlas and Aschheim (1985, p. 301) and Barber (n.d., p. 7).

16 Blaug (1995a, p.1) even points out that the 'roots go all the way back to the sixteenth century in the writings of the Salamanca School, one of the oldest scholarly traditions in the whole of economics'.

17 On the quantity theory, Irving Fisher, Monetarism, Milton Friedman and the controversy about the Chicago Tradition see Patinkin (1969); Tavlas (1975); Tavlas (1997); Humphrey (1971); Humphrey (1973); Patinkin (1990, especially pp. 24-28); Patinkin (1995); Niehans (1987, p. 413); Niehans (1990, p. 277); Blaug (1995a, p. 1); Blaug (1995b, pp. 27, 28, 30-35); Laidler (1991a); Laidler (1991b, pp. 302-303); Fisher ([1912] 1918, pp. 156, 163); Fisher ([1911] 1985, pp. vii, 14, 152, 181-183, 319); and R.L. Allen (1993, pp. 12, 113).

18 See, however, Dimand (1994) who uses a Walras-Keynes-Phillips relationship according to Tobin (1975) to model a debt-deflation situation and who argues that Tobin's WKP model bears little resemblance to Keynes or Phillips but does to Fisher.

19 On the relation between M and M' see Fisher ([1911] 1985, pp. 50, 53 and 54); Fisher ([1912] 1918, pp. 180, 183 and 184) as well as Patinkin (1993, p. 8); Wood (1995, p. 113) and R.L. Allen (1993, p. 115).

20 Compare this to the ideas of Fischer (1977) and Taylor (1979 and 1980) about long-term contracts, staggered wage settings and rational expectations.

21 See also Fisher (1896, 1907 and 1930).

22 See Rutledge (1977, p. 202) and our paper on Knut Wicksell's monetary macroeconomics (Loef and Monissen, 1998).

23 See also Patinkin (1990, p. 13).

24 Niehans (1990, p. 375) and Frisch (1933). Samuelson's short note (1959) giving credit to Alvin Hansen's mathematically incomplete formulation of the multiplier-accelerator principle which led him to formulate it in an exact difference equation form points in the same direction of a rather late introduction of this mathematical tool in economics. We owe this hint to J. Ehlgen.

25 We owe this argument to a comment by V. Alexander on an earlier version of this chapter.

26 See Fisher ([1926] 1973, 1933c, 1936, 1937); Dimand (1993a, p. 161) and Patinkin (1993, p. 4, fn 3). Of course, Fisher did not know the term or the content of what is now called rational expectations. However, he always stressed the point, that people misperceive the actual purchasing power of their currency.

27 First, lag equation (2) once, multiplying it by $\lambda(1-\alpha)$ and add the result to the combination of equation (2) and (4). Second, insert equation (3) and the result of step 1 into equation (1). Re-arranging terms leads to equation (5a). If the condition $1+\lambda \neq \gamma$ is not fulfilled, the price level in the system (1) to (4) will not be determined.

28 On Fisher's distinction between the equation of exchange and the quantity theory of money see Fisher ([1912] 1918, pp. 152 and 156-157); Blaug (1995b, p. 29); Patinkin (1990, pp. 2-3) and Patinkin (1995, p. 123).

29 In a strict sense 'cycles' emerge only if a sine or cosine wave results from an underlying higher order difference equation which cannot happen with a first-order equation as given in (5). Fluctuating values of p around p^{*} as a result of a negative magnitude of $\dfrac{\lambda-\gamma}{1+\lambda-\lambda}$ in equation (7), however, can be interpreted as 'business cycles' accordingly.

30 The same problem and solution results in Laidler's monetaristic business cycle model, but with a somewhat different interpretation. See Laidler (1976, pp. 80-82).

REFERENCES

Allen, R.L. (1993), *Irving Fisher. A Biography*, Cambridge, MA, Basil Blackwell.

Allen, W. (1993), 'Irving Fisher and the 100 percent reserve proposal', *Journal of Law and Economics*, **26**, 703-717.

Barber, W.J., 'Irving Fisher as a policy advocate', *mimeo*, no date.

Barro, R.J. (1986), 'Recent developments in the theory of rules versus discretion', *The Economic Journal, Supplement*, **96**, 23-37.

Barro, R.J. (1989), 'Interest rate targeting', *Journal of Monetary Economics*, **23**, 3-30.

Blaug, M. (1995a), 'Introduction', in M. Blaug *et al.* (eds), *The Quantity Theory of Money. From Locke to Keynes and Friedman*, Aldershot, UK, Edward Elgar, 1-3.

Blaug, M. (1995b), 'Why is the quantity theory of money the oldest surviving theory in economics?', in M. Blaug *et al.* (eds), *The Quantity Theory of Money. From Locke to Keynes and Friedman*, Aldershot, UK, Edward Edgar, 27-49.

Dimand, R.W. (1993a), 'The dance of the dollar: Irving Fisher's monetary theory of economic fluctuations', *History of Economics Review*, **20**, 161-172.

Dimand, R.W. (1993b), '100% Money: Irving Fisher and monetary reform in the 1930s', *History of Economic Ideas*, **20**, 59-76.

Dimand, R.W. (1994), 'Irving Fisher's debt-deflation theory of great depressions', *Review of Social Economy*, **52** , 92-107.

Dimand, R.W. (1995), 'Irving Fisher, J.M. Keynes, and the transition to modern macroeconomics', in A.F. Cottrell and M.S. Lawlor (eds), *New Perspectives on Keynes*. annual supplement to *History of Political Economy*, **27**, 247-266.

Fischer, S. (1977), 'Long-term contracts, rational expectations, and the optimal money supply', *Journal of Political Economy*, **85**, 191-205.

Fisher, I. (1892), *Mathematical Investigations in the Theory of Value and Prices,* Transactions of the Connecticut Academy. Reprinted together with his *Appreciation and Interest* (1896), New York, A.M. Kelley, 1961.

Fisher, I. (1896), *Appreciation and Interest*, published for the American Economic Association, New York, Macmillan, Facsimile reprint. Reprinted together with his *Mathematical Investigation in the Theory of Value and Prices*, New York, A.M. Kelley, 1961.

Fisher, I. (1907), *The Rate of Interest,* New York, Macmillan.

Fisher, I., assisted by H.G. Brown ([1911], [1913] 1985) *The Purchasing Power of Money: Its Determination and Relation to Credit, Interest and Crises,* New York, Macmillan, (1911). New and revised edition 1913. Reprinted 1985 from the 1931 printing, Fairfield, A.M. Kelley, 1985.

Fisher, I. ([1912] 1918), *Elementary Principles of Economics,* New York, Macmillan.

Fisher, I. (1913), 'A compensated dollar', *Quarterly Journal of Economics*, **27**, 213-235, 385-397.

Fisher, I. (1920), *Stabilizing the Dollar. A Plan to Stabilize the General Price Level Without Fixing Individual Prices*, New York, Macmillan.

Fisher, I. (1923), 'The business cycle largely a "dance of the dollar" ', *Journal of the American Statistical Association*, New Series 144, **18**, 1024-1028.

Fisher, I. (1925), 'Our unstable dollar and the so-called business cycle', *Journal of the American Statistical Association*, New Series 149, **20**, 179-202.

Fisher, I. (1926), 'Testimony before the committee on banking and currency', *House of Representatives*, **69:1**, March 26.

Fisher, I. ([1926] 1973), 'A statistical relation between unemployment and price changes', *International Labor Review*, **13**, 785-792. Reprinted as 'Lost and found: I discovered the Phillips curve – Irving Fisher', *Journal of Political Economy*, **81**, 496-502.

Fisher, I. (1928), *The Money Illusion*, New York, Adelphi.

Fisher, I. (1930), *The Theory of Interest*, New York, Macmillan.

Fisher, I. (1932), *Booms and Depressions. Some First Principles*, New York, Adelphi.

Fisher, I. (1933a), 'The debt-deflation theory of great depressions', *Econometrica*, **1**, 337-357.

Fisher, I. (1933b), *Stamp Scrip*, New York, Adelphi.

Fisher, I. (1933c), 'The relation of employment to the price level', in C.F. Roos (ed.), *Stabilization of Employment*, Bloomington, Ind., Principia Press,152-159.

Fisher, I. ([1935a] 1936), *100% Money*, rev. 2nd ed., New York, Adelphi.

Fisher, I. (1935b), assisted by H.R.L. Cohrssen, *Stable Money, A History of the Movement*, New York, Adelphi.

Fisher, I. (1936), 'Changes in the wholesale price index in relation to factory employment', *Journal of the American Statistical Association*, **31**, 496-502, 'Rejoinder', 505-506.

Fisher, I. (1937), 'Note on a short-cut method for calculating distributed lags', *Bulletin de L'Institut International de Statistique*, **29**, 323-328.

Fisher, I. N. (1961), *A Bibliography of the Writings of Irving Fisher*, New Haven, CT, Yale University Library.

Friedman, M. (1956), 'The quantity of money – a restatement', in M. Friedman (ed.), *Studies in the Quantity Theory of Money*, Chicago, University of Chicago Press, 3-21.

Friedman, M. (1960), *A Program for Monetary Stability*, New York, Fordham University Press.

Friedman, M. (1968), 'The role of monetary policy', *The American Economic Review*, **58**, 1-17.

Friedman, M. (1985), 'Monetarism in rhetoric and in practice', in A. Ando, H. Eguchi, R. Farmer and Y. Suzuki (eds), *Monetary Policy in Our Times*, Cambridge, MA, MIT-Press, 15-28.

Frisch, R. (1933), 'Propagation problems and impulse problems in dynamic economics', in *Economic Essays in Honour of Gustav Cassel*, London, Allen and Unwin, 171-205.

Hall, R.E. (1983), 'Macroeconomic policy under structural change', in *Industrial Change and Public Policy*, Federal Reserve Bank of Kansas City, 85-111.

Hotson, J.H. (1987), 'The Keynesian revolution and the aborted Fisher-Simons revolution or the road not taken', *Economies et Sociétés*, **21**, 185-219.

Hume, D. (1752), *Political Discourses*, Edinburgh.

Humphrey, T.M. (1971), 'Role of non-Chicago economists in the evolution of the quantity theory in America 1930-1950', *Southern Economic Journal*, **38**, 12-18.

Humphrey, T.M. (1973), 'On the monetary economics of Chicagoans and non-Chicagoans: Reply', *Southern Economic Journal*, **40**, 460-463.

Humphrey, T.M. (1984), 'Algebraic quantity equations before Fisher and Pigou', Federal Reserve Bank of Richmond *Economic Review*, 13-22.

Humphrey, T.M. (1990), 'Fisherian and Wicksellian price-stabilization models in the history of monetary thought', Federal Reserve Bank of Richmond *Economic Review*, 3-12.

Humphrey, T.M. (1992a), 'A simple model of Irving Fisher's price-level stabilization rule', Federal Reserve Bank of Richmond *Economic Review*, 12-18.

Humphrey, T.M. (1992b), 'Price-level stabilization rules in a Wicksellian model of the cumulative process', *Scandinavian Journal of Economics*, **94**, 509-518.

Laidler, D. (1976), 'An elementary monetarist model of simultaneous fluctuations in prices and output', in Frisch, H. (ed.), *Inflation in Small Countries*, Berlin, Springer, 75-89.

Laidler, D. (1991a), *The Golden Age of the Quantity Theory*, Princeton, Princeton University Press.

Laidler, D. (1991b), 'The quantity theory is always and everywhere controversial – why?', *The Economic Record*, **67**, 289-306.

Loef, H.-E. and Monissen, H.G. (1998), 'Knut Wicksell und die moderne Makroökonomik', in E. Streissler (ed.), *Studien zur Entwicklung der ökonomischen Theorie*, Neue Folge, Band 115/XVIII, Berlin, Duncker und Humblot, 247-274.

Lucas, R.E. (1973), 'Some international evidence on output-inflation-trade-offs', *American Economic Review*, **63**, 326-334.

Marget, A.W. ([1938-1942] 1966), *The Theory of Prices. A Re-Examination of the Central Problems of Monetary Theory*, Vol. I. Reprint, New York, A.M. Kelley.

McCallum, B.T. (1985), 'On the consequences and criticisms of monetary targeting', *Journal of Money, Credit, and Banking*, **17**, 570-597.

McCallum, B.T. (1987), 'The case for rules in the conduct of monetary policy: a concrete example', *Weltwirtschaftliches Archiv*, **123**, 415-429.

Meltzer, A.H. (1984), 'Rules for price stability: an overview and comparison', in *Price Stability and Public Policy*, Federal Reserve Bank of Kansas City, 209-222.

Meltzer, A.H. (1985), 'Variability of prices and money under fixed and fluctuating exchange rates: an empirical study of monetary regimes in Japan and the United States', in Bank of Japan, *Monetary and Economic Studies*, **3**, 1-46.

Meltzer, A.H. (1987), 'Limits of short-run-stabilization policy', *Economic Inquiry*, **25**, 1-14.

Monissen, H.G. (1989), 'Die konjunkturtheoretischen Vermutungen von Irving Fisher', in B. Schefold (Hrsg.), *Entwicklungen der ökonomischen Theorie VII*, Berlin, Duncker und Humblot, 35-64.

Morgan, M.S. (1995), 'Irving Fisher's models of money', *Draft paper*, Department of Economics, University of Amsterdam and Department of Economic History, London School of Economics, Amsterdam and London.

Niehans, J. (1987), 'Classical monetary theory, new and old', *Journal of Money, Credit, and Banking*, **19**, 409-424.

Niehans, J. (1990), *A History of Economic Theory, Classical Contributions, 1720-1980*, Baltimore, Johns Hopkins University Press.

Patinkin, D. (1969), 'The Chicago tradition, the quantity theory, and Friedman', *Journal of Money, Credit, and Banking*, **1**, 46-70.

Patinkin, D. (1972), 'On the short-run non-neutrality of money in the quantity theory', *Banca Nationale del Lavoro Quarterly Review*, **100**, 3-22.

Patinkin, D. (1973), 'On the monetary economics of Chicagoans and non-Chicagoans: comment', *Southern Economic Journal*, **39**, 454-459.

Patinkin, D. (1987), 'Neutrality of money', in J. Eatwell, M. Milgate and P. Newman (eds), *The New Palgrave: A Dictionary of Economics*, London, Macmillan.

Patinkin, D. (1990), 'Irving Fisher, the Cambridge school, and the quantity theory', *mimeo*, Seoul, Korea, Development Institute, Distinguished Lecturer Program Report Series 90-01.

Patinkin, D. (1993), 'Irving Fisher and his compensated dollar plan', *Economic Quarterly*, Federal Reserve Bank of Richmond, **79**, 1-33.

Patinkin, D. (1995), 'Concluding comments on the quantity theory', in M. Blaug *et al.* (eds), *The Quantity Theory of Money. From Locke to Keynes and Friedman*, Aldershot, UK, Edward Elgar, 120-133.

Rutledge, J. (1977), 'Irving Fisher and autoregressive expectations', *The American Economic Review, Papers and Proceedings*, **67**, 200-205.

Samuelson, P.A. (1959), 'Alvin Hansen and the interactions between the multiplier analysis and the principle of acceleration', *The Review of Economics and Statistics*, **41**, 183-184; reprinted in J. Stiglitz (ed.), *The Collected Scientific Papers of Paul A. Samuelson, Vol. II*, Cambridge, MIT-Press, 1966, 2nd printing 1970, 1123-1124.

Schumpeter, J.A. (1948), 'Irving Fisher's econometrics', *Econometrica*, **16**, 219-231.

Tavlas, G. S. (1975), 'Some further observations on the monetary economics of Chicagoans and non-Chicagoans', *Southern Economic Journal*, **42**, 685-692.

Tavlas, G.S. (1997), 'Chicago, Harvard, and the doctrinal foundations of monetary economics', *Journal of Political Economy*, **105**, 153-177.

Tavlas, G.S. and J. Aschheim (1985), 'Alexander Del Mar, Irving Fisher, and monetary economics', *Canadian Journal of Economics*, **18**, 294-313.

Taylor, J.B. (1979), 'Staggered wage setting in a macro-model', *The American Economic Review*, **69**, 108-113.

Taylor, J.B. (1980), 'Aggregate dynamics and staggered contracts', *Journal of Political Economy*, **88**, 1-23.

Taylor, J.B. (1985), 'What would nominal GNP targetting do to the business cycle?', *Carnegie-Rochester-Conference Series on Public Policy*, **22**, 61-84.

Thornton, H. (1802), *A Inquiry into the Nature and Effects of the Paper Credit of Great Britain*, London. Reprinted with an introduction by F.A. von Hayek, London, Allen and Unwin, 1939.

Tobin, J. (1975), 'Keynesian models of recession and depression', *The American Economic Review*, **65**, 195-202.

Tobin, J. (1983), 'Monetary policy: rules, targets, and shocks', *Journal of Money, Credit, and Banking*, **15**, 506-518.

Tolley, G.S. (1962), '100 per cent reserve banking', in L.B. Yeager (ed.), *In Search of a Monetary Constitution*, Cambridge, MA, Harvard University Press, 275-304.

Wood, G.E. (1995), 'The quantity theory in the 1980s: Hume, Thornton, Friedman and the relation between money and inflation', in M. Blaug *et al.* (eds), *The Quantity Theory of Money. From Locke to Keynes and Friedman*, Aldershot, UK, Edward Elgar, 97-119.

Monetary Policy and Monetary Reform: A Note

Volbert Alexander

If we take the UK price index in the year 1630 as 100 and look to the same magnitude in 1930, that is, 300 years later, it is still around 100. The corresponding price index today, 67 years after 1930, has reached around 3000.

Compared with the well-known hyperinflational processes which took place in the first half of the 20th century the British experience is quite moderate. Accelerating hyperinflations occured in Austria, Germany, Greece, Hungary, Poland and Russia showing the following dramatic characteristics and leading to breakdowns of the existing monetary systems within two years:

Table C5.1: Characteristics of accelerating hyperinflations

	Austria	Germany	Greece	Hungary		Poland	Russia
Begin	Oct. 1921	Aug. 1922	Nov. 1943	Mar. 1923	Aug. 1945	Jan.1923	Dec. 1921
End	Aug. 1922	Nov. 1923	Nov. 1944	Feb. 1924	Jul. 1946	Jan. 1924	Jan. 1924
Length (= number of months)	11	16	13	10	12	11	26
Total increase in the price level	69.9	1.02×10^{10}	4.70×10^{8}	44.0	3.81×10^{27}	699.0	124.0×10^{5}
Max. monthly inflation rate in %	134.0	32.4×10^{3}	85.5×10^{6}	98.0	41.9×10^{15}	275.0	213.0

In contrast to these striking short run phenomena of hyperinflations resulting in the destruction of monetary systems, the Latin American history of the last 40–50 years shows another type of monetary disorder: we observe substantial inflationary processes lasting for decades with short run accelerations and decelerations of inflation rates but leaving the monetary systems in tact. They

109

are accompanied by high political instability and substantial cycles in the real sector. The following numbers only give a general impression of these Latin American experiences:

Table C5.2: Consumer price indices of Latin American countries
(1965 = 100)

	1965	1975	1985	1995
Argentina	100	2916	847510399	51130×10^9
Brazil	100	877	662822	1215×10^{12}
Chile	100	88827	3521790	16291456
Mexico	100	189	3889	143862
Source: IMF, International Financial Statistics Yearbook

These impressive empirical observations show the dramatic changes in monetary regimes in the first half of this century stemming from the developments of modern paper money– and credit-systems in which money can be supplied without restrictions from real aggregates like gold, silver or other commodity standards. It also points to the immense instability potential of a mismatched modern monetary sector.

Irving Fisher's contributions to economic theory coincide in time with the beginning of these dramatic changes in monetary sectors of industrialized economies. He was one of the first economists who fully understood the immense dangers and the instability potential of these fundamental changes in monetary conditions. His main conclusion was that monetary developments were the dominant and only source of instability even in the real sector of the economy – that means real output and employment. This conclusion can be interpreted as one of the first examples for overcoming the traditional position of the neutrality of money. Consequently he developed analytically and promoted politically a monetary system in which an extensive creation of money and the political use of large changes in the money supply were impossible as they were in the monetary systems of former centuries.

If we analyse Fisher's contribution to economic theory in the light of recent knowledge and developments two points are of crucial interest:

First, Fisher treats inflationary and deflationary shocks as the main sources of monetary *and* real economic instability. For him the danger of a depression coming from a negative shock in money supply, which means from a negative growth rate of money, is just as important as an inflationary development caused by positive money supply shocks. We know that one of the major reasons for the Great Depression 1929-1932 was the policy of the FED: from 1927-1929 money supply in the U.S. decreased by 30% as a consequence of a very restrictive monetary policy. With our recent knowledge about the effects of monetary policy measures the danger of a recession caused by negative growth rates of money supply is negligible and has not been observed since World War Two.

The discussion about the policy implications of the rational expectations hypothesis which intensified in the 70s shows that slowdowns of economic activity may also be caused by positive growth rates of the money supply: if money growth is overestimated by transactors and unanticipated disinflation occurs, real economic activity goes down. According to the Lucas-supply-equation actual output falls below potential output when the expected inflation exceeds actual inflation. This constellation normally exists in situations of positive growth rates of money supply and prices. A negative money supply growth, therefore, is neither a necessary nor a sufficient condition for creating a recession by monetary policy measures.

On the other hand, Fisher was right in blaming high growth rates of money supply as the main source of substantial inflationary processes. Concerning inflation his analysis and policy consequences even hold up in the light of recent knowledge in economic theory. Up to now the key question for a policy of stable price levels is how to restrict the money creation potential of central banks. This question crucially depends on the degree of independence central banks have vis-à-vis national governments. Empirical studies show that a policy of stable prices is only provided by monetary authorities with an independent legal, instrumental and personal status.

Second, it is always attractive to show that modern ideas and conclusions can be found in very old studies and that many 'new' hypotheses are only a repetition of ideas presented long ago. Fisher is often cited for his modern proposals in controlling the behavior of central bankers. Indeed his suggestion was to fire central bank officers automatically in case the price level should deviate from a target value by more than 10% during three consecutive months.

This reminds us of modern proposals enforcing central bankers to follow an anti-inflationary monetary policy, in general, and of the New Zealand experiment, in particular. But if we analyse this issue in detail we can see substantial differences between Fisher's concept and the proposals discussed today. While Fisher's central bankers will lose their jobs when they fail to reach their target, price stability, for three months the New Zealand law refers to a time period of three consecutive years.

Also other statements in Fisher's publications make clear that his monetary policy game was a relatively short run phenomenon. He often proposes to react immediately on actual shocks in money demand or in velocity.

Modern concepts like, for example, the Meltzer- or McCallum-rules prefer only base money reactions by the central bank as a response to permanent velocity movements like shifts in the four years' average in money demand.

It becomes obvious that Fisher did not consider adequately two central elements of modern monetary and macroeconomic analysis:

- the length and variability of lags in the effect of monetary policy and
- the implications of uncomplete knowledge of economic structures and processes.

6. Constructive Income Taxation: A Modern Interpretation

Clemens Fuest[*]

1 INTRODUCTION: INCOME VERSUS CONSUMPTION TAXATION

The question of finding the adequate base for taxation is a key one in the discipline of public finance. In the twentieth century, a large part of this debate has concentrated on the dichotomy between, on the one hand, comprehensive income taxation, and, on the other hand, the taxation of expenditure or consumption. While the concept of comprehensive or broad-based income taxation has been systematically developed in the work of Schanz (1896), Haig (1921) and Simons (1938), the development of the modern concept of consumption tax systems owes substantial contributions to Irving Fisher (1906, 1937) and Fisher and Fisher (1942). This chapter purposes to give a survey of the main arguments which play a role in the modern debate on the issue of consumption versus income taxation and to highlight the importance of Irving Fisher's contribution to the subject.

The chapter proceeds as follows: the following section reproduces Fisher's proposal for a reform of the classical income tax system; section three discusses efficiency aspects of the consumption versus income tax controversy; section four discusses the implications of international economic integration; section five focuses on equity issues; section six reviews practical possibilities and problems of switching from an income tax system to a consumption tax system; section seven gives the conclusions.

2 CONSTRUCTIVE INCOME TAXATION: THE PROPOSAL

Irving Fisher's proposal to reform the tax system is essentially motivated by what Fisher holds to be the weaknesses of the U.S. Federal Income Tax of his time (which was in its basic principles not too different from today's income tax systems). His main objections to the income tax system are summarized in the following five points:

> (1) They (the tax laws, C.F.) are unfair ... not only because they impose double taxation (by taxing savings and their fruits) and allow double exemption, but also because they thus tax the producers of the nation's wealth more heavily than those who merely spend, especially the 'idle rich'.
> (2) By taxing the increase of capital, they kill the most important geese which lay the most important golden eggs.
> (3) They are unwise, largely because they actually kill much of the revenue which they should produce.
> (4) Their administration is unduly costly and vexatious to the taxpayer; and their uncertainty and complexity require the continuous employment of expensive tax specialists in government, in business, and in private life.
> (5) They keep a sword of Damocles hanging over the head of the taxpayer. Several years after his original return has been filed with great care and in good faith, he is still exposed to the chance of receiving from the Treasury a deficiency notice, which is often difficult and costly to contest (Fisher and Fisher, 1942, pp. 3-4).

This quotation shows that many of the key issues in the modern debate on the income vs. consumption tax controversy have in fact been discussed by Irving Fisher, who, in the introduction to his book, *Constructive Income Taxation*, states that he developed his tax reform proposal in its main components as far back as 1896 (Fisher and Fisher, 1942, p. x).[1] The first point he raises concerns equity issues which will be discussed briefly in section 5 of this chapter. The second and the third point raise issues Fisher seems to have deemed most important in the debate. The effect of the tax system on capital accumulation and economic growth in general, and more specifically, on the development of tax revenue over time. He thought that the income tax system inhibited economic development and growth. This is why he called it 'destructive' and labeled his own proposal as 'constructive'. The consequences of the tax system for economic growth also play a key role in the modern critique of income tax. The last two points raised above are probably most convincing even to the non-specialist, namely that the existing tax systems burden the taxpayer merely by the fact that they are excessively complex. This flaw of the income tax system has survived until today.

What Fisher thought to be a viable solution to all these problems is a very simple reform proposal:

> The essential feature of our proposal is that the proposed tax base is income spent, that is, income used for consumption purposes, excluding all income saved, such as undivided profits and investments, presumably used for productive purposes (Fisher and Fisher, 1942, p. 4).

Of course, the fundamental idea of choosing consumption as the appropriate tax base existed before Fisher. The issue of consumption taxation has been discussed by such prominent philosophers as Thomas Hobbes[2], and consumption taxation has played a role in practical tax policy much earlier. For instance, in the fifteenth and sixteenth century, consumption taxes were discussed in the German Empire as a means to finance the wars against the Turks.[3] However, it was Fisher's contribution to have argued in favor of consumption taxation in the context of modern tax system. In particular, he has explained to a general public in the U.S. that the consumption tax does not involve giving an account of each item of consumption expenditure, which would clearly require a supervision of citizens not acceptable for practical purposes. Instead, Fisher points out (Fisher and Fisher, 1942, p. 4):

> We need only two data:
> 1. The amount of income we had to spend; that is, what we had or received during the day.
> 2. The amount we did not spend; that is, the amount left over as determined by counting at the end of the day.

Clearly, while this is not to say that all tax administration problems are easily solved in this approach, it is more difficult after than before Fisher's contributions to argue that sticking to the income tax system is justified merely for administrative reasons. In fact, Fisher was convinced that his proposal would facilitate the administration of the tax system for both tax payers and the government. What is more important and, at least for an economist, also more interesting, however, is that Fisher argued that the consumption tax system would also be more efficient and more equitable. The problems of overall equity and efficiency of the two alternative tax systems also dominate the modern debate and are therefore addressed in the following two sections.

3   EFFICIENCY ASPECTS OF CONSTRUCTIVE INCOME TAXATION

3.1. Optimal Tax Considerations

According to the theory of optimal taxation, an optimal tax structure should minimize the excess burden of the tax system. The solution to this problem is trivial if the required revenue can be raised by lump sum taxes; these taxes, however, are usually ruled out for equity reasons. Given that lump sum taxes are not available, an optimal tax structure has to take into account that taxes cause welfare losses by inducing distortions. One argument often put forward in favor of the consumption tax system is that it is neutral with respect to the pattern of consumption over time, i.e. it avoids intertemporal distortions. The comprehensive income tax, in contrast, includes income from savings in its tax base and therefore does induce intertemporal distortions by discriminating future relative to present consumption.

Both tax systems, however, distort the (intratemporal) choice between consumption and leisure; as is well known from the theory of the second best, given that both tax systems cause one type of distortion, the mere fact that one of them – the consumption tax system – avoids a second distortion does not allow us to conclude that the latter is superior to the income tax system. The question of whether or not an optimal tax system should discriminate savings, as does the comprehensive income tax, has been studied extensively in the optimal taxation literature (for a survey, see Huber, 1992). One point often made in critique of the income tax and in favor of a consumption tax system is based on a variant of the celebrated Corlett-Hague-rule (see Corlett and Hague, 1953-1954).

The Corlett-Hague rule in its original form applies to a one-period model with two consumption goods and elastically supplied labor. The rule states that an optimal tax system should put a higher tax on the good which is more complementary to leisure. The economic intuition behind this rule is simple. A uniform tax on all consumption goods would induce the household to work less and enjoy more leisure because the tax drives a wedge between the net wage and the opportunity cost of leisure. This distortion can obviously be reduced if goods are taxed more heavily which are complementary to leisure. The Corlett-Hague rule can also be applied to a two-period framework. Assume that a household lives and consumes over two periods but supplies labour in the first period only. In this framework, higher taxes on future consumption would be desirable only if future consumption was more complementary to present leisure than present consumption. Supporters of consumption tax systems argue that it is more plausible to assume that the opposite is the case. According to this view, the discrimination of savings in the existing income tax systems is inefficient.

While the above argument certainly does make an interesting point, it also has an important shortcoming. It holds only under the restrictive assumption that there are just two periods. In the following section, we therefore reconsider the problem of intertemporal neutrality in a simple intertemporal model with more than two periods.

3.2. Optimal Taxation in a Simple Intertemporal Framework

Consider an economy of identical households, each living T periods. The utility function of the representative household is assumed to take the form

$$\sum_{t=0}^{T}(1+\rho)^{-t}(U(C_t)+Q(F_t)) \tag{6.1}$$

where C_t is consumption in period t and $F_t = 1 - L_t$ is leisure, or total available time (normalized to unity) minus working time. The functions $U(\cdot)$ and $Q(\cdot)$ are assumed to have the usual neoclassical properties. The household has no initial endowment but may work to earn labor income and save or dissave across periods. For present purposes, it is sufficient to consider a pure commodity tax system, where the commodity tax (τ) may vary across periods. It is straightforward to show that this tax system is equivalent to a combined tax on wages and savings (see, for instance Huber, 1996). The budget constraint of the representative household can thus be written as

$$\sum_{t=0}^{T}(1+r)^{-t}(1+\tau_t)C_t = \sum_{t=0}^{T}(1+r)^{-t}w_tL_t \tag{6.2}$$

where w_t is the wage rate in period t. Equation (6.2) essentially states that the present value of the household's consumption expenditure is (in equilibrium) equal to his wealth, i.e. the present value of his labor income. The distortions induced by the tax system which have been mentioned in the preceding paragraph can be demonstrated in this model by considering the household's optimal decisions on consumption and the supply of labor. Maximizing (6.1) subject to (6.2) leads to the following first-order conditions:

$$\frac{\partial U}{\partial C_t}(1+\rho)^{-t} + \lambda((1+\tau_t)(1+r)^{-t}) = 0 \quad \text{for} \quad t = 0 \dots T \tag{6.3}$$

and

$$\frac{\partial Q}{\partial L_t}(1+\rho)^{-t} - \lambda w_t(1+r)^{-t} = 0 \quad \text{for} \quad t = 0 \dots T. \tag{6.4}$$

These can be transformed into

$$-\frac{\dfrac{\partial U}{\partial C_t}}{\dfrac{\partial Q}{\partial L_t}} = w_t^{-1}(1+\tau_t) \quad \text{for} \quad t = 0 \dots T \tag{6.5}$$

and

$$\frac{\dfrac{\partial U}{\partial C_t}}{\dfrac{\partial U}{\partial C_0}}(1+\rho)^{-t} = \frac{(1+\tau_t)}{(1+\tau_0)}(1+r)^{-t} \quad \text{for} \quad t = 0 \dots T. \tag{6.6}$$

Equation (6.5) captures the (intratemporal) distortion of the choice between consumption and leisure. This distortion occurs both in the case of the income tax and the consumption tax system. Equation (6.6) shows that the tax system may also distort the intertemporal pattern of consumption if the tax is not constant over time. This distortion occurs in the income tax system, because income from savings is included in the tax base; consumption later in life is therefore discriminated relative to earlier consumption. A consumption tax system, in contrast, avoids this intertemporal distortion.

As has been mentioned in the preceding paragraph, given that both tax systems only allow for second-best allocations, with an intratemporal distortion between leisure and consumption, it is a priori not clear whether it is generally desirable to avoid the second distortion. This question can be answered by deriving the optimal tax structure in the present model. In order to do this, we have to take into account the revenue needs of the public sector and the production side of the economy. For the former, assume that there is an exogenously determined revenue requirement of the government for the period under consideration, with the present value G. The public sector budget constraint can then be written as

$$G = \sum_{t=0}^{T}(1+r)^{-t}\tau_t C_t. \tag{6.7}$$

For the production side of the economy, we consider the case of a small open economy with two factors of production, capital (K) and labor (L). Output in period t (Y_t) is described by the production function

$$Y_t = F(K_t, L_t), \tag{6.8}$$

where F is assumed to be linear-homogenous in K and L. Capital moves freely across borders whereas labor is immobile. The interest rate (r) is determined on the international capital market. In this setting, the wage rate is determined by the interest rate in the world market and constant over time, given that the interest rate does not change. We can therefore normalize the wage rate to unity.[4]

We can now derive the optimal intertemporal tax structure by maximizing the utility of the representative agent subject to the government budget constraint. For the following analysis, it is convenient to use the 'primal' approach to the optimal tax problem (Atkinson and Stiglitz, 1980, p. 377), which is to formulate the problem in terms of quantities instead of considering the dual approach (the formulation in prices), although the latter is more common in the theory of optimal taxation. This can be done by using (6.3) and (6.4) to substitute the tax rates in the budget constraints of the household (6.2) and the public sector (6.7). The problem of the government is thus to maximize

$$\sum_{t=0}^{T}(1+\rho)^{-t}(U(C_t)+Q(1-L_t))$$ (6.9)

over C_t and L_t, subject to
a) the household budget constraint, which, using the first-order conditions of the household's maximization problem, can be written as

$$\sum_{t=0}^{T}(1+\rho)^{-t}\frac{\partial U}{\partial C_t}C_t+\sum_{t=0}^{T}(1+r)^{-t}\frac{\partial Q}{\partial L_t}L_t=0$$ (6.10)

b) the (modified) government budget constraint

$$G=\sum_{t=0}^{T}[((1+\rho)^{-t}\frac{\partial U}{\partial C_t}/\frac{\partial Q}{\partial L_0}+(1+r)^{-t})C_t]$$ (6.11)

and finally c) the condition for an optimal intertemporal allocation of labor:[5]

$$\frac{\dfrac{\partial Q}{\partial L_t}}{\dfrac{\partial Q}{\partial L_0}}=(1+\rho)^t(1+r)^{-t}\quad\text{for}\quad t=0\dots T.$$ (6.12)

Deriving the first-order conditions for the above problem and making some rearrangements leads to the following result:

$$\frac{\tau_t}{1+\tau_t}=\eta_t(1+\frac{\gamma}{\phi})+\frac{1}{\phi}(1-\gamma)\quad\text{for}\quad t=0\dots T$$ (6.13)

where γ and ϕ are the Lagrangean multipliers of constraints (6.10) and (6.11), respectively, and

$$\eta_t=C_t\frac{\dfrac{\partial^2 U}{\partial C_t^{\,2}}}{\dfrac{\partial U}{\partial C_t}}$$ (6.14)

is the elasticity of the marginal utility of consumption in period t. Equation (6.13) immediately reveals that intertemporal neutrality, i.e. holding constant the tax τ across periods is not necessarily optimal. A sufficient condition for intertemporal neutrality to be desirable is a constant elasticity of the marginal utility of consumption. This however, is obviously a rather special case. On the other hand, the above result is of course far from offering support to the type of intertemporal distortion induced by the classical income tax, i.e. the discrimination of income from savings. Depending on the preference structure it may as well be desirable to subsidize savings. The main lesson to be learned from the above result is that the theory of optimal taxation does not offer unambiguous support for an intertemporally neutral tax system.

Two important aspects, however, have been neglected in the above analysis which do support the case against the taxation of savings. The first point concerns the effects of savings taxes on capital accumulation and economic growth. In models which, contrary to the one above, allow savings to affect capital accumulation and output, it turns out that the welfare costs of capital taxation are higher, the longer taxpayers anticipate the tax. If they do anticipate this tax, they will react by consuming out of their accumulated wealth. As a consequence of this, the capital stock declines. In the extreme case, it may be that a capital tax increase leads to a reduction of savings such that the net return on savings remains constant and the burden of the tax entirely falls on labor (see Chamley, 1981).

Taking into account the effects of capital taxes on capital accumulation leads to the conclusion that the welfare cost of capital taxation is much higher than is suggested by studies which abstract from capital accumulation. This point may be interpreted as a refinement of the argument most emphasized by Irving Fisher, namely that capital taxes discourage savings and growth. Fisher mentions this argument many times in his work. Perhaps the most drastic way of making his point is the following paragraph from the chapter on the 'Destructiveness of Tax on Savings' in his book *Constructive Income Taxation* (Fisher and Fisher, 1942, p.73):

> Nothing else in the field of taxation is quite comparable to the tragic harm done by a tax which thus destroys and discourages saving. Perhaps the nearest parallel is the old French window tax, which discouraged windows so that people preferred to live in the dark, thereby falling prey to tuberculosis. The tax collections were light in terms of money, but in terms of distress and disease the tax burden was, so goes the tradition, enormous.

The second argument in favor of intertemporally neutral taxation is the problem of time inconsistency. This problem is related to the fact that un-anticipated capital tax increases have a lump sum element and therefore a lower welfare cost – the latter is simply due to the fact that taxpayers have no time to adjust to the tax. Even if a tax on capital is not desirable *ex ante*, a government has incentives to tax capital *ex post*. As taxpayers know that the government has incentives to deviate from tax policies announced previously, efficiency gains may be achieved if the government could credibly commit to its tax policy. One solution to the problem of time inconsistency with con-siderable practical appeal would be to introduce a constitutional rule stating that the tax system should be intertemporally neutral. Such a solution would be preferable, for instance, to constitutionally guaranteed tax rates or ceilings on tax rates, because it leaves room for the changing revenue needs of the public sector (see Huber, 1992).

Summarizing, this section has shown that, while conventional optimal tax theory does not allow us to draw unambiguous conclusions concerning the relative efficiency of the income tax and the consumption tax systems, the growth effects of capital taxation and time consistency problems both support the case for intertemporally neutral tax systems.

4   THE IMPLICATIONS OF INTERNATIONAL ECONOMIC INTEGRATION

While changing theoretical views on the efficiency of alternative tax systems seem to affect practical tax policies only with large time lags if at all, the fact that traditional income tax has come under pressure in recent years is due to another striking development – the increasing role of international openness.

The influence of international economic integration on tax policies has been most important in the field of capital taxes. These taxes comprise taxes on domestic investment such as, for instance, the corporate income tax, and taxes on income from savings. In a closed economy, there is little difference between these different forms of capital taxation since savings equal investment; the economic effect of a capital tax in a closed economy is basically to reduce savings.

In an open economy, in contrast, the economic consequences of capital taxes are different and depend on the form of capital taxation. A tax on domestic investment, for instance, will have no or little impact on domestic savings. Yet, the distortions it induces are very important. If a small open economy is under consideration, a tax on domestic investment will have no impact on the interest rate in the world capital market. Investors will therefore accept no net return to investment which is lower than the rate of interest of alternative investments. Consequently, the burden of a tax on domestic investment is borne entirely by immobile factors of production. Given that the immobile factors bear the burden of the tax anyway, it is more efficient to abolish the capital tax and to tax the income of the immobile factors directly.[6]

The second type of capital tax, a tax on domestic savings, could, in principle, be more efficient, even in a small open economy. As people are normally much less mobile internationally than capital, the distortions induced by a tax on savings collected according to the residence principle should not be much higher in an open than in a closed economy. The main objection to the taxation of savings in an open economy, however, concerns its implementation. As portfolio investment, which requires little more than setting up a bank account, is almost costlessly mobile, investors may easily avoid domestic taxes by holding financial assets abroad. Due to bank secrecy laws and limited international cooperation and exchange of information by tax administrations, it is practically impossible to force investors to report their capital income earned abroad to the tax authorities in their countries of residence. Although most countries do include income from savings in their income tax bases, the effective taxation of savings within the personal income tax has eroded almost completely during the last two decades.

At least from a theoretical point of view, it thus seems appropriate to conclude that a small open economy should abolish capital taxation completely. Some authors have therefore raised the question of why so many countries do in fact continue to tax capital. In this debate, some reasons have been given why it may still be rational to tax capital income, one reason being that taxpayers would otherwise have strong incentives to declare labor as capital income (see Gordon and McKie-Masson, 1994). On the other hand, it is undeniable that there is a general trend among industrialized countries towards a reduction of capital income taxes.

A consumption tax system, in contrast, would be much less vulnerable to tax competition. In practice, labor taxes may take the form of a) a labor income tax, b) a payroll tax or c) a value added tax. The labor income tax is only affected by international openness if workers move abroad. As labor is much less mobile internationally, it cannot escape the tax burden as easily as capital (however, instead of moving across borders, labor may be relocated to the black economy). The payroll tax will basically have the same effect as the income tax (abstracting from its redistributive potential) but plays only a minor role in most European countries.

The most important alternative to the labor income tax is the value added tax. For the incidence of the value-added tax, it is plausible to assume that it is shifted forward, which means that it raises consumer prices. It is therefore equivalent to a tax on consumption out of labor income, transfers, accumulated wealth and economic rents (or pure profits). It thus differs from the labor income tax by having a broader tax base. The broader base may explain why the importance of the value added tax has increased in many countries during the past twenty years. The implications of international openness for value added tax have been the subject of a long debate in the context of EU tax harmonization and the tax treatment of trade among member states. For the purposes of the present paper, it is sufficient to state that, abstracting from cross-border-shopping, the value added tax can only be avoided by consuming abroad, which is, again, more costly than moving capital.

The pressure of international tax competition thus constitutes another, in the debate on practical tax policy possibly the most convincing, argument in favor of reforming the existing tax systems into the direction of consumption taxation.

5   EQUITY ASPECTS

While there is a tendency in modern economics, especially in the theory of optimal taxation, to concentrate on the efficiency properties of tax systems, the public debate on tax policy attributes much importance to the issue of equity and to the so-called 'social' consequences of tax policies, the latter meaning roughly the impact of the tax system on the wellbeing of the poorest percentiles of the population. There are, of course many different ways of deriving criteria for equity or justice in taxation and Irving Fisher was well aware of the fact that 'justice is a difficult concept' (Fisher and Fisher, 1942, p. 92), but he did present a number of arguments to make a case for his proposal on equity grounds.

First, as a fundamental and rather general point, Fisher argues that the taxation of income from all kinds of savings is a form of double taxation: 'It follows, as the night of the day, that, if a tax on the savings is added to the tax on the fruit of the savings, essentially the same thing is taxed twice' (Fisher and Fisher, 1942, p. 57).

Of course, the question of whether or not taxing income from savings has to be considered as a form of double taxation is a matter of interpretation or definition. Supporters of the traditional income tax would probably argue that there is an undeniable difference between the income saved and income generated by the accumulated savings. Hence, taxing both would not imply double taxation.

The second and perhaps more convincing point Fisher makes concerns the specific question of taxing corporate income. As many modern supporters of a consumption tax system, he argues that the notion of tax burden makes sense only if interpreted as a sacrifice in terms of consumption. In this sense, it is obvious that any debate on the issue of equitable taxation should concentrate on natural persons; corporations, in contrast, are only legal entities and cannot suffer from consumption foregone. Hence, he argued that there was little reason to have corporate income taxes at all (Fisher and Fisher, 1942, chapter 4). Moreover, as dividends were also subject to personal income tax in Fisher's days and remain so in the U.S. until the present day, without deductions granted for corporate income taxes paid, corporate income was taxed twice even in the logic of the income tax system.

The third point raised by Fisher is the fact that his concept '... not only takes off taxes on savings but puts taxes on dissavings' (Fisher and Fisher, 1942, p. 73). This captures a point often neglected in the debate on consumption taxes. In a pure income tax system, people who live off accumulated wealth are not taxed (the source of what has been accumulated should of course be income which has been subject to tax) while they are taxed in a consumption tax system. Clearly, this point has a certain appeal to all those who feel that accumulating wealth is morally superior to spending out of wealth accumulated in the past and possibly by someone else.[7]

Not surprisingly, until today, the equity implications of consumption and income tax systems are subject to an ongoing debate. One fundamental objection against the taxation of capital has been raised by Judd (1987), who shows that the introduction of capital taxes may under certain circumstances lead to a reduction of the capital stock such that the after-tax return on savings remains unaffected. In this case, the tax is borne entirely by other factors, in particular labor. If this is correct, it is hard to defend the capital tax, even if equity reasons would in principle call for a redistribution from 'capital owners' to 'workers'.

Even if one rejects the hypothesis that capital taxes may end up being borne by labor, it is by no means obvious that an equitable tax system should tax capital. One approach which has been quite popular in the theory of public finance is based on the ability-to-pay-principle and distinguishes between a) horizontal equity and b) vertical equity. Horizontal equity states that people of the same capacity, however that capacity is measured, should be treated equally; vertical equity states that people of higher capacity should bear a higher burden than people of lower capacity.

The comprehensive income tax is often defended as being more equitable than other tax systems, in particular the consumption tax system. This, however, is by no means obvious, even if one accepts the basic rationale of the ability-to-pay-principle. In order to apply this principle to real-world tax policy, an indicator for ability to pay or capacity has to be agreed upon. Here, the income tax relates the contribution of an individual to overall production, on a yearly basis. It is now a simple matter to show that the existing income tax systems violate the principle of horizontal equity. Consider two persons of the same 'capacity' who differ only by the fact that one of them has a higher rate of time preference. Although both persons have the same lifetime income, the income tax favors the person who prefers to consume early in his life, while the other person, who saves more of his income, is discriminated against. Choosing lifetime income, in contrast, would make it difficult to explain why the tax system should reward those who consume early in life. If anything, the opposite is likely to be what would conform with general moral standards.

Of course, the above arguments are far from covering the whole extent of the subject, and discussing all objections on equity grounds that have been raised against consumption taxation would be beyond the scope of this paper. It should be clear, however, that a reform towards consumption taxation would by no means imply that equity issues are disregarded.

6 HOW SHOULD 'CONSTRUCTIVE INCOME TAXATION' BE IMPLEMENTED?

The argument of the preceding paragraphs has concentrated on rather abstract issues concerning the fundamental choice between an income tax and a consumption tax system. It has turned out that there are strong arguments in favor of reforming the existing tax systems towards consumption taxation and intertemporal neutrality. This leaves us with the question of how such a consumption tax system should be implemented. While Fisher had in mind some type of personal expenditure tax, the modern debate on capital tax reform has shown that far fewer radical changes are required to achieve the goal of intertemporal neutrality.

As has already been mentioned above, a consumption tax is equivalent to a tax on labor income plus rents. It is now straightforward to show that such a tax system may take the form of a tax on labor income and an appropriately designed capital income tax. The fact that there is a capital income tax at all reflects the fact that the return on real investment projects has to be divided into, on the one hand, intramarginal rents and, on the other, the return covering the opportunity cost of capital. While the former should be taxed in a consumption tax system, the latter should not, because a tax on the return on marginal investment would reduce the capital stock and thus violate intertemporal neutrality.

In order to show how an intertemporally neutral tax on capital or real investment can be designed, it is convenient and, thanks to the separation theorem (which we also owe to Irving Fisher) also theoretically sound to use the well-known concept of capital value in order to check the effect of the tax system on investment. According to this concept, an investment project will be carried out if the present value of the expected 'net earnings' is positive. An intertemporally neutral tax system can be implemented simply by allowing firms an instantaneous depreciation of their investments and taxing future net earnings at the same rate as labor income. The financial structure of the firm, i.e. the share of debt and equity, plays no role for the tax base. Such a tax system, which is known as the 'cash flow tax' boils down to simply raising a uniform tax on the capital value:

$$V_0 = \sum_{t=0}^{T}(1+r)^{-t} R_t (1-\theta), \tag{6.15}$$

where θ is the tax rate which also applies to labor income and R_t is net earnings or the cash flow from the project.[8] Clearly, such a tax would raise no revenue from marginal investment and would therefore be intertemporally neutral, but it would tax intramarginal projects. There are several objections to this type of tax system. First, one can argue that, if the excess burden of the tax system is to be minimized, it is inefficient to tax rents and labor income at the same rate. While the labor income tax distorts the labor-leisure choice, a tax on rents or pure profits is equivalent to a lump sum tax. This is why Sinn (1985) has proposed to introduce a modified cash flow tax system which raises an additional tax on distributed earnings. The revenue may be used to reduce the labor income tax and thus lower the overall excess burden of the tax system.

One objection to this solution is that, especially in small enterprises, a differential taxation of profits and labor income creates incentives for firm owners to declare profits as labor income, if the latter is taxed at a lower rate. A number of Nordic countries have in fact done the opposite and introduced 'dual income tax systems', where labor is taxed at higher rates than profits (see Sorenson, 1994).

On the other hand, taxing labor and profit income at different rates again raises the problem of time inconsistency. In practice, problems of tax evasion and corporate control would imply that the optimal tax on rents would be less than 100%. The government would have incentives, however, to raise the level of this tax once an investment project has been realized. Roughly speaking, the taxation of rents at the level which is optimal under the criterion of minimizing the excess burden of the overall tax system may easily amount to a confiscatory taxation on investors. Again, it would be beneficial, for instance, to have a constitutional rule stating that rents should be taxed at the same rate as labor income.

Another problem of the cash flow tax is that the introduction of instantaneous depreciation would cause considerable short-run revenue losses following the reform. One may of course argue that these revenue losses are largely transitional and that the government may rely on public debt. On the other hand, capital market imperfections and institutional constraints (as, for instance, the Treaty of Maastricht) may impose limits on the financing of government expenditure via public debt. One way to solve this problem would be to replace the cash flow tax with its immediate write-off by a modified version of the existing profit income tax, which has been suggested by Boadway and Bruce (1984).[9] This 'neutral business tax' combines elements of the current corporate (or business) tax system with the neutrality properties of the cash-flow tax.

The crucial modification relative to the cash-flow tax concerns the determination of the profit tax base. Instead of granting an immediate write-off, the neutral business tax is consistent with any type of depreciation rule. The basic idea of this approach is that, whatever the depreciation rule, the present value of the investment project should be the same as in the case of instantaneous depreciation. This obviously requires that (see equation 6.15)

$$V_0 = \sum_{t=0}^{T}(1+r)^{-t} R_t(1-\theta) = \sum_{t=0}^{T}(1+r)^{-t}(R_t - \theta P_t), \qquad (6.16)$$

where P_t is the profit tax base. The concept of the neutral business tax makes sure that (6.16) holds good by granting an interest deduction for the book value of all assets. The profit tax base then becomes

$$P_t = R_t - D_t - rB_t, \qquad (6.17)$$

where D_t is the depreciation in period t and B_t is the book value of the firm's assets at the beginning of period t. This last form of implementing an intertemporally neutral tax system has the practical advantage that it could be implemented by introducing only minor modifications to the existing tax system.

7   CONCLUSIONS

This paper has shown that Irving Fisher's idea of introducing a consumption tax system has survived until today. It has turned out that, using both efficiency and equity arguments, a case can be made for replacing income by consumption taxation. Modern supporters of consumption taxation have modified Fisher's approach mainly as far as the practical implementation is concerned, especially in the field of taxing investment. The basic principles guiding Fisher's concept of 'constructive income taxation', however, have been preserved.

NOTES

*   The author would like to thank Bernd Huber, Hans G. Monissen and Christian Scheer for very helpful comments and suggestions. The usual disclaimer applies.

1   Interestingly, the U.S. Federal Income Tax was only introduced in 1913. The first attempts to introduce such a tax, however, had already been made in the 1890s but were rejected by the Supreme Court. This may explain why Fisher started to think about these issues before the income tax was in fact introduced.

2   'Equality of imposition, consisteth rather in the equality of that which is consumed, than of the riches of the person who consumes the same. For what reason is there, that he which laboureth much, and sparing the fruits of his labour, consumeth little should be more charged, than he that living idle, getteth little and spendeth all he gets; seeing the one has no more protection from the Common-wealth, than the other', Thomas Hobbes in Leviathan (1651), the quotation is taken from Musgrave (1985).

3   See Reichsabschied zu Nürnberg 1466 (1747/1967) and Janssen (1872). I owe this point to Christian Scheer.

4 It would also be possible simply to assume that labor is the only factor of production and that the production technology is linear, such that the wage rate is given.
5 The separability assumptions for the utility function imply that the intertemporal allocation of labor supply is not distorted.
6 This is a direct implication of the production efficiency theorem of Diamond and Mirrlees (1971).
7 As will be explained in the following section, the consequences of consumption taxation for those who live off accumulated wealth are especially relevant when it comes to assessing the effects of a reform towards consumption taxation.
8 The first to propose this type of tax system was Brown (1948).
9 This proposal has been developed independently by Wenger (1983).

REFERENCES

Atkinson, A.B. and Stiglitz, J.E. (1980*), Lectures on Public Economics*, London, McGraw-Hill.

Boadway, R. and Bruce, N. (1984), 'A general proposition on the design of a neutral business tax', *Journal of Public Economics*, **24**, 231-239.

Brown, E.C. (1948), 'Business income taxation and investment incentives', in L.A. Metzler *et al.* (eds), *Income, Employment, and Public Policy. Essays in Honor of A.H. Hansen*, New York, W.W. Norton.

Chamley, C. (1981), 'The welfare cost of capital income taxation in a growing economy', *Journal of Political Economy*, **89**, 468-496.

Corlett , W.J. and Hague, D.C. (1953-1954), 'Complementarity and the excess burden of taxation', *Review of Economic Studies*, **21**, 21-30.

Diamond, P. A. and Mirrlees, J.A. (1971), 'Optimal taxation and public production I: production efficiency', *American Economic Review*, **61**, 8-27.

Fisher, I. (1906), *The Nature of Capital and Income*, New York, Macmillan.

Fisher, I. (1937), 'Income in theory and income taxation in practice', *Econometrica*, **5**, 1-55.

Fisher, I. and Fisher H.W. (1942*), Constructive Income Taxation: A Proposal for Reform*, New York and London, Harper and Brothers.

Gordon, R. and MacKie-Masson, J.K. (1994), 'Tax distortions to the choice of the organizational form', *Journal of Public Economics*, **55**.

Haig, R.M. (1921), *The Federal Income Tax*, New York, Columbia University Press.

Huber, B. (1992), 'Besteuerung, Intertemporale Neutralität und zeitliche Inkonsistenz', *Finanzarchiv*, N.F., **49**, 423-456.

Huber, B. (1996), *Optimale Finanzpolitik und zeitliche Inkonsistenz*, Heidelberg, Springer-Verlag.

Janssen, J. (1872), *Frankfurts Reichskorrespondenz nebst anderen verwandten Aktenstücken von 1376-1519*, Leipzig, Winter.

Judd, K.L. (1987), 'The welfare cost of factor taxation in a perfect foresight model', *Journal of Political Economy*, **95**, 675-709.

Musgrave, R.B. (1985), 'A brief history of fiscal doctrine', in A.J. Auerbach and M. Feldstein (eds), *Handbook of Public Economics*, North-Holland, **1**, 1-59.

Reichsabschied zu Nürnberg 1466 (1747/1967), in *Neue und vollständigere Sammlung der Reichsabschiede*, Osnabrück, Otto Zeller, 204-206.

Schanz, G. (1896), 'Der Einkommensbegriff und die Einkommensteuergesetze', *Finanzarchiv*, **13**, 1-87.

Simons, H. (1938), *Personal Income Taxation: The Definition of Income as a Problem of Fiscal Policy*, Chicago, University of Chicago Press.

Sinn, H.-W. (1985), *Kapitaleinkommensbesteuerung*, Tübingen, J.C.B. Mohr (Paul Siebeck).

Sorensen, P.B. (1994), 'From the Global Income Tax to the Dual Income Tax: Recent Tax Reforms in the Nordic Countries', *International Tax and Public Finance*, **1**, 57-79.

Wenger, E. (1983), 'Gleichmäßigkeit der Besteuerung von Arbeits- und Vermögenseinkünften', *Finanzarchiv*, N.F. **41**, 207-252.

Comment on Fuest
Constructive Income Taxation: A Modern Interpretation

Christian Scheer

My comments will be concerned with three of the five aspects which Clemens Fuest discusses in his stimulating modern interpretation of Irving Fisher's *Constructive Income Taxation*: (1) Fisher's place in the history of the idea of personal consumption taxation, (2) efficiency and (3) implementation.

1 FISHER'S PLACE IN THE HISTORY OF THE IDEA OF PERSONAL CONSUMPTION TAXATION

Though most of them considered the scheme to be 'theoretically sound ... [but] – practically impossible',[1] for more than a century a respectable number of well-known economists has praised the idea of personal taxation on the basis of the amount spent rather than on that of the amount received: John Stuart Mill, Marshall, Pigou, Keynes, Schumpeter, Einaudi *et al.* and Irving Fisher himself developed his concept of personal consumption taxation over a period of more than forty years. Thus it seems appropriate to start by asking three questions about the place of Fisher's *Constructive Income Taxation* in the history of tax theory and tax policy:[2]

(1) Was Fisher the first to claim that an expenditure tax is superior to an income tax? The answer certainly must be no: Proposals of taxation according to personal consumption (instead of taxation on the basis of income received)[3] have been made in many different forms prior to Fisher (and in many cases unknown to Fisher):

The earliest schemes of a personal consumption tax which I could trace were discussed long before Hobbes (1642/1651)[4] on the occasions of the Nürnberg Reichstag of 1466 and the Augsburg Reichstag of 1518, when the introduction of some kind of general taxation was considered to be necessary in order to finance a military campaign against the Turks:[5] According to these plans every

130

inhabitant of the Holy Roman Empire was expected to pay annually a sum corresponding to his personal one week's consumption expenditure for three years.[6] Later, during the nineteenth century, in England John Revans (1847) suggested a personal consumption tax as a single tax.[7] In Germany, inspired by John Stuart Mill's famous and much discussed critique of 'double taxation of savings', Eduard Pfeiffer, a wealthy rentier, protagonist of the idea of consumer cooperative societies and author of a two-volume treatise on 'Public Revenues' (1866), dedicated 26 pages of his book to the 'personal consumption tax',[8] a scheme which he called 'so simple, that it is truly astonishing that it has not been worked out before' (Pfeiffer, 1866, vol. 2, p. 538). After the turn of the century the idea came up again, and in Germany the first two decades of the twentieth century were almost heydays of expenditure tax schemes, with projects from Bendixen (1902) – (see Bräuer, 1928, p. 522), Elster (1913, 1916), Mombert (1916) and Zeiler (1918),[9] later to be followed by Schumpeter (1929, p. 381). For the USA Truxton Beale (1911) and Ogden Mills and his spending tax bill of 1921 (inspired by T.S. Adams and C.A. Jordan) must be mentioned.[10]

(2) Did Fisher bring forward new arguments in favor of a personal consumption tax? Again the answer must be negative. It is well known that already Hobbes (1642, 1651), for reasons of justice, supported taxation on the basis of consumption. Mill (1848)[11] and Pfeiffer (1866) introduced the criterion of equal treatment with respect to life income and consumption while criticizing the annual income tax for not differentiating between 'permanent' income and 'temporary' income which in part must be saved for the future. Mill (1848) also introduced the argument of intertemporal non-neutrality by blaming the income tax for disturbing the 'natural competition between the motives for saving and those for spending' (Mill, 1848, book v, chapt. ii , § 4, p. 814). And as for the expectation that a shift towards consumption taxation should stimulate saving and economic growth, this was a main point in Pfeiffer (1866), Beale (1911) and in particular in Elster (1913/1916) and Mombert (1916). Moreover, Pfeiffer (1866) also put forward simplicity of assessment and lower compliance costs, and almost all of these early authors emphasized that consumption is 'in its own nature more public than income' (Mill) and that a personal consumption tax offers fewer chances for domestic and international evasion.

(3) Was Fisher the first to invalidate the common argument that such a tax is impossible in practice owing to the difficulty of a direct assessment of personal expenditure? Modern authors (including Clemens Fuest; cf. Kaldor, 1955, p. 191; Head, 1979, p. 202; Musgrave, 1980, p. 35) have no doubts that it was Fisher who demonstrated first the 'indirect' calculation of the tax base 'by which a spendings tax may be made practicable without trusting to direct records of the spendings' (Fisher, 1942, p. 219). However, even in this respect Fisher was not the first: an indirect computation of personal consumption was proposed as

early as 1913 by Karl Elster, a German junior civil servant and later freelance writer on monetary matters, and (with reservations) by Paul Mombert (1916)[12].

To sum up this historical outline it can be said that Fisher's 'Constructive Income Taxation' cannot claim the credit for historical priority with respect to its concept, arguments or technical method. Nevertheless Fisher certainly was the first to devote a full book to the subject and his book is a landmark in the history of tax theory, being in its time the most emphatic plea for the case of the personal consumption tax and the profoundest demonstration of the theoretical implications of including saving in the concept of income for tax purposes. Of course, 'Constructive Income Taxation' was published in 1942, when the international flow of ideas was more or less interrupted by the war. More than twelve years later Kaldor (1955) acknowledged the influence of Fisher's ideas on his own 'expenditure tax' concept, but as for the influence of 'Constructive Income Taxation' in its own time Kaldor's diagnosis was: 'Fisher's work attracted no notice whatsoever, and ... as far as I know, his book has never been reviewed in any of the English periodicals' (Kaldor, 1955, p. 13).

2   EFFICIENCY

In its section three, Fuest's article deals with efficiency aspects of 'constructive income taxation'. The traditional argument used to support a personal consumption tax for efficiency reasons is the absence of distortions of intertemporal consumption choice. However, as both tax schemes, income taxation and personal consumption taxation, are not neutral with respect to the labor-leisure choice, intertemporal neutrality does not allow the conclusion that a personal consumption tax is superior. Simply counting the number of distortions is not a sufficient analysis. Critics of personal consumption taxation point out the fact that for a given tax yield wage income has to be taxed more heavily in a consumption tax scheme than in an income tax scheme which also taxes income from capital. Avoiding intertemporal distortions thus might mean introducing additional work-leisure distortions. This of course has been discussed extensively in the optimal taxation literature. Whether a consumption tax still can be considered to be superior depends on the relation between the pattern of consumption over time and the work-leisure decision, and that of course is a question of empirical evidence. As Fuest points out, supporters of personal consumption tax systems argue that future consumption is less complementary to present leisure than present consumption. But what is more important, Clemens Fuest also emphasizes that in an intertemporal framework the effect of capital taxation on capital formation and the problem of time inconsistency support the case for intertemporally neutral tax systems.

However, there might be another problem of non-neutrality which is not dealt with in Fuest's article: In the standard two-period model of consumption choice saving is considered as the accumulation of capital which permits the intertemporal allocation of consumption opportunities towards the second period, and all savings are for future consumption.[13] Within this 'saving-for-future-consumption' model under a specific set of conditions[14] a labor income tax and a consumption tax are equivalent and both are intertemporally neutral. Things are different if savings yield pure accumulation benefits in and of themselves and independent of the increase in future consumption possibilities (cf. Brennan and Nellor, 1982). Thus, by the act of saving the household 'purchases' simultaneously both a psychic return (security, independence, influence etc.) which he receives over the period in which he holds the asset and a future consumption benefit. In this case, as Brennan and Nellor (1982) have demonstrated for a two-period model, a consumption tax is not intertemporally neutral (it encourages saving) while a labor income tax is still neutral. As a consequence of this, the presence of psychic returns to saving a personal consumption tax in the tradition of Fisher *et al.* must be supplemented by an annual wealth tax in order to achieve a more neutral tax system. And indeed, a number of authors suggest combining a consumption tax and a wealth tax,[15] although some of these authors recommend this chiefly for redistributive reasons[16] and some of them for reasons of horizontal equity.[17]

Of course the major difficulty of such a specific supplemental wealth tax is that it requires the estimation of the psychic rate of return. And beside that, there is the problem of human capital which might generate psychic benefits, too. Accordingly, in a world with only two sorts of income (labor income and income from capital) the existence of psychic benefits of saving could be an additional argument in favor of a consumption tax system in the form of a labor income tax instead of the traditional concept of an expenditure tax on income minus saving.

In his modern interpretation of Fisher's *Constructive Income Taxation* Clemens Fuest discusses a taxation of wages and rents by means of a combination of a labor income tax and a cash flow tax at the business level. This leads me to the problem of complexity and to another category of costs of taxation apart from the welfare costs: administrative and compliance costs. That a system of personal consumption taxation is easier to administer and less costly than income taxation has already been claimed by Pfeiffer (1866), and Irving Fisher characterized his scheme as the 'simplest income tax proposal ever made'. But on second glance judging the alternative tax systems by their 'technical' problems is not at all easy.[18] On the occasion of the Heidelberg Congress on Taxing Consumption, Seidl (1980) has taken a very skeptical view of the administration problems of consumption taxation, and what is more, the system he is most critical of is the taxing-business-cash-flows-cum-wages method. Certainly, replacing the income tax (in its existing form or in the 'ideal' Schanz-Haig-Simon version) with a direct tax based on consumption will remove the troublesome problem of valuation and the necessity of complicated special rules with respect to capital gains. Nevertheless, quite a number of serious 'technical' problems will remain. To name just two of them: consumer durables or the problem of determining the boundary line between personal consumption and expenditure deductible as professional expenses.[19] Thus, even with a system of personal consumption taxation 'real' simplicity of taxation will be achieved only if (among other things) there is a departure from the traditional ideal of personal taxation according to 'individual circumstances' and a move towards a more objective definition of the tax base. Whether such a move would be 'easier' with a system of consumption taxation than with a system of income taxation – the answer to that is not easy.

3 IMPLEMENTATION

In 1979 Prest claimed the existence of 'a curious twenty-year periodicity' (Prest, 1979, p. 245) in the discussion of personal consumption taxation, with Irving Fisher in the 30s, Kaldor in the 50s and the Meade Committee (and, so it may be added, the Brookings conference (see Pechman, 1980) and the U.S. Department of the Treasury's 'Blueprints for Basic Tax Reform' (1977)) in the 70s. Today, nearly twenty years later, we truly can speak of a 'return of the cycle', pointing out to the activities of the KSN-group (Rose, Wagner, Wenger) in Germany (cf. Rose, 1990) and to recent discussions of new 'hybrid' consumption-based direct taxes in the U.S.A. (Nunn and Domenici, McLure and Zodrow)[20]. Nevertheless, with the exception of the well-known experiments with Kaldor's concept in India and Ceylon/Sri Lanka and with the exception of the KSN-inspired tax reform in the new-born state of Croatia, Vickrey's dictum of 1947 still holds today, after fifty years: 'The history of the spendings tax is one of discussion only' (Vickrey, 1947, p. 330).

What possible explanation can be found for this rather astonishing fact that such a long-lived idea has not initiated corresponding tax reforms until now? There might be (at least) three explanations:

(1) Policymakers and the public do not care for perfect neutrality and they do not care very much for efficiency of taxation. Politicians, the legal profession, fiscal courts and the voters in the first place think in terms of 'justice' and 'equity' of taxation, and more often than not the distributional effects of proposed tax reforms are measured not by some abstract concept of 'just distribution' but by simple comparison with the existing (supposed) distribution of tax burden.

(2) Economists can explain why a system of personal consumption taxation may not only be efficient, but also fair in terms of the popular 'principle of horizontal equity'. They can do this by assessing the horizontal equity by reference to the opportunities available. Thus, equal treatment of equal opportunities calls for equal reductions in the discounted value of lifetime consumption by people for whom this would be equal in the absence of taxation. However, appreciation of this type of argument requires seeing 'equal circumstances' in a lifetime perspective and comparing individuals 'ex ante', and this requires thinking in terms of present values. There are good reasons for questioning the assumption that politicians and voters look upon tax proposals in this way.[21] Thus, it seems to be rather difficult to communicate the philosophy of personal taxation according to consumption to voters and policymakers. And it may be even more difficult in the case of more sophisticated modern systems of direct consumption taxation, like the labor income tax[22] which Clemens Fuest discusses in his modern interpretation of Fishers 'Constructive Income Taxation'.

(3) In political discussions of tax schemes there seems to be a tendency to compare personal consumption tax systems, not with the imperfect present tax structure, but rather with some idealized income tax system, and to forget how complicated, unfair and unsatisfactory the tax system is at the moment.[23]

All things considered, rather than a replacement of the current income tax by a direct tax based on consumption we shall see more of Prest's 'curious periodicity' in tax discussions at the academic level. In any case, to convince the public of the superiority of consumption tax systems is certainly no easy task for economists. Perhaps success depends on laying more emphasis on explaining the equity aspects than in stressing efficiency ones. Fisher's book could be taken as an example of excellent 'tax promotion', but even Fisher has not been successful – so far.

NOTES

1   J.M. Keynes in his evidence before the Colwyn Committee on National Debt and Taxation; cf. Kaldor, 1955, p. 12.
2   Fisher did not take very much notice of the historical roots of the idea of personal consumption taxation; in fact, even John Stuart Mill's famous arguments were not known to him until 1938; Fisher, 1942, p. 218.
3   Not to mention the various proposals for a personal taxation of 'excess consumption' or 'excess spending' *beside* the existing personal income tax, proposals which in most cases basically meant a more progressive income taxation. (The matter is different with Andrews' scheme (Andrews, 1980) of a 'supplemental expenditure tax' which was suggested as a substitute for the highest rates of tax under the existing individual income tax and which might be considered as an incremental device for ultimately achieving a full scale expenditure tax.)

4   Since Kaldor (1955) it has become the practice to quote Hobbes' 'Leviathan' (1651), chapter 30. In fact Hobbes has already demonstrated his arguments in favor of taxing consumption in his 'Philosophical Rudiments Concerning Government and Society' (1642, chapter XIII, 11, p. 174).

5   Of course the intellectual fathers of these tax plans were not guided by efficiency considerations. Presumably the decisive factor has been the difficulty of defining a workable general tax base even in the case of the rural population. In the end, it was decided to levy a lump-sum tax (1518).

6   Cf. Neue und vollständigere Sammlung der Reichs-Abschiede etc. (1747), vol. 1, p. 206; Janssen (1872, vol. 2, p. 985, 987). Instead of the Middle High German text, which even for German readers of today is quite difficult to understand, the Latin description of the 1518 tax plan may be quoted from the report of the Polish delegation to King Sigismund I. of Poland: '.... ut ... omnes ... solverent quotannis pro expeditione ipsa tantum quantum unius septimanae expensa pro sua quisque et familiae suae provisione valere possit ...'; Liske (1878, p. 643).

7   Cf. Mill (1848, p. 831), Rau (1865, vol. 2, p. 209), and Gothein (1916, p. 249), mention similar tax plans of an anonymous German pamphleteer in 1850 and of a patrician merchant in Cologne 1847.

8   Pfeiffer (1866, vol. 2, pp. 18-26 and 538-554). Pfeiffer's book was called to Fisher's attention only after most of Fisher's book had been written and Fisher, erroneously thinking that the whole of Pfeiffer's treatise was dealing with consumption taxation, called it 'the largest treatise on the subject, in two volumes' (Fisher, 1942, p. 218).

9   While Bendixen's tax should replace a surcharge to the (Prussian) income tax, Elster's and Mombert's 'Consumption Income Tax' was thought to be levied by the Reich in addition to the existing taxes (at that time only the German states levied income taxes). In Zeiler's plan the consumption tax was to be a single tax, substituting all existing taxes.

10 While not mentioning Beale (1911), Fisher explicitly dedicates his 'Constructive Income Taxation' to the memory of the late Ogden Mills – for schemes of a personal spendings tax for Japan in that period (Masao Kambe, [1916] 1926) cf. Bräuer (1928, pp. 524-525).

11 Believing that in practice it would not be possible to assess people on the basis of their expenditure, as a practical compromise John Stuart Mill recommended differentiation of the income tax according to the source of income.

12 In Elster's tax plan the tax base is computed by deducting savings from income; cf. Elster, 1913, p. 791. Mombert, 1916, p. 19, in the first place suggests subtracting net wealth accrual from income, but later on he modifies this by declaring that a direct computation of personal consumption 'might be more appropriate'.

13 Which could be understood to include bequests. For simplicity I assume that there are no gifts and no bequests.

14 Constant tax rates, perfect capital market, only two types of income (labor income and income from capital accumulated).

15 Cf. Shoup, 1969, p. 352; Meade Committee, 1978, p. 351; Head, 1979, p. 217; Musgrave, 1990, p. 36.

16 Meade Committee, 1978, p. 351.

17 Cf. Head, 1979, p. 217. In my opinion, even in the presence of non-pecuniary benefits from accumulation this argument cannot justify a supplemental wealth tax if horizontal equity is interpreted as equal treatment of equal opportunities (*ex ante*); cf. Schneider, 1979, p. 39.

18 Kaldor for instance rather drastically changed his mind on this point in later years; cf. Seidl, 1980, p. 411.

19 Consider e.g. the different treatment of the expense incurred commuting from home to business under German income tax law (deductible) and U.S. tax law (deduction not permitted).

20 Cf. McLure and Zodrow, 1996.

21 Cf. Minarik's description of the failure of the expenditure tax concept in the USA during the 80s: 'A former superior of mine, a lawyer who worked for a number of years on congressional staffs, used to say that his first rule in dealing with members of congress was not to bring up present values' (Minarik, 1989, p. 147).

22 Cf. Musgrave, 1980, p. 36: 'Can it be that the case for taxing consumption ... sounds a lot more appealing than would that for singling out wages as the prime base for income taxation?'

23 Kay and King, 1990, p. 119. It should be noted that some critics of the personal consumption
    tax maintain the opposite with respect to academic discussions and hold that there is a
    'tendency to compare the imperfect present with the perfect future'; Prest, 1979, p. 257.

REFERENCES

Andrews, W.D. (1980), 'A supplemental personal expenditure tax', in J.A. Pechman
    (ed.), 127-151.
Beale, T. (1911), 'The Measurement of Income for Taxation', *Journal of Political
    Economy*, **19**, 655-675.
Bräuer, K. (1928), 'Verbrauchseinkommensteuer und Verbrauchsbelastung im Rahmen
    der Einkommensteuer', in *Handwörterbuch der Staatswissenschaften*, 4th ed., vol. **8**,
    Jena, Gustav Fischer, 521-529.
Brennan, G. and Nellor, D. (1982), 'Wealth, Consumption and Tax Neutrality', *National
    Tax Journal*, **35**, 427-436.
Elster, K. (1913), 'Eine Reichsaufwandsteuer?', *Jahrbücher für Nationalökonomie und
    Statistik* **101**, 785-796.
Elster, K. (1916), 'Nochmals: Eine Reichsaufwandsteuer', *Jahrbücher für National-
    ökonomie und Statistik*, **107**, 800-818.
Fisher, I. and Fisher, H.W. (1942), *Constructive Income Taxation: A Proposal for
    Reform*, New York and London, Harper and Brothers.
Gothein, E. (1916), *Verfassungs- und Wirtschaftsgeschichte der Stadt Cöln vom
    Untergang der Reichsfreiheit bis zur Errichtung des Deutschen Reichs* (Die Stadt
    Cöln im ersten Jahrhundert unter Preußischer Herrschaft 1815 bis 1915, vol. I/1).
    Köln, Paul Neubner.
Head, J.G. (1979), 'Fisher-Kaldor Regained', Report of the Meade Committee in the
    UK, *Finanzarchiv, Neue Folge*, **37**, 193-222.
Hobbes, T. (1642), 'Philosophical Rudiments Concerning Government and Society. The
    English Works of Thomas Hobbes of Malmesbury', ed. by Sir W. Molesworth, vol. 3,
    London 1839. Reprinted Aalen 1966, Scientia.
Janssen, J. (ed.) (1872), *Frankfurts Reichscorrespondenz, nebst anderen verwandten
    Aktenstücken von 1376-1519*, 2 vols., Freiburg i.Br., Herder.
Kaldor, N. (1955), *An Expenditure Tax*, London, Allen and Unwin.
Kay, J.A. and King, M.A. (1990), *The British Tax System*, 5th ed. Oxford, Oxford
    University Press.
Liske, X. (1878), 'Zur Geschichte des Augsburger Reichstages 1518', *Forschungen zur
    Deutschen Geschichte*, **18**, 638-646.
McLure, C.E. and Zodrow, G.R. (1996), 'Advantages of a Hybrid Direct Tax on
    Consumption, in National Tax Association', *Proceedings of the 88th Annual Confe-
    rence on Taxation*, Columbus, Ohio, National Tax Association – Tax Institute of
    America, 47-52.
Meade Committee (1978), *The Structure and Reform of Direct Taxation*, Report of a
    Committee chaired by Professor J.E. Meade (The Institute for Fiscal Studies), London,
    Allen and Unwin.
Mill, J.S. (1848), *Principles of Political Economy with Some of Their Applications to
    Social Philosophy*, ed. Sir William Ashley, London and New York 1909, Longman,
    Green and Company. Reprinted Fairfield, NJ 1987, A.M. Kelley.

Minarik, J.J. (1989), 'How Tax Reform Came about', in D.C. Colander and A.W. Coats (eds), *The Spread of Economic Ideas*. Cambridge, UK, Cambridge University Press, 141-154.

Mombert, P. (1916), *Eine Verbrauchseinkommensteuer für das Reich als Ergänzung zur Vermögenszuwachssteuer*, Tübingen, J.C.B. Mohr (Paul Siebeck).

Musgrave, R.A. (1990), 'On Choosing the 'Correct' Tax Base – A Historical Perspective', in M. Rose (1990), 29-42.

Neue und vollständigere Sammlung der Reichs-Abschiede etc. (1747). 4 vols. Franckfurt am Mayn, Ernst August Koch. Reprinted Osnabrück 1967, Zeller.

Pechman, J.A. (ed.) (1980), *What Should be Taxed: Income or Expenditure?*, Washington, D.C., The Brookings Institution.

Pfeiffer, E. (1866), *Die Staatseinnahmen. Geschichte, Kritik und Statistik derselben*, 2 vols., Stuttgart and Leipzig, A. Kröner.

Prest, A.R. (1979), 'The Structure and Reform of Direct Taxation', *Economic Journal*, **89**, 243-260.

Rau, K.H. (1865), *Grundsätze der Finanzwissenschaft*, 2. Abtheilung, 5th ed. Leipzig and Heidelberg, C.F. Winter'sche Verlagsbuchhandlung.

Revans, K. (1847), *A Per-Centage Tax on Domestic Expenditure to Supply the Whole of the Public Revenue etc.*, London, J. Hatchard and Son.

Rose, M. (1990), *Heidelberg Congress on Taxing Consumption*, Berlin et al., Springer.

Schneider, D. (1979), 'Bezugsgrößen steuerlicher Leistungsfähigkeit und Vermögensbesteuerung', *Finanzarchiv, Neue Folge*, **37**, 26-49.

Schumpeter, J.A. (1929), 'Ökonomie und Soziologie der Einkommensteuer', *Der deutsche Volkswirt*, **4**, 380-385.

Seidl, C. (1980), 'Administration Problems of an Expenditure Tax', in M. Rose (1980), 407-449.

Shoup, C.S. (1969), *Public Finance*, Chicago, Aldine.

U.S. Department of the Treasury (1977), *Blueprints for Basic Tax Reform*, Washington, D.C., 2nd ed. Arlington, Virginia 1984, Tax Analyst.

Vickrey, William (1947), *Agenda for Progressive Taxation*, New York, The Ronald Press Company. Reprinted Clifton 1972, A.M. Kelley.

Zeiler, A. (1918), Einkommensabgaben, gesellschaftlicher Ausgleich und Gesamtverbrauchssteuer, Zweibrücken, F. Lehmann.

PART FOUR:
DEBT-DEFLATION AND
THE GREAT DEPRESSION

7. Irving Fisher's Debt-Deflation Theory of Great Depressions

Robert W. Dimand*

The eminent Yale monetary and capital theorist Irving Fisher is best known in the economics profession for the equation of exchange, the distinction between real and nominal interest rates, and an early analysis of intertemporal allocation. In fact, his contributions as an early macroeconomist were extensive, and his debt-deflation theory of depression both deserves and implicitly gets consideration currently. It is Fisher's misfortune, as well as that of the profession, that his analysis of the debt-deflation process, one of his most insightful contributions to macroeconomics, received little notice from his contemporaries.

Fisher has acquired lasting and unenviable fame for his predictions in September 1929 that 'stock prices have reached what looks like a permanently high plateau' (Barber, 1985, p. 77) and for the consequences to Fisher of his predictive error. As John Kenneth Galbraith (1977, p. 192) remarked, 'In the late nineteen-twenties Fisher went heavily into the stock market and in the Crash lost between eight and ten million dollars. This was a sizable sum, even for an economics professor.' Fisher was known for this even to those, such as Robert Sobel (1968, pp. 97, 132), whose direct knowledge of Fisher and his work was vague enough to identify him as 'Irving Fisher of Harvard'. Kathryn Dominguez, Ray Fair, and Matthew Shapiro (1988) have now shown that even using modern statistical techniques, and adding some retrospectively compiled time series to those available to Fisher and to the Harvard Economic Society, it would not have been possible to predict the onset, length or depth of the Great Depression by time-series analysis.

Dominguez, Fair, and Shapiro have done much to redeem Fisher's reputation as a forecaster relative to that of, for example, Roger Babson, whose successful prediction of a break in stock prices in the fall of 1929 must be balanced against his prediction of a stock price boom in 1930. If one views the bull market of the 1920s as a speculative bubble, all that could be predicted is that the bubble would eventually burst, not when.

Indeed, Fisher's formal statistical forecasting method, as distinct from his more subjective statements about future stock prices, held up quite well. In a series of journal articles, Fisher (1923, 1925, 1926) sought empirical verification of his monetary theory of economic fluctuations by correlating output and unemployment with a distributed lag of past changes in the price level (see Dimand, 1993). He was an innovator in the use of correlation analysis and distributed lags, and constructed his own price indices. His 1926 article was republished in 1973 as 'I Discovered the Phillips Curve'. Fisher (1925) found a correlation of .941 between a trend-adjusted measure of the volume of trade and a distributed lag of monthly inflation rates for the 114 months ending January 1923. Scott Sumner (1990) has found that, using the lag weights from Fisher's 1925 paper, Fisher's equation yielded a correlation of .851 for the period from January 1923 to July 1933, a close out-of-sample fit. The stable relationship between output and inflation collapsed only with the economic policy regime change after Franklin Roosevelt's inauguration, when the United States left the fixed gold value of the dollar for what Maynard Keynes termed 'a gold standard on the booze' and U.S. output recovered sharply. Thus 'updating Fisher's model to the 1923-1935 period', Sumner (1990, p. 721) found that 'The correlation between the predicted and the actual output series was only .256' because of the structural change in 1933.

1   FISHER'S AUDIENCE

Apart from the regrettable impact on his personal finances, the stock market crash and subsequent depression had two important consequences for Fisher as a theorist of economic fluctuations. Fisher's attention was focused on a gap in his analysis in the 1920s of the business cycle as 'a dance of the dollar': the need to explain why sometimes a deep and lasting depression occurred. He offered a brilliant solution of this puzzle in *Booms and Depressions* (1932) and 'The Debt-Deflation Theory of Great Depressions' (1933). Secondly, his mistaken stock market predictions and the attention attracted by books by Keynes and Friedrich Hayek combined to take away Fisher's audience just when he had something important to tell it.

Patrick Deutscher (1990, pp. 188-194) analyzed citations in articles listed under 'Aggregative and Monetary Theory and Cycles' and the non-historical categories of 'Money, Credit and Banking' in the American Economic Association *Index of Economic Journals*. Fisher was the most cited macroeconomist in 1920-1930, cited in 30 articles, compared to 24 citations for second-ranked Wesley Clair Mitchell and 9 for tenth-ranked John Maynard Keynes (mostly references to *A Tract on Monetary Reform*, 1923). In 1931-1935, after the publication of *A Treatise on Money* by Keynes (1930) and *Prices and Production* (1931) by Hayek, Fisher was tied with Ralph Hawtrey for fourth most cited macroeconomist with 30 citations, behind Keynes (66), Dennis Robertson (44), and Hayek (33). The temporary seizure of the profession's attention by Keynes's *Treatise* has been discussed by Dimand (1989). For 1936-1939, after Keynes's *General Theory* (1936), Fisher was tied with Ragnar Frisch, Simon Kuznets, and Gunnar Myrdal for sixteenth most cited macroeconomist with 13 mentions, compared to 125 articles citing Keynes. Fisher did not make Deutscher's list of the ten most frequently cited macroeconomists of 1940-1944 (actually eleven, because of tie for tenth place between Kuznets and Abba Lerner). The effect of Keynes's books in diverting attention from Fisher is ironic, in view of the ten references to Fisher in the index of the *Treatise* (two to passages of six or seven pages) and three in that of the *General Theory*. Keynes, writing from Bretton Woods in July 1944 in reply to Fisher's praise of his world bank proposal, told Fisher that 'You were one of my earliest teachers on these matters and nothing is more satisfactory to any of us than to satisfy one of those from whom we have learned' (I. N. Fisher, 1956, p. 326).

Fisher's decline from first place to disappearance from the list is even more striking when it is noted that Deutscher's tabulation excludes the *IEJ* categories of index numbers and interest. In Deutscher's first period, in which Fisher published *The Making of Index Numbers* (1922a), the *Index of Economic Journals* records an article by Warren Persons on 'Fisher's Formula for Index Numbers' in the *Review of Economic Statistics* (1921), a 23-page review article of Fisher (1922a) by Allyn A. Young in the *Quarterly Journal of Economics*, a review article by Carl Snyder in the *American Economic Review*, and replies by Fisher to Young (in 14 pages), to Snyder, and to reviews by A. L. Bowley in the *Economic Journal* (with a reply by Bowley) and by G. Udney Yule in the *Journal of the Royal Statistical Society*. Fisher's *The Theory of Interest* (1930), a revision of his *The Rate of Interest* (1907), received an 18-page review essay by Gottfried Haberler in the *Quarterly Journal of Economics*, one of 37 pages by Frank Knight in the *Journal of Political Economy*, and one of 14 pages by Arthur W. Marget in German in the *Zeitschrift für Nationalökonomie*, all in 1931. After 1931, there were no more review articles on Fisher, apart from six pages by B.P. Adarkar on 'Fisher's Real Rate Doctrine' (concerning Fisher, 1930) in the *Economic Journal* in 1934.

This extensive attention to slightly earlier writings of Fisher contrasts sharply with the reception of his *Booms and Depressions*. Harold Barger, of University College, London, reviewed it jointly with another book in the *Economic Journal* (1933, p. 681), allotting one paragraph to each. Barger rejected Fisher's debt-deflation theory in a single sentence as being at once nothing new and a deplorable innovation: 'What little theory it contains is in no way novel, while Professor Fisher's contentment with price stability as a policy, and emphasis on over-indebtedness rather than over-investment as the root of all evil, are not encouraging.' In place of Fisher's concern with debt, Barger took it to be obvious that analysis should focus on over-investment, the neo-Austrian/London School of Economics concept of the lengthening of the average period of production during a boom. Since Fisher (1907) had already shown that there may be multiple solutions for the average period of production and given a numerical example of reswitching of techniques (see K. Velupillai, 1975), this alternative would have had little appeal for him.

The Lessons of Monetary Experience, a volume of essays presented to Fisher on his seventieth birthday in 1937, offered an opportunity to offset the lack of attention given Fisher's post-1930 work, but the letter of invitation to contributors specified, presumably in accordance with the wishes of Fisher:

> All contributors are asked merely to present scientific opinions on the lessons of recent monetary policies. Under no circumstances is it contemplated to include any eulogies of Professor Fisher's work. The only reference to him will be in the dedication of this book (Gayer, 1937, p. vi).

Fisher was not mentioned in A.L. Macfie's *Theories of the Trade Cycle* (1934). Fisher's writings, including those on the debt-deflation theory of depressions, were listed in the select bibliography of Raymond Saulnier's *Contemporary Monetary Theory* (1938), but his name did not appear in the index to the book, and appeared in the text only in a footnote appended to the discussion of Hawtrey (Saulnier, 1938, pp. 77-78n.).

2   DIAGNOSIS OF THE DEPRESSION

Fisher addressed the American Association for the Advancement of Science in New Orleans on the first day of 1932 on the subject of 'The Debt-Deflation Theory of Depressions', on which he had lectured at Yale in 1931. With the word 'Great' inserted before 'Depressions' in the title, a revised version of this paper appeared in the first volume of *Econometrica* in October 1933 and in the *Review of the International Statistical Institute* the following January. As Fisher was the founding president of the Econometrics Society, this paper took the place of a presidential address. In these journals the theory would be offered for the consideration of the most technically sophisticated segment of the economics profession. Extended into a book with historical material, a literature survey, and appendixes, Fisher's theory was presented to the general public as *Booms and Depressions* in the fall of 1932.

Even before publishing his theory, Fisher expounded 'the debt disease' to the House Ways and Means Committee at the end of April 1932. As an exposition to an official body of a new theory aimed at understanding and curing current economic problems, Fisher's presentation can be compared only to Keynes's private evidence on his forthcoming *Treatise on Money* to the Macmillan Committee in 1930. Fisher explained to the Congressmen that 'When you have this overindebtedness, and people try to get out of debt by liquidating, ... it causes distressed selling and the contraction of the currency, and therefore a fall in prices', increasing the real burden of debts. In the absence of a policy of reflation through monetary expansion, the economy lacked any automatic mechanism to stop the debt-deflation (Barber, 1985, pp. 160-161).

Fisher (1933, pp. 338-341) rejected 'The old and apparently still persistent notion of "the" business cycle, as a single, simple, self-generating cycle (analogous to that of a pendulum swinging under influence of the single force of gravity)' as 'a myth'. He found some grain of truth in most of the cycle theories (which he had reviewed in Fisher 1932, chapter VI), but often only a small one:

> as explanations of the so-called business cycle, or cycles, when they are really serious, I doubt the adequacy of over-production, under-consumption, over-capacity, price-dislocation, maladjustment between agricultural and industrial prices, over-confidence, over-investment, over-saving, over-spending, and the discrepancy between saving and investment.

Instead, he stressed two dominant factors in serious depressions: 'over-indebtedness to start with and *deflation* following soon after'. Over-investment and over-speculation mattered when carried on with borrowed money, over-confidence 'when, as, and if, it beguiles its victims into debt'. He held that this was the explanation of why business contractions occasionally became deep depressions: 'if debt and deflation are absent, other disturbances are powerless to bring on crises comparable in severity to those of 1837, 1873, or 1929-1933'.

Changes in the real value of inside debt would generally be neglected in later discussions of what came to known as the Pigou-Haberler real balance effect, as being transfers which do not affect aggregate wealth. Fisher, in contrast, emphasized the effect of the real value of nominal debt of changes in the price level that had not been anticipated when the debt was contracted. The possibility of bankruptcy created an asymmetry between the effect of falling prices and of rising prices. The bankruptcies and, even more, the fear of bankruptcy and loan default induced by falling prices and excessive nominal debts would increase risk premia on loans, lead to withdrawal of uninsured deposits from banks with loan portfolios considered in danger of default, and cause liquidation of assets and repayment of loans, all of which would depress asset prices and contract the money supply. The attempt to restore liquidity by selling assets to repay loans and increase bank reserves would be self-defeating, warned Fisher (1933, p. 346): 'By March, 1933, liquidation had reduced the debts about 20 per cent, but had increased the dollar about 75 per cent, so that the *real* debt, that is debt measured in terms of commodities, was increased about 40 per cent.'

Fisher summarized the process expounded in Chapters II and III of *Booms and Depressions* in nine links. First, debt liquidation, resulting from some random shock such as the bursting of a bubble in stock prices, 'leads to *distress selling* and to (2) *Contraction of deposit currency*, as bank loans are paid off, and to a slowing down of velocity of circulation', so that (3) the price level drops, causing (4) '*A still greater fall in the net worths of business*, precipitating bankruptcies.' Profits are reduced (5), so that firms curtail production and employment (6). 'These losses, bankruptcies, and unemployment, lead to (7) *Pessimism and loss of confidence*, which in turn lead to (8) *Hoarding and slowing down still more the velocity of circulation*.' The ninth link was 'a fall in the nominal, or money, rates and a rise in the real, or commodity, rates of interest' (Fisher, 1933, p. 342).

It is noteworthy that Fisher's analysis predicts contraction of the money supply during the debt-deflation process without the monetary base having fallen, due to repayment of bank loans and loss of confidence, which causes both banks and the public to hoard cash. This is consistent with U.S. experience during the Great Depression, in which the money supply fell by about a third while the monetary base rose.

These things would only occur 'Assuming, as above stated, that this fall of prices is not interfered with by reflation or otherwise.' Turning to the policy implications of his analysis, Fisher (1933, pp. 346-347) insisted that

> Those who imagine that Roosevelt's avowed reflation is not the cause of our recovery but that we had 'reached the bottom anyway' are very much mistaken. ... If reflation can now so easily and quickly reverse the deadly down-swing of deflation after nearly four years, when it was gathering increased momentum, it would have been still easier, and at any time, to have stopped it earlier. In fact, under President Hoover, recovery was apparently well started by the Federal Reserve open-market purchases, which revived prices and business from May to September 1932. The efforts were not kept up and recovery was stopped by various circumstances, including the political 'campaign of fear'.

Fisher's support for reflation (raising the price level back to its previous level) and price stabilization is opposed to the neo-Austrian view of Lionel Robbins (1934) and Murray Rothbard (1975) that falling prices would bring about needed readjustment, lower wage rates would restore full employment, and a growing economy should have falling prices. Rothbard (1975, pp. 157-163, 272-274) is particularly critical of Fisher's views on reflation and stabilization, although it was Hawtrey rather than Fisher whom he named as 'one of the evil geniuses' of the stabilizationists. Fisher's emphatic endorsement, in his 1933 article and in several other publications, of Roosevelt's monetary expansion, which raised the price of an ounce of gold from $20.67 in several erratic jumps to $35, contradicts the claim by Fisher's associate Hans Cohrssen (1991, p. 827) that Fisher was an opponent of what Cohrssen regards as 'Roosevelt's Marxist economic measures'. Fisher's opposition to the National Recovery Administration's scheme of raising prices by restricting output (Sumner, 1990, p. 724) was offset by his support for devaluing the dollar against gold. Among Yale's full professors of economics, Fisher and his closest former student, James Harvey Rogers, a special adviser to the Roosevelt administration, stood apart from the anti-New Deal views of Fred Fairchild, Edgar Furniss, and Norman Buck (see Fairchild, Furniss, Buck, and Whelden, 1935; and W.R. Allen, 1977).

Fisher's concern about deflation causing bankruptcy and the fear of bankruptcy parallels that expressed by John Maynard Keynes (1931, p. 33; 1973, XIII, p. 361) in his Harris Foundation lectures at the University of Chicago in 1931 (see Dimand, 1991). Keynes opposed the wage and price deflation advocated by O.M.W. Sprague of Harvard, then economic adviser to the Bank of England and later to the U.S. Treasury, on the grounds that 'all this financial structure would be deranged by the adoption of Dr Sprague's proposal. A widespread bankruptcy, default, and repudiation of bonds would necessarily ensue.' A drastic rise in the real value of inside debt would have depressing consequences, such as higher risk premia, increased liquidity preference (increased hoarding in Fisher's terms), and disruption of the financial structure. These effects would be likely to exceed the stimulative real balance effect of a higher real value of outside money (of which Keynes was well aware by 1925 at the latest – see Presley, 1986).

Keynes argued, in chapter 19 of the *General Theory*, that increased downward flexibility of wages and prices would not necessarily eliminate unemployment. Even though an economy with a given stock of (outside) money and a given price level would have a larger real aggregate effective demand for output than another economy with the same money stock and a higher price level, it does not follow that swiftly falling prices will stimulate aggregate demand. Keynes and Fisher agreed on the contractionary effect of deflation when there are nominal debts, and on the role of fear of bankruptcy in raising real interest rates and disrupting the financial system. In addition, as emphasized by Robert Mundell (1963), the higher real return on holding money during deflation would cause a contractionary increase in demand for real money balances. James Tobin (1980, p. 10) noted what he termed the Fisher effect on spending of transferring wealth from debtors to creditors through lower prices: 'Debtors have borrowed for good reasons, most of which indicate a high marginal propensity to spend from wealth or from current income or from any liquid resources they can command.' Fisher's account of the debt-deflation process (1932, 1933) and Keynes's analysis of the contractionary potential of deflation (1936, chapter 19) have been taken up by contemporary macroeconomists, with Tobin (1975, 1980) and J. Bradford De Long and Lawrence Summers (1986) emphasizing the implications for aggregate demand

and Hyman Minsky (1975, pp. 64, 126; 1982; 1986, pp. 172, 177) stressing the fragility of the financial system.

3   THE EXPERIENCE OF THE 1920s AND 1930s

The experience of the 1920-1921 deflation and recession helped shape analysis of the Great Depression. Britain began a contractionary monetary policy to raise the pound sterling from its 1920 low of $3.20 towards its prewar parity of $4.86, which was finally reached in 1925, even though the United States was itself undergoing a sharp deflation at the time. A.W. Phillips (1958, p. 115) records that in the United Kingdom unemployment rose from 2.6 percent in 1920 to 17.0 percent in 1921 and 14.3 percent in 1922, while wage rates declined by 22.2 percent in 1921 and 19.1 percent in 1922, and the cost of living index fell by 12.8 percent in 1921 ('largely a result of falling import prices') and 17.5 percent in 1922. Phillips was concerned to explain changes in wage rates by unemployment and cost of living changes. From the point of view of Fisher (1926), concerned with explaining unemployment, these figures suggest that the unemployment of this period cannot be blamed on downward rigidity of either money or real wages. Rapid wage deflation did not eliminate British unemployment in the early 1920s, contrary to what the analysis of Edwin Cannan (1932, 1933) and Robbins (1934) would have predicted. This experience was also inconsistent with the argument in Keynes's *General Theory* (1936, chapter 2) that real wages are countercyclical (moving in the opposite direction to procyclical money wages), a claim from which Keynes (1939) retreated in the face of evidence advanced by John Dunlop, Michal Kalecki, and Lorie Tarshis. Because the 1921 drop in the cost of living largely reflected lower import prices (as the exchange value of sterling rose), the decline in the product wage (the real wage cost to firms) would have exceeded the decline in the purchasing power of money wages. The 1921-1922 British experience of high unemployment and falling real wages recurred in many countries in the Depression: real weekly earnings in manufacturing in 1932 were 15 percent lower than in 1929 in Germany, 14 percent lower in the United States (Temin 1989, p. 121).

If rapidly falling British wage rates in 1921 and 1922 did not prevent high unemployment during deflation, what was the link from deflation to output and employment? Keynes drew attention in his *Tract on Monetary Reform* (1923) to the inability to reduce money interest rates below zero, if money is costless to store, so that deflation raises real interest rates, and to the existence of outstanding nominal contracts. On the latter point, he drew attention to an article by Fisher (1922b) estimating the average maturity of outstanding nominal contracts (about a year). Fisher's article had appeared in the *Manchester Guardian Commercial*'s series of supplements on 'Reconstruction in Europe' . Keynes had edited the supplements, and based his *Tract* on four of his articles in the series. Keynes (1936, chapter 2) considered one particular variety of unexpired nominal contract, staggered money wage bargains when workers care about relative wages, as an explanation of involuntary unemployment and of the real effects of demand stimulus. Fisher (1932, 1933) went further in exploring how the existence of unexpired contracts in money terms, typified by debts, provided a channel for price changes to affect real spending. The larger the outstanding volume of nominal debts and other contracts in money terms, the more sensitive real spending would be to changes in expected prices, and hence changes in the perceived real burden of debts and real value of assets.

This dependence of the sensitivity of real spending to price changes on the extent of nominal indebtedness is the key to the debt-deflation theory of great depressions. Peter Temin (1989, p. 59) expressed skepticism about the 'premise that the deflation caused the Depression' because the United States experienced a decline of wholesale prices by about one quarter over each of the two-year periods 1920-1921 and 1929-1930, yet the Depression did not begin in 1921. (Britain did experience high unemployment throughout the 1920s, dipping below 10 percent in only one year, but the British deflation in 1921-1922 was more severe than that in the U.S. because of the exchange appreciation.) Fisher's predictions in 1929 and 1930, as well as those of the Harvard Economic Service, reflected recollection of the briefness and mildness of the 1921 American recession. Fisher (1932, 1933) was able to explain why his earlier predictions were wrong and why the deflation of 1929-1930 was followed by so much more economic disruption than a similar amount of deflation in 1920-1921: the growth of nominal indebtedness associated with the intervening stock boom.

Fisher (1932, chapter VII) attempted to measure 'The Over-Indebtedness that led to the World Depression.' He found the growth of debt closely linked to margin buying of stocks beginning in 1923, and noted that 'All security loans [loans with negotiable securities as collateral] increased from October 3, 1928, to October 4, 1929, by 36 percent and reached on that date a peak just under 17 billions' (1932, pp. 72-73, 81). Urban mortgages tripled to $37 billion from 1920 to 1929, and commercial bank loans rose 50 percent to $39 billion from 1922 to 1929, even though commodity prices remained roughly constant from 1923 to 1929, after their sharp drop in 1921. The deflation following the stock market crash of October 1929 had a greater effect on real spending than the deflation of 1921 had, because nominal debt was much greater in 1929, including debt secured by stocks.[1]

4   A FISHER MODEL OF DEFLATION
AND DEPRESSION

For Fisher, the sensitivity of real expenditure to deflation depended on the extent of nominal indebtedness. The importance of his approach can be seen clearly in the context of a three-equation model used by James Tobin (1975). Tobin called the model the Walras-Keynes-Phillips (or WKP) model, but, although it captures the concern of Keynes (1936, chapter 19) that increased wage and price flexibility might be destabilizing, it has more to do with Fisher than with Keynes or Phillips. Tobin (1975, p. 198) posited desired real aggregate expenditure E as a function, given the money stock M, of the price level p, expected inflation x,[2] and real income Y, so that $E = E(p,x,Y)$. He included in the model a 'Phillips curve' equation relating the output gap $(Y - Y^*)$ to the gap between actual and expected inflation, and assumed that expected inflation adjusts adaptively to the difference between actual and expected inflation. He remarked that 'I do not mean necessarily to associate myself – much less Keynes! – with the natural-rate hypothesis in all its power and glory.' Fisher, however, as a believer in the long-run neutrality of money, would not have objected to association with the natural-rate hypothesis (that $Y = Y^*$ when inflation is correctly expected, and Y^* is independent of the inflation rate). Tobin's equation 2.2.1, the 'Phillips curve' linking the output gap to unexpected inflation, recalls the correlation of output and a distributed lag of price changes in Fisher (1923, 1925), not the dependence of wage changes on unemployment in Phillips (1958). The adaptive expectations hypothesis, Tobin's equation 2.3.1, is consistent with the practice of Fisher, who, after explaining the dependence of money interest rates on expected inflation, correlated money interest rates with a distributed lag of past price changes in *The Theory of Interest* (1930). Neither Keynes nor Phillips used adaptive expectations. The Walrasian aspect of Tobin's WKP model was equation 2.1.1, which made the rate of change of output a function of excess demand $E - Y$, in place of the more Marshallian assumption that the rate of change of prices depends on $E - Y$. Since the 'Phillips curve' (2.2.1) and adaptive expectations (2.3.1) are Fisherian, and the choice of variables to explain E in 2.1.1 fits Fisher (1932, 1933), the Walras-Keynes-Phillips model would be better termed a Fisher model.

$$\dot{Y} = A_y(E - Y) \qquad\qquad\qquad\qquad [7.1, (2.1.1)]$$

$$\pi = A_p(Y - Y^*) + x \qquad\qquad\qquad [7.2, (2.2.1)]$$

$$\dot{x} = A_x(\pi - x) \qquad\qquad\qquad\qquad [7.3, (2.3.1)]$$

Tobin investigated the local stability of his WKP model around its equilibrium at potential output, at which $E(p, x, Y) = E(p^*, 0, Y^*) = Y^*$. If the model was stable, M/p would automatically move back toward Y^* after a perturbation. He found that the 'critical necessary condition for stability is:

$$p^* E_p + A_x E_x < 0'. \qquad\qquad [7.4, (3.4)]$$

The second term would be positive: a higher expected rate of inflation would increase spending (that is, $E_x > 0$) both because of the 'flow Pigou effect' named by Tobin (1975) and also because of the reduced demand for real money balances discussed by Mundell (1963). Tobin suggested that E_p, and hence the first term of the stability condition, would be negative because of the 'stock Pigou effect' (the wealth effect on consumption of lower M/p due to higher p) and the 'Keynes effect' of higher interest rates[3]. Discussion in the literature of Tobin's stability condition 3.4 has concentrated on its implication that more rapid adjustment of expectations (larger A_x) makes instability more likely, and on the related question 'Is Price Flexibility Destabilizing?' (see Driskill and Sheffrin, 1986; De Long and Summers, 1986, 1988).

Fisher's debt-deflation theory has implications for both terms of Tobin's stability condition 3.4. With sufficient inside debt denominated in money, what Tobin (1980, pp. 9-11) termed the Fisher effect on inside debt could dominate the stock Pigou effect on outside money, so that E_p would be positive (a higher price level would increase real expenditure, a lower price level reduce it), the model would necessarily be unstable: Y and p move further away from their equilibrium values after an initial shock. (The Keynes effect would cease once deflation reduced nominal interest rates nearly to zero – as with the U.S. Treasury bill rates of three eighths of one percent in the 1930s.) The size of E_x, the derivative of desired expenditure with respect to expected inflation, could also be expected from Fisher's analysis to depend on the amount of nominal indebtedness. The larger the amount of nominal debt in this model relative to the scale of other variables, the less likely it is that the model is stable. This interpretation of the model captures Fisher's explanation of why the U.S. economy returned to potential output quickly after the deflation of 1921, but did not do so after the deflation of 1929-1930 due to over-indebtedness.

Unfortunately, these implications of Fisher's debt-deflation theory have not been brought out in the literature proceeding from Tobin (1975). De Long and Summers (1986), for instance, cited Fisher's 1923 and 1925 articles, but not his 1932 book or 1933 article. Their discussion led to an exchange between Sumner (1990) and De Long and Summers (1990), in which Sumner very usefully extended Fisher's 1925 analysis to the period 1923-1935 as a byproduct of arguing that price rigidities due to New Deal policies, especially the National Industrial Recovery Act, depressed output from July 1933 to August 1935 (with some mention of reflation and a nearly 50 percent rise in industrial output in the first half of 1933; Sumner 1990, pp. 723-725).

5 FISHER'S DEBT-DEFLATION THEORY AND THE LITERATURE

As often happened with Fisher, he was overly enthusiastic about the reception and acceptance of his theory. He reported (1933, p. 337) that

Since the book [*Booms and Depressions*] was published its special conclusions have been widely accepted and, so far as I know, no one has yet found them anticipated by previous writers, though several, including myself, have zealously sought to find such anticipations. Two of the best-read authorities in this field assure that those conclusions are, in the words of one of them, 'both new and important'.

In fact, published contemporary discussion of his debt-deflation theory was very limited, the most important being the summary in 1937 in Gottfried Haberler's League of Nations survey of theories of *Prosperity and Depression* (1946, pp. 113-116). Fisher's name was even missing from the index of Albert Gailord Hart's *Debts and Recovery, A Study of Changes in the Internal Debt Structure from 1929 to 1937* (1938), an empirical study for which Fisher's debt-deflation theory might have been expected to be of central importance.

In the final footnote of his *Econometrica* article, Fisher (1933, p. 350n.) reported that Wesley Mitchell, to whom *Booms and Depressions* was dedicated, had drawn his attention to Thorstein Veblen's *Theory of Business Enterprise* (1904, Chapter VII) as the work that 'probably comes nearest to the debt-deflation theory. Hawtrey's writings seem the next nearest.' While Veblen (1904, pp. 100-101, 105) stressed the importance of outstanding nominal debt in explaining fluctuations, this was not a recurrent theme in his writing and, unlike Fisher, he did not view monetary shocks as the source of instability.

Ralph Hawtrey of the British Treasury was the only prominent interwar economist with a theory of economic fluctuations as thoroughly monetary as that of Fisher. His account of the 'vicious circle' of distress selling increasing the real burden of debt by depressing asset prices, although not at the heart of his theory, was closely related to Fisher's debt-deflation process. Fisher's acknowledgement of affinity to Hawtrey failed to satisfy Raymond Saulnier (1938, pp. 77-78n.) who, in his only mention of Fisher, criticized Fisher (1933, p. 350n.) for failing to remark that his complaint of the absence of the word 'debt' from the indexes of monetary treatises did not apply to Hawtrey's *Currency and Credit* (1927). The affinity of the two approaches was not noted by Hawtrey, who in 1950 cited Fisher in the fourth edition of *Currency and Credit* only for the equation of exchange and *The Making of Index Numbers*.

Fisher's debt-deflation theory enabled him to explain why some deflations, such as that of 1929-1930, were followed by severe depressions, while others were not, as in 1921. His emphasis on the importance of unanticipated changes in the real value of inside debt and on the asymmetry created by the risk of bankruptcy was shared by later macroeconomic theorizing, notably by Minsky and Tobin, and recently by Bernanke (1995), King (1994), and Wolfson (1996). His theory of the debt-deflation process gave Fisher a powerful insight into the nature and remedy of the Great Depression, and of his personal financial disaster, just when his audience had walked out on him, repelled by his mistaken stock predictions and attracted elsewhere by the spectacularly successful new books of Keynes and Hayek.

NOTES

* First published in slightly different form in the *Review of Social Economy* 52:1 (Spring 1994). I am grateful to William J. Barber and Mary Ann Dimand for helpful comments.
1 That the stock crash of October 1987 was not followed by a depression may be explained by the concerted central bank response to the crash, in an institutional setting of deposit insurance and restrictions on margin buying of stocks.
2 Because of the 'flow Pigou effect', the consumption effect of expected capital gains on money holdings, $-xM / p$.
3 The lower M / p implies an LM curve further to the left, and higher interest rates reduce investment.

REFERENCES

Allen, W.R. (1977), 'Irving Fisher, F.D.R. and the great depression', *History of Political Economy*, **9**, 560-587.
Barber, W.J. (1985), *From New Era to New Deal: Herbert Hoover, the Economists, and American Economic Policy, 1921-1933*, Cambridge, UK, Cambridge University Press.
Barger, H. (1933), Review of Fisher (1932) and *Money* by Francis Hirst, *Economic Journal*, **3**, 681.
Bernanke, B.S. (1995), 'Money, credit, and banking lecture: the macroeconomics of the great depression: a comparative analysis', *Journal of Money, Credit, and Banking*, **27**, 16-29.
Cannan, E. (1932), 'The demand for labour', *Economic Journal*, **42**, 357-370.
Cannan, E. (1933), 'Unemployment', in his *Economic Scares*, London, King.
Cohrssen, H. (1991), 'Working for Irving Fisher', *Cato Journal*, **10**, 825-833.
De Long, J.B. and Summers, L. (1986), 'Is increased price flexibility stabilizing?', *American Economic Review*, **76**, 1031-1044.

De Long, J.B. and Summers, L. (1988), 'Is increased price flexibility stabilizing? Reply', *American Economic Review*, **78**, 273-276.

De Long, J.B and Summers, L. (1990), 'Price-level flexibility and the coming of the new deal: reply to Sumner', *Cato Journal*, **9**, 729-735.

Deutscher, P. (1990), *R. G. Hawtrey and the Development of Macroeconomics*, Ann Arbor, University of Michigan Press.

Dimand, R.W. (1989), 'The reception of Keynes's *Treatise on Money:* a review of the reviews', in D.A. Walker (ed.), *Perspectives on the History of Economic Thought*, Volume II, Aldershot, UK, Edward Elgar.

Dimand, R.W. (1991), 'Keynes, Kalecki, Ricardian equivalence and the real balance effect', *Bulletin of Economic Research*, **43**, 289-92, Reprinted in M. Blaug, (ed.), *Pioneers of Economics*, **39**, *Michael Kalecki (1899-1970)*, Aldershot, UK, Edward Elgar, 1992.

Dimand, R.W. (1993), 'The dance of the dollar: Irving Fisher's monetary theory of economic fluctuations', *History of Economics Review*, **20**, 161-173.

Dominguez, K.M., Fair, R.C. and Shapiro, M.D. (1988), 'Forecasting the depression: Harvard versus Yale', *American Economic Review*, **78**, 595-612.

Driskill, R.A., and Sheffrin S.M. (1986), 'Is price flexibility destabilizing?', *American Economic Review*, **76**, 802-807.

Fairchild, F.R., Furniss E.S., Buck N.S.and Whelden C. H., Jr. (1935), *A Description of the 'New Deal'*, rev. ed., New York, Macmillan.

Fisher, I. (1907), *The Rate of Interest*, New York, Macmillan. Reprinted in I. Fisher, 1997, Volume 3.

Fisher, I. (1922a), *The Making of Index Numbers*, Publication No. 1 of the Pollak Foundation for Economic Research. Cambridge, MA, Houghton Mifflin. Reprinted in I. Fisher , 1997, Volume 7.

Fisher, I. (1922b), 'Devaluation versus deflation', *Manchester Guardian Commercial*, 'Reconstruction in Europe', Section 11, December 7.

Fisher, I. (1923), 'Business cycle largely a "dance of the dollar"', *Journal of the American Statistical Association*, New Series , **18**, 1024-1028. Reprinted in I. Fisher, 1997, Volume 8.

Fisher, I. (1925), 'Our unstable dollar and the so-called business cycle', *Journal of the American Statistical Association*, New Series 20, **150,** 179-202. Reprinted in I. Fisher, 1997, Volume 8.

Fisher, I. (1926), 'A statistical relation between unemployment and price changes', *International Labour Review* 13, 785-792. Reprinted as 'Lost and found: I discovered the Phillips curve – Irving Fisher', *Journal of Political Economy,* **81,** 1973, 496-502, and in I. Fisher, 1997, Volume 8.

Fisher, I. (1930), *The Theory of Interest*, New York, Macmillan. Reprinted in I. Fisher, 1997, Volume 9.

Fisher, I. (1932), *Booms and Depressions*, New York, Adelphi. Reprinted in I. Fisher, 1997, Volume 10.

Fisher, I. (1933), 'The debt-deflation theory of great depressions', *Econometrica*, **1,** 337-57. Reprinted in I. Fisher, 1997, Volume 10.

Fisher, I. (1997), *The Works of Irving Fisher*, 14 Volumes, edited by W.J. Barber, assisted by R.W. Dimand and K. Foster, consulting editor J. Tobin, London, Pickering and Chatto.

Fisher, I. N. (1956), *My Father, Irving Fisher*, New York, Comet.

Galbraith, J.K. (1977), *The Age of Uncertainty*, Boston, Houghton Mifflin.

Gayer, A.D. (ed.) (1937), *The Lessons of Monetary Experience*, New York, Farrar and Rinehart.

Haberler, G. (1946), *Prosperity and Depression*, 3rd ed., Lake Success, NY, United Nations.

Hart, A.G. (1938), *Debts and Recovery*, New York, The Twentieth Century Fund. As reprinted in A.G. Hart and Mehrling P., *Debt, Crisis, and Recovery: The 1930s and the 1990s*, Armonk, NY, M.E. Sharpe, 1995.

Hawtrey, R.G. (1927), *Currency and Credit*, 3rd ed., London, Longmans.

Hayek, F.A. von (1931), *Prices and Production*, London, Routledge.

Keynes, J.M. (1923), *A Tract on Monetary Reform*, London, Macmillan.

Keynes, J.M. (1930), *A Treatise on Money*, London, Macmillan.

Keynes, J.M. (1931), 'An economic analysis of unemployment', in Q. Wright, (ed.), *Unemployment as a World Problem*, Chicago, University of Chicago Press, 1-42.

Keynes, J.M. (1936), *The General Theory of Employment, Interest and Money*, London, Macmillan.

Keynes, J.M. (1939), 'Relative movements of real wages and output', *Economic Journal*, **49**, 34-51.

Keynes, J.M. (1973), *Collected Writings*, Vol. XIII, (ed.) D.E. Moggridge, London, Macmillan, and New York, Cambridge University Press, for the Royal Economic Society.

King, M. (1994), 'Presidential address: debt deflation: theory and evidence', *European Economic Review*, **38**, 419-445.

Macfie, A. L. (1934), *Theories of the Trade Cycle*, London, Macmillan.

Minsky, H.P. (1975), *John Maynard Keynes*, New York, Columbia University Press.

Minsky, H.P. (1982), 'Debt-deflation processes in today's institutional environment', *Banco Nazionale del Lavoro Quarterly Review*, **143**, 375-393.

Minsky, H.P. (1986), *Stabilizing an Unstable Economy*, New Haven, CT, Yale University Press.

Mundell, R.A. (1963), 'Inflation and real interest', *Journal of Political Economy*, **71**, 280-283.

Phillips, A. W. (1958), 'The relation between unemployment and the rate of change of money wage rates in the United Kingdom, 1861-1957', *Economica*, **25**, 283-300, as reprinted in J. Lindauer, (ed.), *Macroeconomic Readings*, New York, The Free Press, 1968, 107-119.

Presley, J.R. (1986), 'J.M. Keynes and the real balance effect', *The Manchester School*, **54**, 22-30.

Robbins, L. (1934), *The Great Depression*, London, Macmillan.

Rothbard, M. (1975), *America's Great Depression*, 3rd. ed., Kansas City, Sheed and Ward.

Saulnier, R. (1938), *Contemporary Monetary Theory*, New York, Columbia University Press.

Sobel, R. (1968), *The Great Bull Market*, New York, Norton.

Sumner, S. (1990), 'Price-level stability, price flexibility, and Fisher's business cycle model', *Cato Journal*, **9**, 719-727.

Temin, P. (1989), *Lessons from the Great Depression*, Lionel Robbins Lectures, Cambridge, MA, MIT Press.

Tobin, J. (1975), 'Keynesian models of recession and depression', *American Economic Review*, **65**, 195-202.

Tobin, J. (1980), *Asset Accumulation and Economic Activity*, Yrjo Jahnssen Lectures, Chicago, University of Chicago Press.

Veblen, T. (1904), *The Theory of Business Enterprise*, New York, Charles Scribner's Sons, as reprinted New York, Mentor Books, no date.

Velupillai, K. (1975), 'Irving Fisher on "switches of techniques" ', *Quarterly Journal of Economics*, **89,** 679-680.

Wolfson, M.H. (1996). 'Irving Fisher's debt-deflation theory: its relevance to current conditions', *Cambridge Journal of Economics*, **20,** 315-333.

8. Irving Fisher, the Quantity Theory, and the Great Depression

Frank G. Steindl*

As this conference well illustrates, Irving Fisher continues to be a fascinating figure, one with a wealth of interests and first-rate professional discoveries. Though there may well be dispute about his most important contribution, the equation of exchange of *The Purchasing Power of Money* (1911a) *(PPM)* surely is one. When reference is made to the equation, one can be reasonably sure his name will not be far behind.

The equation, in fact, formed the basis for his quantity theory oriented investigations, particularly the 'dance of the dollar' (Fisher, 1923, 1925) and Phillips curve (Fisher, 1926 [1973]) explorations. In the two decades prior to the Depression, there was little doubt that the quantity theory was the basis for his macroeconomics, which in his and the profession's case came down to a theory of the price level. The litmus test for that theory was the Great Depression, particularly the 1929-1933 Contraction.

The focus of this paper is on Fisher's lifelong quantity theory orientation during the years of the Great Depression, specifically his attempts to understand the dramatic 1929-1933 contraction. After the spring, 1933 trough, his attention focused on the pressing needs of his crusades, of which a campaign to promote explicitly the ongoing recovery was not one.[1]

1 FISHER'S PRE-DEPRESSION QUANTITY THEORY

The basis for his quantity theory orientation was his equation of exchange – $MV + M'V' = PT$. As he repeatedly maintained, the two were different: 'The equation of exchange implies no causal sequence' (1911a, p. xix). The link was that the equation was the vehicle with which to implement quantity theoretic analyses, that 'the quantity theory [could] be made more clear by the equation of exchange' (1911a, p. 15). Consequently, much effort was expended in *PPM* to develop the ingredients in and the factors affecting the six elements in the equation – M, M', V, V', P, and T.[2] Illustrative of this were the fulcrum arrays 'determining' the price level, i.e., the purchasing power of money, as the required balance given the left-side amounts of money M (symbolized by a purse) and deposit currency M' (for which a bank book was the symbol) and right-side volume of trade T ('the grocer's tray') for the years 1896-1912 (1911a, p. 306 insert), a practice he continued for the rest of the decade.[3]

In developing the equation of exchange, he had to consider the perennial question: what is money.[4] To that end, it was currency, denoted M, and its associated velocity was V. 'Bank deposits transferable by check', though a form of 'circulating media' (Fisher, 1911a, pp. 10-11), were not money; they were 'deposit currency', denoted as M' for which the relevant velocity was V'.

In subsequent work, Fisher never aggregated M and M' into a single money supply series. They were always considered separately as money and deposit currency, with the latter the most frequently used monetary measure, largely because of the relative ease of obtaining data, particularly after the formation of the Federal Reserve System. He further assumed that the currency-deposit ratio, M/M', was constant (1911a, pp. 50, 151-154).

This assumption allowed him to sidestep questions of money supply mechanisms, ones in which he appears never to be seriously interested. Under the gold standard, the monetary regime when *PPM* was written, the 'exogenous' M generated reserves which then determined M'. Under a managed money standard, the monetary authorities determined the reserve base which via a deposit multiplier then gave M'. With the fixed currency-deposit ratio, M/M', the quantity of Fisherian money M was then determined.

The economic analysis in *PPM* was essentially comparative statics as Fisher examined the effects of movements in one variable at a time. The price level was, almost without fail, the endogenous variable – after all, 'the chief object of this book is to explain the causes determining the purchasing power of money' (1911a, p. 13). The singular exception to the comparative statics exercises was in chapter 4 – 'Transitions Periods' (1911a, pp. 55-73). It was here that he outlined a monetary business cycle framework, one in which the interplay of nominal and real interest rates was basic. That chapter apparently justified his later assertion that 'the vast field of "business cycles" is one on which I had scarcely entered before, and I had never attempted to analyze it as a whole' (1932b, p. vii). It is important to note that the analysis of the transition, though initially considered as relating to movements between successive equilibria, also generated a cycle: 'We have found that one such "boom" period leads to a reaction, and that the action and reaction complete a cycle of "prosperity" and "depression" ' (1911a, p. 72).

His quantity theoretic orientation can be seen in two mid-1920s' empirical investigations, one dealing with cycles, the other with (un)employment. The first attempts to understand the cycle in terms of the rate of change of the price level, one 'of the two components of the real rate of interest' (1923, p. 1024). The model is a linear distributed lag of the rate of change of prices on which is regressed an index of the physical volume of trade. They are 'correlated [at] 79 per cent' (1923, p. 1027). The behavior of prices is implicitly assumed to be the result of proportionate movements of the quantity of money, in that no monetary data are explicitly considered.

The project's final results, appearing two years later, reported a correlation coefficient of '94.1 per cent. ... Seldom before has a correlation so high been found in the efforts to explain "the business cycle" ' (1925, p. 179). Again, the quantity theory was implicitly employed in that no monetary data were formally considered. There was little doubt in his mind that the business cycle was largely a monetary phenomenon and that monetary stabilization was the key to mitigating its more pronounced movements: 'Probably much of the remaining fluctuation of T, not explained by the factors here studied, is due to non-cyclical factors also. There can be little left in the fluctuations of T which can be said to be truly cyclical in character' (1925, p. 201).

In the second project, Fisher applied his distributed lag framework to deal with employment – the Phillips curve question. The correlation between the distributed lag of rates of price change and employment was '90 percent' (1926, p. 791).[5] Here again, there was an implicit quantity theory strand from which the 'independent' price changes explained movements in the index of employment, leading to the conclusion that 'the "dance of the dollar" [is] the key ... to the major fluctuations in employment. [Thus] we have in our power, as a means of substantially preventing unemployment, the stabilization of the purchasing power of the dollar, pound, ... and any other monetary units' (1926, p. 792).

By the latter half of the decade, the validity of the quantity theory as a theory of prices was so established in his mind that he began referring to inflation and deflation not as movements of the price level but as movements of the quantity of money (Allen, 1993, p. 200), as is most clearly seen in *The Money Illusion*, a tract for the general public.

The interesting interpretation emanating from his empirical forays is that Fisher's quantity theory was not just a theory of prices and a framework for investigating price movements. Rather, the quantity theory, for which the equation of exchange was an effective tool for empirical implementation, was also a theory of output and employment. For him, price stability was a monetary phenomenon and from price stability came output and employment stability. These notions were to be put to the test with the advent of the 1930s, particularly the 1929-1933 slide.

2   DEPRESSION

Though initially slow to realize the severity of the depression, Fisher felt that a satisfactory understanding necessitated a return to the theory of business cycles. His focus now was principally on depressions, in part no doubt because of his dramatically diminished personal fortune (Allen, 1993, pp. 234-238). That reappraisal appeared in September, 1932 as *Booms and Depressions* (1932b) (*BD*), the origins of which were 'first stated in my lectures at Yale in 1931' (Fisher, 1933a, p. 350). It represented 'a brilliant solution of this puzzle' between his earlier dance of the dollar empirical forays and that of 'a deep and lasting depression' (Dimand, 1994, p. 93).

BD is a strange book. Its audience appears to be professional economists. It reads, however, like a popular tract intended to educate the general public.[6] Thus, it is not surprising that it received poor reviews in the professional journals (Allen. 1993, pp. 241-242). The subtitle, 'Some First Principles', is instructive because it suggests he would return to basics, namely to an examination of the behavior of the quantity of money, and to a limited extent that is what he did. The theory's principal theme is that deflation increases the real value of debt, thereby causing bankruptcies, which in turn reduces aggregate demand and, thus, plunges the economy further into depression.

The central feature causing the depression was over-indebtedness. Though not the sole explanation of the depression, it 'seems to me highly probable' that it and 'deflation were strong and indeed the dominating factors' (1932b, p. 85). He was primarily concerned with its consequences, not with its causes: 'I am not, mind you, trying to explain how the over-indebtedness came about. That is another chapter' (Fisher, 1932a, p. 197). He did however single out 'Investing in Equities on Borrowed Money' (1932b, pp. 72-73), the strategy largely responsible for wrecking his family finances. In an aside, but one intended to give an element of generality to his concentration on the importance of over-indebtedness, he argued that 'Monetary Inflation *without* any unusual debts to begin with' led to over-indebtedness as 'unwonted profits [caused] business men ... to extend themselves in new enterprises, requiring *more* debts' (1932b, p. 48).

The attempt to reduce over-indebtedness resulted in '*contraction of deposit currency*, as bank loans are paid off, and to a slowing down of velocity of circulation [thereby causing] *a fall in the level of prices*' (1933a, p. 342) – that is, a decline in the efficiency of money. A further round of attempts to repay brought additional declines in prices.

The formal debt-deflation framework had nine factors in the sequence, with debt liquidation as the first in the logical order (1932b, pp. 8-38; Dimand, 1994, p. 97). Several points must be emphasized. First, and least important for present purposes, the interplay between real and nominal interest rates, which was central to his *PPM* cyclical mechanism, was no longer of much consequence, appearing at the end of the sequence, with changes in the earlier eight factors causing '*complicated disturbances in the rates of interest*' (1933a, p. 342) in which nominal rates fell and real rates increased.

Of more interest was his clearer, and altered, view of the money supply mechanism. In previous writings, he held to the view that the supply of money – both currency and deposit currency – was essentially determined 'exogenously,' in that the changes in the price level, hence the purchasing power of money were the result of changes in the individual monetary aggregates, given that velocity, being determined by institutional patterns, was slow to change. That is, the money supply was independent of the demand for loans.[7] With *BD*, this changed.

He now explicitly modeled currency, his *M*, as exogenous; it was determined by the Federal Reserve. The wave of bank failures in late 1931, for instance, with its consequent increased demands for currency 'more than defeated the [greater than 80 per cent increase in] new issues of Federal Reserve notes' (1932b, pp. 103-104). Accordingly, the increase in Money in Circulation during 1930-1931 was dismissed as 'misleading' because the 'increased quantity of Federal Reserve notes' was 'in stockings or in other hoarding places and not circulating at all' (1932b, p. 96).[8] He reiterated the same point the following year, using virtually identical phrasing (1933b, p. 57 n. 8). That the System was accommodating an increase in the demand for currency was not something he acknowledged. Rather, he repeatedly had currency being determined by the monetary authorities. As yet another instance, he had individual Reserve Banks issuing and circulating 'Federal Reserve notes' (1932b, p. 132), as a further recovery mechanism.

Of more consequence in his money supply framework, the attempt at debt liquidation, the first step in the debt-deflation sequence, led to a fall in the level of deposits as loans were repaid. Incidentally, deposit currency now was frequently referred to as currency (1932b, pp. 14-16, 31, 96, 127). But Fisher's framework did not have banks responding by acquiring other assets; they now were passive agents whose asset acquisition activities were dictated by the demand for loans.[9] That is, in a 'stampede of liquidation' arising from 'a general state of *over*-indebtedness', the 'new borrowings will by no means suffice to restore the balance, and there must follow a net shrinkage of deposits' (1932b, p. 15). To underscore this, Fisher maintained that central bank policy on interest rates was the vehicle by which to 'regulate' the supply of deposit currency, such that 'a lowered rate increases the borrowing and a raised rate decreases [it]' (1932b, p. 126).

The hypothesis that banks were passive – that is, that they effectively subscribed to the real-bills doctrine – evidently was accepted by him because he never looked at Federal Reserve data to see if the fall in deposit currency could be understood from the supply side. Had he done so, he would have seen that member bank reserves *fell* 21 percent (an annual rate of 9.8 percent) while Federal Reserve Credit increased *only* 12 percent (a 5.3 percent annual rate) between the fourth quarter, 1929 and the first quarter, 1932, the last one for which data were available to be included in the book. Ironically, his list of proposed remedies featured open-market purchases as a recovery vehicle (1932b, pp. 128-131, 213); yet System actions as summed up either in Federal Reserve Credit or in member bank reserves were evidently not something worth addressing as a potential cause of the slide.

The final point to be made about *BD* is that it was here that Fisher returned to the monetary data in order to document that the depression was in fact associated with a decline in his monetary measures. The data were presented and discussed in an appendix (1932b, pp. 178-181) and depicted on a semi-logarithmic graph showing the behavior of net demand deposits – Fisher's deposit currency – and time deposits, (1932b, pp. 93-95). The former fell 16 percent from the end of June, 1929 to the end of 1931.

Fisher's preferred method now was not, however, calculating rates of monetary change. He, instead, coupled the money change with its respective estimated velocity movement, hence he looked at MV rather than M and similarly $M'V'$ rather than M'. These were his 'efficiency of money' notions. They were calculated in the following manner. Between October, 1929 and February, 1932 'deposit currency of the member banks ... fell ... 21 per cent ... and the velocity in the same period fell 61 per cent, so that the efficiency of deposit money [was] only 31 per cent of what it had been in 1929' (1932b, p. 96), that is, deposit currency's efficiency was $(1 - .21)(1 - .61) = .31$.

It was these declines in the efficiency of deposit currency, and not the behavior of deposits alone, which impressed Fisher as the by-product of the desire to reduce indebtedness, the initiating cause of the slump. Ironically, the move to liquidation, the desire to reduce indebtedness, 'left unpaid balances *more* burdensome ... than the whole debt burden had been in 1929. ... In a word, despite all liquidations, the 234 ¼ billions of 1929 became over 302 billions in 1932, if measured in 1929 dollars' (1932b, pp. 107-108).

Fisher thus saw that the desire to reduce indebtedness, with its consequent reduction in deposits, resulted in a decline in wholesale prices.[10] The price decline was not, however, interpreted as the direct result of Federal Reserve policy, that is, as due to reductions in the supply of reserves and deposits; rather it was understood as resulting from the desire to reduce over-indebtedness, that is, as due to increases in the demand for money.

The quantity theory view of price level movements has them originating from a disequilibrium in the money market. In the present case, the dramatic fall in prices would be attributed to a sharp increase in the excess demand for money. But how to gauge such an excess demand? The typical way is to take the price decline as prima facie evidence of excess demand, the method used at Chicago, particularly by Simons (Steindl, 1995, pp. 79-83). This approach is tautological. An empirical measure of the excess demand would be preferable. Another approach looks at the behavior of the money supply, to see if it fell, which of course it did, and Fisher's deposit currency data documented this. Still another approach, and this is a noteworthy discovery, is Fisher's efficiency of money calculation. It combines in a single number the joint effect of money supply and demand movements, that is, it captures the notion of an excess demand for money! Decreases in the stock of money and increases in the demand, as captured by falling velocity, define excess demand, and Fisher's efficiency of money does just that.

A quantity theory explanation of the decline in prices would therefore take the falling efficiency of money as evidence of an excess demand for money. To combat the excess demand, the appropriate policy would be to increase the money supply, with the extent of the increase being gauged by the movement of the measured efficiency of money to the point where it would register neither an increase nor a decrease.

This, however, was not Fisher's approach. The decline in velocity was taken to imply a 'liquidity trap' with its associated asymmetry in the effectiveness of monetary policy. Accordingly, the appropriate policy in times of rising prices is

> taking the surplus M out of the overflooded circulation; for people cannot spend what they do not have. [With falling prices, however] people *can* hoard what they *do* have; so that ... a mere new supply of money, to replace what has been liquidated or hoarded, might fail to raise the price level by failing to get into circulation. ... For a prompt boost of the price level, therefore, a mere increase in M might prove insufficient, unless supplemented by some influence exercised directly on the moods of people to accelerate V – that is, to convert the public from hoarding. (1932b, p. 140)

And, typical of Fisher, he was not at a loss to suggest a velocity-enhancing policy. The anti-hoarding plan – the strategy to increase velocity – with which he came increasingly to be enamored was the Silvio Gesell inspired stamp scrip – *Schwundgeld* – the stamped dollar, 'a sort of stamp tax on hoarding' (1932b, p. 142). Though 'this plan did not come to my attention until after this book had been finished' (1932b, p. 142), he felt strongly enough attracted to it to devote four pages in an appendix as well as to write the following year a short book espousing its merits (Fisher, 1933c).[11]

The chapter in which the liquidity trap, hence stamp scrip, analysis was presented is titled 'Remedies'. One of the ironies of that chapter is that he advocates Federal Reserve actions – rediscount rate and open market purchases (1932b, pp. 126-131) – prior to his stamp scrip proposal. The set-up for the discussion of monetary policy actions is an equation of exchange lead-in to the quantity theory as a vehicle to raise the price level, being that Fisher's overriding concern was raising the price level in order to reduce indebtedness (1932b, pp. 122-124). The discussion of rediscount rate and open market operations is conventional, though he adds two empirical sidelights. First, he suggests that rediscount rate policy 'is relatively slow'; open market operations are 'a supplementary instrument which works faster' (1932b, p. 128). Second, reserves generated through open market purchases would initially be used to repay indebtedness to the Federal Reserve Banks, but after a commercial bank's 'indebtedness is paid off, any further excess in its [reserve] balance is pretty sure to be used as reserve for further loans to the public' (1932b, p. 129).[12] His summary assessment of Federal Reserve actions is that the 'Reserve Banks can powerfully regulate the volume of the country's deposit currency – for good or ill' (1932b, p. 130).

Yet, given this lead-in to the importance of reserves, he did not feel it necessary to examine Federal Reserve data to see what was actually happening. Had he done so, he would have seen the aforementioned (21 percent) reduction in member bank reserves from the fourth quarter, 1929 through the first quarter, 1932. Even if reserves had increased – as they did in the last nine months of 1932 (to a level 2½ percent less than three years earlier), too late for inclusion in the book – there was the issue of the growing volume of excess reserves. Many took this as evidence of the impotency of monetary policy, as substantiation of a 'shortage' of borrowers. Would he have fallen in line with those or did he in fact understand that those excess reserves were desired by banks for precautionary, liquidity purposes? He, in fact, never addressed excess reserves during the Depression proper, more than likely because their dramatic growth occurred after he completed *BD*. [13]

The point, however, is that his strongly argued advocacy of the potency of monetary policy actions was not followed up by examination of actual Federal Reserve actions as they affected bank reserves. True, he faulted the System in general terms, specifically for failure to 'exercise it['s power] without due reference to the price level' (1932b, p. 151), but he did not investigate systematically actual policy actions.

More to the point, if Fisher believed that Federal Reserve induced monetary expansion was the appropriate course for recovery, why did he then advance the falling velocity – liquidity trap – hypothesis with its stamp scrip solution? This possibility, it should be emphasized, was not simply one on a shopping list of potential explanations; it was a desideratum, one about which he felt strongly enough that in the exigencies of the circumstances he took time to devote a book to it. If the issue was simply one of an excess demand for money, then sufficiently aggressive monetary expansion would be all that would be required. Instead, he added the conjunctive condition of a reasonably unbounded increase in the demand for money, that is, a situation in which money supply increases would not be sufficient.

The foregoing indicates that Fisher's analysis of the Great Depression parted company from the quantity theory approach with which he was so intimately linked since *PPM*. The departure rests on his monetary mechanism. Formerly, the monetary aggregates were exogenous and an excess demand for money could be eliminated by monetary expansion, that is, the price level was controllable. Now the deposit component was endogenous, as banks were perceived to adhere to the real-bills doctrine; thus, the fall in deposits due to attempts to liquidate borrowings at banks could not be offset by acquisition of other earning assets – new loans or securities. Further, Federal Reserve actions could not be counted on to eliminate the excess demand for money because of liquidity trap considerations.

With the Depression, Fisher demonstrated his empirical monetary bent in that he formally considered the actual behavior of money measures. In these efforts, he however wandered from the accepted notion of the quantity theory, which is that changes in the independently determined supply of money gave rise to changes in the price level, and in the short-run to changes in real activity. For him, money was now endogenously determined with the slide in prices and output resulting from attempts to reduce an exogenously given state of general over-indebtedness. He also became enamored of the likelihood that monetary expansions were impotent because of increases in the demand for money, as measured by his efficiency of money calculations.

During much of the rest of the Depression he turned his attention to crusades to raise the price level to its 1926 level – reflation (1933b, esp. p. 67 n. 3), that is, there was not to be any base drift – and to a restructuring of monetary arrangements – 100% reserves (1945). In the Debt-Deflation paper, which is largely a summary of *BD*, as well as in *After Reflation, What?* (1933b, p. 58), he included a graph (1933a, p. 356) depicting the September, 1932–August, 1933 movements of net demand deposits and money-in-circulation, the latter being inverted because 'the more of it when hoarded, the worse. Hence to indicate improvement, the curve of it is here inverted' (1932b, p. 57 n. 8). The graph showed vividly the sharp declines of the money and deposit series to March, 1933 and the clear rebound thereafter.

Though inverting money-in-circulation can be interpreted as a clever way of underscoring the decline and subsequent increase in the quantity of money, such an interpretation suffers because Fisher never aggregated the two. More likely, his purpose in inverting money-in-circulation was to underscore that the Federal Reserve's 'exogenous' increase in currency was being thwarted by hoarding. With his orientation that the System determined Money in Circulation, it is unlikely that he saw hoarding by the public as the reason for the increase in currency M. Being that he regarded M as exogenous, a liquidity trap interpretation of the public's demand for money was not implausible.

Among the other variables included in that graph were commodity prices and industrial production The sharp declines in each to March, 1933 and the strong rebound thereafter stand out. There was, however, neither discussion nor interpretation of those movements, other than a cryptic comment 'that immediate reversal of deflation is easily achieved by the use ... of appropriate instrumentalities' (1933a, p. 346).

3 CONCLUDING COMMENTS

This paper has argued that the quantity theory orientation which characterized Fisher's previous analyses of prices, output, and employment was essentially abandoned with the onslaught of the Great Depression. Those earlier explorations convinced him that monetary actions dictated price movements, which themselves were fundamental to understanding changes in output and employment. Furthermore, the price level was controllable by the monetary authorities, hence his late-1920s tendency to refer to monetary changes as inflation and deflation.

As the Depression marched on, he markedly revised his views. The decline now was due to attempts at liquidation from over-indebtedness; that was the basic reason. The increase in currency was due to Federal Reserve actions, not to increased demands for it on the part of the public. Associated with the repayment of bank loans was a consequent ratcheting down of deposits. As bank loans were repaid, banks did not acquire other assets. They most likely were acting as the real-bills doctrine would have them. Flawed Federal Reserve policy, as documented by an examination of actual System actions, was not considered.

His efficiency of money notion was an ingenious device whereby an excess demand for money, and the degree thereof, could be calculated. But the excess demand was not to be eliminated by Federal Reserve policy. Although he indicated that Reserve policy through the rediscount window and open market operations would stimulate recovery, he followed shortly thereafter with the empirical judgment that increases in the demand for money were rendering policy ineffective. Why else would he then have been so attracted to the stamp scrip proposal?

This change of emphasis stands at odds with his earlier quantity theory views. His discerning scientific mind, responsible for so many fruitful discoveries, led to an interpretation of the Depression and a proposed solution which contrasted fundamentally with that for which the pre-depression Fisher would have crusaded.

NOTES

* An earlier version was presented at the Universities of Bamberg, Central Oklahoma, Mainz, and Siegen. I thank the participants for their comments. Parts of the paper appeared in Steindl (1997), for which permission to reprint is gratefully acknowledged.
1 The recovery is a fascinating period on its own. From the spring, 1933 trough until the economy fully recovered in summer, 1942, industrial production increased at a 13.5 percent annual rate. Though Fisher saw signs of recovery in late summer, 1932 – 'as this book goes to press' (1932b, p. 157) – it was not until somewhat more than two years after the trough that in a speech promoting his debt-deflation hypothesis, he acknowledged, 'the growing conviction the depression is nearing its end is justified' (1935, p. 38).
2 Chapter 10 is concerned with index numbers for the price level. The chapter's forty-five page appendix analyzes forty-four different price index number formulae.
3 In 1911, Fisher published a note, 'The Equation of Exchange', clarifying calculations made in *PPM*. Annually thereafter, until 1919, he reported in the *American Economic Review* an additional year's data on the equation's six elements in articles entitled 'Equation of Exchange for 19xx', see for instance Fisher (1911b). These were accompanied by a somewhat more insightful version of the fulcrum charts of *PPM*.
4 The discussion in this section is developed is greater length in Steindl (1997).
5 Fisher did not formally investigate an inflation-unemployment connection. Rather, he dealt with an employment series based on data from the Harvard Committee on Economic Research (Fisher 1926, p. 790 n. 2).
6 His zeal in attempting to stir the public can be seen in the exaggerated tone which runs through the book. He notes that 'among the "chief inciters to over-indebtedness" were "high-pressure salesman" of financial firms whose efforts were in part responsible for 'steadily and enormously [inflating] the deposit currency' (1932b, pp. 73-74). In fact, the data reported by Fisher show negligible rates of increase in net demand deposits – six-tenths of a percent annual rate for the December, 1924-June, 1929 period, for instance.
7 As indicated, Fisher was never much concerned with money supply mechanisms, a point underscored by Laidler (1991, p. 65). The model Fisher used was essentially a simple Phillips *Bank Credit* multiple deposit expansion framework with its emphasis on bank reserves (1932b, p. 37 n. 3). He later based the decline in deposit currency on Rogers (1933), who in a testament to the times titled his article 'The Absorption [rather than the seemingly more natural heading, "The Expansion"] of Bank Credit'.
8 As to the formal measure of currency, he used Money in Circulation (MIC), a series initially employed when he constructed his monetary data in *PPM*. That MIC series was 'the total amount of money (coin and paper) outside of the federal treasury and outside the banks of deposit and discount' (1911a, p. 280); this differed from the latter Federal Reserve MIC series he used in analyzing the thirties. That one – currently called Currency in Circulation – is currency outside the Treasury and Federal Reserve; that is, it includes banks' vault cash.
9 As he pointed out the following year, 'almost all checking accounts ... grow out of the business loans made by commercial banks. But in order to maintain these borrowed accounts, business men must have the confidence to borrow' Fisher (1933b, p. 22).
10 The index peaked in November, 1925 at 104.5 (1926 = 100). It then fell at a two percent annual rate until summer, 1929, after which the decline accelerated to a fourteen percent annual rate to the time he wrote *BD*.
11 Some details of the proposal were considered in the appendix which was concerned with 'Other Plans for Reflation and Stabilization' (1932b, pp. 225-243). A fuller discussion had to wait until the following year when in response to having 'answered four or five hundred

inquiries about it' (Fisher 1933c, p. 1), he laid out the case for such scrip.

12 He also proposes that reserve requirements be 'temporarily relaxed' (1932b, p. 131), a suggestion much in keeping with the menagerie of remedies to combat the depression. And, in character with his reformer-crusader image, he advocates changing the structure of reserve requirements to correspond to the activity in deposit accounts rather than to the geographical location of banks.

13 As excess reserves grew – from $46 million in the first quarter, 1932 to $0.5 billion in the three months prior to the March, 1933 trough, to $2.1 billion in the first quarter, 1935 – Fisher took note as he prepared his *100% Money*. He, however, was agnostic as to the reason: for him, it was both a shortage of borrowers – 'borrowers fail[ing] to come forward' (1945, p. 44) – and a credit crunch – banks 'afraid to lend' (1945, p. 104). Curiously, the excess reserves growth did not dismay him, because such growth made implementation of 100% reserves easier. Hence he was not opposed to the subsequent doubling of reserve requirements beginning in August, 1936 (Fisher 1936, p. 106).

REFERENCES

Allen, R.L. (1993), *Irving Fisher: A Biography*, Cambridge, MA, Blackwell.

Dimand, R.W. (1994), 'Irving Fisher's debt-deflation theory of great depressions', *Review of Social Economy*, **52**, 92-107.

Fisher, I. (1911a), *The Purchasing Power of Money*, New York, Macmillan. Reprint 2d ed., 1922, 1971, New York, A.M. Kelley.

Fisher, I. (1911b), 'The equation of exchange: 1896-1910', *American Economic Review*, **1**, 296-305.

Fisher, I. (1923), 'The business cycle largely a "dance of the dollar" ', *Journal of the American Statistical Association*, **18**, 1025-1028.

Fisher, I. (1925), 'Our unstable dollar and the so-called business cycle', *Journal of the American Statistical Association*, **20**, 179-202.

Fisher, I. (1926), 'A statistical relation between unemployment and price changes', *International Labour Review*, **13** (no. 6), 785-92. Reprinted in I. Fisher (1973), 'I discovered the Phillips curve', *Journal of Political Economy*, **81**, 496-502.

Fisher, I. (1932a), 'What should be done in the present emergency?', in Norman Wait Harris Foundation, Round Table Conference on *Gold and Monetary Stabilization*, University of Chicago, January 29, 193-253

Fisher, I. (1932b), *Booms and Depressions*, New York, Adelphi.

Fisher, I. (1933a), 'The debt-deflation theory of great depressions', *Econometrica*, **1**, 337-357.

Fisher, I. (1933b), *After Reflation, What?*, New York, Adelphi.

Fisher, I. (1933c), *Stamp Scrip*, New York, Adelphi.

Fisher, I. (1935), 'Fisher backs view recovery is near', *The New York Times*, May 24, 38.

Fisher, I. (1936), 'The depression, its causes and cures', *Abstracts of Papers Presented at the Research Conference on Economics and Statistics Held by the Cowles Commission for Research in Economics*, Colorado College Publication, General Series No. **28**, Study Series, No. 21, Colorado, CO, Colorado College, 104-107.

Fisher, I. (1945), *100 Per Cent Money*, 3rd ed., New Haven, CT, The City Printing

Company.

Laidler, D. (1991) *The Golden Age of the Quantity Theory*, Princeton, NJ, Princeton University Press.

Rogers, J.H. (1933), 'The absorption of bank credit', *Econometrica*, **1**, 119-129.

Steindl, F.G. (1995), *Monetary Interpretations of the Great Depression*, Ann Arbor, MI, University of Michigan Press.

Steindl, F.G. (1997), 'Was Fisher a practicing quantity theorist?' *Journal of the History of Economic Thought*, **19**, 241-60. Reprinted in J.M. Buchanan and B. Monissen, *The Economists' Vision, Essays in Modern Economic Perspectives*, Frankfurt, Campus Verlag, 209-226.

PART FIVE:
STATISTICS, ECONOMETRICS, AND INDEX NUMBERS

9. Irving Fisher's Contributions to Economic Statistics and Econometrics

John S. Chipman

I have valued statistics as an instrument to help fulfill one of the great ambitions of my life, namely, to do what I could toward making economics into a genuine science. – Irving Fisher (1947a)

1 INTRODUCTION

Irving Fisher was unusual among great economists in that he not only made lasting contributions to economic theory (particularly the theory of interest and of intertemporal economics in general), but he took care to confront his theories with the facts in a way that no economist had done before. In this chapter I have selected three of Fisher's contributions to this end. The first is his attempt to find a way to measure marginal utility from data on consumer demand in competitive markets. The second is his attempt to test the quantity theory of money. And the third is his pioneering work on disequilibrium dynamics, in particular, his method of relating cyclical fluctuations in output and employment to distributed lags of rates of inflation – thus providing quantitative confirmation of an important insight that goes back to Hume (1752).

As will become apparent in the following analysis, Fisher was not perfect. In the first of these investigations, ingenious as it was, he concluded that (with hypothetical data) a progressive income tax would be justified, whereas a contradiction between his assumptions and his hypothetical data brings to light the fact that had he made use of his implicit assumptions (in particular, the assumption that expenditure shares are independent of prices), his own analysis would have concluded that the optimal income tax was proportional. In the second of these investigations, somehow he overlooked, or allowed himself to overlook, the fact that his method of testing the equation of exchange violated his own 'factor reversal test' of index-number theory, so that he ended up testing whether a Laspeyres price index furnished a good approximation to a Paasche price index. In the third of these investigations, his

failure to predict and explain the downturn of output and employment in the
Great Depression appears to have been the result of his failure to believe in
his own theory, which turned out to explain the circumstances remarkably
well.

Can this be the work of a great economist? My answer is yes, for the following reasons. Fisher never played it safe. He stuck his neck out in ways that
few economists have dared to do. I think of my experience in the classroom:
the brightest students are those who dare to ask stupid questions. Fisher dared
to tackle the important issues, and he pursued them relentlessly, even though
often subjected to ridicule. Despite the errors that one can find in his work,
there was a steadfastness and courage in daring to pursue his ideas to their
logical conclusion that mark the truly original scientist. This, I think, will be
apparent in the analysis to follow.

2   MEASURING THE MARGINAL UTILITY OF MONEY

Approaching economics from the perspective of mechanics, Fisher in his
doctoral dissertation (1892) showed himself to be a firm believer in measurable utility. However, he strongly disagreed with the psychophysical argument used by Edgeworth (1881, p. 99): 'Just perceivable increments of pleasure are equatable'. Instead, Fisher countered:

> I have always felt that utility must be capable of a definition which shall connect it
> with its positive or objective commodity relations. A physicist would certainly err
> who defined the unit of force as the minimum sensible of muscular sensation.
>
> ...
>
> This foisting of Psychology on Economics seems to me *in*appropriate and vicious
> (1892, p. 5, emphasis in original).

He thus set himself the task of justifying the measurability of utility on the
basis of economic considerations alone.

He started out by stating that: 'The laws of economics are framed to explain
facts' (p. 11). The fallacy of equating utility with pleasure was exposed by the
example, 'the last dollar's worth of sugar (we are told) represents the same
quantity of pleasurable feeling as the last dollar's worth of dentistry'. Instead
of pleasure, he argued, the correct criterion was 'desire', and this was to be
inferred simply from the 'economic act of choice'.

The basis of Fisher's construction is the hypothesis of *independence* of
commodities in the sense that the consumer's utility function has the additively separable representation

$$U(q_1, q_2, ..., q_n) = \sum_{i=1} u_i(q_i),$$ (9.1)

where q_i is the quantity consumed of commodity i . This implies that the marginal utility of any commodity depends on the quantity of that commodity alone, i.e., $\partial U / \partial q_i = u_i'(q_i)$. Fisher proceeded to argue that on this hypothesis it would be possible to measure utility, in the sense that, given an arbitrary value for $u_1'(q_1^1)$, then for any other q_1, say q_1^2 one could determine the value of $u_1'(q_1^2)$, i.e., one could determine the *ratio* of marginal utilities $u_1'(q_1^1) / u_1'(q_1^2)$. His argument for this was, however, very perplexing. He proceeded as follows, where 'utility' means 'marginal utility' unless preceded by the adjective 'total', and 'infinitesimal utility' means the same as 'marginal utility':

> Our first problem is to find the ratio of two infinitesimal utilities. If an individual I consumes 100 loaves of bread in a year the utility ... of the last *loaf* is (presumably) greater than what it would be if he consumed 150 loaves. What is their *ratio*? It is found by contrasting the utilities of the 100th and 150th loaves with a third utility. This third utility is that of oil (say) of which let B gallons be consumed by I during the year. Let β be that infinitesimal or small increment of B whose utility shall equal that of the 100th loaf (1892, pp. 10-11, emphasis in original).

Already there is a problem. Let us say that the marginal utility of the 100th loaf of bread is $u_1'(100)$ and that of the Bth gallon of oil $u_2'(B)$. Fisher does not define B units of oil as that number whose marginal utility is equal to that of 100 loaves of bread; rather, the quantity B is apparently chosen independently (prices are not mentioned), and it must be $B + \Delta B = B + \beta$ whose marginal utility is equal to that of 100 loaves of bread; but there is no reason why β should be 'small' – and it would be 'infinitesimal' only if $u_2'(B) = u_1'(100)$. Fisher continues:

> Now in substituting the hypothesis of 150 loaves *let us not permit our individual to alter B,* his consumption of oil. The utility of the 150th loaf will be pronounced by him equal (say) to the utility of $\frac{1}{2}\beta$. Then the utility of the 150th loaf is said to be half the utility of the 100th (emphasis in original).

But on what basis can our individual 'pronounce' that the marginal utility of 150 loaves of bread is equal to $\frac{1}{2}\beta$? Already there is a confusion: the marginal utility of the 100th loaf of bread is now said to be β , and that of the 150th $\frac{1}{2}\beta$, whereas β was previously defined as *that increment in $q_2 = B$* whose marginal utility is equal to that of the 100th loaf of bread. Further, so long as u_1' and u_2' are decreasing functions, obviously a *larger* increment in q_2 (say 2β) would be needed in order for $u_2'(B + 2\beta) = u_1'(150)$.[1] A continuation of Fisher's text confirms the basic confusion:

That is, if:

ut. of 100th loaf = ut. of β, B being the total,

and   ut. of 150th loaf = ut. of $\beta/2$, B being the total again,

the ratio is defined:

$$\frac{\text{ut. of 100th loaf}}{\text{ut. of 150th loaf}} = \frac{\beta}{\beta/2} = 2.$$

Thus, 'ut. of β' in the first displayed formula is replaced by 'β' in the second, and 'ut. of $\beta/2$' is replaced by '$\beta/2$' in the second. Perhaps the ambiguity in the phrase 'the utility of $\frac{1}{2}\beta$' is what led Fisher astray; it could mean either '$u_2'(B + \frac{1}{2}\beta)$' or 'the utility to the amount of $\frac{1}{2}\beta$'. But it is curious indeed that one who argued so strongly in favor of the precision of mathematical statements should in this case have allowed his mathematics to be corrupted by ambiguities of language.

Two separate aspects of 'measurability' need to be kept in mind in connection with Fisher's problem. One is that the additively separable form of the utility function (9.1) is invariant with respect to linear transformations; that is, if $W(q) = F(U(q))$, where F is a monotone increasing function, then $\partial W / \partial q_1 \partial q_2 = 0$ if and only if F is linear. On the other hand, the question of the magnitude of the ratio $u_1'(q_1^1) / u_1'(q_1^2)$ has to do with the particular functional form specified for $u_1(q_1)$, and this is a separate question. One possible form is $u_1(q_1) = \alpha_1 \log q_1$, yielding $u_1'(q_1^1) / u_1'(q_1^2) = q_1^2 / q_1^1$; another is $w_1(q_1) = \alpha_1 q_1^\rho$ where $0 < \rho < 1$, yielding $w_1'(q_1^1) / w_1'(q_1^2) = (q_1^2 / q_1^1)^{1-\rho}$; these are related by the transformation $w_1(q_1) = \alpha_1(\exp\{u_1(q_1)\})^{\rho/\alpha_1}$, which is certainly not linear. The problem of finding the right functional form for each $u_i(q_i)$ – given the hypothesis (9.1) – is essentially the integrability problem of utility theory (specialized to this case), and for this one needs data on prices and demand functions. In thinking that it was possible to measure marginal utility without any data on prices and consumers' choices in competitive markets, Fisher went quite far astray.

One might have expected this subject to come up again in Fisher's 'little treatise' on the calculus (1897) which appeared five years later; but most of the illustrations in that book were from physics.[2] In his elementary textbook (1912) there was a thorough treatment of the principle that '*the market price of any good is equal to the ratio between its marginal desirability* [read: marginal utility] *and the marginal desirability of money for each and every buyer*' (p. 295, emphasis in original) – but no attempt to show how this 'desirability' could be measured.

We may surmise that Fisher became unconvinced by his own 1892 argument and sought a method of measuring utility on the basis of observed data on quantities purchased at various prices and incomes. This is the problem he set himself in his contribution to the Clark volume (Fisher, 1927b).[3]

Fisher (1927b) furnished an illustration of how one could measure the marginal utility of income ('money') of identical consumers whose preferences for two or more commodities could be represented by the additively separable utility function (9.1) where $u_i'(q_i) > 0$ and $u_i''(q_i) < 0$ for $i = 1, 2,...,n$. He assumed in his illustration that there were sets of observations on two prices p_1^t, p_2^t, income Y^t, and two expenditure shares $\theta_i^t = p_i^t q_i^t / Y^t (i = 1,2)$ for $t = 1, 2, 3$ (in fact, a subset of these, as will be made clear). Observation set 2 was interpreted as that of a family in 'Evenland', used as a 'yardstick' (p. 159) or 'measuring rod' (p. 166), while observation sets 1 and 3 were interpreted as drawn from 'Oddland' in such a way that, prices differing as between the two countries, family incomes were such that family 1 in Oddland consumed the same amount of food, and family 3 in Oddland the same amount of housing, as family 2 in Evenland (I shall identify food and housing as commodities 1 and 2 respectively).

Setting marginal utilities proportional to prices we have

$$\frac{\partial}{\partial q_i^t} U(q_1^t, q_2^t,...,q_n^t) = u_i'(q_i^t) = \omega^t p_i^t, \tag{9.2}$$

where ω^t is the marginal utility of income of family t. Further, defining the demand functions by $q_i = h_i(p, Y)$, where $p = (p_1, p_2,..., p_n)$, the share of commodity i in the consumer's expenditure (assumed equal to income) is defined as

$$\theta_i^t = \frac{p_i^t q_i^t}{Y^t} = \frac{p_i^t h_i(p^t, Y^t)}{Y^t}. \tag{9.3}$$

The quantities demanded are therefore obtained from[4]

$$q_i^t = h_i(p^t, Y^t) = \frac{\theta_i^t Y^t}{p_i^t}. \tag{9.4}$$

Observation set 2 consists of data from family 2 in Evenland on all five variables $p_1^2, p_2^2, \theta_1^2, \theta_2^2$, and Y^2, hence q_1^2 and q_2^2. Data are assumed available from family 1 in Oddland on p_1^1 and θ_1^1 (but not p_2^1, θ_2^1, or Y^1), and from family 3 in Oddland on p_2^3 and θ_2^3 (but not p_1^3, θ_1^3, or Y^3). Since it is assumed that the special hypothesis

$$q_1^1 = q_1^2 \text{ and } q_2^2 = q_2^3 \tag{9.5}$$

holds, it follows of course from (9.4) that

$$\frac{\theta_1^1 Y^1}{p_1^1} = \frac{\theta_1^2 Y^2}{p_1^2} \text{ and } \frac{\theta_2^2 Y^2}{p_2^2} = \frac{\theta_2^3 Y^3}{p_2^3}. \tag{9.6}$$

From (9.5) and the assumption of identical preferences it follows immediately that

$$u_1'(q_1^1) = u_1'(q_1^2) \quad \text{and} \quad u_2'(q_2^2) = u_2'(q_2^3),$$

hence by (9.2),

$$\omega^1 p_1^1 = \omega^2 p_1^2 \quad \text{and} \quad \omega^2 p_2^2 = \omega^3 p_2^3. \tag{9.7}$$

Now, given the additively separable form of the utility function (9.1), we have from (9.2),

$$\omega^2 = \frac{u_1'(q_1^2)}{p_1^2} = \frac{u_2'(q_2^2)}{p_2^2}, \tag{9.8}$$

and this marginal utility is taken by Fisher as *numéraire*, hence equations (9.7) and (9.6) constitute four equations in the four unknowns ω^1, ω^3, Y^1, and Y^3, which are easily solved to obtain

$$\omega^1 = \omega^2 \frac{p_1^2}{p_1^1} \quad \text{and} \quad \omega^3 = \omega^2 \frac{p_2^2}{p_2^3} \tag{9.9}$$

and

$$Y^1 = \frac{\theta_1^2 p_1^1}{\theta_1^1 p_1^2} Y^2 \quad \text{and} \quad Y^3 = \frac{\theta_2^2 p_2^3}{\theta_2^3 p_2^2} Y^2. \tag{9.10}$$

From (9.9) and (9.10) as well as data on Y^2 and the arbitrary choice of ω^2, one can interpolate a curve through the points (Y^t, ω^t), $t = 1, 2, 3$, to obtain the marginal utility of income as a function of income.

While Fisher's method is ingenious, it is rather strange, since conditions (9.5) are completely gratuitous – one would never expect to find them fulfilled unless the prices and family incomes in the two countries were experimentally chosen precisely to achieve this outcome.[5] On the other hand, the assumption that data on p_2^1, θ_2^1, and Y^1, as well as p_1^3, θ_1^3, and Y^3 are missing seems equally artificial. Let us consider, however, what Fisher does with the above assumptions.

First let us examine precisely how Fisher justified taking ω^2 as given. Before quoting his text it is necessary to comment on his terminology. The expression 'marginal utility' appears in the title of his paper in quotation marks, since it was a terminology of which he had come to disapprove (cf. Fisher, 1918a). Being a staunch prohibitionist, he was unwilling to describe a person's preference for alcohol by any term that conveyed the suggestion of usefulness. He thus replaced 'marginal utility' of a commodity by 'want-for-one-more-unit' of the commodity, and 'marginal utility of money' by 'want-for-one-more-dollar'. 'Marginal utility' generally was referred to as 'wantability', and the unit of measurement of utility was called a 'wantab'; in his words (1927b, p. 164):

> To coin a word, we may call this latter unit [one unit of ω^2] a 'wantab' (which may be regarded as an abbreviation either of 'wantability', or of 'want tab' (i.e. a unit for keeping tab on the strength of a want).

Returning now to equations (9.6) and (9.7), but replacing Fisher's notation by the above, we have in his words (p. 171):

> What has been done is to solve these four equations to obtain the four unknowns $\omega^1, \omega^3, Y^1, Y^3$, assuming Y^2 and ω^2 as known, the former in dollars and the latter being, for convenience, taken as the standard for measuring wantability since no other unit has previously been established.

Let us then take ω^2 in (9.8) as a fixed number, say $\omega^2 = 1$; then the remaining two ω' are obtained from (9.9). To find how they relate to income one must evaluate (9.10). Here we must note how Fisher supposes the θ_i' to be obtained. Regarding θ_1^2 he states (p. 167):

> This percentage is readily found from the budget tables. Suppose it to be 50%. That is, the budget tables of Evenland show that in a family there which has an income and annual expenditure of only $600, 50% thereof is spent for food.

Likewise for θ_1^1 (p. 168):

> The family budget tables in Oddland show, let us say, that a family which spends $400 for food is one which spends thereon 40% of its total expenditure; that is, $\theta_1^1 = .4$.

What these two quotations show is that Fisher is making the implicit assumption that the share of a commodity in total expenditure depends on that total expenditure only, independently of the prices; but since the shares $\theta_i(p,Y)$ must be homogeneous of degree 0, it follows that they are also independent of total expenditure (income), that is, constant. It follows in turn from this that (9.1) must be of the loglinear type

$$U(q) = a\sum_{i=1}^{n}\theta_i \log q_i, \text{ where } a > 0, \ 0 < \theta_i < 1, \text{ and } \sum_{i=1}^{n}\theta_i = 1. \tag{9.11}$$

This is proved in the following theorem, which may be skipped by the reader interested only in the result.

THEOREM: Let a system of demand functions $q_i = h_i(p,Y)$ be generated by maximizing an additively separable utility function (9.1) subject to the budget constraint $\sum_{i=1}^{n}p_i q_i = Y$, and suppose the expenditure shares

$\theta_i(p,Y) = p_i h_i(p,Y)/Y$ are constants, θ_i. Then the utility function (9.1) has the form (9.11). Furthermore, the marginal utility of income has the form

$$\omega(p,Y) = \frac{a}{Y}. \tag{9.12}$$

PROOF: From the demand functions $h_i(p,Y) = \theta_i Y / p_i$ we have the indirect utility function

$$V(p,Y) = U[h(p,Y)] = \sum_{i=1}^{n} u_i\left(\frac{\theta_i Y}{p_i}\right). \tag{T.1}$$

Applying the Antonelli-Allen-Roy partial differential equation $\partial V / \partial p_j = -h_j \partial V / \partial Y$ we obtain

$$-u_j'\left(\frac{\theta_j Y}{p_j}\right)\frac{\theta_j Y}{p_j^2} = -\frac{\theta_j Y}{p_j}\sum_{i=1}^{n} u_i'\left(\frac{\theta_i Y}{p_i}\right)\frac{\theta_i}{p_i}.$$

Cancelling like terms from both sides and introducing the transformation of variables $p_j = \theta_j Y / q_j$, this becomes

$$u_j'(q_j)q_j = \theta_j \sum_{i=1}^{n} u_i'(q_i)q_i. \tag{T.2}$$

Now differentiating this equation with respect to q_k for $k \neq j$, we obtain

$$0 = \theta_j[u_k'(q_k) + q_k u_k''(q_k)], \quad \text{hence} \quad \frac{d \log u_k'(q_k)}{d \log q_k} = \frac{q_k u_k''(q_k)}{u_k'(q_k)} = -1$$

Since j was arbitrary, this must hold for every $k = 1, 2,...,n$. Integrating this equation we get

$$u_k'(q_k) = \alpha_k / q_k \text{ for } \alpha_k > 0, \tag{T.3}$$

and integrating once again gives

$$u_k(q_k) = \alpha_k \log q_k + \text{constant} \ (\alpha_k > 0). \tag{T.4}$$

Substituting (T.3) into (T.2) for $k = j$ we see that

$$\alpha_j = a\theta_j \text{ where } a = \sum_{i=1}^{n}\alpha_i.$$

Consequently, substituting (T.4) into (9.1) but ignoring the superfluous constant term, we obtain the sought result. Likewise, substituting (T.4) into (T.1) we obtain $\omega(p,Y) = \partial V(p,Y)/\partial Y = a/Y$. Q.E.D.

This implication of constant expenditure shares (combined with his assumption of identical tastes within and between Oddland and Evenland) is in fact violated by Fisher's numbers, which show $\theta_1^2 = 0.5 > 0.4 = \theta_1^1$ (likewise $\theta_2^2 = 0.20 < 0.25 = \theta_2^3$) in Table 9.1 below. Likewise, (9.12) shows that $\omega' Y^t = a - a$ property not satisfied by Table 9.2 below.

The following table displays the numerical values assumed by Fisher:

Table 9.1: Values assumed by Fisher for the prices, income, expenditure shares, and marginal utility of income

t	p_1^t	p_2^t	Y^t	θ_1^t	θ_2^t	ω^t
1	4/3			0.4		
2	1	1	600	0.5	0.20	1
3		3			0.25	

From these values we fill in $\omega^1 = 3/4$ and $\omega^3 = 1/3$ from (9.9) and $Y^1 = 1000$ and $Y^3 = 1440$ from (9.10). This allowed Fisher to draw a curve through the points (Y^t, ω^t) given by the following completed table for these variables:

Table 9.2: Values implied by Fisher's assumptions of income and the marginal utility of income in the three observation sets

t	Y^t	ω^t
2	600	1.00
1	1000	0.75
3	1440	$0.33\frac{1}{3}$

(1927b, p. 170, Chart II, except that Fisher shows only the curve through the last two of these points).

Although Fisher did not explicitly mention it, his method also allows measurement of the marginal utilities of the individual commodities, provided additional data are available. From formula (9.2), it is clear that to obtain these measurements one must infer what the missing price data must have been in order to bring about condition (9.5). If data were available on q_2^1 and θ_2^1 one could infer p_2^1, and similarly if data were available on q_1^3 and θ_1^3 one could infer p_1^3. Then one could tabulate pairs $(q_i^t, u_i'(q_i^t)) = (q_i^t, \omega^t p_i^t)$ for $t = 1, 2, 3$ and interpolate a marginal utility function, and in particular determine $u_i'(q_i^1) / u_i'(q_i^2)$ provided $q_i^1 \neq q_i^2$, thus solving the problem he posed in 1892.

There is one aspect of Fisher's model that I have not mentioned, in order to avoid mixing up pure theory and the problem of aggregation. Fisher thought of the price variables in the above analysis as *price indices* of groups of commodities. With statistical application in view, this is only reasonable. But he did not comment on the difficulties that might be faced in formulating the pure theory in terms of aggregates. On the other hand, he did use aggregation as a way of defending his hypothesis of independent marginal utilities. Thus (1927b, p. 176), he considered it reasonable to assume that there were no substitutes or complements (in the intuitive sense of positive or negative signs of $\partial^2 U / \partial q_i \partial q_j (i \neq j)$) *between* the food group and housing group, etc., while this would not apply *within* groups.

Another aspect of Fisher's model that requires comment is that, while it is described as a 'statistical method', it is not statistical in the usual meaning of the term, since it has exactly enough observations to estimate the parameters and no more; in other words, the model has zero degrees of freedom. In contemporary terminology it would be described as a method of 'calibration' rather than 'estimation'. Fisher himself used the term 'triangulation' to describe his procedure (1927b, p. 187). In fact on several occasions he stated that he considered Frisch's procedure (1926, 1932) superior to his own; cf. Fisher (1930a, p. 238; 1933b, p. 11; 1941, p. 190). And there is no doubt that he would have approved heartily the modern progress that has been attained in estimating systems of demand functions.

The third aspect of Fisher's model that deserves comment is the objective he proposed of 'testing the justice of a progressive income tax'. Since the time of Robbins (1938), the economics profession has been fairly reticent about making interpersonal comparisons of utility. These were made unabashedly by Fisher, on the ground that 'philosophic doubt is right and proper, but the problems of life cannot, and do not, wait' (1927b, p. 180).

In comparing satisfactions among different families, Fisher (unwittingly or not) found himself foisting psychology on economics in a way that he had previously characterized as 'inappropriate and vicious'. He argued (1927b, p. 175) that 'it seems reasonable to assume that [two families'] psychological reactions to the same 'physical' food rations, or to the same 'physical' housing accomodation will be the same'. Again (1927b, p. 180):

> By common sense we cut our gordian knots. We may not know really what goes on in the mind of a dog, but practically we can tell by his behavior when he is hungry, or pleased. We have somehow learned to interpret the wagging of his tail, and the sound of his bark. Even more have we learned to interpret the feelings of another human being.

A return to Fisher's approach may be said to have been made by Samuelson (1947) (but not with Fisher's special assumptions) in his positing of a social welfare function. Fisher's *principle of equal sacrifice* (1927b, p. 186), which assumed that 'taxes are small so as not appreciably to affect the income and the want-for-one-more-dollar' (an assumption that could not be accepted today), entailed that for two different families in Oddland, their sacrifices $\omega^1 \tau_1 Y^1$ and $\omega^3 \tau_3 Y^3$ must be equal, where τ_i is the proportionate tax on income (strictly speaking, expenditure) Y^i. By a series of simple deductions from (9.9) and (9.10) (pp. 184-186) he was able to arrive at the second equality of the following formula:

$$\frac{\tau_3}{\tau_1} = \frac{\omega^1 Y^1}{\omega^3 Y^3} = \frac{\theta_1^2 / \theta_1^1}{\theta_2^2 / \theta_2^3}. \qquad (9.13)$$

From the third term in (9.13) he was able to compute, as we see from Table 9.1,

$$\frac{\theta_1^2 / \theta_1^1}{\theta_2^2 / \theta_2^3} = \frac{0.5 / 0.4}{0.20 / 0.25} = 1.5625.$$

Thus, he concluded:

> By formula [9.13] we can now find the theoretically just rate of progression (or regression, as the case may be) of an income tax. This formula gives, in our hypothetical example, 1.56. Thus, if out of $Y^1 = \$1000$, a tax of 1%, or $10 is paid, then out of $Y^3 = \$1440$ a tax of 1.56% or $22.46 should be paid (instead of $14.40 as would be the case under proportional taxation).

What, however, would Fisher have concluded if instead of using the right-most expression of (9.13) he had used the middle expression? Consulting Table 9.2 we see that

$$\frac{\omega^1 Y^1}{\omega^3 Y^3} = \frac{600}{480} = 1.25.$$

What can account for this contradiction?

The formula (9.13) is certainly correct. Therefore, some of the numbers in Tables 9.1 and 9.2 must be incorrect! Recalling the above discussion, we may conclude that the error committed by Fisher was in choosing the expenditure shares θ_i^j arbitrarily when by his own assumptions they were independent of the prices, and therefore (from homogeneity), also independent of income, hence constant. It is indeed surprising that Fisher did not check whether the second equality in his formula (9.13) was satisfied by his own numbers. From the above discussion it follows that $\theta_1^2 = \theta_1^1$ and $\theta_2^2 = \theta_2^3$, hence both numerator and denominator are equal to unity, and the fraction is equal to unity. Therefore, on Fisher's own (implicit) assumptions, the optimal tax is neither progressive nor regressive, but proportional!

3 TESTING THE QUANTITY THEORY OF MONEY

Central to Fisher's concerns throughout his career were (1) the scientific problem of explaining variations in the purchasing power of money, or its reciprocal, the 'price level' or 'cost of living' and (2) the policy problem of stabilizing the above. A curious feature of his writings is that, although they took place during the same period, there was a notable lack of integration between these two endeavors. I shall start with the first.

In Fisher (1911b, 1911c, 1913d) we have the formulation of the scientific problem. It starts with the basic 'equation of exchange' first written in the form

$$M'V' + M''V'' = \sum_{i=1}^{n} p_i^t q_i^t \tag{9.14}$$

where M' denotes the quantity of 'money' (hand-to-hand currency) and V' its velocity of circulation, both at time t (I have added the time superscripts), M'' denotes the quantity of deposits in checking accounts and V'' their velocity of circulation, both at time t, and p_i^t and q_i^t denote the price and quantity traded of commodity i at time t.[6] It must be kept in mind that although Marshall (1891) had introduced the concept of 'national dividend', it was not until Kuznets's researches in the 1930s, culminating in his monograph (Kuznets, 1941), that there were any data available on national income or product, hence Fisher's equation of exchange (9.14) referred to the sum total of transactions including those in intermediate goods and financial securities.

Fisher's first task was to obtain data on the two stock variables M' and M'' and the two flow variables $M'V'$ and $M''V''$; V' and V'' were estimated by taking the quotient of the flow variables and the corresponding stock variables. If t stands for a year, $M''V''$ was estimated by the total of checks drawn in year t, it being assumed that 'each check circulates against goods once and but once' (Fisher, 1911c, 1913d, p. 282). $M'V'$ was estimated by means of a very careful graph-theoretic analysis of the flows of money to and from (as well as within) three groups – commercial depositors, other depositors, and non-depositors (chiefly wage-earners) – using the 'reservoir principle' (1909, pp. 611-612) that the net outflow of a reservoir 'must equal the net decrease in its contents during the same time' (this latter being judged to be relatively small). He divided $M'V'$ into eight components for which he provided rough statistical estimates, and came to the conclusion that the first two, constituting 95% of the total, formed a good 'first approximation'; these were (1) all money deposited and (2) money expenditures of non-depositors. He then concluded that V' could be estimated on the assumption that money paid in wages circulates twice but that all but a small percentage of the remaining stock of money circulates only once (1909, p. 615; 1911c, 1913d, pp. 287-288, 473).

Fisher's second task was to replace the right side of (9.14) by a product of a price index and a quantity index. As he made clear in the Appendix to Chapter X of *The Purchasing Power of Money* (1911c, 1913d, pp. 385-429), these indices should satisfy the condition that their product be equal to the total value. This principle was stressed again in his *Making of Index Numbers* where it was referred to as the 'factor reversal test' (1922, p. 72), and elaborated in a subsequent study under the appellation 'total value criterion' (1927c). Thus, he stated (1911c, 1913d, p. 385):[7] 'Each form of price index, P', applicable to the equation of exchange, implies a correlative trade index, T', such that the product of the two is equal to $\sum p'q'$, the right side of the equation of exchange.' Further (p. 386):

Conversely any particular formula for T' implies a correlative form for P'. For, since

$$P'T' = \sum p'q',$$

it follows that

$$P' = \frac{\sum p'q'}{T'}.$$

By means of this equation, if we have given any particular formula for T', we may obtain a resultant particular formula for P'.

...

As [an] example illustrating the derivation of the formula for P' from a given formula for T', let T' be defined as $\sum p^0 q'$; then

$$P' = \frac{\sum p'q'}{T'} = \frac{\sum p'q'}{\sum p^0 q'}.$$

Here, the formula for the index of trade, $T' = \sum p^0 q'$, is the numerator of a Laspeyres quantity index, and the above formula for P' is of course that of a Paasche price index. While the names Laspeyres and Paasche were not yet attached to these formulae by Fisher (1911c, 1913d) – although the attribution had long before been made by Walsh (1901, p. 99) – the distinction between the two concepts was certainly very clear to him.

The data used by Fisher for the volume of trade T_0' were expressed in 'billions of dollars at the prices of 1909' (1911c, 1913d, p. 290; cf. pp. 478-486); thus, the formula he used for the volume of trade in year t may be expressed as

$$T_0^t = \sum_{i=1}^n p_i^0 q_i^t,\tag{9.15}$$

where $t = 0$ corresponds to the base year 1909. According to his principles, the correlative price index should therefore be the Paasche price index

$$P_t^t = \frac{\sum_{i=1}^n p_i^t q_i^t}{\sum_{i=1}^n p_i^0 q_i^t}.\tag{9.16}$$

This satisfies

$$\sum_{i=1}^n p_i^t q_i^t = \frac{\sum_{i=1}^n p_i^t q_i^t}{\sum_{i=1}^n p_i^0 q_i^t} \cdot \sum_{i=1}^n p_i^0 q_i^t = P_t^t T_0^t,\tag{9.17}$$

hence Fisher's equation of exchange (9.14) becomes

$$M'V' + M''V'' = P_t^t T_0^t.\tag{9.18}$$

Fisher's procedure for testing the quantity theory of money, following Kemmerer (1907), was to compute a time series for the variable

$$\frac{M'V' + M''V''}{T_0^t},\tag{9.19}$$

which of course is an estimate of the Paasche price index (9.16), and compare it with an independent price-index series. Unlike his description of the construction of the index of trade, Fisher's description of his method for calculating the price index was quite vague. He stated (1913d, p. 486): 'The table in the text for index numbers is taken from the last column of the table on page 487.'[8] The data in the last column of this table are a rebasing to 1909 of a weighted average of three series: wholesale prices for 258 commodities obtained from the United States Labor Bureau, wages per hour obtained from the *Bulletin of the Bureau of Labor*, and prices of forty stocks obtained from Wesley C. Mitchell, 'The Prices of American Stocks, 1890-1909', *Journal of Political Economy*, May 1910, the weights being 30:1:3. No mention was made by Fisher of the method of constructing the component price indices, but from the subsequent discussion in Fisher (1920, p. 4) it may be assumed that at least the first one was a Laspeyres price index. Consequently, we may assume that the price index with which Fisher compared (9.19) was a Laspeyres index, which may be written as

$$P_0^t = \frac{\sum_{i=1}^n p_i^t q_i^0}{\sum_{i=1}^n p_i^0 q_i^0}.\tag{9.20}$$

Thus, Fisher's method of testing the quantity theory of money consisted in seeing how well a Paasche price index (9.16) is approximated by a Laspeyres price index (9.20)! It seems inconceivable, given the precise attention he paid to the need to choose a price index of a 'correlative form' to the chosen quantity index, that Fisher was unaware of this inconsistency. He could have pointed out the inconsistency and pleaded that the relevant Paasche price-index series were not available; but instead he seems to have papered over the inconsistency, hoping perhaps that the reader would not notice it.[9]

There are other discrepancies between the price-index series that Fisher chose to compare. While wages and stock prices were included in the price index, labor and securities were not included in the series for the volume of trade. The price index P_0^t rose by 58% from 1896 to 1909 whereas the estimated price index P_t^t rose by 85% during the same period (1911c, 1913d, p. 293); since there is a theoretical presumption that a Laspeyres price index will rise faster than a Paasche price index,[10] the reversal of this relationship further detracts from the confidence that one may place in Fisher's calculations.

There is of course another severe objection that can be raised to Fisher's procedure, namely that the equation of exchange (9.18) – as Haberler (1924) was subsequently to point out in his criticism of a similar formulation by Schumpeter (1918) – is a mere tautology. If the data correctly cover the indicated variables, the equation should hold identically; any departure from equality can only be attributed to measurement error. But Fisher went even beyond this, to fit not this tautology to the data, but to fit *a bad approximation of this tautology* to the data! To be sure, Fisher was well aware of the objection that (9.18) was a tautology, but defended himself in the following terms (1911c, 1913d, p. 157):

> One of the objectors to the quantity theory attempts to dispose of the equation of exchange ... by calling it a mere truism. While the equation of exchange is, if we choose, a mere 'truism', based on the equivalence, in all purchases, of the money or checks expended, on the one hand, and what they buy, on the other, yet in view of supplementary knowledge as to the relation of M to M', and the non-relation of M to V, V', and the Q's, this equation is the means of demonstrating the fact that normally the p's vary directly as M, that is, demonstrating the quantity theory. 'Truisms' should never be neglected. The greatest generalizations of physical science, such as that forces are proportional to mass and acceleration, are truisms, but, when duly supplemented by specific data, these truisms are the most fruitful sources of useful mechanical knowledge.

One can agree with this and still raise the question, does a truism require empirical verification, and the 'supplementary knowledge' not require it? The equation of exchange is consistent, for example, with the possibility (during a period of unemployment and excess reserves) of an exogenous rise in the volume of trade bringing about an increase in M'; in fact, the events leading to Fisher's subsequent proposal for 100% money (1935b) suggest that the 'supplementary knowledge' could have benefited from more systematic empirical study.

In what is perhaps Fisher's last published work (1947b), he challenged 'the idea that the velocity of the circulation of money has no theoretical principle behind it' and expressed the opinion that (p.173):

> there is no other situation in the whole economic realm that is subject to so much adjustment and readjustment as the cash balance in relation to its use. This adjustment seeks to make the marginal utility of each person's cash balance equal to the marginal utility of its outflow. In other words, the numerator and denominator, constituting the velocity ratio, must for equilibrium have an equality of marginal utilities.

He proceeded to further develop his 1909 approach to the statistical estimation of various velocity concepts.

I turn now to the relation between Fisher's scientific investigations and the policy recommendations he proposed for stabilization of the price level. These latter are contained in his proposal for a 'compensated dollar' (1913a-c, 1918b) culminating in his *Stabilizing the Dollar* (1920). This book, calling to mind a similar claim by Gossen (1854), forecast (pp. xxv-xxvi) that 'there is coming, slowly but surely, a revolution in economic thought similar to the revolution in astronomic thought begun by Copernicus' owing to the fact that we now possess 'in the "index number" of prices the necessary instrument for measuring the value of the dollar in terms of its power to purchase goods'. His proposal was that in each month, say, the level of the index number would be used to change the amount of gold the government would give or take for a gold certificate. A fixed market basket corresponding to the weights in the price index would retain a fixed value.

Leaving aside the disadvantage later pointed out by Haberler (1927, 1929) and Frisch (1936) that the Laspeyres price index overestimates the true rise in the cost of living, Fisher's scheme assumes that there is a determinate relationship between the stock of money (defined in his case as currency) and the price level. This is what is usually considered to be the quantity theory of money, as opposed to Fisher's formula which replaces the stock of money (M) by the quantity $(MV + M'V')/T$. In his *Stabilizing the Dollar* Fisher in fact adhered to the theory in the first sense, saying (1920, p. xxxii): 'The price level fluctuates largely with the fluctuation in the quantity of money', and displaying a graph (p. 31) exhibiting the quantity of 'money in circulation and in banks', and the 'index number of [prices of] responsive commodities' between 1914 and 1919 (but not providing data sources), and remarking that 'changes in the price level [seem] usually to follow changes in the quantity of money one to three months later'. As far as I know, this is the only attempt on Fisher's part to confront the quantity theory of money (as usually understood) with empirical evidence. But Fisher adopted a strange terminology, as the following passage indicates (1920, pp. 215-216):

> The impression that the plan is dependent on acceptance of the quantity theory of money is presumably due to the fact that I have espoused that theory (in a modified form) in my *Purchasing Power of Money*. But there is nothing in the plan itself which could not be accepted equally well by those who reject the quantity theory altogether. On the contrary, ... the plan should seem even simpler to those who do not accept the quantity theory but believe that a direct relationship exists between the purchasing power of the dollar and the bullion from which it is made, than to believers in the quantity theory.
>
> It will be clear to any one who follows the reasoning and explanations in this book, that the only money theory assumed is that common to all theories, and accepted universally; namely, that a large quantity of gold will buy more goods than a small quantity ... and that an increase of gold in a dollar will, somehow, increase the dollar's purchasing power. As to the exact process by which this acknowledged result is attained we need have no concern.

A clearer idea of what Fisher meant by the quantity theory may be obtained by considering the distinction he made between comparative statics and dynamics. Regarding the first, he stated:

> We have emphasized the fact that the strictly proportional effect on prices of an increase in M is only the *normal* or *ultimate* effect after transition periods are over. The proposition that prices vary with money holds true only in comparing two imaginary periods for each of which prices are stationary or are moving alike upward or downward and at the same rate (1911c, 1913d, p. 159, emphasis in original).

Fisher's principal concern, however, was with transition periods in which a rise in M would bring about, in addition to a rise in M', a rise in T and increases in V and V', leading to a more than proportionate rise in the price level, P. His analysis was based on the theory developed in his earlier works (1896, 1907) relating interest rates to price changes. Thus, he argued (1911c, 1913d, pp. 55ff.) that the initial effect of an increase in the money supply (M) was to cause banks to increase their loans (M'), which would put upward pressure on commodity markets and therefore raise prices; however, since rents and wages are set on a contractual basis, profits will increase more than proportionately to prices, and businesses will be stimulated to increase their activities. Most important of all, the real rate of interest

$$r = \frac{1+i}{1+\dot{P}/P} - 1 \approx i - \frac{\dot{P}}{P}, \tag{9.21}$$

(where i is the nominal rate of interest, P is the price level, and $\dot{P} = dP/dt$ its rate of change over time) will have fallen, since the money rate of interest is sluggish, too, in adjusting upwards. In this, Fisher was of course influenced by Wicksell (1897, 1898). But this type of analysis actually goes as far back as Hume (1752, p. 50):

> A nation, whose money decreases, is actually, at that time, much weaker and more miserable, than another nation, who possesses no more money, but is on the encreasing hand. This will be easily accounted for, if we consider, that the alterations in the quantity of money, either on the one side or the other, are not immediately attended with proportionable alterations in the prices of commodities. There is always an interval before matters be adjusted to their new situation; and this interval is as pernicious to industry, when gold and silver are diminishing, as it is advantageous, when these metals are encreasing. The workman has not the same employment from the manufacturer and merchant; tho' he pays the same price for everything in the market. The farmer cannot dispose of his corn and cattle; tho' he must pay the same rent to his landlord.

The Hume-Wicksell-Fisher process just described is highly complex, since one has to account for the short-term changes in commodity prices resulting from the initial change in the money supply, as well as the gradual adjustment of factor prices to commodity prices and of the nominal interest rate to the rate of inflation. Perhaps Fisher found the challenge of formulating this entire model mathematically too daunting, and instead considered it more fruitful to study first the individual adjustment relationships themselves. Thus, if the driving force is the real interest rate r, then various adjustment variables such as the volume of trade (Fisher's T) and employment (E) may be postulated to vary inversely with (9.21), and these relationships may be studied empirically. In fact, this is just what Fisher did in the studies to be described in the next section.

4   THE DISTRIBUTED LAG OF REAL OUTPUT, EMPLOYMENT, AND INTEREST RATES BEHIND THE INFLATION RATE

Let R be any response variable such as T (volume of trade) or E (employment). If it depends inversely on (9.21), then it depends inversely on the nominal interest rate and directly on the rate of inflation, $\dot{P}/P$. Likewise, from (9.21) the nominal interest rate, i, will vary directly with the rate of inflation. Fisher in his series of fourteen studies (1923b, 1924, 1925, 1926a, 1926b, 1927a, 1930b, 1931, 1932, 1933a, 1933d, 1935a, 1936a,b, 1937) investigated the relationships of the above three variables to the rate of inflation; he mentioned (1931, p. 154) that a similar study of the influence of the nominal interest rate would be 'well worth doing', but this was never accomplished.

Fisher made the interesting comment (1925, p. 181n) that 'the idea of [using] the *rate of change* of the price level, or of its reciprocal, the purchasing power of the dollar, was emphasized in my *Appreciation and Interest* (1896). ... It was used by Prof. J. M. Clark (1917) ... .' I do not think he was claiming credit for Clark's 'acceleration principle'; Clark did not refer to Fisher (1896), nor did he discuss prices. I think that Fisher was simply struck by the analogy between Clark's model in which the rate of net investment varied as the *rate of change* of consumption, and his own in which the levels of 'trade' and employment varied as the *rate of change* of prices. If one of them could provide an explanation for turning-points in the business cycle (e.g., a slackening of the rate of growth of consumption leading to an actual decline in net investment, according to Clark), so of course could the other. In fact, the Fisher relationship is not subject to the criticism of Clark (1917) made by Frisch (1931) that the acceleration principle does not hold for *gross* investment, so it is rather curious that Fisher never specifically pointed out that his law could explain turning-points in the business cycle on the basis of slackening in the rate of change in the price level.[11] Perhaps it was his strong aversion to the concept of the 'business cycle' that prevented him from making the specific observation that a mere slackening of the rate of inflation would tend to depress output and employment, and a mere slackening in the rate of deflation would tend to stimulate output and employment.

The first of Fisher's series of studies affirmed (1923b, p. 1024) that 'the principal force affecting the cycle is the *real* rate of interest, the sum of the *money* rate of interest and the rate of appreciation (positive or negative) of the purchasing power of the dollar'. He then presented 'some preliminary findings as to one only of the two components of the real rate of interest, namely, ... the rapidity of fall (or rise) of the price level'. He exhibited a time series of the price level, P_t, on his favorite device, the 'ratio chart' (cf. Fisher, 1917), so that he could refer to the rate of inflation $P'_t = d \log P_t / dt = \dot{P}_t / P_t$ as the 'derivative' or 'slope' of this curve (1923b, pp. 1024-1025), with this logarithmic derivative plotted underneath using a difference rather than ratio scale. His method of measuring the rate of inflation statistically was explained in a footnote (p. 1026) as follows: 'found for each month by taking the two index numbers for the months following and preceding, dividing the former by the latter, and subtracting unity', i.e.,

$$P'_t = \frac{P_{t+1}}{P_{t-1}} - 1 = \frac{\Delta P_t + \Delta P_{t-1}}{P_{t-1}} = \frac{\Delta P_t}{P_{t-1}} + \frac{\Delta P_{t-1}}{P_{t-1}} \tag{9.22}$$

where $\Delta P_t = P_{t+1} - P_t$. This is a rather curious definition, when the definition

$$P_t' = \frac{P_{t+1}}{P_t} - 1 = \frac{P_t + \Delta P_t}{P_t} - 1 = \frac{\Delta P_t}{P_t},$$ (9.23)

would seem so much more natural as an approximation to the instantaneous percentage rate of change, or logarithmic derivative, $P_t' = \dot{P}_t / P_t = d \log P_t / dt$.

Fisher took as the dependent variable a series for the volume of trade T_t in month t, namely the business barometer of the American Telephone and Telegraph Company; the great innovation introduced in this paper was the formula

$$\overline{P}_t' = \sum_{i=0}^{n-1} w_i P_{t-i}' \text{ where } w_i = \frac{n-i}{(n+1)n/2}$$ (9.24)

of a distributed lag of past *rates of change* of the price level, the coefficients descending linearly by month (he took $n = 8$).[12] In his picturesque language, Fisher described $\overline{P}_t'$ as the 'dance of the dollar', and the dependent variable T_t as the 'dance of business'. He found a 79% correlation between T_t and $\overline{P}_t'$ over the period 1914-1922, using monthly observations. A graph in which the ordinates of $\overline{P}_t'$ were plotted four months ahead of those for T_t showed close agreement except for the months following the outbreak of the First World War in 1914 and the months preceding the entrance of the United States into the War in 1917, as well as the period from June 1921 to December 1922 which he attributed to the overly simple weighting scheme in the distributed lag, which he promised to modify 'according to probability principles' in future work.

In his second contribution (1924) Fisher replaced the linear weighting scheme of (9.24) by a 14-month scheme that was unimodal and very slightly skewed to the right, defined by the sequence of lag coefficients

(0, 2, 6, 11, 18, 23, 25, 23, 18, 12, 7, 4, 2, 1)

divided by their sum, 152, with mode 7 and mean 7.24, and replaced the AT&T series by the volume series that had recently been issued by the Harvard Committee on Economic Research (presumably this is Persons' (1923) series, not yet published when this paper was presented). The correlation for the period 1915-1922 was 86%; a very good fit was obtained for the period 1920-1922, with a correlation of 94.4%. The latter fit was depicted in a chart with the $\overline{P}_t'$ series magnified three times and 'projected ahead about seven months'. He promised continued improvements.

The definitive contribution in this series was the third (1925), which must be considered one of Fisher's finest and most brilliant works. Here, the terminology 'distributed lag' is first introduced (p. 183), and the lag distribution chosen 'which, among the many tried, best fits the facts' (p. 184), was the lognormal, yielding

$$\overline{P}_t' = \int_0^\infty l(w; \mu, \sigma^2) P_{1-w}' dw, \tag{9.25}$$

where

$$l(w; \mu, \sigma^2) = \frac{1}{w\sigma\sqrt{2\pi}} e^{-\frac{1}{2}(\log w - \mu)^2/\sigma^2} \tag{9.26}$$

is the density function of the (two-parameter) lognormal distribution of the random variable W, μ and σ^2 being the mean and variance of $X = \log W$ which has the corresponding normal density

$$n(x; \mu, \sigma^2) = \frac{1}{\sigma\sqrt{2\pi}} e^{-\frac{1}{2}(x-\mu)^2/\sigma^2}$$

(see for instance Aitchison and Brown, 1957, or Johnson and Kotz, 1970, chapter 14). Fisher transformed the parameters μ and σ^2 to two new parameters T ('target distance' – not to be confused with the 'trade' variable) – defined by $T = e^\mu$, and A ('accuracy ratio') – defined by $A = e^{-0.6745\sigma}$.[13] He estimated the 'target distance' to be $9\frac{1}{2}$ months and the 'accuracy ratio' to be 0.53. The latter (according to his discussion on p. 189) derives from the first quartile of the normal distribution, $v = \mu - 0.6745\sigma$ (the factor 0.67449σ was known at that time as the 'probable error' – cf. R.A. Fisher, 1958, p. 45), and e^v was estimated to be 5 months; consequently, the accuracy ratio is $A = e^v / e^\mu = e^{v-\mu} = e^{-0.6745\sigma} = 5/9.5 = 0.5263$.

Fisher remarked further that:

> It is therefore quite possible that the type finally chosen is not absolutely the best. But we may be sure that it is not far from it, if for no other reason than simply because there remains so little *room* for improvement, between the extraordinary high correlation which this method yields and 100 per cent (p. 185, emphasis in original).

It is interesting to observe that this is precisely the point of view of contemporary optimization heuristics in cases where computation of a precise optimum is known to be impossible in finite time.

Fisher slightly changed his definition of the approximation to P_t' to the following (1925, p. 182, note 3, emphasis in original):

> The slope for any given month is measured by subtracting the index number for the *preceding* month from that for the *succeeding* month and reducing the result to a percentage of the given or intervening month. This percentage, being for two months, is multiplied by six to give a *per annum* rate.

This new definition was

$$P'_t = \frac{P_{t+1} - P_{t-1}}{P_t} = \frac{\Delta P_t}{P_t} + \frac{\Delta P_{t-1}}{P_t}, \tag{9.27}$$

multiplied by 6. This definition, like the previous one (9.22), contains a built-in two-month moving average, so that the distributed lag is an average not of past monthly inflation rates, but of two-month moving averages of past inflation rates. The monthly index of trade that he used, from Persons (1923), and which he smoothed by a three-month moving average (with weights $\frac{1}{4}, \frac{1}{2}, \frac{1}{4}$), covered the period August 1915 to March 1923, and the monthly price data went back to January 1903; the correlation was 0.941. The same numerical lag distribution was applied to different periods, going back as far as 1877, with high correlations as well. Fisher stated (1925, p. 198) that he had thought of using the real rate of interest (formula (9.21) above), following Fisher (1896, 1906), but had decided against it because 'the rate of interest (in money) is always perceived while the rate of appreciation of money is not', hence they were best studied separately (whether this meant jointly as distinct independent variables or separately after correction for the other influence was not made clear); however, this was never done.[14] He noted (1925, p. 199) that Alvin Hansen and Holbrook Working had 'pointed out that, conformably to the quantity theory, the price level follows bank deposits with a few months' lag', but no such published work was cited;[15] however, the discussion made clear that he regarded the general question of studying the dynamics of the monetary system as one of highest importance and one that had just begun. He expressed his strong opinion that such a complete system, when subject to random outside forces, would still not exhibit regular cycles, but would be much more akin to a theory of 'the swaying of the trees'.

In Fisher's next two studies (1926a, 1926b) the dependent variable was employment. Both papers reported on the same research. Because of the computational labor,[16] Fisher reverted to the 'short-cut' method of approximating the lognormal lag distribution by the above linear one (9.24); he nevertheless found a correlation of 90% in the relationship. The same numerical lag distribution was applied to different periods with equally satisfactory results. This led him to reiterate his belief that since such a large proportion of business fluctuations could be explained by price changes, the prevailing emphases in business-cycle theory were misplaced. A sixth paper (1927a, pp. 65-66) applied his methodology to bankruptcies, showing a very good fit between bankruptcies and a distributed lag of rates of increase in the value of the dollar between 1911 and 1927. No correlation coefficient or other technical details were provided; however, the correlation coefficient was subsequently (1931, p. 152) reported as 0.76.

The seventh study was an analysis contained in the *Theory of Interest* (1930b, pp. 416-442) of a relation between money interest rates and a distributed lag of inflation rates, using data from 1890 to 1927, embedded in a much broader discussion of the relation between interest and prices (chapter XIX, pp. 399-451). The theory was stated as follows (p. 400):

> If the price level falls in such a way that [merchants] may expect for themselves a shrinking margin of profit, they will be cautious about borrowing unless interest falls, and this very unwillingness to borrow, lessening the demand in the money market, will tend to bring interest down. On the other hand, if inflation is going on, they will scent rising prices ahead and so rising money profits, and will be stimulated to borrow unless the rate of interest rises enough to discourage them, and their willingness to borrow will itself tend to raise interest.

He proceeded to cite historical events supporting this theory, but was especially interested in applying his distributed-lag analysis to obtain definite quantitative results.

For Great Britain, using bond yields from Gibson (1923), he obtained a correlation of 0.87 in a distributed lag of interest behind price changes 'when effects of price changes are assumed to be spread over 28 years or for a weighted average of 9.3 years' (1930b, p. 423), while for the United States, using bond yields taken from the *Statistical Bulletin*, 1928-1929, of the Standard Statistics Company, the highest correlation obtained (0.857) was 'for a distribution of the influence due to price changes over 20 years or a weighted average of 6.7 years'. The British data were yearly, and the American data quarterly. He concluded (1930, p. 425, emphasis in original):

> the results and other evidence indicate that, over long periods at least, interest rates *follow* price movements. The reverse, which some writers have asserted, seems to find little support. Experiments, made with United States short term interest rates, to test the alternative hypothesis of distributed influence of interest rate changes instead of price changes, gave results of negligible significance. Our investigations thus corroborate convincingly the theory that a direct relation exists between P' and i, the price changes usually preceding and determining like changes in interest rates.

These findings, which were either ignored or forgotten for forty years, had to be rediscovered by macroeconomists in the 1970s. Fisher provided the following explanation for the long lag length (1930, p. 429): 'A further probable explanation of the surprising length of time by which the rate of interest lags behind price change is that between price changes and interest rates a third factor intervenes. This is business, as exemplified or measured by the volume of trade. It is influenced by price change and influences in turn the rate of interest.'

An eighth, largely retrospective, study (1931) noted that the correlations of trade, employment, interest, and bankruptcies with $\overline{P}'$ had become much lower following 1923. In particular, using the Federal Reserve Board index of manufactures and mining as the variable for the volume of trade, corrected for secular trend, he noted that for the period January 1923 to June 1930 (p. 153):

The highest correlation obtained was only +.459, when price change influence was assumed to be lagged and distributed over a range of 30 months or a weighted average of 10 months. This indicates that price played a subordinate rôle from 1923 to the present. Other factors predominated and shoved the influence of prices into the background.

He turned his attention to 'internal forces' such as the level of indebtedness, which was the main theme of studies 9 and 11 (1932, 1933e). Thus (1931, p. 153): 'The stock market crash of 1929, and the commodity market crash of 1920-1921 were due largely to the fact that the profit-taker was in debt'. However, the crash of 1920-1921 was one that was perfectly explained by his 1925 analysis. Panic and distress selling might have been partly the *cause* of the large price decline of that period; but the explanation of the volume of trade by past rates of inflation, based on a distributed lag over 33 months with a weighted average of $9\frac{1}{2}$ months, held up perfectly in the 1925 analysis. The only question is whether he needed a better explanation of price changes than the purely monetary one.

In the tenth of the series of studies (1933a), Fisher found that the relation between $\overline{P}'$ and employment persisted up to 1932. He quoted a correlation coefficient of 0.84 (p. 156), though his exposition did not make clear whether this referred to the relation over the entire period 1903-1932, or just to the period 1919-1932. While he referred to his *Booms and Depressions* (1932), the *rationale* that he presented for the relationship between employment and $\overline{P}'$ did not differ from that presented in his 1925 paper. This presents an interesting paradox. His 1931 analysis – in which he had concluded that the previous empirical relationships he had found between trade and employment and the distributed lag of previous inflation rates no longer held up after 1923 – at least provided him with a good excuse for his failure to predict the 1929 depression. Now, however, it turned out that the relationship between employment and $\overline{P}'$ stood up extremely well at least up to the middle of 1932 (1933a, p. 155, Chart III). This suggests that if he had had by the fall of 1929 the data on inflation rates up to that time that he employed in Fisher (1933a), he should have been able to predict the Great Depression without having to resort to the debt-deflation hypothesis; and by the end of 1930 he should at least have been able to explain it. This 1933 study employed data up to close to the end of 1932, so the explanation cannot be that there was a substantial delay in the availability of data. It is truly a puzzle that he felt the need to resort to new hypotheses to explain the Great Depression when his 1925 'law' (as he had called it) already explained it so well.

Another puzzle is that if his distributed-lag explanations of trade and employment are to be reconciled with his equation of exchange, it must be assumed that rises in trade and employment induced by inflation must be financed by either an increase in the money supply and deposits or by an increase in velocity, and declines in trade and employment must be accompanied by either a fall in the money supply and deposits or a decline in velocity. Unless the entire accommodation is to be provided by changes in velocity, currency and deposits must be considered to some extent as endogenous variables during the transition process. To be sure, the price changes that lead to the changes in trade and employment are precipitated by changes in the money supply; but since the changes in trade and employment occur with a lag, and the equation of exchange must hold identically at all points of time, some change in $MV + M'V'$ must take place *following* the initial change in M or M' that precipitated the price change.

In the twelfth of this series of studies, Fisher showed that countries on the gold standard had similar patterns of price changes over time, as was also the case with countries in the sterling area, whereas these groups had quite distinct price patterns; thus (1935a, p. 6):

> From all the above comparisons, we conclude that the divergence between the price levels of any two countries that differ in monetary standards corresponds with the divergence between those two monetary standards. This principle really includes, as a special case, the case of countries on the same monetary standard, where the divergence is practically zero. In short, price levels among nations behave, in general, according to their monetary standards.

Fisher also took the opportunity to establish his priority over Cassel (pp. 7-8):

> We conclude that, with a few exceptions ..., a rise or fall in the price of gold is accompanied immediately by a rise or fall in the level of commodity prices.
>
> This principle was stated and verified statistically in *Stabilizing the Dollar* [Fisher (1920)] (see, especially, pp. 26-28). It was discussed and further verified by Professor Gustav Cassel in *Money and Foreign Exchange After 1914* [Cassel (1922)], published in 1922 – he called it the principle of purchasing power parity.

Fisher took the opportunity in this 1935 article to return to his distributed-lag analysis for the United States (1935a, pp. 8-10), which he brought down to the end of 1933 (starting at the beginning of 1903), for both employment and trade. In the case of employment, in which he had obtain a correlation of 0.9 in the first study (1926a, 1926b) and 0.84 in the second (1933a), he stated:

> This makes the third time that the original study of 1922 [*sic*] as to employment (E) has been extended; and each time the correlation between the two curves continues to be striking, despite the fact that in no case was any attempt made to change, or improve upon, the original method of distributing the lag.

No figure for this 'striking' correlation coefficient was quoted, however. In the case of the volume of trade, in which he reverted to Persons' index, he stated that 'this relationship has, for the first time, been calculated beyond 1922 and brought down to date. For the whole period the same striking correspondence is found, again sustaining the conclusion that deflation depresses trade and reflation revives it', although again no correlation coefficient was quoted. The upbeat spirit is in stark contrast to his pessimistic assessment of 1931. The charts (1935a, pp. 24-25) indicated that the predictive power of $\overline{P}'$ was still strong for trade and employment (the weighted average covering the preceding 25 months), except for the period mid-1931 to mid-1932. For this period he concluded that '*some non-monetary factor dominates* and was present almost all over the world' (p. 12, emphasis in original).

His suggested explanation, offered with great diffidence, was that, on the basis of a comparison of time series on 'business conditions' with time series on $\overline{P}'$ for sixteen countries (pp. 26-27, emphasis in original), the curve of business conditions 'was put out of line by *new tariffs and other trade impediments following the growth of "nationalism", and also by the sudden and unforseen developments in the international debt situation*'. As far as I know, this was the only case in which Fisher attributed a specific failure in his 'law' to hold to the debt situation. His explanation was as follows: 'Not only do debts and debt-liquidation affect business conditions indirectly through the medium of deflation, so as to register in $\overline{P}'$ in the chart, but they doubtless also affect business directly, especially if the business world suddenly awakens with a shock to their dangerous magnitude.' He concluded, however (p. 14), that 'with the exception of 1931-32, it seems that the depression has been, in each country, chiefly ruled by its changes of price level'.

The thirteenth of the series of studies (1936a,b) returned to the distributed-lag analysis, brought up to the end of 1935. Only charts for employment were shown, and no correlation coefficients were reported. But some light on the puzzles alluded to above is thrown by Fisher's observation that (p. 498, emphasis in original):

> the correspondence between the actual and the computed fluctuation in employment is naturally far from exact; since many other causes operate concurrently.
>
> Among other influences is the *direct* influence of money-shortage on T irrespective of the intermediation of P... .

Some quite convincing specific reasons were advanced as to why his 1925 relationship did not hold up during certain periods (1936, pp. 499-500): (1) the failure of *factory* employment to rise with $\overline{P}'$ during 1917-1918 was attributed to the military draft; (2) the falling-off of employment in 1931-1932 while $\overline{P}'$ was rising was explained as previously (1935a); (3) the apparent lack of any relationship between E and $\overline{P}'$ from August 1933 to November 1935 was attributed to the quantitative restrictions on production and trade introduced by the federal government (reducing hours but not pay in the N.R.A., the dole and relief work, and governmental restrictions on production), counterbalancing the favorable effects of price increases. It is interesting that the amount of debt was invoked only in the second of these three cases (in Fisher, 1935a). His chart (1936, p. 499) showed a turn-down of $\bar{P}$ in 1935 which might have foreshadowed the depression of 1937.

One of the contributions of this 1936 article of Fisher's is his reiteration (also made in Fisher, 1935a, p. 9) of an important methodological point from his 1925 article (1936, p. 498):

> Some critics, unfamiliar with mathematical statistics, have argued that to adjust the parameter or parameters, so as to get the best fit, is making the fit to suit. This is answered in the 1925 article referred to. Suffice it here to say that, for such critics, a convincing answer is that, after finding the best fit for one period, if the very same formula, thus found best for that period, be then applied to any other period, it is found to give almost as good a result as if it had been based on the statistical data for this second period.

This article was criticized by Copeland (1936) who among other points raised the following (p. 504):

> Thus, E is shown to lag behind the curve of monthly increments in the price index. ... It may conceivably be true at the same time that P lags analogously behind the curve of monthly increments in factory employment. When two time series, A and B, can be represented by synchronous sine curves, the curve of monthly increments in each will lead the other curve. But one would not be justified in noting that the curve of monthly increments in A leads the B curve and then concluding, as Fisher does, that changes in A cause changes in B.

He went on to say: 'Assuming that Fisher had established that cyclical movements in the wholesale price index precede those in the factory employment index ..., would this show anything except that prices respond more quickly than employment to a common influence?' Fisher responded (1936b, p. 506) that Copeland had not shown that the two series were cyclical, but agreed that it would be worth while to examine the reverse relationship (thus anticipating the type of causality analysis later employed by Sims, 1972).

Fisher's fourteenth and final contribution to his distributed-lag methodology was his article (1937) explaining his short-cut method for computing distributed lags of the form (9.24). This paper needs to be read in conjunction with the work of Fisher's long-time collaborator, Sasuly (1934). Fisher made clear that the method consisted in regressing the dependent variable on (9.24) for successive values of $n = 1, 2,...$ until a (local) maximum of the correlation coefficient was obtained. For large n the computational burden increased, and for this calculation Sasuly's formula

$$\sum_{t=1}^{n} ta_t = (n+1)S_n^0 - S_n^1 \text{ where } S_{t'}^0 = \sum_{t=1}^{t'} a_t \text{ and } S_n^1 = \sum_{t'=1}^{n} S_{t'}^0 = \sum_{t''=1}^{n} \sum_{t=1}^{t'} a_t$$

proved very useful (Fisher, 1937, p. 326; Sasuly, 1934, pp. 135, 147). With today's high-speed computers such formulae are hardly needed, but in Fisher's time they were clearly highly advantageous. Fisher provided few clues as to how he proceeded in the case of the lognormal lag other than to refer the reader to Chapter X of Sasuly (1934). From the discussion there (especially pp. 201-202) one may conjecture that a piecewise linear approximation to the lognormal density may have been used.

As Fisher noted (1937, p. 327), the distributed lag was used by Roos (1934) in the analysis of building construction. Fisher's work stimulated Alt's (1942) article on distributed lags, which was followed by Tinbergen's (1949) study in which Fisher's idea was applied to the estimation of long-term foreign-trade elasticities; instead of following Fisher's method, however, Tinbergen estimated the lag coefficients essentially freely without constraining them by any form of lag distribution. Koyck (1954) criticized Tinbergen's procedure and suggested instead (without knowledge of Fisher's work) a lag distribution in which the lag coefficients decline proportionately instead of linearly. This was soon followed by Berger's paper (1953) which compared Koyck's method with Fisher's, and found that they led to very similar estimates, but that Koyck's method appeared more natural and was computationally simpler. Koyck's monograph (1954) soon followed, and included a discussion of Berger's comparisons (pp. 30-32) between Fisher's approach and his own. With Koyck's monograph, the topic of distributed lags became a standard tool of econometrics, and there soon followed important contributions by Klein (1958), Solow (1960), Almon (1965), Jorgenson (1966), Leamer (1972), Shiller (1973) and many others. It is clear that Fisher had introduced an important and influential econometric technique.

Discussion of Fisher's innovative distributed-lag studies would not be complete without some comment on his so-called anticipation of the Phillips curve. Donner and McCollum (1972) were the first to suggest that Fisher (1926b) had discovered the Phillips curve; independently, this had also been pointed out by Jacob Mincer to the editors of the *Journal of Political Economy*, who published Fisher's 1926 paper under the title 'I Discovered the Phillips Curve' in 1972, and remarked in their editorial note: 'It is not generally known that the first statistical investigation of the relationship between inflation and the unemployment rate was performed not by A.W. Phillips in 1958 but by Irving Fisher in 1926.' What Phillips (1958) discovered, however, was a declining relationship between the rate of change of the money wage rate (as dependent variable) and the level of unemployment (as independent variable). The rationale for Phillips's relationship was clearly expressed in his opening sentence (1958, p. 283):

> When the demand for a commodity or service is high relative to the supply of it we expect the price to rise, the rate of rise being greater the greater the excess demand. Conversely when the demand is low relatively to the supply we expect the price to fall, the rate of fall being greater the greater the deficiency of demand. It seems

plausible that this principle should operate as one of the factors determining the rate of money wage rates, which are the prices of labour services.

Thus stated, the relationship in question can be said to go back at least to John Stuart Mill, if not long before. Quantitatively expressed by Samuelson (1947) as a differential equation expressing the rate of change of a price as an increasing function of the excess demand for the corresponding commodity, this has been well known in economic theory for a long time, and was given statistical precision by Phillips. However, Fisher's relationship differs from this one in a number of important respects. In the first place, Fisher dealt with a relation not between money wages and employment, but between money prices and employment; secondly, in Fisher's theory, the rate of inflation of commodity prices was a component of the *independent variable*, while employment was the *dependent* variable; thirdly, Fisher stated many times that he had tried to find a significant relationship between employment (as well as the volume of output) and the concurrent (or even past) rate of inflation of commodity prices, but without success, and found a significant relationship only between employment (or 'trade') and *a distributed lag* of past rates of inflation. The rationale behind Fisher's relationship was that when prices rise, wages (and other cost components) *lag behind*, raising profits and inducing firms to expand output and employment (and conversely when prices fall). If money wages rose in response to a rise in prices, most of the Fisher effect would be removed. Put another way, the Fisher effect depends on the *real wage* to *fall* in order to stimulate employment.

There was no distributed lag in Phillips's relationship, although he had employed distributed lags in a previous study (1956). The only thing Fisher's and Phillips's relationships have in common is that employment is one of the variables (dependent and independent respectively), and that a rate of change of a price (commodity prices and money wage rates respectively) is an element of the other variable. It is difficult to understand how anybody could confuse such different relationships. It is akin to confusing a supply relationship with a demand relationship.

I close with an unanswered question. Fisher passionately advanced the cause of price stability, and advocated reflation as a means to restore previous debtor-creditor relationships (Fisher, 1932, p. 125; 1933d). If everybody knows that the price level will be increased and restored to a previous level, such reflation could presumably be brought about effectively. But under Fisher's theory, a reflation would itself stimulate output and employment, but since the rate of inflation would have to slow down as the target price level is approached, his own relationship (the acceleration principle as applied to prices) would predict a recession as a consequence of the price increase slowing down to its new stationary level. It seems that Fisher overlooked this important dynamic aspect of his price-stabilization schemes.

NOTES

1   This assumes $\beta > 0$. If, however, $u_2'(B) < u_1'(100)$ then $u_2'(B+\beta) = u_1'(100)$ requires $\beta < 0$. It is then logically possible that $u_1'(150) = u_2'(B+\frac{1}{2}\beta) < u_2'(B+\beta) = u_1'(100)$. Even if this is so, however, so long as the functional form of u_2 (q_2) is not known – hence there is no numerical determination of $u_2'(B+\beta) / u_2'(B+\frac{1}{2}\beta)$ – there is then no numerical determination of $u_1'(100) / u_1'(150)$ by this method. The second ratio can no more be determined than the first; all we can say is that the ratios are equal.

2   There was one example of compound interest (p. 32n), one of a profit-maximizing competitive firm (p. 48), and one from demography (pp. 50-51), but the rest were from geometry and physics. The only discussion of utility was the mention of the distinction between marginal and total utility (p. 65).

3   The circumstances that led Fisher to publish this study are recounted in a circular enclosed by Fisher with a reprint of his article sent to a group of interested economists, which included Jacob Marschak – who quoted an extract from it in his habilitation thesis (1931, pp. 128-129n). The following excerpt from Marschak's footnote seems worth reproducing here:

> After the enclosed paper was published I learned, for the first time, of Dr. Ragnar Frisch's 'Sur un Problème d'Economie Pure' [(1926)] in which, by different methods, the same problem has been attacked. Dr. Frisch not only devised a method but applied it to obtain definite statistical estimates with which my own tentative and unpublished figures are, at least, consistent.
>
> To Dr. Frisch, therefore, belongs the honor of being, so far as I know, the first to publish anything on this difficult subject.
>
> Although the publication of my own method comes later, I had, in unpublished lectures, employed it at least as early as 1912. In an article [Fisher (1918a)] I referred to the intention of publishing this method; but publication was put off from year to year in the hope of first making a full statistical application. Publication would have been still further delayed had it not been for the invitation to furnish immediately a paper for the volume of Economic Essays in honor of Professor J. B. Clark. This led to the decision to publish my method by itself and defer the statistical application to a later time.

4   As will be mentioned later in this section, in practice one can obtain data only on *groups* of commodities, and for these one can generally obtain data on price indices and expenditure shares but not quantity indices other than those defined by (9.4), which explains Fisher's set-up.

5   This criticism was made by Marschak (1931, p. 139), who also provided a nice graphical exposition of Fisher's procedure. Marschak also was quite critical (p. 138n) of an article by Bilimovič (1930) commenting on Fisher's method, so I have not thought it necessary to add my own comments.

6   Fisher used Q in place of q to denote a commodity quantity.

7   For consistency with the notation being used in the text I have taken the liberty of replacing Fisher's Q by q and his time subscripts by the corresponding superscripts, in this and the following quotation.

8   The first ed. (1911c) contains the misprint 'page 103'.

9   There was of course the further inconsistency that while the price index was rebased to 1909, the weights were presumably those of an earlier year, perhaps 1896. Even if the weights had been those of 1909 (the final year), it would of course still have been a Laspeyres price index, since the crucial property of a Paasche price-index series is that the weights change from year to year.

10 It was shown by Bortkiewicz (1923, pp. 376-378) that if the p_i' / p_i^0 and q_i' / q_i^0 are

negatively correlated for $i = 1, 2,...,n$, then $P'_t = \frac{\sum_{i=1}^{n} p'_i q'_i}{\sum_{i=1}^{n} p^0_i q'_i} < \frac{\sum_{i=1}^{n} p'_i q^0_i}{\sum_{i=1}^{n} p^0_i q^0_i} = P'_0$.

See also the discussion in Haberler (1927, p. 93), as well as the later and more elaborate treatment by Bortkiewicz (1932).

11 An effect analogous to those of Clark and Fisher is that cited by Carver (1903) who observed, following Marshall (1891, p. 657), that a small percentage rise in a firm's revenues could lead to a large percentage rise in its profits; hence, capitalizing the expected stream of profits at the going discount rate, a proportionate rise in the price of the firm's product would lead to a magnified rise in the value of the firm. This influenced Aftalion (1909, p. 249) in his original formulation of Clark's subsequent acceleration principle.

12 Fisher's exposition was ambiguous; P'_t was described merely as 'a weighted average, the weights being 1, 2, 3, 4, 5, 6, 7, 8, for each eight consecutive ordinates of the "derivative" P' ' (1923b, p. 1027), but his later exposition (1924, p. 50) confirmed that the weights were in descending order. Since $\sum_{i=0}^{n-1} i = (n+1)n/2$, the coefficients w_i of the P'_{t-i} sum to 1.

13 Fisher's footnote on pp. 186-187 states that log $A = .6745\sigma$, which is clearly a misprint for $-.6745\sigma$; there is another obvious misprint in the typesetting of the formula for the lognormal density. Fisher omitted the factor $1/(\sigma\sqrt{2\pi})$ needed for (9.26) to be true density functions.

14 It seems that the idea of *multiple* correlation (or multiple regression) was not well-known among economists at the time; not until the the publication of Ezekiel's text (1930), and the studies of Frisch (1934), Koopmans (1937), and Tinbergen (1939), did the idea become part of the stock-in-trade of the profession.

15 The reference is evidently to Working (1923), who concluded that there was approximately an eight-month lag between circulating medium ($M + M'$) and the price level (I am indebted to Thomas Humphrey for this reference). Hansen's (1921) contribution was the establishment of the close relation between cash reserves and bank deposits.

16 Fisher remarked (1926b, p. 786): 'During the last three years ... I have had at least one computer in my office almost constantly at work on this problem ....' In those days the word 'computer' referred to a live human being working with pencil and paper and, no doubt, a slide rule. It seems that the 'computer' referred to was Max Sasuly. The phrasing in Fisher (1926a, p. 26) was: 'During the last two years I have had someone at work on this problem, doing statistical computations quite constantly.'

REFERENCES

Aftalion, A. (1908), 'La réalité des surproductions générales', *Revue d'économie politique*, **22**, (October 1908) 696-706; **23** (February 1909), 81-117; **23** (March 1909), 201-229; **23** (April 1909), 241-259.

Aitchison, J. and Brown, J. A. C. (1957), *The Lognormal Distribution*, London, Cambridge University Press.

Almon, S. (1965), 'The distributed lag between capital appropriations and expenditures', *Econometrica*, **33**, 178-196.

Alt, F.L. (1942), 'Distributed lags', *Econometrica*, **10**, 113-128.

Amid-Hozour, E., Dick, D.T. and Lucier, R.L. (1971), 'Sultan schedule and Phillips curve: An historical note', *Economica*, N.S., **38**, 319-320.

Berger, J. (1953), 'On Koyck's and Fisher's methods for calculating distributed lags', *Metroeconomica*, **5**, 89-90.

Bilimovič, A. (1930), 'Irving Fishers statistische Methode für die Bemessung des Grenznutzens', *Zeitschrift für Nationalökonomie*, **1**, 114-128.

Bortkiewicz, L. von (1923), 'Zweck und Struktur einer Preisindexzahl', *Nordisk Statistisk Tidsskrift*, **2** (1923), 369-408; **3** (1924), 208-251, 494-516.

Bortkiewicz, L. von (1932), 'Die Kaufkraft des Geldes und ihre Messung', *Nordic Statistical Journal*, **4**, [*Nordisk Statistisk Tidsskrift*, **11**], 1-68.

Carver, T.N. (1903), 'A suggestion for a theory of industrial depressions', *Quarterly Journal of Economics*, **17**, 497-500.

Cassel, G. (1922), *Money and Foreign Exchange After 1914*, London, Constable.

Clark, J.M. (1917), 'Business acceleration and the law of demand: a technical factor in economic cycles', *Journal of Political Economy*, **25**, 217-235.

Copeland, M.A. (1936), 'Changes in the wholesale price index in relation to factory employment: discussion', *Journal of the American Statistical Association*, **31**, 503-505.

Davis, H.T. (1941), *An Analysis of Economic Time Series*, Bloomington, IN, The Principia Press.

Davis, H.T. (1941), *The Theory of Econometrics*, Bloomington, Indiana, The Principia Press.

Donner, A. and McCollum J.F. (1972), 'The Phillips curve: an historical note', *Economica*, N.S., **39**, 323-324.

Douglas, P.H. (1947), 'Irving Fisher', *American Economic Review*, **37**, 661-663.

Edgeworth, F.Y. (1881), *Mathematical Psychics*, London, C. Kegan Paul.

Evans, G.C. (1930), *Mathematical Introduction to Economics*, New York, McGraw-Hill.

Ezekiel, M. (1930), *Methods of Correlation Analysis*, New York, J. Wiley and Sons, 2nd ed., 1941.

Fisher, I. (1892), *Mathematical Investigations in the Theory of Value and Prices*, in *Transactions of the Connecticut Academy*, **9**, 1-124. Reprinted, New Haven, Yale University Press, 1925. Facsimile reprint, New York, A.M. Kelley, 1961.

Fisher, I. (1896), *Appreciation and Interest*, Publications of the American Economic Association, Third Series, Vol. XI, No. 4. New York, Published for the American Economic Association by Macmillan. Facsimile reprint, bound with *Mathematical Investigations in the Theory of Value and Prices*, New York, A.M. Kelley, 1961.

Fisher, I. (1897), *A Brief Introduction to the Infinitesimal Calculus. Designed Especially to Aid in Reading Mathematical Economics and Statistics*, New York, Macmillan, 3rd ed., 1909.

Fisher, I. (1899), 'Mortality statistics of the United States census', in *The Federal Census*. Critical Essays by Members of the American Economic Association, Collected and Edited by a Special Committee. *Publications of the American Economic Association*, New [second] Series, No. **2**, 121-169.

Fisher, I. (1906), *The Nature of Capital and Income*, New York, Macmillan, Facsimile reprint, Düsseldorf, Verlag Wirtschaft und Finanzen GmbH, 1992.

Fisher, I. (1907), *The Rate of Interest*, New York, Macmillan. Facsimile reprint, Düsseldorf, Verlag Wirtschaft und Finanzen GmbH, 1994.

Fisher, I. (1909), 'A practical method of estimating the velocity of circulation of money', *Journal of the Royal Statistical Society*, **72**, 604-618.

Fisher, I. (1911a), 'The "impatience theory" of interest', *Scientia (Rivista di Scienza)*, **9**, 380-401.

Fisher, I. (1911b) 'Recent changes in price levels and their causes', *Bulletin of the American Economic Association*, 37-45. 'Discussion', 46-70.

Fisher, I., assisted by H.G. Brown, (1911c), *The Purchasing Power of Money*, New

York, Macmillan. German translation, *Die Kaufkraft des Geldes*, Berlin, Druck und Verlag Georg Reimer, 1916.

Fisher, I. (1912), *Elementary Principles of Economics*, 3rd (first public) ed.. New York, Macmillan.

Fisher, I. (1913a), 'A compensated dollar', *Quarterly Journal of Economics*, **27**, 213-235, 385-397.

Fisher, I. (1913b), 'Standardizing the dollar', *American Economic Review* [Supplement], **4**, 20-28. 'Discussion', 29-51.

Fisher, I. (1913c), 'La hausse actuelle de la monnaie, du crédit et des prix, comment y remédier', *Revue d'Economie politique*, **27**, 419-434.

Fisher, I., assisted by H.G. Brown, (1913d), *The Purchasing Power of Money*, New and revised (2nd) ed., New York, Macmillan. Facsimile reprint, New York, A.M. Kelley, 1985.

Fisher, I. (1914), *Why Is the Dollar Shrinking? A Study in the High Cost of Living*, New York, Macmillan.

Fisher, I. (1917), 'The "ratio" chart', *Publications of the American Statistical Association*, **15**, 577-601. Reprinted as a pamphlet, Yale University, 1917, 1-24.

Fisher, I. (1918a), 'Is "utility" the most suitable term for the concept it is used to denote?' *American Economic Review*, **8**, 335-337.

Fisher, I. (1918b), 'Stabilizing the dollar in purchasing power', in E.M. Friedman (ed.), *American Problems of Reconstruction*, New York, E.P. Dutton and Company, 361-390.

Fisher, I. (1919), 'Economists in public service', *American Economic Review* [Supplement], (Papers and Proceedings of the first Annual meeting of the American Economic Association, Richmond, Va., 1918) **9**, 5-21.

Fisher, I. (1920), *Stabilizing the Dollar. A Plan to Stabilize the General Price Level Without Fixing Individual Prices*, New York, Macmillan.

Fisher, I. (1922), *The Making of Index Numbers*, Boston and New York, Houghton Mifflin, 2nd ed., 1923, 3rd ed., 1927.

Fisher, I. (1923a), 'Stabilizing the dollar', in L.D. Edie (ed.), *The Stabilization of Business*, New York, Macmillan, 54-112.

Fisher, I. (1923b), 'The business cycle largely a "dance of the dollar" ', *Journal of the American Statistical Association*, **28**, 1024-1028.

Fisher, I. (1924), 'Fluctuations in price-levels', in W.M. Persons, W.T. Foster and A.J. Hettinger, Jr. (eds), *The Problem of Business Forecasting*, ('Pollak Foundation volume'), Papers presented at the Eighty-Fifth Annual Meeting of the American Statistical Association, (Washington D.C.), December 27-29, Boston and New York, Houghton Mifflin, 50-52.

Fisher, I. (1925), 'Our unstable dollar and the so-called business cycle', *Journal of the American Statistical Association*, **20**, 179-202.

Fisher, I. (1926a), 'Banking policy and unemployment', *American Labor Legislation Review*, **16**, 24-29.

Fisher, I. (1926b), 'A statistical relation between unemployment and price changes', *International Labour Review*, **13**, 785-792. Reprinted as 'Lost and Found: I discovered the Phillips Curve – Irving Fisher', *Journal of Political Economy*, **81**, (1973), 496-502.

Fisher, I. (1927a), 'The unstable dollar as a factor in the credit man's problem', *Monthly Bulletin of the Robert Morris Associates*, July, 54-70.

Fisher, I. (1927b), 'A statistical method for measuring marginal utility and testing the justice of a progressive income tax', in J.H. Hollander (ed.), *Economic Essays, Contributed in Honor of John Bates Clark*, New York, Macmillan, 157-193.

Fisher, I. (1927c), 'The "total value criterion", a new principle in index number construction', *Journal of the American Statistical Association*, **22**, 419-441.

Fisher, I. (1928), *The Money Illusion*, New York, Adelphi.

Fisher, I. (1930a), 'The application of mathematics to the social sciences', (Seventh Josiah Willard Gibbs Lecture 1929), *Bulletin of the American Mathematical Society*, **36**, 225-243.

Fisher, I. (1930b), *The Theory of Interest*, New York, Macmillan. Facsimile reprint, New York, Kelley and Millman, Inc., 1964.

Fisher, I. (1930c) *The Stock Market Crash – and After*, New York, Macmillan.

Fisher, I. (1931), 'Business cycles as facts or tendencies', in *Economische Opstellen, aangeboden aan Prof. Dr. C. A. Verrijn Stuart*, Haarlem, De Erven F. Bohn N. V., 140-157.

Fisher, I. (1932), *Booms and Depressions. Some First Principles*, New York, Adelphi.

Fisher, I. (1933a), 'The relation of employment to the price level', in C.F. Roos (ed.), *Stabilization of Employment*. Papers presented at the Atlantic City Meeting of the American Association for the Advancement of Science, Bloomington, Indiana, The Principia Press, 152-159.

Fisher, I. (1933b), 'Statistics in the service of economics', *Journal of the American Statistical Association*, **28**, 1-13.

Fisher, I., assisted by H.W. Fisher, (1933c), *Inflation?*, New York, Adelphi.

Fisher, I., assisted by H.W. Fisher, (1933d), *After Reflation, What?*, New York, Adelphi.

Fisher, I. (1933e), 'The debt-deflation theory of great depressions', *Econometrica*, **1**, 337-357.

Fisher, I., assisted by H.R.L. Cohrssen, (1934), *Stable Money. A History of the Movement*, New York, Adelphi.

Fisher, I. (1935a), 'Are booms and depressions transmitted internationally through monetary standards?', *Bulletin de l'Institut International de Statistique*, (Rapports et communications présentés à la XXIIème session de l'Institut International de Statistique, Londres 1934), **28** (2ème Livraison), 1-29.

Fisher, I. (1935b), *100% Money*, New York, Adelphi, 2nd ed. (1936), 3rd ed. (1945), New Haven, The City Printing Company.

Fisher, I. (1936a, b), 'Changes in the wholesale price index in relation to factory employment', *Journal of the American Statistical Association*, **31**, 496-502. 'Rejoinder', 505-506.

Fisher, I. (1937), 'Note on a short-cut method for calculating distributed lags', *Bulletin de l'Institut International de Statistique*, (Rapports et communications présentés à la XXIIème session de l'Institut International de Statistique, Athènes (2ème partie) **29**, (3ème Livraison), 323-328.

Fisher, I. (1941), 'Mathematical method in the social sciences', *Econometrica*, **9**, 185-197.

Fisher, I. (1947a), 'Response to Professor Frisch', *Econometrica*, **15**, 73-74.

Fisher, I. (1947b), 'The statistics of the velocity of circulation: a progress report', *Econometrica*, **15**, 173-176.

Fisher, Sir R.A. (1958), *Statistical Methods for Research Workers*, 13th ed., New York, Hafner Publishing Company Inc.

Frisch, R. (1926), 'Sur un problème d'économie pure', *Norsk Matematik Forenings Skrifter*, Serie I, Nr. 16, 1-40. Reprinted in *Metroeconomica*, **9**, 1957, 79-111. English translation, 'On a problem in pure economics', in J.S. Chipman, L. Hurwicz, M.K. Richter, and H.F. Sonnenschein (eds), *Preferences, Utility, and*

Demand, New York, Harcourt Brace Jovanovich, Inc., 1971, 386-423.

Frisch, R. (1931), 'The interrelation between capital production and consumer-taking', *Journal of Political Economy,* **39,** 646-654.

Frisch, R. (1932), *New Methods of Measuring Marginal Utility,* Tübingen, J.C.B. Mohr (Paul Siebeck).

Frisch, R. (1934), *Statistical Confluence Analysis by Means of Complete Regression Systems,* Oslo, Universitetets Økonomisk Institutt, Publikasjon nr. 5.

Frisch, R. (1936), 'Annual survey of general economic theory: the problem of index numbers', *Econometrica,* **4,** 1-38. 'Errata', 192.

Frisch, R. (1947), 'Irving Fisher at eighty', *Econometrica,* **15,** 71-73.

Frisch, R. (1959), 'A complete scheme for computing all direct and cross demand elasticities in a model with many sectors', *Econometrica,* **27,** 177-196.

Gibson, A.H. (1923), 'The future course of high class investment values', *The Bankers', Insurance Managers' and Agents' Magazine,* **515,** 15-34. Reprinted in revised form in *The Spectator,* 7 March, 1925.

Gossen, H.H. (1854), *Entwickelung der Gesetze des menschlichen Verkehrs,* Braunschweig, Druck und Verlag Friedrich Vieweg und Sohn. Reissued, Berlin, Verlag R.L. Prager, 1889. English translation: *The Laws of Human Relations and the Rules of Human Action Derived Therefrom,* Cambridge, MA, The MIT Press, 1983.

Haberler, G. (1924), 'Kritische Bemerkungen zu Schumpeters Geldtheorie. Zur Lehre vom "objektiven" Tauschwert des Geldes', *Zeitschrift für Volkswirtschaft und Sozialpolitik,* Neue Folge, **4,** 647-668. English translation: 'Critical notes on Schumpeter's theory of money – the doctrine of the "objective" exchange value of money', in A.Y. Koo (ed.), *Selected Essays of Gottfried Haberler,* Cambridge, MA, The MIT Press, 1985, 531-546.

Haberler, G. (1927), *Der Sinn der Indexzahlen. Eine Untersuchung über den Begriff des Preisniveaus und die Methoden seiner Messung.* Tübingen, J.C.B. Mohr (Paul Siebeck).

Haberler, G. (1929), 'Der volkswirtschaftliche Geldwert und die Preisindexziffern. Eine Erwiderung', *Weltwirtschaftliches Archiv,* **30,** 6-14.

Hansen, A.H. (1921), *Cycles of prosperity and depression in the United States, Great Britain and Germany: A study of monthly data 1902-1908,* Madison, University of Wisconsin Studies in the Social Sciences and History, Number 5.

Hume, D. (1752), 'Of money', Discourse III, 41-59, of *Political Discourses,* Edinburgh, printed by R. Fleming, for A. Kinkaid and A. Donaldson. Facsimile reprint, Düsseldorf, Verlag Wirtschaft und Finanzen GmbH, 1987.

Johnson, N.L. and Kotz S. (1970), *Continuous Univariate Distributions - 1,* New York, J. Wiley and Sons.

Jorgenson, D.W. (1966), 'Rational distributed lag functions', *Econometrica,* **34,** 35-149.

Kemmerer, E.W. (1907), *Money and Credit Instruments in their Relation to General Prices,* New York, Henry Holt and Co., 2nd ed., 1909.

Klein, L.R. (1958), 'The estimation of distributed lags', *Econometrica,* **26,** 553-565.

Koopmans, T.C. (1937), *Linear Regression Analysis of Economic Time Series,* Haarlem, De Erven F. Bohn N.V.

Koyck, L.M. (1953), 'Long-term foreign trade elasticities. A note', *Metroeconomica,* **5,** 61-67.

Koyck, L.M. (1954), *Distributed Lags and Investment Analysis,* Amsterdam, North-Holland Publishing Company.

Kuznets, S. (1941), *National Income and Its Composition, 1919-1938,* New York,

National Bureau of Economic Research.

Laughlin, J.L. (1911), 'Causes of the changes in prices since 1896', *Bulletin of the American Economic Association*, (Papers and Discussions of the Twenty-third Annual Meeting, St. Louis, Missouri, 1910), Fourth Series, No. 2, 26-36, 'Discussion', 46-70.

Leamer, E.E. (1972), 'A class of informative priors and distributed lag analysis', *Econometrica*, **40**, 1069-1081.

Marschak, J. (1931), *Elastizität der Nachfrage*, Tübingen, J.C.B. Mohr (Paul Siebeck).

Marshall, A. (1891), *Principles of Economics*, London, Macmillan, 2nd ed..

Mirrles, J. (1971), 'An exploration in the theory of optimum income taxation', *Review of Economic Studies*, **38**, 175-208.

Persons, W.M. (1923), 'An index of trade for the United States', *Review of Economic Statistics*, **5**, 70-78.

Phillips, A.W. (1956), 'Some notes on the estimation of time-forms of reactions in interdependent dynamic systems', *Economica*, N.S., **23**, 99-113.

Phillips, A.W. (1958), 'The relation between unemployment and the rate of change of money wages in the United Kingdom, 1861-1957', *Economica*, N.S., **25**, 283-299.

Robbins, L. (1938), 'Interpersonal comparisons of utility: a comment', *Economic Journal*, **28**, 635-641.

Roos, C.F. (1934), *Dynamic Economics. Theoretical and Statistical Studies of Demand, Production and Prices*, Bloomington, Indiana, The Principia Press.

Samuelson, P.A. (1947), *Foundations of Economic Analysis*, Cambridge, MA, Harvard University Press.

Sasuly, M. (1934). *Trend Analysis of Statistics. Theory and Technique*, Washington, D.C., The Brookings Institution. Facsimile reprint, Westport, CT, Greenwood Press, 1973.

Sasuly, M. (1947), 'Irving Fisher and social science', *Econometrica*, **15**, 255-278.

Schumpeter, J.A. (1918), 'Das Sozialprodukt und die Rechenpfenninge. Glossen und Beiträge zur Geldtheorie von heute', *Archiv für Sozialwissenschaften und Sozialpolitik*, **44**, 627-715.

Schumpeter, J.A. (1948), 'Irving Fisher's econometrics', *Econometrica*, **16**, 219-231.

Shiller, R.J. (1973), 'A distributed lag estimator derived from smoothness priors', *Econometrica*, **41**, 775-788.

Sims, C.A. (1972), 'Money, income, and causality', *American Economic Review*, **62**, 540-552.

Solow, R.M. (1960), 'On a family of lag distribution', *Econometrica*, **28**, 393-406.

Tinbergen, J. (1939), *Statistical Testing of Business-Cycle Theories*. Vol. 1, *A Method and Its Application to Investment Activity*, Vol. 2, *Business Cycles in the United States of America, 1919-1932*, Geneva, League of Nations. Facsimile reprint, New York, Agathon Press, 1968.

Tinbergen, J. (1949), 'Long-term foreign trade elasticities', *Metroeconomica*, **1**, 174-185. Reprinted in J. Tinbergen, *Selected Papers*, Amsterdam, North-Holland Publishing Company, 1959, 124-137.

Tinbergen, J. (1951), *Business Cycles in the United Kingdom 1870-1914*, Amsterdam, North-Holland Publishing Company.

Walsh, C.M. (1901), *The Measurement of General Exchange-Value*, New York, Macmillan.

Westerfield, R.B. (1947), 'Irving Fisher', *American Economic Review*, **37**, 656-661.

Wicksell, K. (1897), 'Der Bankzins als Regulator der Warenpreise', *Jahrbücher für Nationalökonomie*, **68**, 228-243.

Wicksell, K. (1898), *Geldzins und Güterpreise. Eine Studie über die den Tauschwert des Geldes bestimmenden Ursachen,* Jena, Verlag Gustav Fischer. English translation by R.F. Kahn: *Interest and Prices. A Study of the Causes Regulating the Value of Money,* London, Published on behalf of the Royal Economic Society by Macmillan, 1936.

Working, H. (1923), 'Prices and the Quantity of Circulating Medium, 1890-1921', *Quarterly Journal of Economics,* **37**, 228-256.

10. A Statistical Relation Between Employment and Price Changes in the United States and Germany, 1960-1995: Fisher's Discovery of the 'Phillips Curve' Reconsidered

Horst Entorf[*]

---

1 INTRODUCTION

A long time before A.W. Phillips (1958) (re-)discovered the negative relationship between price changes (wages) and unemployment, Irving Fisher had analyzed the correlation between these time series for the period 1903 to 1925.

The results were published in the article 'A Statistical Relation Between Unemployment and Price Changes' (1926). The article was reprinted in the *Journal of Political Economy*, under a section called 'Lost and Found' in the issue of March/April 1973. In an attempt to do posthumous justice to Fisher, the article was appropriately retitled 'I discovered the Phillips Curve'.

The question of a potential inflation-unemployment trade-off has remained one of the key points in macroeconomics. It is a worthwhile experiment to replicate Fisher's search for statistical facts on this relationship. Using his correlation methods and current data, this article shows that Fisher's way to analyze the inflation-unemployment trade-off is still valid. However, Fisher would not be able to confirm the lead of price changes over employment, as he did in his article. In other words, he would have problems in providing empirical evidence in favor of the hypothesis that unstable currencies (the 'dance of the dollar') cause business cycle fluctuations. Instead, more in accordance with Phillips (1958), who considered the tightness of the labor market as a cause of changes in nominal wages, the data reveal that shocks to labor demand anticipate price instability.

2   FISHER'S STATISTICAL APPROACH

Fisher's article has to be seen in the light of his fight for a stable purchasing power of the dollar. The 'dance of the dollar', as he puts it, causes inflation or deflation:

> inflation carries with it a great stimulation of trade and an increase in employment (or decrease in unemployment). And yet, strange as it may seem, when applied to the so-called 'business cycle', these relationships have been almost wholly overlooked (Fisher, 1973, p. 497).

Fisher, on the contrary, studied these relationships very carefully.[1] First, he noted that the simultaneous analysis of trending and stationary data should be avoided. He noted that it is not the price level that is important:

> In running an automobile we know that it takes no more petrol on a high plateau than on the lowlands, but it does take much more petrol when we are going uphill; and, on the other, takes less when we are going downhill. It is the going uphill or downhill of the price level on which we should fix attention (Fisher, 1973, p. 499).

Second, Irving Fisher was the first who applied the idea of 'distributed lags': '... the effect on employment will not certainly wait for seven months and then suddenly explode ...' (Fisher, 1973, p. 500).

Instead, he proposed a lag structure that looks like a 'normal' probability curve. It seemed to be best suited to show the effects of price changes on unemployment or employment. In other words, Fisher conjectured a first small, then increasing and finally decreasing effect of price changes on employment. He reported a high correlation of 90 percent between (the delayed and distributed) price changes and employment for the (sub-)period 1915-1925.[2]

Fisher was particularly interested in lead-lag relationships between economic variables, as can be seen from the careful treatment of the distributed effects of price changes on employment. In a footnote (Fisher, 1973, p. 501, n. 6), he was very specific with respect to the lead-lag structure of price changes and employment. He reported that the highest cross-correlation with a fixed lag was 79 percent. The lag of four months confirmed that employment had followed price changes. This lag of employment corroborated Fisher's view that the business cycle was largely a reflection of the unstable dollar.

Moreover, he drew attention to the fact that there was no fixed lag between the constructed time series of distributed effects and employment that would have led to a higher correlation. Thus, in the language of modern statistics, the maximum of cross-correlation function between employment and the distributed effects of price changes was at zero.

3   THE REPLICATION OF FISHER'S ANALYSIS

The replication is based on employment and consumer price changes for the United States and West Germany for the period 1960 to 1995.[3] Figure 1 reveals the strongly divergent employment trends in the U.S. and Germany. Employment in Germany is upward trending only after 1984, whereas U.S. employment almost doubled from 66 million people in 1960 to 125 million people in 1995. Since naive correlation analysis would be misleading in the presence of such trending time series,[4] the analysis is based on deviations from employment trends, i.e. on the cyclical component of employment. Figure 2 presents the adjustment to the long-run trend.[5]

The 'Fisher relationship', i.e. the relationship between cyclical employment and price changes, turns out to be surprisingly robust. As can be seen from Figures 3 and 4, the cross-correlation functions reveal that employment *leads* one year over price changes. The corresponding correlation coefficient is positive. Both the lag and the positive correlation can be observed for both countries and for all sample periods (1960-1995, 1960-1984, 1984-1995). The negative correlation coefficients with minima found for a lead of price changes of about 3 years would contradict the positive correlation found by Fisher. However, the lead of 3 years is much too long to be reasonable. Since we are considering cyclical data, this observed lead of price changes is nothing but the reflection of the one-year lag. In general, considering a cycle with the duration of c periods, the lag of p periods in combination with a negative correlation is equivalent to the lead of $(c / 2 - p)$ in combination with a positive correlation (see Entorf, 1993, for details). Figure 2 reveals about 4.5 cycles during the period 1960 to 1995, so that the average cycle length is about 8 years. Thus, the one-year lag exactly coincides with the lead of 3 years.[6]

Thus, in terms of Fisher's arguments, the 'causation' has changed. Shocks to the labor market seem to be the origin of adjustment processes, and pressures from the labor markets have led to wage and price changes. Furthermore, following Fisher's methodology, the distributed effects of such changes in the level of employment need to be calculated. Assuming that the bargaining process is based on employment data experienced during the last two years, it seems reasonable to assume that the simultaneous effect of employment is 25%, and that 50% and 25% of the total effect follow within the first and second year, respectively.[7] Now, there is no fixed lag between the constructed distributed effects series and price changes that would lead to a higher correlation.[8] Figure 5 gives a visual impression of the highly correlated co-movement of price changes and projected employment.

4 SUMMARY AND CONCLUSIONS

Fisher's (1926) article 'A Statistical Relation Between Unemployment and Price Changes' is a pioneering contribution to the analysis of macroeconomic instability. According to Fisher's hypothesis, 'the dance of the dollar', as he put it, causes price changes that would lead to macroeconomic fluctuations. Fisher confirmed the hypothesis. Using U.S. data of the period 1903 to 1925 and calculating cross-correlations, he showed that price changes and employment were positively correlated and that price changes had a lead over employment.

The question of a potential inflation-unemployment trade-off has remained one of the key points in macroeconomics. This article replicates Fisher's analysis. If Fisher could apply recent German and U.S. data, he would find a confirmation of the inflation-unemployment trade-off rediscovered by Phillips (1958), but he would not confirm the lead of price changes over employment. Instead, he would find a surprisingly robust lead of (cyclical) employment over price changes.

Thus, if we agree with Fisher's view that leading variables 'foreshadow' lagging variables,[9] then recent evidence suggests that shocks to the labor market are the source of macroeconomic price instability. Moreover, from a general equilibrium view and taking into account the positive correlation between price changes and cyclical employment, destabilizing shocks to the economy seem to be dominated by labor demand shocks.[10]

Of course, this result must be taken with a certain proviso, namely the danger of spurious correlation. It seems advisable to finish in the spirit of Irving Fisher (1973, p. 502):

> We may, therefore, feel certain that changes in the [employment] level do definitely foreshadow or anticipate changes in [prices]. Of course, this relationship might conceivably not be causal ... [It] ... might conceivably be caused by some third influence.[11]

Figure 10.1: Employment and consumer price changes

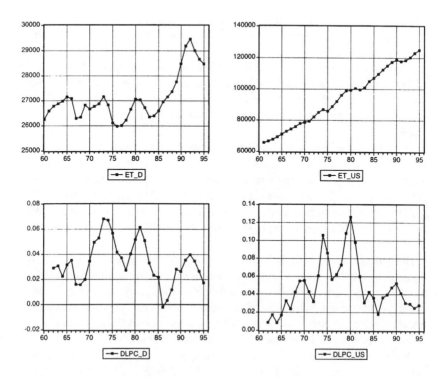

Note: ET_D = employment in Germany, ET_US = employment in the U.S., DLPC_D = consumer price changes in Germany, DLPC_US = consumer price changes in the U.S.

Figure 10.2: Construction of cyclical employment

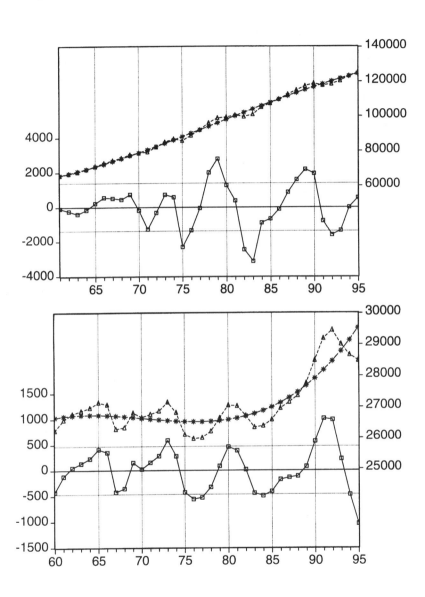

Note: Upper panel: United States, lower panel: Germany

Figure 10.3: Cross correlograms, Germany

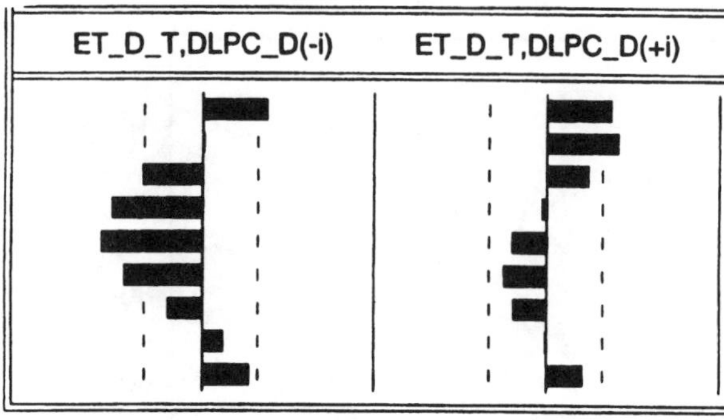

ET_D_T,DLPC_D(-i)	ET_D_T,DLPC_D(+i)	i	lag	lead
		0	0.3908	0.3908
		1	0.0155	0.4315
		2	-0.3501	0.2481
		3	-0.5326	-0.0165
		4	-0.5959	-0.1981
		5	-0.4581	-0.2524
		6	-0.2008	-0.1934
		7	0.1237	-0.0023
		8	0.2867	0.2164

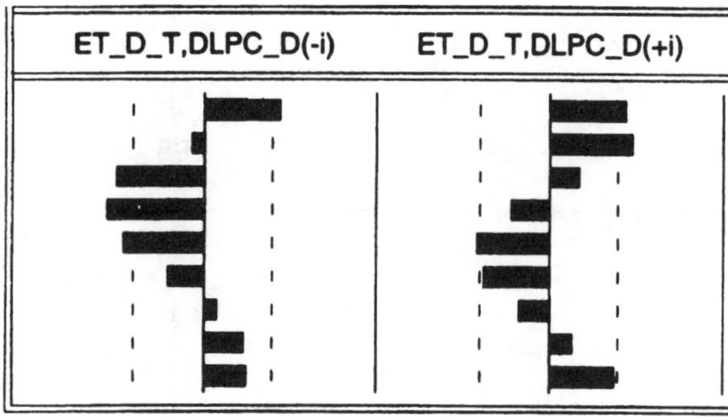

ET_D_T,DLPC_D(-i)	ET_D_T,DLPC_D(+i)	i	lag	lead
		0	0.4510	0.4510
		1	-0.0671	0.4983
		2	-0.5096	0.1787
		3	-0.5700	-0.2254
		4	-0.4742	-0.4308
		5	-0.2080	-0.3872
		6	0.0741	-0.1802
		7	0.2396	0.1385
		8	0.2585	0.3858

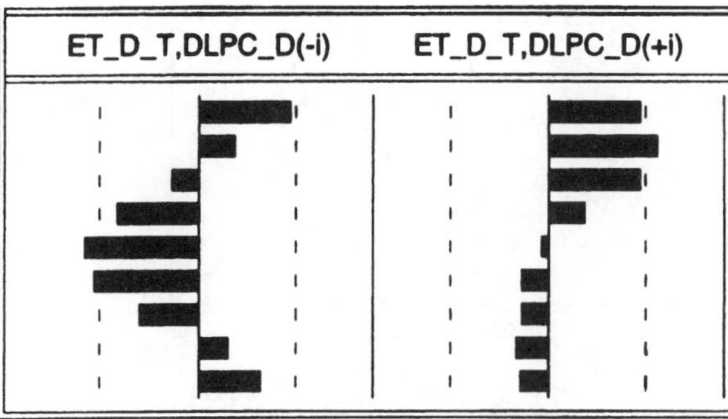

ET_D_T,DLPC_D(-i)	ET_D_T,DLPC_D(+i)	i	lag	lead
		0	0.5466	0.5466
		1	0.2151	0.6442
		2	-0.1493	0.5467
		3	-0.4736	0.2145
		4	-0.6690	-0.0395
		5	-0.6125	-0.1555
		6	-0.3392	-0.1545
		7	0.1745	-0.1866
		8	0.3719	-0.1617

Note: ET_D_T = cyclical employment, DLPC_D = consumer price changes; from above to below: 1960-1995, 1960-1984, 1984-1995

Figure 10.4: Cross correlograms, United States

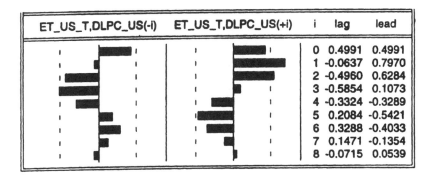

ET_US_T,DLPC_US(-i)	ET_US_T,DLPC_US(+i)	i	lag	lead
		0	0.2837	0.2837
		1	-0.1634	0.4837
		2	-0.4218	0.2954
		3	-0.3743	0.0090
		4	-0.1612	-0.2232
		5	-0.0184	-0.2571
		6	0.0044	-0.1400
		7	0.0319	-0.0686
		8	0.1052	-0.0173

ET_US_T,DLPC_US(-i)	ET_US_T,DLPC_US(+i)	i	lag	lead
		0	0.3376	0.3376
		1	-0.1545	0.5423
		2	-0.4316	0.2700
		3	-0.3413	-0.1078
		4	-0.0731	-0.3012
		5	0.0374	-0.2172
		6	-0.0290	-0.0050
		7	-0.1322	0.1231
		8	-0.1877	0.0972

ET_US_T,DLPC_US(-i)	ET_US_T,DLPC_US(+i)	i	lag	lead
		0	0.4991	0.4991
		1	-0.0637	0.7970
		2	-0.4960	0.6284
		3	-0.5854	0.1073
		4	-0.3324	-0.3289
		5	0.2084	-0.5421
		6	0.3288	-0.4033
		7	0.1471	-0.1354
		8	-0.0715	0.0539

Note: ET_US_T = cyclical employment, DLPC_US = consumer price changes; from above to below: 1960-1995, 1960-1984, 1984-1995

Horst Entorf

Figure 10.5: Distributed employment effects and price changes

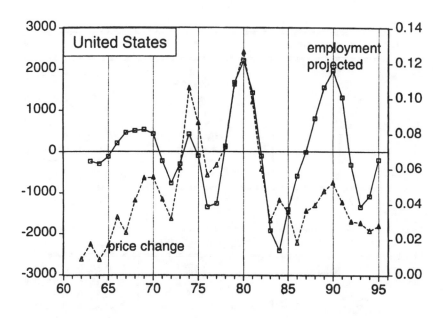

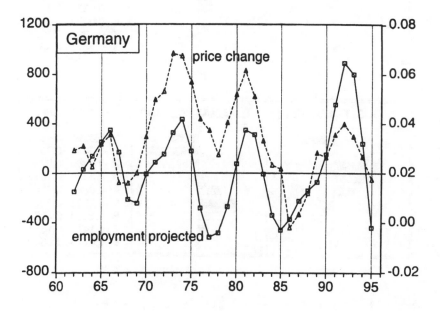

NOTES

*   I am grateful to Bettina and Hans G. Monissen for helpful comments and suggestions.

1   In fact, he mentioned the very time intensive use of (human) 'computers': 'During the last three years in particular I have had at least one computer in my office almost constantly at work on this problem ...' (Fisher, 1973, p. 497).

2   Fisher graphed data from 1903 to 1925, but reported a correlation coefficient only for 1915-1924. More examples for this kind of 'data mining' are presented by Dimand (1993, p. 169), who tried to explain this practice by Fisher's enthusiasm for his theory: 'Fisher's enthusiasm for his theory of the business cycle as a dance of the dollar appears to have led him to seek higher correlations in ways that would now be regarded as questionable.'

3   Source: Sachverständigenrat (German council of economic experts), 1996.

4   The variance of the long-run employment trend would dominate the cross-correlation function. There would be a persistent cross-correlation pattern such that cyclical lead-lag relationships cannot be identified. Fisher's analysis is based on original data that, however, does not reveal any significant trend.

5   Both time series are adjusted to a time polynomial of third order.

6   In more detail:
    a) Germany, 1960-1995, has 4 cycles. This implies that the average cycle length is about 9 years, and the transformation leads to $9 / 2 - 1 = 3.5$. This result is confirmed by the minimum of the empirical cross-correlation function which is found at 4 years for the lead of price changes over employment.
    b) Germany, 1960-1984, 3 cycles imply that the average cycle length is about 8 years, $4 - 1 = 3$, the minimum is found at 3.
    c) Germany, 1984-1995, 1 cycle of about 12 years, $6 - 1 = 5$, the minimum is found at 4.
  For the U.S., the cross-correlation function is dominated by the higher variance of price changes (see Figures 10.1 and 10.2). Inspection of Figure 10.2 gives:
    a) U.S., 1960-1995, 6 cycles imply an average cycle of 6 years, $3 - 1 = 2$, the minimum is found at 2.
    b) U.S., 1960-1984, 4 cycles imply an average cycle of 6 years, $3 - 1 = 2$, the minimum is found at 2.
    c) U.S., 1984-1995, 2 cycles imply an average cycle of 6 years, $3 - 1 = 2$, the minimum is found at 3.

7   Results are robust as long as one does not give too much weight to lags zero or two.

8   For the period 1960-1984 the zero-lag correlations are 0.55 (U.S.) and 0.57 (D), for 1984-1995 the correlations are 0.54 (U.S.) and 0.76 (D), and for 1960-1995 they are 0.49 in both countries. Only in the case of 'U.S., 1984-1995' the maximum of the cross-correlation function is not at zero but at the one-year lag of price changes.

9   This principle of 'Granger-causality' has been (re-) introduced by Granger (1969).

10   Assuming upward bending labor supply and downward bending labor demand curves, supply shocks (i.e. shifts of the labor supply curve) lead to a negative correlation between short-run fluctuations of prices and employment, demand shocks (shifts of the demand curve) can be identified by a positive correlation.

11   Of course, in Fisher's original conclusion of his own article, the words 'prices' and 'employment' are interchanged.

REFERENCES

Dimand, R.M. (1993), 'The dance of the dollar: Irving Fisher's monetary theory of economic fluctuations', *History of Economics Review*, **20**, 161-172.

Entorf, H. (1993), 'Constructing leading indicators from non-balanced sectoral business survey series', *International Journal of Forecasting,* **9**, 211-225.

Fisher, I. (1926), 'A statistical relation between unemployment and price changes', *International Labour Review*, **13**, 785-792.

Fisher, I. (1973), 'I discovered the Phillips curve', *Journal of Political Economy*, **81**, 496-502.

Granger, C.W.J. (1969), 'Investigating causal relations by econometric models and cross-spectral methods, *Econometrica*, **37**, 424-438:

Phillips, A.W. (1958), 'The relationship between unemployment and the rate of change of money wages in the United Kingdom, 1861-1957', *Economica*, **25**, 283-299.

Sachverständigenrat (1996), *Reformen voranbringen*, Stuttgart, Metzler-Poeschel, (Data Appendix).

11. Irving Fisher and the Modern Theory of Index Numbers

János Barta

From the beginning and throughout my life 'I have tried' to help build economics into a genuine science, comparable with the physical sciences, as well as to apply its principles to help solve certain practical economic problems pressing for solution – Irving Fisher (1947).

This paper brings to mind Irving Fisher as a pioneer in mathematical economics and shows some of his main achievements in the domain of price index theory. The well-known price indices of Laspeyres, Paasche and Fisher are presented in a mathematical framework. Furthermore, the Divisia indices and their specializations by Vogt are treated (Sections 2 and 3). Section 4 deals with the 'two great reversal tests' of Fisher: the time reversal test and the factor reversal test. Fisher also introduced the idea of antitheses of price indices, which, many years later, led to the discovery of astonishing mathematical properties in price index theory. The need of a rigorous definition of price indices induced the search for a suitable axiom system. This question provoked many answers, but no definitive and universally accepted solution (Section 5). Some of the most recent contributions to the axiomatics of price index theory are discussed in the paper.

1 FISHER BETWEEN MATHEMATICS AND ECONOMICS

The above quotation comes from Fisher's manuscript called *My Economic Endeavours*, a work that Fisher planned to publish in 12 chapters as his scientific testament and summary of his research. The quotation expresses Fisher's deep scientific inclination, which underlay his research in economics during his whole life.

Originally Fisher was a mathematician, and his view of economics was always deeply related to mathematical methods. At the time he entered the field of mathematical economics, 'in the so-called gay nineties', Fisher was one of the first scientists in America to come from mathematics to economics. Remembering his early years Fisher (1941, p. 185) wrote:

> One day I confided to William Sumner my growing perplexity as to how I was to write my doctor's dissertation, since only about half my time had been spent on mathematics, the other half having been mostly in economics. He immediately said: 'Why not write on mathematical economics?' I replied, 'I never heard of it.'

In this sense Fisher can be considered a pioneer in mathematical economics. It's remarkable that the systematic use of mathematical models in social sciences is more recent than in natural sciences, like physics, for example.

An interesting question is why this delay took place in the history of social sciences. The economist Mitchell (1938, p. 10) wrote for the case of the measurement of price changes:

> It is a curious fact that men did not attempt to measure changes in the level of prices until after they had learned to measure such subtle things as the weight of the atmosphere, the velocity of sound. ... Their tardiness in attacking that problem is the more strange because price changes had frequently been a subject of acrimonious debate among publicists and a cause of popular agitation. Perhaps disinclination on the part of 'natural philosophers' to soil their hands with such vulgar subjects as the prices of provision was partly responsible for the delay.

As the title of this paper indicates, we will focus on price index theory. This was one of the main domains in which Fisher accomplished his program of explaining economical phenomena using mathematical models.

Fisher is therefore the father of the modern price index theory; indeed his work opened the way for a great mathematical development, which went on to the present day. It is fascinating how the theory behind price indices became more and more abstract, involving surprisingly many domains of pure mathematics, like functional analysis, group theory, axiomatics and so on. This wide use of sophisticated mathematical tools led to the so-called modern theory of index numbers.

2   THE PRICE INDEX PROBLEM

The economic concept of price index can be modeled mathematically as follows:

We consider a function with four n-dimensional vectors as arguments:

$$P: R_{++}^{4n} \to R_{++}, \quad (\vec{q}^0, \vec{p}^0, \vec{q}^1, \vec{p}^1) \mapsto P(\vec{q}^0, \vec{p}^0, \vec{q}^1, \vec{p}^1),$$

prices in the base situation $= (p_1^0, p_2^0, \ldots, p_n^0) = \vec{p}^0$,

quantities in the base situation $= (q_1^0, q_2^0, \ldots, q_n^0) = \vec{q}^0$,

prices in the observed situation $= (p_1^1, p_2^1, \ldots, p_n^1) = \vec{p}^1$ and quantities in the observed situation $= (q_1^1, q_2^1, \ldots, q_n^1) = \vec{q}^1$.

Figure 11.1: The quantity-price diagram

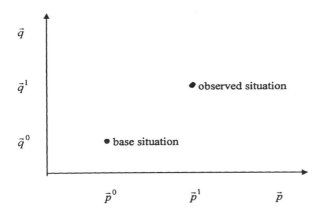

There is a base situation $(\vec{p}^0, \vec{q}^0)$ and an observed situation $(\vec{p}^1, \vec{q}^1)$ (see Figure 11.1). The price index $P(\vec{q}^0, \vec{p}^0, \vec{q}^1, \vec{p}^1)$ is a function which gives a positive real number expressing the comparison of these two situations. This number is called the price index number.

The essence of the price index problem consists of finding for several commodities a suitable continuation of the price relative defined for one commodity into a higher dimension. The continuation has to be thought of as, e.g. the continuation of a function defined on the real axis to a function defined in the complex plane. The price relative appears when one considers only one good. The price index then is simply the price in the observed situation p^1 divided by the price in the base situation p^0. In this case, the price index is the following function of the 4 real variables p^0, q^0, p^1, q^1, whereby q^0 is the quantity in the base situation and q^1 that of the observed situation:

$$P(q^0, p^0, q^1, p^1) = \frac{p^1}{p^0}. \tag{11.1}$$

3   SOLUTIONS TO THE PRICE INDEX PROBLEM

3.1 Laspeyres, Paasche Solutions and Their Arithmetic and Geometric Mean

There are many possible solutions to the price index problem Among the most well-known ones are Laspeyres index and the Paasche index:

$$P_{Laspeyres} = \frac{\vec{q}^0 \vec{p}^1}{\vec{q}^0 \vec{p}^0} = \frac{\sum_{i=1}^{n} q_i^0 p_i^1}{\sum_{i=1}^{n} q_i^0 p_i^0}, \qquad (11.2)$$

$$P_{Paasche} = \frac{\vec{q}^1 \vec{p}^1}{\vec{q}^1 \vec{p}^0} = \frac{\sum_{i=1}^{n} q_i^1 p_i^1}{\sum_{i=1}^{n} q_i^1 p_i^0}. \qquad (11.3)$$

The Drobisch arithmetical mean of the Laspeyres index and Paasche index

$$P_{Drobisch} = \frac{P_{Laspeyres} + P_{Paasche}}{2} \qquad (11.4)$$

and Fisher's geometrical mean

$$P_{Fisher} = \sqrt{P_{Laspeyres} \cdot P_{Paasche}} \qquad (11.5)$$

are other suitable solutions to the price index problem. Fisher called Laspeyres and Paasche indices 'very good', the Drobisch index 'superlative' and Fisher's index 'ideal'.

3.2 The Divisia Solution and Two Special Cases

3.2.1 The Index of Divisia

We regard the base point $(\vec{q}^0, \vec{p}^0)$ and the observed point $(\vec{q}^1, \vec{p}^1)$ as connected by a path $\{\vec{q}(t), \vec{p}(t)\}$ parameterized by the 'time parameter' $t \in [t_0, t_1]$ with

$$\vec{q}(t_0) = \vec{q}^{\,0}, \quad \vec{p}(t_0) = \vec{p}^{\,0},$$

$$\vec{q}(t_1) = \vec{q}^{\,1}, \quad \vec{p}(t_1) = \vec{p}^{\,1}.$$

(11.6)

The whole path $\{\vec{q}(t), \vec{p}(t)\}_{t \in [t_0, t_1]}$ will be denoted by C. We treat all components $q_i(t)$ and $p_i(t)$ as differentiable with regard to t. We denote these derivatives by $\dot{q}_i(t)$ and $\dot{p}_i(t)$ respectively.

The resulting Divisia indices for quantities and prices

$$Q_{Divisia}^{(C)} = \exp \int_{t_0}^{t_1} \frac{\dot{\vec{q}}(\tau)\vec{p}(\tau)}{\vec{q}(\tau)\vec{p}(\tau)} d\tau$$

(11.7)

and

$$P_{Divisia}^{(C)} = \exp \int_{t_0}^{t_1} \frac{\vec{q}(\tau)\dot{\vec{p}}(\tau)}{\vec{q}(\tau)\vec{p}(\tau)} d\tau$$

(11.8)

are dependent on the path C from the base point to the observed point in the $2n$-dimensional quantity-price space:

Figure 11.2: An arbitrary path in the quantity-price diagram

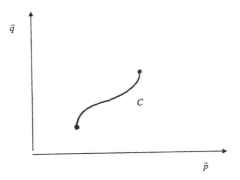

One can conceive of some of the traditional indices as Divisia line integrals on fictitious paths between the base point $(\vec{q}^{\,0}, \vec{p}^{\,0})$ and the observed point $(\vec{q}^{\,1}, \vec{p}^{\,1})$ in the two n-dimensional quantity-price space. Laspeyres' index, Paasche's index and Edgeworth-Marshall's (and Walsh') index, for example, can be interpreted as Divisia indices (see Vogt and Barta, 1997) on the paths given in figures 11.3.1, 11.3.2 and 11.3.3 respectively:

Figure 11.3.1: The index of Laspeyres seen as Divisia index

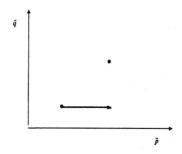

Figure 11.3.2: The index of Paasche

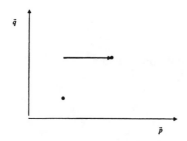

Figure 11.3.3: The index of Edgeworth-Marshall

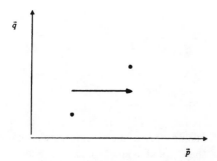

3.2.2 The Divisia Index on the Straight Line

The straight line can be regarded as a special path between the base point and the observed point in the $2n$-dimensional quantity-price space. It can be parameterized as follows:

$$
\begin{aligned}
q_1(t) &= q_i^0 + t \cdot (q_i^1 - q_i^0) \\
p_i(t) &= p_i^0 + t \cdot (p_i^1 - p_i^0)
\end{aligned}
\quad,\text{ with } i = 1, 2, ..., n \text{ and } t \in [0, 1]
\tag{11.9}
$$

Analytically, the evaluation of the Divisia price (11.8) index on the straight line leads to the following index:

$$
P_{Vogt\,I}^{(C_{lin})} =
\begin{cases}
\sqrt{\dfrac{\vec{q}^1\vec{p}^1}{\vec{q}^0\vec{p}^0}}\left(\dfrac{\vec{q}^0\vec{p}^1+\vec{q}^1\vec{p}^0+\sqrt{D}}{\vec{q}^0\vec{p}^1+\vec{q}^1\vec{p}^0-\sqrt{D}}\right)^{\frac{\vec{q}^1\vec{p}^0-\vec{q}^0\vec{p}^1}{2\sqrt{D}}} & D>0 \\[2em]
\sqrt{\dfrac{\vec{q}^1\vec{p}^1}{\vec{q}^0\vec{p}^0}}\,\exp\dfrac{\vec{q}^0\vec{p}^1-\vec{q}^1\vec{p}^0}{\vec{q}^0\vec{p}^1+\vec{q}^1\vec{p}^0} & D=0 \\[2em]
\sqrt{\dfrac{\vec{q}^1\vec{p}^1}{\vec{q}^0\vec{p}^0}}\,\exp\left(\dfrac{\vec{q}^0\vec{p}^0-\vec{q}^1\vec{p}^0}{\sqrt{-D}}\arctan\dfrac{\sqrt{-D}}{\vec{q}^0\vec{p}^1+\vec{q}^1\vec{p}^0}\right) & D<0
\end{cases}
\tag{11.10}
$$

where

$$
D = (\vec{q}^0\vec{p}^1 + \vec{q}^1\vec{p}^0)^2 - 4\vec{q}^0\vec{p}^0 \cdot \vec{q}^1\vec{p}^1.
\tag{11.11}
$$

3.2.3 The Divisia Index on the Exponential Path

One might prefer the exponential path $C_{\exp}$ displayed in figure 11.4 to the straight line.

Figure 11.4: The exponential path

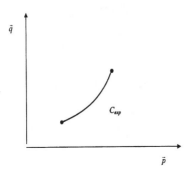

This exponential path can be parameterized as follows:

$$q_i(t) = q_i^0 \cdot \left(\frac{q_i^1}{q_i^0}\right)^t$$

$$p_i(t) = p_i^0 \cdot \left(\frac{p_i^1}{p_i^0}\right)^t$$

, with $i = 1, 2, ..., n$ and $t \in [0, 1]$ \qquad (11.12)

and the Divisia price index on this path is given by

$$P_{Vogt\,II}^{(Cecp)} = \exp \int_0^1 \frac{\sum\limits_{i=1}^n q_i^0 p_i^0 \left(\dfrac{q_i^1 p_i^1}{q_i^0 p_i^0}\right)^t ln\left(\dfrac{p_i^1}{p_i^0}\right)}{\sum\limits_{i=1}^n q_i^0 p_i^0 \left(\dfrac{q_i^1 p_i^1}{q_i^0 p_i^0}\right)^t} dt. \qquad (11.13)$$

The analytic integration of (11.13), however, was evaluated only for the situation with two commodities:

$$P_{Vogt\,II}^{(C_{exp})2} = \left(\frac{p_1^1}{p_1^0}\right)^E \qquad (11.14)$$

with

$$E = \left(1 + \frac{ln(\frac{p_2^1}{p_2^0})\left(ln(\frac{q_2^1 p_2^1}{q_1^1 p_1^1}+1) - ln(\frac{q_2^0 p_2^0}{q_1^0 p_1^0}+1)\right)}{ln\left(\frac{p_1^1}{p_1^0}\right) \cdot ln\left(\frac{\frac{q_2^1 p_2^1}{q_1^1 p_1^1}}{\frac{q_2^0 p_2^0}{q_1^0 p_1^0}}\right)} + \frac{ln(\frac{q_2^0 p_2^0}{q_1^0 p_1^0}+1) - ln(\frac{q_2^1 p_2^1}{q_1^1 p_1^1}+1)}{ln\left(\frac{\frac{q_2^1 p_2^1}{q_2^0 p_2^0}}{\frac{q_1^1 p_1^1}{q_1^0 p_1^0}}\right)} \right).$$

$$(11.15)$$

It remains to investigate if such an evaluation is possible for $n > 2$. From the above figures it is clear that the indices Vogt I and Vogt II are crossings of the indices of Laspeyres and Paasche, namely 'geometric crossings'.

4   TESTS FOR PRICE INDICES: FROM FISHER TO THE PRESENT

4.1 Fisher's Great Reversal Tests

The words 'suitable' and 'good' for price indices should be clarified: a criterion is needed in order to distinguish good from bad functions.

In 1922 Fisher was aware of this problem. In his book *The Making of Index Numbers* (1922, p. 9) we find that:

> The multiplicity of formulae for computing index numbers has given the impression that there must be a corresponding multiplicity in the results of these computations, with no clear choice between them. But this impression is due to a failure to discriminate between index numbers which are good, bad, and indifferent. By means of certain tests we can make this discrimination.

Fisher (1911, 1922) is known for his test-theoretical approach in the statistical index theory. By test he understood a desired property of an index. The above quotation shows clearly his desire to have rational criteria in order to discriminate good from bad index numbers.

The use of tests is again a scientific method, typical in statistics or other applied sciences. The two most important tests introduced by Fisher are the so-called 'great reversal tests'. The first one is the *time reversal test*

$$P(\vec{q}^{\,0},\vec{p}^{\,0},\vec{q}^{\,1},\vec{p}^{\,1}) = \frac{1}{P(\vec{q}^{\,1},\vec{p}^{\,1},\vec{q}^{\,0},\vec{p}^{\,0})} \qquad (11.16)$$

stating that when the two situations are interchanged, the price index yields the reciprocal value. For instance, when the index is 2 with 1980 as the base and 1990 as the observed situation, it should be 1/2 when reversed with 1990 as the base and 1980 as the observed situation. The second great reversal test is the

factor reversal test

$$P(\vec{q}^{\,0},\vec{p}^{\,0},\vec{q}^{\,1},\vec{p}^{\,1}) = \frac{\vec{q}^{\,1}\vec{p}^{\,1} / \vec{q}^{\,0}\vec{p}^{\,0}}{P(\vec{p}^{\,0},\vec{q}^{\,0},\vec{p}^{\,1},\vec{q}^{\,1})}. \qquad (11.17)$$

The factor reversal test states that a price index P multiplied with its analogous quantity index Q should yield the value ratio

$$V = \vec{q}^{\,1}\vec{p}^{\,1} / \vec{q}^{\,0}\vec{p}^{\,0}. \qquad (11.18)$$

Tests help us to classify indices; they give informations about the quality of the chosen price index. For example, it is remarkable that the well-known and most used indices of Laspeyres (11.2) and Paasche (11.3) satisfy neither the time reversal test nor the factor reversal test; the index of Drobisch (11.4) satisfies the time reversal but not the factor reversal test and finally Fisher's index (11.5) which satisfies both. This fact supports the widely accepted conviction that Fisher's index is the ideal price index. In the following section we will give further arguments for calling it 'ideal'.

4.2 Fisher's Antitheses and Fisher's Group of 16 Elements

4.2.1 The Group of 4 Antitheses

Fisher (1922) called the time and the factor reversal test 'finders of new formulae'. For each price index $P(\vec{q}^{\,0},\vec{p}^{\,0},\vec{q}^{\,1},\vec{p}^{\,1})$ there exists its

time antithesis

$$AT(P(\vec{q}^{\,0},\vec{p}^{\,0},\vec{q}^{\,1},\vec{p}^{\,1})) = \frac{1}{P(\vec{q}^{\,1},\vec{p}^{\,1},\vec{q}^{\,0},\vec{p}^{\,0})} \qquad (11.19)$$

and its

factor antithesis

$$AF(P(\vec{q}^0,\vec{p}^0,\vec{q}^1,\vec{p}^1)) = \frac{\vec{q}^1\vec{p}^1 / \vec{q}^0\vec{p}^0}{P(\vec{p}^0,\vec{q}^0,\vec{p}^1,\vec{q}^1)}. \tag{11.20}$$

Fisher's reversal tests (4.1) and (4.2) state that an index should be equal to the corresponding antithesis. From a mathematical point of view AT and AF are two functionals, which when applied to an index function P generate a new index function, $AT(P)$ and $AF(P)$ respectively. The composition of AT and AF yields the

simultaneous time and factor antithesis

$$AS(P) = AT(AF(P)) = AF(AT(P)). \tag{11.21}$$

By considering also the

identity antithesis

$$AE(P) = P \tag{11.22}$$

we get a set of 4 antitheses (AE, AT, AF, AS). This set is interesting because it has a group structure, which is a property that plays a central role in mathematics. Armstrong (1988, p. VII) says about the beauty of the group structure: 'Groups measure symmetry as numbers measure size'.

4.2.2 Fisher's Group of 16 Antitheses

Irving Fisher was the first to introduce time and factor antitheses in price index theory, but the intriguing connection between concrete economic objects and abstract mathematical structures was found out many years later by Vogt (1987). The main results obtained in this domain are shown in chapter 3 of Vogt and Barta (1997). In 1993 Arthur Vogt extended to 16 the original set G of 4 antitheses (see Vogt, 1993):

$$F = \{AE, AQ, AP, AT, AF, AS, f7, f8, f9, f10, f11, f12, f13, f14, f15, f16\}$$

The following group table was obtained by using the computer program *Mathematica*. This group F is called Fisher's group. Many interesting mathematical properties and symmetries are contained in the group F. But from a practical point of view also, Fisher's index has been considered as ideal since 1922 because it passes all the sixteen reversal tests (obtained by the above 16 antitheses) and is the only possible index with this property! (cf. Vogt 1991, p. 12). This is a point in favor of these sixteen reversal tests.

Table 11.1: Fisher's group

	AE	AQ	AP	AT	AF	AS	7	8	9	10	11	12	13	14	15	16
AE	AE	AQ	AP	AT	AF	AS	7	8	9	10	11	12	13	14	15	16
AQ	AQ	AE	AT	AP	10	9	11	12	AS	AF	7	8	16	15	14	13
AP	AP	AT	AE	AQ	9	10	12	11	AF	AS	8	7	15	16	13	14
AT	AT	AP	AQ	AE	AS	AF	8	7	10	9	12	11	14	13	16	15
AF	AF	7	8	AS	AE	AT	AQ	AP	13	14	15	16	9	10	11	12
AS	AS	8	7	AF	AT	AE	AP	AQ	14	13	16	15	10	9	12	11
7	7	AF	AS	8	14	13	15	16	AT	AE	AQ	AP	12	11	10	9
8	8	AS	AF	7	13	14	16	15	AE	AT	AP	AQ	11	12	9	10
9	9	12	11	10	AP	AQ	AT	AE	15	16	13	14	AF	AS	8	7
10	10	11	12	9	AQ	AP	AE	AT	16	15	14	13	AS	AF	7	8
11	11	10	9	12	15	16	14	13	AP	AQ	AE	AT	8	7	AF	AS
12	12	9	10	11	16	15	13	14	AQ	AP	AT	AE	7	8	AS	AF
13	13	16	15	14	8	7	AS	AF	11	12	9	10	AE	AT	AP	AQ
14	14	15	16	13	7	8	AF	AS	12	11	10	9	AT	AE	AQ	AP
15	15	14	13	16	11	12	10	9	8	7	AF	AS	AP	AQ	AE	AT
16	16	13	14	15	12	11	9	10	7	8	AS	AF	AQ	AP	AT	AE

Finally, Fisher's group could also be classified on the basis of its algebraic structure: the result was that F is isomorphic to the group

$$D_4 \times Z/_{2Z} \tag{11.23}$$

where D_4 is the dihedral group with 8 elements and $Z/_{2Z}$ is the cyclic group with 2 elements. Later interesting information about this group, in particular the subgroup structure and the order of each element, were found, e.g. Fisher's group G has altogether 35 subgroups: 1 subgroup with 16 elements, 7 with 8 elements (4 of these are isomorphic to D_4), 15 with 4 elements, 11 with 2 elements and finally 1 subgroup with 1 element. It is important to remember that the dihedral group plays an important role in Euclidean geometry; in fact the 8 possible isometries of a square (that is 4 symmetries and 4 rotations) correspond to a dihedral group.

4.3 Antitheses of Properties of Indices

The research into antitheses continued with the introduction of a new idea: the antithesis of a property of price indices.

Let P be a given index and E any property of indices. Then let $A(P)$ be a given antithesis of the index P. The following question arises: which property has to hold for P, so that $A(P)$ satisfies E ? This property is called $A(E)$, i.e. the antithesis of the property E.

An example: What is the factor antithesis of the

proportionality property

$$P(\vec{q}^{\,0}, \vec{p}^{\,0}, \vec{q}^{\,1}, \lambda\vec{p}^{\,0}) = \lambda \ ? \tag{11.24}$$

If proportionality holds for the factor antithesis of the index P, we have

$$\frac{\dfrac{\vec{q}^{\,1} \cdot \lambda\vec{p}^{\,0}}{\vec{q}^{\,0} \cdot \vec{p}^{\,0}}}{P(\vec{p}^{\,0}, \vec{q}^{\,0}, \lambda\vec{p}^{\,0}, \vec{q}^{\,1}} = \lambda \tag{11.25}$$

by canceling the factor λ

$$P(\vec{p}^{\,0}, \vec{q}^{\,0}, \lambda\vec{p}^{\,0}\vec{q}^{\,1}) = \frac{\vec{q}^{\,1}\vec{p}^{\,0}}{\vec{q}^{\,0}\vec{p}^{\,0}}. \tag{11.26}$$

By rewriting (4.11) in the usual sequence $\vec{q}^{\,0}, \vec{p}^{\,0}, \vec{q}^{\,1}, \vec{p}^{\,1}$ the

strong value-index-preserving test

$$P(\vec{q}^{\,0}, \vec{p}^{\,0}, \lambda\vec{q}^{\,0}, \vec{p}^{\,1}) = \frac{\vec{q}^{\,0}\vec{p}^{\,1}}{\vec{q}^{\,0}\vec{p}^{\,0}} \tag{11.27}$$

emerges. The strong value-index-preserving test is the factor antithesis of the proportionality property.

The definition of antithesis of a property can be formalized in the following implication:

$$P \text{ satisfies } A(E) \Leftrightarrow A(P) \text{ satisfies } E. \tag{11.28}$$

Section 3.2 of Vogt and Barta (1997) treats this idea and shows several interesting properties following from the above definition.

5 AXIOMATICS

The use of tests shows Fisher's scientific approach to price index theory. The next natural question to ask is: 'What essential properties have to be satisfied by a function in order for it to be considered a price index?' This is nothing else than looking for a suitable axiom system for price indices. The axiomatic approach of price indices is actually a modern evolution of Fisher's original program, that is, treating economics with the same rationality as physical sciences, and therefore we might say that axiomatics belong to the modern theory of index numbers. It follows a short overview of the axiomatic approach of price indices. One of the best-known axiom system is the one Eichhorn and Voeller proposed in 1978. It consists of the following 5 properties:

Monotonicity axiom

$$P(\vec{q}^{\,0},\vec{p}^{\,0},\vec{q}^{\,1},\vec{p}^{\,1}) > P(\vec{q}^{\,0},\vec{p}^{\,0},\vec{q}^{\,1},\hat{\vec{p}}^{\,1}) \quad if \quad \vec{p}^{\,1} > \hat{\vec{p}}^{\,1},$$

$$P(\vec{q}^{\,0},\vec{p}^{\,0},\vec{q}^{\,1},\vec{p}^{\,1}) < P(\vec{q}^{\,0},\hat{\vec{p}}^{\,0},\vec{q}^{\,1},\vec{p}^{\,1}) \quad if \quad \vec{p}^{\,0} > \hat{\vec{p}}^{\,0}. \tag{11.29}$$

This axiom states that the function P is strictly increasing with respect to $\vec{p}^{\,1}$ and strictly decreasing with respect to $\vec{p}^{\,0}$.

Dimensionality axiom:

$$P(\vec{q}^{\,0},\lambda\vec{p}^{\,0},\vec{q}^{\,1},\lambda\vec{p}^{\,1}) = P(\vec{q}^{\,0},\vec{p}^{\,0},\vec{q}^{\,1},\vec{p}^{\,1}) \quad for \ \lambda \in R_{++}. \tag{11.30}$$

This axiom states that a dimensional change in the unit of currency in which all prices are measured does not change the value of the function P.

Commensurability axiom

$$P(\frac{q_1^0}{\lambda_1},...,\frac{q_n^0}{\lambda_n},\lambda_1 p_1^0,...,\lambda_n p_n^0,\frac{q_1^1}{\lambda_1},...,\frac{q_n^1}{\lambda_n},\lambda_1 p_1^1,...,\lambda_n p_n^1) =$$

$$P(\vec{q}^{\,0},\vec{p}^{\,0},\vec{q}^{\,1},\vec{p}^{\,1}) \ for \ \lambda_1,...,\lambda_n \in R_{++}. \tag{11.31}$$

This axiom states that a change in the units of measurement of commodities does not change the value of the function P.

Identity theorem

$$P(\vec{q}^{\,0},\vec{p}^{\,0},\vec{q}^{\,1},\vec{p}^{\,0}) = 1. \tag{11.32}$$

According to this theorem the value of the function P equals one if all prices remain constant.

Linear homogeneity test

$$P(\vec{q}^{\,0},\vec{p}^{\,0},\vec{q}^{\,1},\lambda\vec{p}^{\,1}) = \lambda P(\vec{q}^{\,0},\vec{p}^{\,0},\vec{q}^{\,1},\vec{p}^{\,1}) \quad for \ \lambda \in R_{++}. \tag{11.33}$$

According to this test the value of the function P changes by the factor λ if all prices of the observed situation change λ-fold.

This can be considered as the basic axiom system for price indices, so that the later proposals of new systems are mainly attempts to correct or improve the original axiom system.

Olt (1995) proposed an axiom system consisting of the dimensionality axiom (11.30), the commensurability axiom (11.31), the

symmetry theorem

$$P(\vec{q}^{\,0},\vec{p}^{\,0},\vec{q}^{\,1},\vec{p}^{\,1}) = P(\tilde{\vec{q}}^{\,0},\tilde{\vec{p}}^{\,0},\tilde{\vec{q}}^{\,1},\tilde{\vec{p}}^{\,1}) \tag{11.34}$$

(stating that the same permutation of the components of the four vectors does not change the value of the index) and the

strong mean value theorem:

For   every $(\vec{q}^{\,0},\vec{p}^{\,0},\vec{q}^{\,1},\vec{p}^{\,1}) \in R^{4n}_{++}$ there   exists   a $\lambda = \lambda(\vec{q}^{\,0},\vec{p}^{\,0},\vec{q}^{\,1},\vec{p}^{\,1};P) \in (0,1)$ so that the value of the price index can be represented as a convex combination of the smallest and the biggest price relative:

$$P(\vec{q}^{\,0},\vec{p}^{\,0},\vec{q}^{\,1},\vec{p}^{\,1}) = \lambda \cdot \min_i \left\{ \frac{p_i^1}{p_i^0} \right\} + (1-\lambda) \cdot \max_i \left\{ \frac{p_i^1}{p_i^0} \right\}. \tag{11.35}$$

Price index theory produced many other axiom systems; each in an attempt to represent the idea of price index or a specific aspect of it in the best possible way. As Eichhorn and Pfingsten (1984) have pointed out price indices are not functions but sequences of functions $\left\{ P_n \right\}_{n \in N}$; a price index function for any possible number of commodities n. However, the idea of price index implies that this should behave 'the same way' for any number of commodities n, therefore there must be a strong relation between P_n (the index for n commodities) and P_{n+1} (the index for $(n + 1)$ commodities), that is, an extension rule is needed. This fact represents a difference from other classical mathematical measures like norms and metrics, which are usually defined in a fixed n-dimensional vector space. It would be reasonable to define an analogous extension rule also for norms and metrics; in this way they would also become sequences of functions like price indices according to Eichhorn and Pfingsten (1984, cf. Section 2.5.3 of Vogt and Barta, 1997).

It is remarkable that the above two axiom systems would accept as a price index the following alternating sequence

$$P_n(\vec{q}^{\,0},\vec{p}^{\,0},\vec{q}^{\,1},\vec{p}^{\,1}) = \begin{cases} P_{Laspayres}(\vec{q}^{\,0},\vec{p}^{\,0},\vec{q}^{\,1},\vec{p}^{\,1}), \ for \ n = 2,4,6,..., \\ \\ P_{Paasche}(\vec{q}^{\,0},\vec{p}^{\,0},\vec{q}^{\,1},\vec{p}^{\,1}), \ for \ n = 1,3,5,.... \end{cases} \tag{11.36}$$

However, with this index the calculating authority could manipulate the value of the index by introducing an $(n+1)^{th}$ 'phantom commodity' with $q_{n+1}^0 = 0$ and $q_{n+1}^1 = 0$. That's why in chapter 4 of Vogt and Barta (1997) the natural extension axiom for price indices is introduced. This extension rule permits the extension of P_n to P_{n+1} and at the same time excludes undesired indices like the above alternating sequence.

6 CONCLUSION

Once more it must be underlined that the present state of price index theory deeply connected with sophisticated mathematical structures had its origin in Fisher's scientific efforts. Therefore, coming back to the initial quotation, it can be said that Fisher was in fact able to 'help built economics into a genuine science' as he desired.

REFERENCES

Armstrong, M. (1988), *Groups and Symmetry*, New York, Springer-Verlag.

Barber, W.J. (ed.), assisted by R.W. Dimand and K. Foster, consulting editor J. Tobin, (1997), *The Works of Irving Fisher*, 14 Volumes, London, Pickering and Chatto.

Barta, J. (1996), *Methods of Automated Theorem Proving Applied to Several Measures of Descriptive Statistics. An Approach to Axiomatics with a New Tool of Computer Logic*, Zürich, Diploma Thesis at the Federal Institute of Technology.

Eichhorn, W. and Pfingsten, A. (1984), 'Sequences of Mechanistic Price Indices', in H. Hauptmann and W. Krelle (ed.), *Operations Research and Economic Theory; Essays in Honour of Martin Beckmann*, Berlin, Springer-Verlag.

Eichhorn, W. and Voeller, J. (1976), *Theory of the Price Index*, Lecture Notes in Economics and Mathematical Systems, Berlin, Springer-Verlag.

Fisher, I., assisted by H.G. Brown (1911), *The Purchasing Power of Money. Its Determination and Relation to Credit, Interest and Crises*. New and revised edition 1913. Reprint, New York, A.M. Kelley, 1985. German translation, Reimer-Verlag, Berlin, 1916. Reprint in I. Fisher, 1997, Volume 4.

Fisher, I. (1922), *The Making of Index Numbers. A Study of Their Varieties, Tests, and Reliability*. Reprint of the third edition of 1927, New York A.M. Kelley, 1967. Reprint in Fisher, 1997,Volume 7.

Fisher, I. (1941), 'Mathematical method in social sciences', *Econometrica*, **9**, 185-197.

Fisher, I. (1947), *My Economic Endeavours*, Manuscript in the Fisher Papers, Series III, Box 26 , Folder 414-417, Yale University Library.

Fisher, I. (1997), cf. W.J. Barber, 1997.

Mitchell, W.C.(1938), *The Making and Using of Index Numbers*, Originally published in 1915 as part of Bulletin 173, Bureau of Labour Statistics, Reprints of Economic Classics, New York, 1965, A.M. Kelley.

Olt, B. (1995), *Axiom und Struktur in der statistischen Preisindextheorie*, Dissertation an der Universität Karlsruhe.

Thomas, A.D. and Wood, G.V. (1980), *Group Tables,* University College of Swansea, UK, Shiva Publishing Ltd.

Vogt, A. (1980), 'Der Zeitumkehr- und der Faktorumkehrtest als "finders of tests" ', *Statistische Hefte*, **21**, 66-71.

Vogt, A. (1981), 'Die Zeit- und die Faktorantithesen von Eigenschaften von Indices', *Statistische Hefte*, **22**, 142-143.

Vogt, A. (1987), 'Some suggestions concerning an axiom system for statistical price and quantity indices', Commun. Statist.-Theory Meth., **16**, 3641-3663.

Vogt, A. (1991), *The Making of Tests for Indices,* discussion paper 91-2 of the University of Bern, Volkswirtschaftliches Institut.

Vogt, A. (1993), 'The ghost and the machine', in W.E. Diewert, K. Spremann and F. Stehling (eds), *Mathematical Modelling in Economics, Essays in Honour of W. Eichhorn*, Berlin, Springer-Verlag.

Vogt, A. and Barta, J. (1997), *The Making of Tests of Index Numbers, Mathematical Methods of Descriptive Statistics,* published in Honour of the 50th Anniversary of the Death of Irving Fisher, Heidelberg, Physica-Verlag.

Wolfram, S. (1988), *Mathematica, a System for Doing Mathematics by Computer*, Addison-Wesley, Belmont, CA.

PART SIX:
CAPITAL, INCOME, AND INTEREST

12.　The Nature of Capital and Interest

Bertram Schefold

1　THE MAIN QUESTIONS

Irving Fisher was arguably the first American theorist who ranks high in the top group of the great economists of all time. This indicates how young the international significance of American science still is. Just prior to the turn of the century the United States began to be recognized as one of the world powers after their victory over Spain in the Cuban war. The dynamics of American economic growth, the rapid succession of inventions, and finally American science began to impress and to challenge Europe. European cultural ideas, adopted by American students who had spent several years at European universities – many of them in Germany – stood in contrast to the American way of life. There emerged an American form of institutionalism, kindred with, and yet distinct from, the historical school in Germany. Irving Fisher was a leading author among those who chose a different path of theoretical economics, with its applications solidly based on a quantitative basis. The veneration of Irving Fisher, expressed by great modern American economists, is a tribute not only to his outstanding originality, but also to the fact that he was a pioneer of modernity in economics. It is significant that Irving Fisher became president of the 'American Economic Association' in 1918, succeeding the generation of Ely and other members of the founding period of the Association who had still studied in Germany and had represented the link between American institutionalism and the historical school.

It should be stressed that Fisher's choice of the modernist approach was not dictated by a narrowness of his intellectual culture. He was a man of many gifts, with literary interests and literary talents. The scientific outlook, however, predominated. He knew a great deal about mathematics and physics. He would discuss the Theory of Relativity with Einstein when he was old, but, as a young man, he had the original idea of creating a physical analogue of his theory of general equilibrium, as expressed in his famous dissertation of 1892 (*Mathematical Investigations in the Theory of Value and Prices*) in the form of a kind of machine which showed the equilibration of marginal utility for each consumer, the level of the uniform price for every good, the proportionality of marginal utilities and prices in the form of the movements of the constituent elements of the machine. A photograph of the apparatus, but not the apparatus itself, has been preserved (Monissen, 1989, pp. 211-230).

Fisher's dissertation on general equilibrium theory was independent from Walras and represented a development of the work by Jevons and Auspitz and Lieben. It also contributed to the development of utility theory, away from hedonistic calculus – Fisher refused to anchor the theory of demand in psychology. He remained always intent to provide clear definitions which would allow measuring quantities used in the theory – a major example was his endeavor to construct an index for the purchasing power of money. He insisted that the primary effect of an increase in the quantity of money was not to lower the rate of interest but to increase prices. Already in his *Appreciation and Interest* (Fisher, ([1896] 1965), Fisher had observed that interest on capital and interest on money are different not only because of different elements of risk but also because the purchasing power of money changes. He further observed that each standard is associated with an own-rate of interest in intertemporal exchange.

> The rate of interest is, as Prof. Böhm-Bawerk shows, an agio on present goods exchanged for future goods of the same kind. It is a simple corollary of this theorem, though Prof. Böhm-Bawerk does not express it, that this agio may be in theory and must be in practice a different agio for every separate kind of goods. (Fisher, [1896] 1965, p. 90).

The difference between the own-rates of interest implies a change of relative prices over time. In the simplest and most important case this is an appreciation or depreciation of all goods relative to money, and this induced Fisher to differentiate between nominal and real interest. I have shown elsewhere, in my introduction to Böhm-Bawerks *Positive Theorie des Kapitales*, why Böhm-Bawerk equated all own-rates of interest by assuming constant relative prices: it is a condition of long-run equilibrium; we shall have to reflect on why Fisher does not make this assumption. Here, as a preliminary, we only note that Fisher, who was educated in the natural sciences, was used to be precise with regard to the problems of dimensionality. The formulation used seems to suggest that it was this problem of dimensionality which helped him to abandon the traditional notion of *one* rate of interest governing the structure of prices, and to turn to a multiplicity of own-rates of interest, more than thirty years before the problem of the multiplicity of the own-rates of interest surfaced in the debate between Hayek and Sraffa, and almost forty years before own-rates of interest became a major theme in Keynes's *General Theory*.

2   THE NATURE OF CAPITAL AND INCOME

The Nature of Capital and Income begins, seemingly traditionally, with the concept of wealth. A broad definition is used: wealth includes all material things which are objects of property. Land and human beings are also wealth. In the case of free persons, 'the owner and the thing owned ... coincide' (Fisher, 1906, p. 5); a slave is the possession of somebody else. The discussion of the value of persons (each for himself, or for others, or according to the income generating powers of populations) at the end of the first chapter sounds like a provocative late echo of the American Civil War.

The second chapter is concerned with the modern theme of property rights; they are all to be reduced to entitlements – entitlements to use the services of wealth. Immaterial wealth is to be interpreted as a service in terms of material wealth. The procedure may seem somewhat forced but enhances the coherence of the Fisherian system.

In the fourth chapter he arrives at his neat distinction between stocks and flows. A stock of wealth, existing at any one time, is capital. A flow of services during a period is an income. This distinction may be compared to others. If raw materials or fuels are used in the process of production, there appears not only a service of capital in the form of a flow, but there is a flow of capital goods which allows production of a flow of outputs. Classical economists treated capital as a joint product and this approach has been taken up again in this century by von Neumann. In this view, capital goods enter production at the beginning of each period; they leave it again as durable means of production in a changed form. The difference in value between the new machine and the same machine, one year older, is equal to its depreciation. Depreciation then is a consumption of the original value of the machine and analogous to the consumption of raw materials or fuels in production. In view of this second interpretation Fisher's polemics against classical authors are not always valid and justified. Depreciation is a flow, and circulating capital may also be regarded as such. Fisher's insistence on the treatment of capital as a stock leads to a consistent approach but the joint production approach offers an alternative which he seems not to have understood.

Fisher makes interesting observations on the correct aggregation of the values of capital and then arrives at his impressive argument explaining why the concept of income should be reduced to consumption. Consider sporadic gains like an inheritance or the winning of a lottery: do they represent increases of income or of personal wealth? Inherited wealth is only an entitlement to future income, it seems to Fisher.

He tries to avoid double counting and the confusion of income and capital. This is to be achieved by means of the general concept: income 'consists of services rendered by capital' (Fisher, 1906, p. 118). It must be presupposed that persons are part of capital. He had shown that debts and assets cancel, as far as capital is concerned. It follows accordingly that the incomes of fictitious persons like cooperations also cancel; in fact they do not consume. What a natural person earns is, at first, an increase in wealth. What is taken away for consumption represents income. The consumption goods so obtained finally generates a psychic income, a 'stream of consciousness' (Fisher, 1906, p. 168) which is what Fisher is really concerned with. One is reminded of a biographical element – his health problems – when one reads his rather extensive deliberations on the tension between the desirability and the difficulties of enjoyment in the case of certain objects of consumption (his example is the treatment by a dentist).

This approach led Fisher to become one in the long chain of authors who have advocated an expenditure tax and who wish to tax people according to their use of resources, not according to their income or ability to pay. Kaldor, an eminent post-war author on expenditure taxation, cites Hobbes, J.S. Mill, Marshall, Pigou and Einaudi as important advocates of expenditure taxation, apart from Fisher. In their view, the capitalization of incomes represents the values of means of production used (including capitalized land values and the specific abilities of labor) which render consumption possible. Saving then is not a use of income but formation of capital.

An argument frequently put forward in this context regards double taxation, i.e. the taxation of personal incomes based on incomes from profits which have already been taxed. The solution to this is very simple: incomes from profits and other incomes are, if they are saved, not incomes at all, according to Fisher; the tax is levied only on expenditure for the purposes of consumption. The tax therefore shall help to favor saving and discourage consumption from existing wealth.

As is well-known, the introduction of an expenditure tax would pose administrative problems and implies that marginal tax rates would have to rise considerably. For Fisher, it was a matter of principle, not of expediency, although he recognized the practical problems involved. The necessary definitions and distinctions had already been developed in *The Nature of Capital and Income*; he returned to the question in 1942 when he saw new possibilities for the realization of the project (Fisher and Fisher, 1942; Kaldor, 1955, pp. 191-223). He now emphasized that the expenditure tax would not have to be based on a complete list of all expenditure for consumption of the person to be taxed, but that it would essentially suffice to take the difference between income (in the ordinary sense) and net saving of a person as an indicator of consumption during a period.

3   INTEREST

Returning to *The Nature of Capital and Income*: the subsequent chapters may be interpreted as demonstrating the conceptual foundation of Fisher's theory of interest. He again starts with a distinction of dimensions, of the productivity of capital, which may be productive in the physical sense or in terms of value. The value of capital now is equal to discounted future earnings and this aspect of valuation is the only one which is really important. According to Fisher's one-sided interpretation of classical theory, the value of capital is determined by the cost of production which is irrelevant for decisions concerning the future if discounted expected returns are different. In fact, objective costs of production are not recognized for the economy as a whole (Fisher, 1906, p. 173), for what represents costs to the one are incomes for the other. The costs of the baker are a revenue to the miller and the wage costs of an entrepreneur are the revenues of many households. Only incomes of the latter kind are eventually used for the satisfaction of individuals, to be balanced against the sacrifices of labor. Health may be one of the reasons why the 'superficial' objective income may differ from the subjective.

Setting aside the personal element in Fisher's exposition, we must ask how his determination of the value of capital by looking at discounted returns – an idea of great and now obvious importance – is related to the determination of the rate of interest in equilibrium, according to his theory. Fisher expands on this determination in *The Nature of Capital and Income* by treating the element of risk in an innovative fashion. I do not want to pursue this aspect, however, but prefer to concentrate on the problem of the determination of interest in equilibrium. Fisher in this regard stands in an interesting contrast to Böhm-Bawerk with his *Positive Theorie des Kapitales*. The question requires to go beyond *The Nature of Capital and Income* and to consult some later writings of Fisher, his *The Rate of Interest* in particular. Since these two books belong together, not only chronologically – being published in 1906 and 1907 respectively – but also in substance, we shall deal with both of them here, and the title of this presentation reflects this.[1]

Fisher was far superior to Böhm-Bawerk in his mathematical knowledge. Böhm-Bawerk's weapon was his logic (he was trained in law and extremely well-versed in the history of economic thought). Fisher was used to regarding a mathematical determination as an explanation. Böhm-Bawerk demanded more when he spoke of causality. He once gave an example, addressed to Fisher:

> Wenn mir als Daten gegeben sind der Fassungsraum eines Bassins und die Zahl der Tage, die seine Füllung aus einer Wasserquelle erfordert, so kann ich daraus die Reichlichkeit der Quelle berechnen; sie ist durch die bekannten Daten 'eindeutig bestimmt'. Hier ist also die Größe der Ursache durch Größendaten der Wirkung eindeutig bestimmt. Umgekehrt könnte ich natürlich, wenn mir die Reichlichkeit der Quelle und die Füllungsdauer bekannt wäre, einen rechnungsmäßigen Schluß auf den

Fassungsraum und die Wasserfüllung des Bassins ziehen, also von der Größe der Ursa-
che auf die Größe der Wirkung schließen. Die eindeutige Bestimmtheit ist gegenüber
der Kausalitätsfrage neutral ... (Böhm-Bawerk, 1961, p. 315).

Economics is concerned with human action; causality follows from the effects
of changing activities of the economic agents. It is therefore for instance not
sufficient to prove the existence of a full employment equilibrium but the point
is to analyze how it can be shown to be stable in the face of change, such as the
change caused by an immigration of workers. The entire chain of events, with
their actions and reactions, must be traced in such a case if the equilibrium is
disturbed and, if all goes well, restored. The reader of Böhm-Bawerk can verify
that for him the relevant equilibria are in fact those in which stability is obtained
with respect to specific disturbances. It is not necessary to analyze the chain of
events up to the ultimate cause – in the example, we do not know what causes
the migration of labor. It is precisely the strength of the equilibrium concept that
the outcome is the same in the face of a multiplicity of possible causes. If full
employment is disturbed because trade unions press for higher wages, the
equilibrium will again prove to be stable, as Böhm-Bawerk shows, because the
resulting unemployment will weaken trade union power so that wages may
eventually be expected to fall back to the equilibrium level. Fisher's equilibrium
concept seems to have been different. His interpretation of equilibrium made it
more difficult to say what a long-run equilibrium was and to establish its
stability. Yet both authors thought that they were essentially trying to grasp the
same phenomenon, hence the strange mixture of mutual respect and criticism
which was only in part due to the different personalities and stations and which
is so difficult to disentangle. We consider their contributions to two problems of
the theory of capital: the productivity of a system as yielding an upper limit for
the rate of interest and the period of production as an expression of the capital-
labor ratio, used to determine the actual rate of interest.

Fisher, at first, seemed to have no reason in his theory of interest of 1907 to
argue polemically against his predecessor since he thought that his own theory
was only a little different from that of Böhm-Bawerk; he revered him and John
Rae as precursors of his own ideas. An introductory chapter is concerned with a
specific American development: the productivity theory of interest as developed
by Henry George. It points to the growth potential of nature as an explanation.
Fisher objects that the rates at which forests or herds of animals grow – if they
are managed economically – depend in their turn on the rate of interest since
investment undertaken on the basis of plans for the future in agriculture. It can
therefore not be said that the rate of interest is determined by an exogenous rate
of growth. It is true, on the other hand, that the growth potential of nature limits
the possibilities of choice of the investors, insofar as they in fact influence the
rate of interest (Fisher, 1907, p. 28). One might add that, for a given technique

with constant returns, the maximum rate of growth of the system as a whole is an upper limit for the rate of interest.

It is clear to us that the maximum rate of growth is equal to the maximum rate of profit, in a long-run equilibrium with normal prices, and it has been pointed out in the classical tradition that the rate of interest is limited by the rate of profit. Ricardo and Marx knew this. In fact, Marx once asked what the rate of profit would be if the workers could live from nothing – he thus asked what the maximum rate of profit was. We know today that the maximum rate is positive if and only if the system is productive. How did this link between the technique employed and the upper limit to interest show in the approaches of Fisher and Böhm-Bawerk?

It is remarkable that Fisher raises the question of the productivity of the system indirectly when he asks whether the series which Böhm-Bawerk uses in order to calculate the period of production as a characterization of the technique will always converge. The period of production is obtained by taking the sum of the dated labor inputs over time, each multiplied by the number of years which have elapsed since that amount of labor was furnished. The construction is similar to the so-called reduction of prices to dated inputs of labor which had already been considered by Adam Smith, and the question had always been whether it was legitimate to neglect labor inputs which date far back in time and which enter a good now under production. Here it is necessary to consider two contrary tendencies. A labor input of the distant past will be of little significance in the calculation of the costs of a commodity available today since the amount of labor is likely to be small. If a tree was planted one hundred years ago, and used fifty years ago in order to produce an axe, and if that axe was used twenty years ago in order to produce a chair on which the tailor is seated who produces our commodity, a suit, it is obvious that the planting of the tree represents only a very small amount of the total amount of labor necessary to the production of the suit. However, this labor input is weighted by a very high interest factor, if the rate of interest is positive at all. The factor is, if the rate of interest is 5%, equal to $1.05^{100}=131.5$. If the rate of interest is 6%, the factor is equal to 339.3.

The point is easy to explain, if one uses a modern formalization. If A is an input-output-matrix, l the associated labor vector of a given system, we may interpret l as direct labor, expended in the current year, Al is the labor expended one year ago, to the extent that it entered the products indirectly which are produced today, A^2l is the labor expended two years ago, to the extent that it enters the commodities of today, etc. If w is the wage rate and p the vector of commodity prices, we have the series (Schefold, [1971] 1989, p.15)

$$p/w = l+(1+r)Al+(1+r)^2 A^2l+\dots . \tag{12.1}$$

A^nl will fall rapidly, as n tends to infinity, but $(1+r)^n$ will rise. Today, it is well known that the series converges for positive r only if r is smaller than the maximum rate of profit R. If r is varied for a given system, small r implies relatively small prices in terms of the wage rate (the net produce can be bought primarily out of wages), while prices in terms of the wage rate rise as r rises towards R because the net produce is increasingly absorbed by profits. The series diverges in the transition from r to R.

Such a problem of convergence was posed by Böhm-Bawerk in connection with the definition of the average period of production, but it was not analyzed properly, as Fisher pointed out. The rate of interest does not enter the definition since the rate of interest is to be determined by means of that average period of production (Böhm-Bawerk [1888] 1961, p. 71).

If the levels of activity of our system are given by a vector x, the average period of production of the system as a whole may be defined as, taking into account all indirect inputs of labor, back to infinity (in logical time and on the hypothetical assumption that the technique and the levels of activity have never changed):

$$T = \frac{0xl + 1xAl + 2xA^2l + 3xA^3l + \ldots}{xl + xAl + xA^2l + xA^3l + \ldots}. \tag{12.2}$$

It can be shown that the period of production, defined by (12.2), exists if and only if R is positive.[2] Böhm-Bawerk used to formulate his average period of production only for systems in which the reduction to dated labor breaks off after a finite number of steps. He therefore assumed that everything was originally produced by labor alone, without assistance of material inputs of production. This assumption was only made for simplification and is clearly not legitimate. Labor has never been unassisted by 'capital' – Eve needed a tree to pluck an apple – but the series is not to be based on historical inputs, with changing technologies over time, anyway. The average period of production was supposed to be a measure of the intensity of capital for a given technique so that, if we consider the technique of the economy as a whole, one has to assume that this same technique has been used ever since time began, as is expressed by formula (12.2), in the same way as normal prices are to be calculated on the hypothetical assumption of an unchanged technique according to formula (12.1).

Now it turns out that there is a relevant special case in which the three magnitudes, Böhm-Bawerk's period of production, the coefficient of capital and the inverse of the maximum rate of profit coincide.[3] For a proof, we need the following series which, with z being a real number, always converges for $|z| < 1$:

$$(1-z)^{-1} = 1 + z + z^2 + \ldots$$

and

$$z(1-z)^{-2} = z + 2z^2 + 3z^3 + \ldots .$$

These series are easily obtained. We have Sraffa's standard proportions or balanced growth at a rate equal to R if the vectors of activity levels q fulfil equation $(1 + R)qA = q$. Formula (12.2) then yields:

$$T = \frac{qAl + 2qA^2l + 3qA^3l + \ldots}{ql + qAl + qA^2l + \ldots} = \frac{(1+R)^{-1} + 2(1+R)^{-2} + 3(1+R)^{-3} + \ldots}{1 + (1+R)^{-1} + (1+R)^{-2} + \ldots}$$

$$= \frac{(1+R)^{-1}[1-(1+R)^{-1}]^{-2}}{[1-(1+R)^{-1}]^{-1}} = 1/R.$$

We obtain the same for the coefficient of capital:

$$K/Y = \frac{qAp}{q(I-A)p} = \frac{(1+R)^{-1}qp}{R(1+R)^{-1}qp} = 1/R.$$

Hence we can see that Fisher's question whether Böhm-Bawerk's series converged implicitly concerned the question of the existence of the maximum rate of profit and of the productivity of the system. It turns out that Böhm-Bawerk was correct insofar as systems which are capable of producing a surplus (and only such systems are economically meaningful) are associated with a positive maximum rate of profit; hence they have a period of production defined according to (12.2). But Fisher nevertheless shows in the appendix to his book (Fisher, 1907, p. 352) that the period of production is no meaningful measure of the rate of interest if the dated inputs and outputs are distributed very unevenly over time.

In order to understand this second problem of capital theory, it is necessary to realize that the rate of profit (or the rate of interest) is *a priori* indeterminate in the interval between zero and the maximum rate of profit associated with the given technique. If we have an entire spectrum of techniques $(A^{(i)}, l^{(i)})$; $i = 1, \ldots, s$; from which one technique may be chosen, a specific technique will minimize costs for each given r. Böhm-Bawerk's conception was, expressed in our modern terminology, that it is possible to associate a period of production $T(i)$ with each of those techniques at given levels of production, according to (12.2). As we have seen, this is possible, for we may draw the wage curve for each of the techniques, and it is then clear that that technique will minimize costs which exhibits the highest wage (and is on the envelope of the wage curve) at the given rate of profit or interest. A critical point concerns the second assumption by Böhm-Bawerk: he thought that, with lower rates of interest, a technique i with a longer period of production $T(i)$ would be chosen, and that this would correspond to a higher intensity of capital. The period of production, given with the technique actually ruling, thus was supposed to become an indicator of the prevailing rate of profit or interest.

We can now see that Böhm-Bawerk would have been right exactly under those conditions under which the surrogate production function of Samuelson can be constructed. Samuelson assumed (Samuelson, 1962, pp. 193-206)[4] that the wage curve of each technique in the spectrum was linear. At higher rates of profit, linearly wage curves pertaining to techniques with higher maximum rates of profit would turn up. In conditions of balanced reproduction, the higher maximum rates of profit would imply a lower intensity of capital and a shorter average period of production. Hence, the inverse relationship between the period of production and the rate of interest at which a technique became profitable would be obtained, as postulated by Böhm-Bawerk. The stability of equilibrium could be demonstrated for various kinds of disturbances: an increase of labor (the immigration mentioned above) could be accommodated by lowering the wage, increasing the rate of interest, lowering the period of production and employing more labor, and similarly for the other familiar cases of an equilibrium disturbed by wage rates being too high, etc.

It was one of Fisher's most remarkable achievements to disprove Böhm-Bawerk's conjecture of an inverse relationship between the rate of interest and the period of production, at least for a special case. However, it was characteristic of Fisher not to look backwards, as in the reduction according to formula (12.2), but to look ahead in time. He assumes in his example that one technique consists in the application of a unit of labor which in ten years' time will yield $5 and in one hundred years time $100, while another application of this same labor yields $15 once in twenty-five years.

> In this case it becomes impossible to call one of the production periods longer than the other; ... it is not true that one of the alternatives will be chosen if the rate of interest is low, as would be the case if they were subject to Böhm-Bawerk's series. The application of labour which issued in the $5 and $100 would, oddly enough, be the most economical if the rate of interest were either very high or very low, whereas the other alternative would be chosen in the case the interest were at a more moderate rate (Fisher, 1907, p. 352).

Obviously, this example is quite similar to that of wine and the oak chest which Sraffa discussed and which has been taken up by a variety of authors (Sraffa, 1960, p. 37; Kurz and Salvadori, 1995, p. 446). Examples of this type are the simplest in order to show the existence of reswitching, i.e. the return of the same technique as cost minimizing at a high rate of profit which had already been cost minimizing at a low rate, or to show that there is no inverse relationship between the period of production and the rate of interest or between capital intensity and the rate of interest. However, the examples have to be extended to the consideration of techniques of closed economies, whereas the example given by Fisher only concerns partial equilibrium. In fact, the reswitching debate centered precisely on the return of techniques in the general equilibrium sense, since Samuelson's surrogate production function had been presented as a defense of traditional neoclassical theory; the paradox exhibited by Fisher was known to specialists and other forms of it had been discussed by authors as diverse as Hayek (1976, p. 200) and Joan Robinson ([1956] 1969, pp. 109-110) (she called it the Ruth Cohen-curiosum). Levhari then claimed to be able to show that reswitching was impossible for techniques representing closed economies, and it was the error in his proof which really launched the debate and made the profession aware that the problem of reswitching had been well described by Sraffa, though he had not provided a numerical example beyond that of the wine and the oak chest, i.e. beyond partial equilibrium.

We can thus see how close the authors of the turn of the century were to key concepts of modern capital theory: to the maximum rate of profit, to the reduction of dated quantities of labor or to reswitching, as if they were searching for the exit in a dark building, and how impossible it was for them to comprehend the connections because they interpreted a given technique not as a self-reproducing system, as it is represented by von Neumann and Sraffa. Their modern models of reproduction have shed a new light on the entire discussion of capital so that the plan of the building, which had previously remained in the dark, now is plain to see (Samuelson, 1994, pp. 43-74).[5]

4   OWN-RATE OF INTEREST AND MONEY-RATE OF INTEREST

As already indicated, one of the most significant innovations contributed by Fisher was his relation between monetary interest and real interest. Keynes introduced own-rates of interest as is now done in the classroom, by referring to interest on different currencies. Employing a given exchange rate between D-Marks and Dollars today, where the rate of interest on Dollars is higher than that on D-Marks, the futures market must express an appreciation of D-Marks. An analogous connection between money (gold) and a commodity (wheat) was postulated by Fisher in his *Appreciation and Interest*, where an appreciation or depreciation of gold is expected. If i represents the money rate of interest, r the own-rate of interest, d the rate of change of prices, we must have the relation

$$1 + i = (1 + r)(1 + d) = 1 + r + d + rd$$

so that we get, with r and d being small

$$i = r + d,$$

the interest on money is not equal to real interest but equal to this, augmented by the rate of inflation (Fisher, [1896] 1965, p. 8; Fisher, 1907, p. 359).

Fisher was not the first to consider such a relation but it is justifiably referred to by his name because of the excellent use which he made of it. He had emphasized that there are as many own-rates of interest as there are commodities, in principle, but most of his subsequent considerations are based on the assumption that a real rate of interest, based on the construction of an index, and the money-rate of interest can be compared. It would seem that Fisher was induced to consider divergent own-rates of interest not so much because of a concern with the problem of capital in intertemporal equilibrium but because he tried to understand the relationship between interest as a monetary and a real phenomenon.

It is easy in a one-good world to represent the intertemporal equilibrium in a diagram – in the form which is to be found in all elementary textbooks. The transformation curve shows that the less we consume of the good in the present, the more we can have of it in the future. The rate of transformation is equal to the intertemporal rate of substitution; together they determine the rate of interest. The rate of time preference is often defined as the intertemporal rate of substitution *minus* 1, measured on the 45^0-line, on which consumption in the present and consumption expected for the future are equal (Blaug, 1978, p. 561).[6]

But in a general intertemporal equilibrium with many commodities and a finite time horizon, of the type which has been rendered famous by Arrow and Debreu, the relative prices may change from period to period so that the own-rates of interest are different, as Fisher had emphasized in *Appreciation and Interest*. The complete system has not been fully formalized by Fisher. Milgate has ascribed priority in the construction of intertemporal equilibrium to Hayek, and Malinvaud is said to have taken his clues from him in 1953 in formulating the ideas which then led to Arrow-Debreu (Milgate, 1982, S. 133; Kurz and Salvadori, 1995, pp. 455-467).

Sraffa interpreted the inequality between the different own-rates of interest which he discovered in Hayek's conception in 1932 as the expression of a disequilibrium. The modern development of economic theory has justified this interpretation to the extent that, even in a neoclassical context, the inequality between different own-rates of interest tends to vanish under suitable conditions if the time horizon is shifted towards infinity. For – but this is only a very general consideration – the inequality between different own-rates of interest is due to the arbitrariness of given endowments which are more or less abundant or scarce (directly in the case of consumption goods, indirectly in the case of means of production) relative to the needs of agents, so that there are scarcity prices in the initial periods of the intertemporal equilibrium which are high if endowments are small relative to what turns out to be the need of the agents in later periods when production will have made good for the initial scarcity, with preferences of consumers remaining stationary. Hence, it is possible to visualize that the own-rates of interest tend to equality and that relative prices converge towards a determined vector of relative prices which corresponds to a stationary equilibrium and which is to be reached asymptotically. Although this result is by no means general, we shall later see how it may be obtained under special conditions. Sraffa interpreted the initial state with diverging own-rates of interest as a deviation from long period equilibrium. Hayek, by contrast, seems to have interpreted the difference of the own-rates of interest as a manifestation of an intertemporal equilibrium, therefore as an equilibrium phenomenon, and this is the common interpretation today (Malinvaud, 1953).[7]

Samuelson takes a more positive view of Fisher's contribution to intertemporal theory regarding the construction of a general equilibrium than Milgate (Samuelson, 1972, pp. 653-667). But Fisher's *Theory of Interest* is in the foreground based on the curve of transformation to express the production of one good, which represents the streams of incomes of an individual in the present and in the future. It is then shown how this may lead to an exchange between individuals with different preferences, but the interdependence between markets for different commodities is not rendered explicit.

Now it is ironic that in this case, Böhm-Bawerk was the one to discover limitations in the treatment of capital in Fisher's book. According to Böhm-Bawerk, Fisher mistakenly asserted that a fall in the rate of interest had to result in a rise of all capital values. Böhm-Bawerk realizes that a given future income will result in a higher capital value, the lower the rate of interest. But he points out that a partial analysis is inadmissible because the rate of interest regulates not only capitalization but also costs. Böhm-Bawerk thus leads the discussion back to a world in which there is a long period equilibrium, all own-rates of interest are equal and prices are normal prices. We know that relative prices change with distribution for a given technique in a complicated manner in this case. We also know that these changes of relative prices are at the root of a problem of capital.

Böhm-Bawerk compared Fisher's error with the error which had been criticized already by Mill, according to which all goods could rise in price in a real sense with a rise of wages (Böhm-Bawerk, [1888] 1961, p. 112).[8]

We may again avail ourselves of the modern formalization in order to express Böhm-Bawerk's criticism. If the future real services rendered by capital remain unchanged, the formalization involves a given technique with fixed capital; the rate of interest is lowered while production remains the same. A single process of production may therefore be represented as follows:

$$(1+r)(a_1 p + M_0 p_{m0}) + w l_1 = p_1 + M_1 p_{m1},$$

where a_1 is a vector of raw materials, p the corresponding vector of prices, p_1 the price of the good produced, M_0, M_1 are a new and a one year old machine respectively, p_{m0}, p_{m1} the corresponding prices and l_1 the labor input to this process. If all raw materials, consumption goods or new machines are produced by such processes while old machines emerge as joint products from them and if every machine is of finite duration for technical reasons while its economic duration is determined by the criterion of the minimization of costs, it can be shown that, for all rates of profit between 0 and some maximum, all prices will be positive.

According to this picture, at least the prices of new machines appear to be determined by the costs of production. But the system may also be transformed so that the price of every machine is equal to the income it generates, discounted by r and interpreted as the rate of interest. For the new machine we have (at once):

$$M_0 p_{m0} = [1/(1+r)]\{p_1 + M_1 p_{m1} - wl_1 - (1+r)a_1 p\},$$

the machine is equal to its discounted income generated in the next year. It is also possible to include the yields of later years by recursively eliminating old machines from the equations; the corresponding future yields then are multiplied by the corresponding powers of $1/1+r$ as discount factors. If one now raises the rate of profit or interest on the right hand side in the nominator and if one arbitrarily leaves the prices constant and the rate of profit or interest as it appears in the denominator, the result claimed by Fisher is in fact obtained: the value of capital falls as the rate of profit or interest rises. But, in the comparison of equilibria, the rate of profit must be taken to be uniform and all prices must change simultaneously. It is then possible that the rise of the rate of profit will also lead to rising prices of capital. If the wage rate is chosen as the *numéraire*, at least new machines will *rise* in price with every rise of the rate of profit or interest. Intuitively, each investor expects that a fall in the rate of interest will lead to rising values of capital, of land, etc. But if the fall of the rate of interest is lasting, the prices of the goods produced by means of those capitals will also fall, in particular, rents will fall, so that the effect on the prices of capital goods and of land may, in the long run, move in both directions.

Again we see how difficult the problem of capital must have appeared to the economists of Fisher's time and how much it has been simplified through modern formalizations.

5 INTERTEMPORAL AND LONG PERIOD EQUILIBRIUM

From Böhm-Bawerk's criticism, we return to Fisher and his own major concern. So far, we have emphasized the problem of production. But it may be argued that Fisher was primarily interested in the subjective side.

> Years after *The Rate of Interest* was published, I suggested the more popular term 'impatience' in place of 'agio' or 'time preference'. This catchword has been widely adopted, and, to my surprise, has lead to a widespread but false impression that I had overlooked or neglected the productivity or investment opportunity side entirely (Fisher, [1930] 1972, p. VIII).

Of course, Fisher had already considered the side of investment in 1907. But I, like other readers, was struck how the subjective side is stressed. This impression is reinforced by Fisher's 'inductive verification (economic)', the subject of his Chapter 15, where the fates of entire nations are related in broad historical comparisons to their time preferences, their propensities to save and their abilities to accumulate. Fisher does not fail to indicate that dangers are associated with such generalizations and he also points to other factors like property and distribution and to the general methodological problem of induction. These doubts are reinforced and expanded in the edition of 1930; there the chapter is more cautiously entitled 'Some illustrative facts' (Fisher, [1930] 1972, Chapter XVIII).

This quarrel regarding an alleged preponderance of the subjective element is nonsense from a purely logical point of view, since equilibrium always involves both aspects, the subjective as well as those of production. But it seems to be the essence of Austrian theory, in the most general sense of the term, to interpret the social rate of time preference as the key variable to the understanding of the growth of an economy – in much the same way as one may regard the Keynesian image of 'animal spirits' of entrepreneurs as the key variable determining the process of investment, if one follows the post-war Cambridge tradition. To the extent that such generalizations are meaningful, Fisher's theory is Austrian and in this perspective, the subjective side played a more important role in the 1907-version of his book than in that of 1930.

We can speak of a social rate of time preference only because the individual rates adapt to each other, the monetary rate of interest being a measuring rod. Fisher (1907, p. 328) speaks of

> the tendency of the rates of time-preference for different individuals to become equal to each other and to the rate of interest, through the loan market, or through buying and selling property.

On the one hand, Fisher here speaks of *the* rate of interest. On the other hand, it had been one of his main achievements to show that there is a specific own-rate of interest to each commodity:

> There are therefore just as many rates of interest in goods as there are forms of goods diverging in value. (Fisher, 1907, p. 84).

Which rate of interest is relevant? Fisher cuts the Gordian Knot by treating the monetary rate of interest as exogenous in the consideration of convergence and it is questionable whether he disposed of a theory of the monetary rate of interest as a specific phenomenon in the way Keynes had his liquidity theory of interest. Of course, in Fisher such a theory emerges if money is a commodity and the money rate of interest equals the own-rate of interest of the money commodity. We have already met with this idea in *Appreciation and Interest* and we shall return to the corresponding formalism, but the specific monetary properties of the money commodity are then not treated.

The following quotation brings Fisher's recourse to the money rate of interest into focus:

> From this explanation it is very evident that if we seek to postulate an absolute standard of value in which the rates of interest are to be reckoned, we cannot fix one which will be uniform for all the individuals in the market. Supply and demand operate only to make *objective* rates equal. Hereafter we shall confine ourselves to a study of objective interest; and since the objective standard usually employed is money, the rate of interest, unless otherwise specified, will be taken in this book to mean the rate of interest in terms of the money standard. (Fisher, 1907, p. 86).

What determines which commodity becomes money? There is a theoretical possibility of circumventing this question, as far as the theory of value (not of money) is concerned: the own-rates of interest converge towards one rate of interest under certain conditions in an intertemporal equilibrium, as we already have indicated and as we shall now show in greater detail. It then does not matter in the long run which own-rate of interest serves as a reference for the market participants (Caspari, 1998, forthcoming).[9]

Let $a_{k,t}$ be the vector of inputs in period t in process k and $b_{k,t+1}$ be the vector of outputs which are produced by the same process in the subsequent period. Let p_t and p_{t+1} be the vectors of prices in intertemporal equilibrium, discounted to the present. Constant returns to scale and perfect competition then imply

$$a_{k,t}p_t = b_{k,t+1}p_{t+1}.$$

Let s be the vector for a *numéraire* – it may be the unit vector for one *numéraire*-commodity; this *numéraire* may be called 'gold'. If gold earns interest in period t at a rate of interest i_t^s, an amount s of gold in period t is equivalent to the promise of the delivery of an amount of gold of $(1+i_t^s)s$ in period $t+1$. This equivalence implies an equality of the values of those quantities, in terms of discounted prices, therefore

$$[(1+i_t^s)s]p_{t+1} = sp_t.$$

The increment of gold 'tomorrow' which is paid over a unit of gold 'today' is the own-rate of interest of gold:

$$i_t^s = sp_t / sp_{t+1} - 1.$$

The own-rates of interest depend on the scarcity relationships in intertemporal equilibrium. Usually, the price for a unit of a commodity promised for 'tomorrow' is lower than a unit of the same commodity, available 'today'; the own-rate of interest is then positive. But if the initial endowment of this commodity is abundant, the price must be low in the very first period and will increase with consumption in subsequent periods. If it cannot be stored free of cost, a negative own-rate of interest is then possible. Storage, causing costs at a rate z in terms of the commodity itself, per unit and period, implies that $1-z$ units of s can be transferred from period t to period $t+1$. The own-rate of interest is then greater or equal to $-z$, for the amount of gold to be delivered against one unit today has a lower limit

$$(l+i_t^s)s \geq (1-z)s,$$

since otherwise the lender would prefer to store the gold himself.

It seems not yet generally known that the several processes of production are all equally profitable, if the comparison is made in undiscounted prices $\bar{p}_t$ which are defined for each period by means of *numéraire s*:

$$\bar{p}_t, = p_t / sp_t.$$

This definition allows to transform the equation for production in terms of discounted prices into one in terms of undiscounted prices:

$$a_{k,t}\bar{p}_t(sp_t) = b_{k,t+1}\bar{p}_{t+1}(sp_{t+1}),$$

therefore

$$(1+i_t^s)a_{k,t}\bar{p}_t = b_{k,t+1}\bar{p}_{t+1}$$

where we can now see that profits are made according to a uniform rate in all processes, but the rate depends on the *numéraire s*. If the own-rate of interest on gold is 4%, an owner of gold can therefore make a profit by lending gold at 4% or he can attain the same level of interest by selling the gold, investing in any process and selling the products of the process again eventually against gold. If the own-rate of silver happens to be 3%, the same processes, measured in terms of the same prices, but expressed in silver, will yield the silver rate of 3%.

A transformation allows us to deduce Fisher's equation. Dividing the last equation by $b_{k,t+1}\bar{p}_t$, and defining

$$\frac{b_{k,t+1}\overline{p}_t}{a_{k,t}\overline{p}_t} = 1 + r_t^k,$$

and

$$\frac{b_{k,t+1}\overline{p}_{t+1}}{b_{k,t+1}\overline{p}_t} = 1 + d_t^k,$$

we obtain

$$1 + i_t^s = (1 + r_t^k)(1 + d_t^k).$$

This is a variant of the Fisher equation. We may interpret r_t^k as a rate of profit in the classical sense since the inputs $a_{k,t}$ and the outputs $b_{k,t+1}$ are both measured by means of the *same* price vector $\overline{p}_t$. It is an evaluation of the success of the process *ex ante*. If input prices were still the same at the end of the process, the profit would be equal to r_t^k. On the other hand, d_t^k measures the change of relative prices, using $b_{k,t+1}$, the vector of outputs, as the vector of weights for this index of prices. We thus verify that the own-rate of interest of the monetary commodity is approximately equal to the sum of the rate of profit obtained in process *plus* the rate of change of prices, using the outputs of process k for the weights of the index of prices.

But this formal analogy, taken in itself, does not really solve the problem of finding *the* rate of interest, since the *numéraire* is arbitrary and the rates of profit r_t^k differ according to the process chosen because relative prices change. Fisher's vision of an economy governed by a rate of time preference must be based on the idea that all rates of profit are uniform and that, accordingly, all own-rates of interest are equal to one another. Input prices are then equal to output prices and we have

$$(1 + r)a_k p = b_k p$$

in all processes that are activated. The index for the time period can then be omitted and a uniform rate of profit, corresponding to all own-rates of interest $r = i^s$ is found.

Does such a convergence obtain? That depends both on technology and on preferences. Neoclassical economists often focus on the latter but it may be pointed out that technology dictates such a convergence if we have single product systems and all inputs are produced. In this case, prices will converge to those of the system:

$$(1 + R)Ap = p$$

(A indecomposable input-output-matrix, R rate of profit), for the price system is in this case without choice of technique given by

$$Ap_t = p_{t+1},$$

so that prices may be expressed by the sequence

$$A^t p_0 = p_t,$$

which is known to converge to p if the *numéraire* for p_0 and p is the same.[10] Convergence does not necessarily obtain if there are primary factors – something is needed to stabilize distribution (Schefold, 1997, pp. 425-501).[11] The question then is whether the rate of time preference actually will govern distribution – if a unique rate of time preference prevails at all.

I feel the need to stress that the intertemporal equilibrium, which thus converges to a long period equilibrium with a uniform rate of profit, determined by technology and by time preference, is a very special construction from a classical or traditional point of view. In classical or early neoclassical theory, the long period equilibrium would be regarded as the fundamental phenomenon, and the intertemporal equilibrium is only a special representation of a convergence of market prices towards the long-run prices, and of the quantities towards those of the terminal state. The process of gravitation is special in that markets always clear under conditions of perfect foresight – there are neither stocks nor Keynesian elements of speculation. Full employment is preserved throughout. The long period equilibrium itself is essentially determined by the neoclassical theory of distribution and also characterized by full employment. Classical and Keynesian equilibria could be different, both in the short run (as models of gravitation) and in the long run.

It may also be mentioned that the problem of reswitching recurs in this context. I have shown that intertemporal equilibria with reswitching can be constructed, i.e., equilibria in which a transition is made from one stationary state to another. The transition is represented as one intertemporal equilibrium with perfect foresight, and it involves a change of technique such that a lower rate of interest in the terminal state involves a lower, not a higher, intensity of capital than in the initial state. Accordingly, it is a transition in which a higher real wage eventually is associated with a higher level of employment. It thus turns out that reswitching does not preclude the existence of an intertemporal equilibrium which stretches from the initial to the terminal state, but that such an equilibrium is associated with counterintuitive *parallel* movements of factor prices and factor quantities so that the stability of such an equilibrium is highly questionable (Schefold, 1997, pp. 483-501).

The discovery of reswitching was one of Fisher's most original contributions. He discovered it in a partial equilibrium context and directed it against Böhm-Bawerk's period of production. It has now turned out that reswitching is also a problem for intertemporal models, precisely if they are developed in the direction corresponding to Fisher's vision: as intertemporal equilibra which converge towards a long period equilibrium.

Fisher's emphasis on an evaluation of capital by looking at expected returns prevented him from seeing the influence of changes of distributions on capital value in long run equilibrium. This is where Böhm-Bawerk scored a point against Fisher. By combining both criticisms, much of the ground of the modern critique of capital theory can be covered and we realize that the complexity of the relationship between distribution and relative prices, first analyzed by Ricardo, has remained a serious obstacle to the analysis of general equilibrium and distribution in terms of supply and demand.

But we do not want obscure Fisher's great achievements by looking only at what seems topical in capital theory today. He characterized his procedure in the following manner, contrasting it to that of Walras and Pareto:

> Walras and Pareto determine the rate of interest simultaneously with all the other unknowns of the problem - the quantities of the commodities exchanged and the services used in their production and the prices of the commodities and the services, while I try to isolate the interest problem by assuming that most of such unknowns have already been determined and confine my discussion to the special factors directly affecting the rate of interest.

In the pursuit of this limited program, Fisher was exceptionally successful.

NOTES

1 This article takes up the arguments which I have presented in my 'Introductions' (written in German) to the companion volumes of the reprints of the works of Fisher and Böhm-Bawerk in the series *Klassiker der Nationalökonomie*, of which I am the managing editor. The companion volumes are mentioned below.

2 For let $1/(1+R)$ be the dominant root of the semipositive matrix A which we assume to be indecomposable for simplicity. If $R > 0$, there is for each r with $0 < r < R$ a positive number $N(r)$ so that $(1 + r)^n > n$ for all $n \geq N(r)$, hence the series (12.1) – which converges – is for $n \geq N(r)$ larger in each single term than the series in the denominator and in the nominator of (12.2). Conversely: if the system is not productive, we may write $qA = \mu q$, with $\mu \geq 0$ and $q > 0$ and such that $ql = 1$. If $x > 0$, we could find $\alpha > 0, \beta > 0$ such that

$$T \geq \frac{\alpha(qAl + 2qA^2l + ...)}{\beta(ql + qAl + ...)} = \frac{\alpha(\mu + 2\mu^2 + ...)}{\beta(\mu + \mu^2 + ...)} = \frac{\alpha(\mu + \mu^2 + ...)(1 + \mu + \mu^2 + ...)}{\beta(\mu + \mu^2 + ...)},$$

but then the formula for T diverges.

3 I believe I was the first to point this out in the first German version of this paper in (Schefold, 1991, pp. 5-29). The point was also taken up in (Schefold, 1997, p. 444).

4 Samuelson had to assume equal capital-intensities in all sectors for each technique, i.e. the proportionality of labor values and prices. Since the labor vector will then be a right-hand eigenvector of the input matrix, the equality of the period of production, of the capital coefficient and of the inverse of the maximum rate of profit will again be obtained.

5 Samuelson himself has related the reswitching debate to Fisher's example in his contribution (Samuelson, 1994, pp. 43-74).

6 Mark Blaug (1978, p. 561) discusses the Fisher-diagram in a historical perspective.

7 This is Milgate's supposition, and he therefore ascribes the influence of Hayek on Malinvaud which has been mentioned. Arguably, the role of Lindahl was more important.

8   Sraffa's introduction to the *Principles* by Ricardo showed, however, that the consideration of the movement to relative prices in function of changes in distribution was not pioneered by Mill but was one of Ricardo's central concerns, essential in particular in his transition from the corn-model to the *Principles* (Hollander, Pasinetti, Schefold, and Skourtos, 1996).
9   My understanding of the relation between intertemporal equilibrium and long period equilibrium has been greatly enhanced by discussions with Volker Caspari and the results of his forthcoming *Gleichgewicht und Kapitalzins*.
10 We assume that the matrix is primitive.
11 For an extended discussion of this and the following points see (Schefold, 1997, pp. 425-501).

REFERENCES

Blaug, M. (1978), *Economic Theory in Retrospect*, 3rd ed., Cambridge, Cambridge University Press.

Böhm-Bawerk, E. von. (1888), *Positive Theorie des Kapitales, Zweiter Band (Exkurse)*, Jena, Gustav Fischer. Reprint of the 4th ed., Meisenheim, Hain, *Kapital und Kapitalzins*, Volume 2, Meisenheim, Hain, (1961).

Caspari, V. (1998, forthcoming), *Gleichgewicht und Kapitalzins*, Berlin, Duncker und Humblot.

Fisher, I. (1896), *Appreciation and Interest*, New York, The American Economic Association. Reprinted with *Mathematical Investigations in the Theory of Value and Prices*, New York, A.M. Kelley, 1961.

Fisher, I. (1906), *The Nature of Capital and Income*, New York, Macmillan.

Fisher, I. (1907), *The Rate of Interest*, New York, Macmillan.

Fisher, I. (1930), *The Theory of Interest*. Reprinted Philadelphia, Porcupine Press, 1972.

Fisher, I. and Fisher H.W. (1942), *Constructive Income Taxation: A Proposal for Reform*, New York, Harper and Brothers.

Hayek, F.A. (1976), *The Theory of Capital*, London, Routledge.

Hollander, S., Pasinetti, L.L., Schefold, B. and Skourtos, M. (1996), *Vademecum zu den Klassikern der Differentialrenten-Theorie*, companion volume to the reprint of the *Corn-Law-Pamphlets* of 1815, Düsseldorf, Verlag Wirtschaft und Finanzen.

Kaldor, N. (1955), *An Expenditure Tax*, London, Allen and Unwin.

Kurz, H. and Salvadori, N. (1995), *Theory of Production*, Cambridge, Cambridge University Press.

Malinvaud, E. (1953), 'Capital accumulation and the efficient allocation of resources', *Econometrica*, **26**, 233-268.

Milgate, M. (1982), 'Capital and Employment', in J. Eatwell (ed.), *Studies in Political Economy*, London, Academic Press.

Monissen, H.G. (1989), 'Irving Fisher', in J. Starbatty (ed.), *Klassiker des ökonomischen Denkens*, Band 2, München, Beck, 211-230.

Robinson, J. ([1956] 1969), *The Accumulation of Capital*, London, Macmillan.

Samuelson, P.A. (1962), 'Parable and realism in capital theory: the surrogate production function', *Review of Economic Studies*, **29**, 193-206.

Samuelson, P.A. (1972), 'Irving Fisher and the theory of capital', in R.C. Merton (ed.), *The Collected Scientific Papers of Paul A. Samuelson*, Volume III, Cambridge, MA., The M.I.T. Press, 653-667.

Samuelson, P.A. (1994), Zwei Klassiker in heutiger Sicht: Böhm-Bawerks *Positive Theorie* und Fishers *The Rate of Interest*, in R. Dorfman, M. Neumann, C. Panico, P.A. Samuelson and B. Schefold, *Vademecum zu einem Klassiker der Zinstheorie*, companion volume to the reprint of I. Fisher: *The Rate of Interest*, Düsseldorf, Verlag Wirtschaft und Finanzen, 43-74.

Schefold, B. (1971), *Mr. Sraffa on Joint Production and Other Essays*, London, Allen and Unwin.

Schefold, B. (1991), Einleitung zur Neuausgabe von Irving Fishers *The Nature of Capital and Income* in P.A. Samuelson, B. Schefold and J. Tobin, *Vademecum zu einem Klassiker der amerikanischen Nationalökonomie*, companion volume to the reprint of I. Fisher: *The Nature of Capital and Income*, Düsseldorf, Verlag Wirtschaft und Finanzen, 5-29.

Schefold, B. (1997), *Normal Prices, Technical Change and Accumulation*, London, Macmillan.

Sraffa, P. (1960), *Production of Commodities by Means of Commodities*, Cambridge, Cambridge University Press.

Comment on Schefold
The Nature of Capital and Interest

Volker Caspari

There are two topics in B. Schefold's paper on *Capital and Interest* which deserve further qualification: first, the relation between intertemporal and long period equilibrium, and second, that between the money rate of interest and the commodity rates. Let me begin with the latter.

One of Fisher's most significant contributions to economic theory was the relation he made between the money rate of interest and the real or commodity rates of interest. Whether or not he was the first to consider this relation is of minor importance. More important is that his contribution in *Appreciation and Interest* clarifies the relationship between interest as a monetary and as a real phenomenon. He had already emphasized the multiplicity of own rates of interest in a multi-commodity world; an observation which became important in the Hayek-Keynes-Sraffa debate about thirty years later. Although Fisher had not fully analyzed the complete system of intertemporal equilibrium, he had pointed out in *Appreciation and Interest* that in an intertemporal equilibrium the commodity rates of interest are different, as long as relative prices change from period to period.

In his *Prices and Production* (1931), Hayek combined the concept of intertemporal equilibrium with Wicksell's theory of the business cycle. Wicksell's approach focuses on the difference between the market rate of interest on money loans and the natural rate of interest, determined by the demand for and supply of savings. Obviously, Hayek had not realized that a single natural rate of interest does exist in a multicommodity world if and only if relative prices do not change from period to period. So when Sraffa argued in his review of *Prices and Production* that in a world of heterogeneous commodities there 'may exist as many "natural" rates as there are commodities' (1932, p. 50), he just repeats an argument put already forward by Fisher: 'There are ... just as many rates of interest as there are forms of goods diverging in value'. (Fisher, 1907, p. 84). Fisher, it seems, was not so much concerned with the problem of capital in intertemporal equilibrium but with the relation between 'money and the real world', a view also held by J.M. Keynes.

In chapter 17 of the *General Theory*, Keynes inspired by Sraffa's critique of Hayek made use of the commodity rates (or own rates) of interest. Although Keynes seemed to agree with Sraffa's critique, he drew a different conclusion. Sraffa interpreted the inequality between the different commodity rates of interest as an expression of a disequilibrium. The movement towards a long period equilibrium is conceived as a process of equalization of the commodity rates. This process is accompanied by unemployment of resources (for instance labor), but this misallocation will have vanished as the process converges to its long period equilibrium. If there is one commodity rate that is 'sticky', this rate sets a limit to the profitable production of commodities. According to Keynes, the peculiarity of the money rate of interest seems to lie in its relative stickiness. Because of its stickiness, the money rate of interest becomes 'essential' for the determination of an equilibrium of output and (un-)employment. It is well-known that Keynes tried to isolate the causes for the stickiness of the money rate of interest (c.f. Barens and Caspari, 1997, pp. 283-303).

1   INTERTEMPORAL AND LONG PERIOD EQUILIBRIUM

An intertemporal equilibrium is an equilibrium in the sense that all (future) markets clear at the prevailing vector of prices. It is a disequilibrium in the sense that the proportion of the stock of capital goods agents want to hold changes from period to period as long as the real rate of profit on each capital good is not uniform. In a neoclassical world, both conditions – market clearing and a uniform rate of profit – are fulfilled in stationary or steady state equilibrium. From a classical and also from an early neoclassical point of view, a long period equilibrium would be regarded as the full or fundamental equilibrium position, while an intertemporal equilibrium would be conceived as a special representation of a convergence of market prices (market clearing) to 'natural' or long run normal prices. The process of convergence can, in a very general sense, be described in the following way: at the initial period different commodity rates of interest are due to the arbitrariness of the given endowments relative to the demand of the different agents. Prices reflect the relative scarcity of the commodities. Prices are relatively high for those commodities whose endowments are low in relation to demand and they are relatively low for commodities whose endowments are abundant in relation to demand. Taking production into consideration, the system moves away from the proportions given by the arbitrary endowments and prices become more and more determined by input-output relations as long as the preferences of the consumers remain stationary. How competition will lead to equal commodity rates cannot easily be conceived, because agents are not actually used to calculating in terms of discounted prices. Discounted prices are defined in terms of an intertemporal constant *numéraire*, while undiscounted prices are defined in terms of a current *numéraire*. Discounting a current price of a commodity *i* by the own discount rate of the *numéraire* (for instance gold) $\beta_{g,t}$ yields the discounted price of this commodity *i*, $p_{i,t}$:

$$p_{i,t} = \beta_{g,t} \cdot \overline{p}_{i,t} \,,$$

where $\overline{p}_{i,t}$ is the current price of commodity *i*.

Profit of period t in process k in terms of discounted prices is given by

$$G_t^k = b_{t+1}^k p_{t+1} - a_t^k p_t \,, \tag{C12.1}$$

where b_{t+1}^k is the output vector of the period *t*, a_t^k is the input vector of the same period, and p_t is the price vector of period t. Now transforming profit of period *t* in terms of current prices yields (omitting the index *k*):

$$G_t = b_{t+1} \beta_{g,t+1} \overline{p}_{t+1} - a_t \beta_{g,t} \overline{p}_t \,. \tag{C12.2}$$

Division by $\beta_{g,t+1}$ gives current profit $\overline{G}_t$:

$$\overline{G}_t = b_{t+1} \overline{p}_{t+1} - a_t \frac{\beta_{g,t}}{\beta_{g,t+1}} \overline{p}_t \tag{C12.2a}$$

since $\dfrac{\beta_{g,t}}{\beta_{g,t+1}} = (1 + \rho_{g,t})$, where $\rho_{g,t}$ is the commodity rate of interest of the *numéraire* (gold). If all contracts are made in terms of the *numéraire*, its own rate becomes the rate of interest of the system. In order to express this, we set $\rho_{g,t} \equiv i_t$, and we assume that i_t is exogenously determined. Now current profit is

$$\overline{G}_t = b_{t+1} \overline{p}_{t+1} - (1 + i_t) a_t \overline{p}_t. \tag{C12.3}$$

Constant returns and perfect competition then imply

$$\frac{b_{t+1} \overline{p}_{t+1} - a_t \overline{p}_t}{a_t \overline{p}_t} = i_t. \tag{C12.4}$$

All processes are equally profitable in terms of the *numéraire* and the rate of profit (left hand) in production is equal to the rate of interest. Now, let us assume that the rate of interest is constant, $i_t = i_{t+1} = i_{t+2} = \ldots \; \forall t$, then the rate of profit must also be constant and uniform over time. Although the rate of

profit is uniform and constant over time, the system may not be in a long
period (or steady state) equilibrium, because the commodity rates of interest
may neither be uniform nor constant over time.

According to (C12.4), profits may be due to either a physical surplus and/or
output prices in $t + 1$ being higher than input prices in t. Both effects can be
separated by a simple decomposition of the left hand side of (C12.4):

$$\frac{b_{t+1}\overline{p}_{t+1} - a_t\overline{p}_t}{a_t\overline{p}_t} \equiv \frac{b_{t+1}\overline{p}_t - a_t\overline{p}_t}{a_t\overline{p}_t} + \frac{b_{t+1}(\overline{p}_{t+1} - \overline{p}_t)}{a_t\overline{p}_t} = i_t. \tag{C12.5}$$

The second term of (C12.5) gives the return over costs on the basis of
constant prices. In a one-commodity world with output and input being the
same physical commodity, e.g. grain, prices cancel and the rate measures the
physical surplus over physical input; in other words, the net amount of grain
at the *end* of period t over the amount of grain at the *beginning* of period t.
This rate has the same dimension as the commodity rate of grain in period t,
ρ_t. The third term gives the increase (or decrease) of revenue due to price
changes from t to $t + 1$ over the value of inputs at the beginning of period t.
This rate, we may call it the revenue gain rate, is positive if $\overline{p}_{t+1} > \overline{p}_t$ and vice
versa. Since i_t is taken as exogenously determined, the higher the revenue
gain, the lower must be the 'real' rate of profit and vice versa.

Furthermore, if $\overline{p}_{t+1} = \overline{p}_t$, the 'real' rate of profit is equal to *the* rate of interest, and all commodity rates of interest are equal to *the* rate of interest.
Thus, it turns out, that as long as $\overline{p}_{t+1} \neq \overline{p}_t$, the 'real' rate of profit is not equal
to the rate of interest indicating that within an intertemporal equilibrium there
is a disequilibrium element that keeps the system going on to adjust to a long
period equilibrium position.

The convergence goes along with the elimination of revenue gains. Revenue gains emerge because current intertemporal prices are still influenced by
scarcities. Processes with a positive and high revenue gain have a low 'real'
rate of profit, while in processes with a high 'real' rate the revenue rate must
be low or even negative. High revenue gains signal that the current prices of
the output of this process rise faster than the price of the *numéraire*, while
negative revenue gains indicate that current prices of the output of this process rise slower than the price of the *numéraire*. Since intertemporal prices
move in inverse proportion to quantities, processes with a negative revenue
gain have a high rate of expansion (growth) and a high 'real' rate of profit,
while processes with high revenue gains have a small rate of expansion
(growth) and low 'real' rate of profit. If, from period to period, scarcities are
more and more reduced, processes tend to expand with the same rate, so that
the 'real' rates of profit in the different processes tend to equalize. Differ-
ences in intertemporal prices, e.g. $\overline{p}_{t+1} > \overline{p}_t$, may still occur, but now they are
uniform over all processes due to the quantity expansion of the *numéraire*.

This is the case of *pure* inflation. If the expansion or contraction of the *numéraire* commodity cannot strictly be kept out of the system, inflation or deflation cannot be *pure* in the sense, that it does not influence the adjustment process. However, this stylized process of convergence is far from being completely unraveled. It needs further theoretical investigations to understand which forces govern this process.

REFERENCES

Barens, I. and Caspari, V. (1997), 'Own-rates of interest and their implications for the existence of underemployment equilibrium positions', in G.C. Harcourt and P.A. Riach (eds), *A 'second edition' of the General Theory*, Volume 1, London, Routledge, 283-303.

Fisher, I. (1896), 'Appreciation and interest', *American Economic Association Publications,* **3**, 331-442.

Fisher, I. (1907), *The Rate of Interest: Its Nature, Determination and Relation to Economic Phenomena*, New York, Macmillan.

Hayek, F.A. (1931), *Prices and Production*, London, Routledge.

Sraffa, P. (1932), 'Dr. Hayek on money and capital', *Economic Journal,* **42**, 42-53.

13. Capital and Income in the Theory of Investment and Output: Irving Fisher and John Maynard Keynes

Jan A. Kregel

The second war produced a watershed in twentieth-century economics. Together with the dominance of the profession by purely academic economists came the disappearance of what might be called financial macroeconomists whose principal concern was the explanation of the interaction of finance and investment in the context of economic fluctuations. Although there has been a renewed interest in business cycles, it has concentrated on 'real' factors, while 'finance' has become a separate discipline concentrating on the microeconomics of efficient markets and some aspects of rational expectations.

One of the founders of the financial macroeconomics approach was Irving Fisher. He was part of a group of economists which included Hayek, Böhm-Bawerk, Schumpeter, Wicksell, Hawtrey, Robertson and Keynes to name a few. Although these economists came from diverse theoretical backgrounds, a common denominator was active participation in financial markets, either through private or public sector experience. This background of institutional knowledge provided support of their distinctive theoretical approach, which recognized that monetary and financial factors are important determinants of the behavior of the economy. This common background may also be noted from the fact that despite theoretical difference, Keynes was outspoken in acknowledgment that 'it was Irving Fisher who ... first influenced me strongly towards regarding money as a "real" factor' (1973, pp. 202-203, n.2). In particular, Keynes suggested that his theory of investment, based on the marginal efficiency of capital, 'was first introduced by Irving Fisher in his *Theory of Interest* (1930) under the designation "the rate of return over cost". This conception of his is, I think, the most important and fruitful of his recent conceptions' (Fisher, 1930, p. 103). Indeed, the modern financial analyst would be surprised to discover in *The Nature of Capital and Income* (1906) and *The Theory of Interest*, most of the basic tools of time value analysis of investment including spot and forward yield curves.

It is unfortunate that much of this part of Fisher's work has fallen from the standard economics curriculum. In the post-war view of economics, Fisher is generally characterized as a forerunner of modern monetarism in which money has no permanent influence, and as the proponent of the rule that nominal interest rates reflect the adjustment of underlying, stable real rates of interest to rationally anticipated inflation. These suggest the rather extreme position that the rate of interest is determined by productivity and that monetary factors have no permanent impact.

But, anyone who has studied Fisher's work will recall the importance of his definition of income for his entire work, as well as the scientific caution in which Fisher always couched his positions. In particular his concern to combat the extreme positions of the 'psychology school' or the 'productivity school' (1930, p. 312), by joining time preference and investment opportunity as dual determinants of the rate of interest. They will also recall his admonition that his theory was only representative of 'rational tendencies', that are based on 'rational and empirical laws ... analogous to rational and empirical laws of physics and astronomy' (p. 321).

Outside these conditions, where actuarial risk is replaced by uncertainty and in which the value of money is unstable Fisher recommended that 'We must ... give up as a bad job any attempt to formulate completely the influences which really determine the rate of interest' (p. 321). Although he did consider it possible to do take steps to reduce the problems caused by unstable money, and made numerous proposals to that effect.

Before someone questions my representation of Fisher as an expert in the operation of financial markets by reference to his role as the public antidote to Roger Babson's continued predictions of an impending stock market crash in early September 1929 and his subsequent declarations that stock prices remained undervalued, I will also draw attention to the fact that Fisher quickly learned from the experience and by 1931 has worked out his theory of debt deflation. Indeed, it is interesting to note the absence of a conference session devoted to this topic. This approach lives on in the work of a small group of Wall Street analysts who rediscovered it through Hyman Minsky's financial instability hypothesis. Although Minsky's theory is often presented as Keynesian, his use of Keynes and Kalecki is primarily the aggregate profits equation, and serves more to explain why 1929 has not recurred, than why it is still a clear and present danger. The endogenous generation of depression from excessive lending and the process by which reducing indebtedness increases indebtedness are both clearly derived from Fisher. And like Keynes, Minsky has clearly acknowledged this debt to Fisher.

However, the particular Fisherian themes that I would like to emphasize will perhaps surprise you. It is 'time'. Indeed, time is a factor that unites the group of pre-war financial macroeconomists. These economists took the impact of time seriously. To draw on an aphorism of Dennis Robertson, the short-run is not the same length in both directions, forward and back. By which I assume he meant that what is unclear in anticipation, appears obvious and self-evident in retrospect. What has been done in anticipation can never be recovered. Fisher's theory of capital is based on the distinction between the theory of what occurs during the passage of time, and what occurs at a point in time. Thus the distinction between capital as a stock, income as a flow, and the value of capital as the value at a point in time of the income flow expected from it. Indeed, at one point Fisher suggests that the theory of capital might better be described as a theory of income. It is a flow theory, a theory that occurs over the passage of time. And the rate of interest is of crucial importance to theory because it is the linkage between two points in time, it brings the future to the present point in time that allows the calculation of capital values. Since the rate of interest relates to flows over time, its specification requires at least two points in time.

The rate of interest on a loan is thus the price of a spot-forward swap of money, or what we today would call a repo contract. Interest can be represented by swap points over spot, as in a foreign currency swap, or repo agreement. Or Fisher would say, by the excess over par. Alternatively, it may be represented by the discount from the maturity or face value, as in a foreign exchange bill or a Treasury bill. Both come to the same thing. It is instructive to note that Keynes also defined the rate of interest as 'nothing more than the percentage excess of a sum of money contracted for forward delivery .. over what we may call the "spot" or cash price of the sum thus contracted for forward delivery' (Keynes, 1936, p. 222).

Since there are spot-forward swaps of different maturity, there will be interest rates referring to different periods, extending not only from today to different future dates, but from future dates to farther future dates. It was following this line of reasoning that led Fisher to the concepts of zero-coupon rates as well as forward rates which have come to play such an important role in modern financial analysis. But, more importantly, Fisher also notes that there is no reason why 'interest rates' cannot also be applied to individual commodities, so that a spot-forward swap of say gold or wheat would also produce a rate of interest, only it would be measured in terms of the commodity itself. Fisher thus notes that

> We thus need to distinguish between interest expressed in terms of money and interest expressed in terms of other goods. But no two forms of goods can be expected to maintain an absolutely constant price ratio towards each other. *There are, therefore, theoretically just as many rates of interest expressed in terms of goods as there are kinds of goods diverging from one another in value* (emphasis in original, 1930, p. 42).

To keep the comparison with Keynes, the sentence that follows the once quoted above reads: 'It would seem, therefore, that for every kind of capital asset there must be an analogue of the rate of interest on money' and he goes on to specify a wheat-rate of interest and a steel-plant rate of interest, finally referring the reader in a note to Sraffa's use of the concept in his debate with Hayek.

Starting from this specification of the rate of interest it is easy to see how Fisher extended it to his opportunity theory of investment and the concept of rate of return over cost. It is important to remember that the discussion is in terms of project selection. The rate of return over cost is that rate which equalizes the net present value of the stream of cash flows from two alternative opportunities of investment. The decision to use the option of an alternative opportunity will then be determined by comparing it to the market rate of interest. The concept is also used to determine incremental investments in a single line, similar to the decision over capital intensity of a project. It also generates what we would now call 'switching' rates of return, that is, changes in market rates of interest which cause one project to be preferred to another. There are also indications that Fisher entertained the possibility of reswitching, caused by multiple solutions and increasing returns, but discarded them as unlikely curiosa.

When Keynes deals with the concept, it has been reduced to the option of shifting from a fixed interest security to an additional unit of a capital investment project and the marginal rate of return over cost becomes the marginal efficiency of capital. But, the important point for both of them is the independent determination of the rate of interest (leaving aside any differences between the psychological determinants of time preference and liquidity preference) and the rate of return over costs (or the efficiency of capital) which allows the determination of equilibrium in terms of the equality between the two. It also leads, for both, to the importance of distinguishing between short and long rates of interest. Fisher cites as a corollary of his theory 'the necessity of positing a theoretically separate rate of interest for each separate period of time ... the divergence between the rate for short terms and for long terms' (1930, p. 313) and Keynes' belief in the difference between short and long-period expectations, citing 'The mistake of regarding the marginal efficiency of capital primarily in terms of the *current* yield of capital equipment, which would be correct only in the static state where there is no changing future to influence the present ...' pointing out in a footnote that 'the relation between rates of interest for different periods depends on expectations' (1936, p. 145).

Up to this point, both Keynes and Fisher propose an equilibrium determined by the equality of the appropriate rate of interest with the return on investment, and propose a similar procedure to decide on the investment projects which will be implemented. The specification of this equilibrium raises another important point – given the possibility noted by both of specifying rates of interest in terms of individual commodities there is the question of whether arbitrage across different rates will produce the same results when specified in different standards. Fisher notes that the arbitrage process cannot determine the rate of interest, but it only 'enables us ... to calculate the rates in other standards' on the assumption 'that the rate is *some one* standard is already known.' (1930, p. 45). Keynes also notes that even when calculating own rates, since they are quoted in money terms, 'it also brings in the money-rate of interest'. Thus, some rate has to be known from outside the system, and that rate for both is the money rate of interest.

First, let us consider the arbitrage process. Fisher argues that market arbitrage should act to eliminate any changes in the relative values of the standards used to express the multiple possible rates of interest. Thus if there are two commodities, say gold and wheat, each showing the same ratio between spot and forward prices, but one of them, say wheat, is appreciating in terms of gold, then there should be a market preference to hold wheat, irrespective of the preferences for the two goods. The increased demand for wheat would them drive up its spot price relative to its forward price, reducing its premium over par and causing a reduction in its interest rate. (Keynes would have identified this as backwardation). The rate of interest on wheat thus adjusts until it is brought into equality with the rate on gold.

Now, one of the implications of considering the interest rate as a spot-forward swap is that it creates a known future value. It fixes a future action and thus makes the future less difficult to predict. But, even if every economic action takes the form of a spot and a predetermined forward transaction, this does not mean that the future is perfectly known or that it will represent a position of equilibrium. Fisher always starts out his theory by assuming perfect foresight, and then explains why this is impossible, even in the present of full forward contracting.

Thus Fisher's description of the arbitrage process between gold and wheat argues that if the forward price of wheat were perfectly known to be at a 10% premium, while the forward price of money were known to be at a 4% premium (the spot and forward price of wheat in money is 1 : 1, then the arbitraged forward price of wheat in money is 1.10/1.04), it would pay to borrow money at 4%, buy a bushel of wheat at the current spot price which can be lent today against 1.10 bushels forward. The wheat can then be sold for 1.10 to repay the money loan with interest of 1.04, giving a positive carry of 6%. If the forward price ratio between gold and wheat is fixed at unity, this would drive up the current price of wheat until it stood at 1.1 / 1.04 = 1.057% premium over money. 1.057 in money invested at 4% just yields 1.10.

Now, this is the relation that Keynes worked out in the *Manchester Guardian* and republished in the *Tract on Monetary Reform*, known today as the interest rate parity theorem. I have suggested (Kregel, 1997) that it forms the core of Keynes' analysis of income determination. If we substitute dollars for gold and marks for wheat, with the dollar interest rate 4% relative to the mark interest rate of 10% it says that the proportional difference between the spot and forward prices of the two currencies should be the spot rate times 1 plus the dollar interest rate divided by 1 plus the mark interest rate or 1 times (1.04/1.10). In Fisher's example the forward dollar mark rate is fixed at 1:1, so we have to rearrange the formula to find the spot rate as the forward rate times 1 plus the mark interest rate divided by 1 plus the dollar rate or 1 times (1.10/1.04). Thus, wheat sells at a spot premium or a forward discount. This means that wheat bought at 1.057 can only be sold at 1 at the end of the contract. It is clear that the arbitrage may occur via adjustment of either the spot or forward prices, i.e. the rate of appreciation or depreciation of one standard in terms of the other, or in terms of the rates of interest in each standard, or in all three.

Of course, the determination of the rate of interest in Fisher's approach to the theory of income is the rate which brought about equality of present and future incomes. It is the extension to real income of the arbitrage process described above that leads directly to the relation between money and real rates of interest. As noted, there are three factors at work, the appreciation or depreciation of one standard in terms of the other, which we can clearly recognize as the rate of inflation, when measured in terms of the money standard, the rate of interest in terms of money and the rate of interest in terms of time preference for present over future income.

Now, if we substitute income for 'wheat' and money for 'gold', then Fisher's arbitrage argument says that it is only possible that the money rate of interest should be 4% when the (real) income rate of interest is 10% if money is expected to exchange for 5.8% more income in the future than in the present so that $1.0578 \cdot 1.04 = 1.10$. Thus, if there is a forward discount on income (the inverse of the forward premium of 1 : 1.057 on money), the rate of return on income (10%) must be higher than that on money (4%), but if income is at a forward premium, then the rate of return on money must be higher than the return on income. This, of course, is just reversing the process noted above, by substituting money and income, for gold and wheat, or for dollars and marks. The relation between the real and the money interest rates given by the rate of appreciation of the standard thus descends directly for the arbitrage relation that insures that the rate of interest is equal to the rate of return over costs or from the interest rate parity theorem.

Now, this precise formal equivalence between Fisher' and Keynes's analysis of the equality between rates of interest and rates of return is really not such a great discovery. Everyone who has taught a course in international finance draws a four-corner diagram in which the two corners of one side (usually the top) represent Keynes's (covered) interest rate parity theorem and Fisher's real-nominal interest rate relation And that is what we have just done here. This is the standard proposition from interest rate parity.

Of course, the actual process of adjustment can come in any of the variables. For example, if the interest rate on income and the discount or premia are fixed, then all of the adjustment must come in the money rate of interest. On the other hand, if only the return on income is fixed, say by time preferences, then the money rate will have to adjust to any changes in the forward discount or premium on money. The proposition that $(1 + p)(1 + r) = (1 + i)$, where p is the rate of inflation, r the rate of increase in real income, and i the rate of interest on money, is just a different way of expressing the interest rate parity theorem for a closed economy, or that there is full arbitrage. Rewriting the relation as $(1 + p) = (1 + i) / (1 + r)$, and writing S as the spot rate of exchange of money for wheat and F the forward rate of exchange of money for wheat, then $F / S = 1 + p$ and we have $F = S [(1 + i) / (1+r)] = .945 \, S$ or given $F = 1$, $S = 1 / .945 = 1.057$, which is the price of wheat in money terms that eliminates arbitrage profit.

But not only is there a formal similarity, Keynes also accepted the general validity of the empirical data in support of Fisher's proposition in the form of what has come to be known as the Gibson Paradox – higher rates of inflation tend to produce higher rates of interest. However, despite this similarity in approach, and agreement on the empirical basis, Keynes takes issue with Fisher on the relation between the rate of interest and the rate of inflation. Thus, there is more than a Gibson Paradox, there is the paradox of how two economists who adopted virtually similar basic analytical systems could reach radically opposed solutions.

Part of the solution to the paradox is to be found in Fisher's discussion of the relation between the rates of interest measured in terms of the various possible commodity standards. He notes the difficulty in transferring the idea of a rate of interest on an individual commodity to income as a whole. In principle 'a rate of interest in terms of fundamental income itself would seem to come as near as we can practically come to any basic standard in which to express a real rate of interest' (1930, pp. 42-3), however, in the absence of such a measure, the practice is to fall back on the use of 'a practical objective standard' represented by 'a cost of living index' which Fisher spent most of his career trying to perfect.

> By means of such an index number we may translate the nominal, or money rate of interest, into a goods rate or real rate of interest, just as we translate money wages into real wages. The cost of living plays the same role in both cases although the process of translating is somewhat different and more complicated in the case of

interest from what it is in the case of wages, for the reason that interest involves two points of time, instead of only one; so that we must translate from money into goods not only in the present, when the money is borrowed, but also in the future, when it is repaid (1930, p. 42).

Fisher was concerned by this point because in his theory the rate of interest to which rate of return over cost should be equated was determined by present relative to future income–time preference. Keynes did not have this problem because liquidity preference referred to present relative to future delivery of money.

This difference is important because the definition of a rate of return in terms of 'fundamental income' (or of an amount of nominal income which can be deflated by a price index) eliminates any possibility of a market-based process of arbitrage which ensures the equilibrium relation. Since there are no markets for 'fundamental income', it is impossible to argue that individuals will buy and sell fundamental income spot against forward or to arbitrage it against a money relative given by a price index. A theory which is based on a real financial market process of arbitrage when applied to individual commodities, has no direct counterpart when looked upon in the aggregate. But, it is precisely such an arbitrage process that Fisher invokes to establish the inflation adjustment of nominal interest rates.

Fisher's solution of 'fundamental income' and aggregate price indices is subject to the criticism of von Mises and Hayek concerning the inadequacies of index numbers, as well as Sraffa's criticism of Hayek's use of a 'neutral' rate of interest. Attempts to deal with these difficulties have moved economists in two directions. Both seem to converge on the same point.

The first is to find a suitable measure of 'fundamental income'. The concept of fundamental income is related to Ricardo's invariable standard of value, and links up with Sraffa's standard commodity and Hicks's definition of income and its 'average period' in his *Value and Capital* (Chapter XIV and note). At this point, we may note that it is a bit more complicated than finding the appropriate price index by which to deflate nominal income.

The second is to analyze the importance of the assumption of perfect foresight for the arbitrage process which establishes the equality of real and nominal rates. This is where Keynes had difficulties with Fisher's version of interest parity (cf. *Treatise on Money*, Volume II, pp. 202-203 and *General Theory*, pp. 142-143*)*. Keynes argues that Fisher's argument that the money rate of interest should automatically reflect a perfectly foreseen rise in the rate of inflation overlooked the impact on long-term bond prices of a rise in interest rates. While it would be true that a perfectly foreseen rise in inflation for the coming year of 2% producing a 2% rise in interest rates on one-year Treasury bills would keep real returns constant, the same would not be true of a holder of a longer-term instrument if it were sold after one year (or even if it were held to maturity). But, it should be true that the one-year return should be the same for any instrument held for one year.

Keynes uses the example of a £100 par value British consol paying £10 per annum to yield 10% which falls to £81.96 (a decline of 1.8% and a capital loss of over £18) when interest rates rise to 12.2%. While the 'variations in the rate of interest earned during the year in question are too small to make much difference' (e.g. the extra 2.2% on the £10 coupon), the holder of fixed interest assets will have a substantial capital loss. The investor will have the benefit of being able to invest the future £10 interest coupon payments at the higher rate of 12.2%, but over a single year this will not be sufficient to cover the £18 decline in the capital value of the bond, and thus by definition could not compensate for any rise in the inflation rate equal to the increased rate of interest. Thus, Keynes suggests that Fisher's relation goes in the wrong direction to the extent that a higher inflation rate increases bond yields and causes absolute losses in capital values which more than offset the rise in the rate of interest which is supposed to compensate for the fall in the value of money. Full inflation coverage should provide for an adjustment in capital value as well as in the income from the bond. But, here we are led back to the concept of income. Keynes is arguing that since the principal value of the bond is impaired even when interest rates adjust to inflation, an individual will have a lower total real income from the original investment. This is particularly easy to see in the case of the consol, for its price is permanently reduced.

The point seems obvious, given Fisher's concern to derive capital values from income flows. Yet, it is the theory of income that prevents Fisher from taking it into account. This is because, if capital is just discounted future income, then an appreciation or depreciation of capital value, i.e. a capital gain or loss, must represent an increase or decrease in expected future income. But, this has no impact on present income. Fisher notes that

> Consols and rentes fluctuate in value every day with every change in the money market. Yet the income they actually yield flows on at the same rate. ... A rise in the market is a capital gain, but it is not income (1930, p. 27).

Fisher had already discussed the point in *The Nature of Capital and Income*:

> Expressed in a single sentence, the general principle connecting realized and earned income is that they differ by the appreciation or depreciation of capital. It is thus possible to describe earned income as realized income less depreciation of capital, or else as realized income plus appreciation of capital. We may therefore state anew the fallacy of confusing realized income with earned income: the fallacy consists in reckoning depreciation of capital as a part of outgo, or appreciation of capital as a part of income. (1906, p. 238).

Thus, the case of a capital loss caused by an increase in the rate of interest is equivalent to the case of realized income exceeding earned income, or the depreciation of capital, due to the rise in the rate of interest. In order to keep capital constant, a deduction will have to be made to income received in future periods. This is the reduction to future income which is represented by the capital loss. A higher rate of inflation, which reduces real future income will also require an increase in future income to offset it.

An alternative way of looking at the problem would be to note that insofar as capital gains and losses for the economy as a whole net to zero, there should be no impact on either present or future income streams due to the change in nominal interest rates. Thus, there need not be any impact on the overall rate of time preference linking present and future incomes. This seems to be what Hayek had in mind with his conception of neutral money, for the money rate of interest would then be managed so as to leave the real rate unchanged. This suggests the second difference, and that is that Fisher implicitly assumes that real incomes are unchanged, while Keynes is looking at a theory to explain the movement in incomes.

> Indeed Professor Fisher's theory could be best rewritten in terms of a 'real rate of interest' defined as being the rate of interest which would have to rule, consequently on a change in the state of expectation of the future value of money, in order that this change should have no effect on current output (1936, p. 143).

Keynes then goes on to make his basic criticism of Fisher's relation, that the most important impact of inflation will be not in the interest rate, but on the incentive to invest – the marginal efficiency of capital. Fisher's account of the impact of a rise in the rate of inflation makes no mention of the impact on either long-term bond values or on the rate of return over costs.

This brings us back to the question of the definition of fundamental income, or just exactly what it means to have income constant when changes in interest rates have an influence on capital values. This is the question that Hicks sought to answer in his 'average period' of income and is now better known as 'McCauley duration', which was worked out in an attempt to assess the Fisher relation with respect to the Gibson Paradox.

Against this background it is interesting to assess Fisher's theory of debt deflation, for here it seems quite clear that he accepted that income would not be constant. Fisher had already noted that his theory required that 'the performance of contracts corresponds to promises and expectations' and that 'because of defaults, the equations fail of being precisely true' (1930, p. 320), and this is precisely the case of debt deflation. This process is propagated by a failure of interest rates to fall in order to keep real rates constant, and thus produces an increase in real indebtedness. This requires the process of forced liquidation which drives prices down. '...the liquidation of debts cannot keep up with the fall of prices which it causes. In that case, the liquidation defeats itself. While it diminishes the number of dollars owed, it may not do so as fast as it increases the value of each dollar owed.' ... '*The more debtors pay, the more they owe*' (1933, p. 344, emphasis in original). Which is simply another way of saying that nominal interest rates have not fallen sufficiently rapidly and have not become sufficiently negative. The failure of lenders to make direct payments to borrowers means that they experience the reduction in terms of default and total loss of principal. The result is that income does not remain constant. The general implication is that when interest rates fail to keep up with inflation there is a boom and when they fail to keep down with deflation there is a debt deflation. Which looks very much like Wicksell. When the interest-inflation rule is met, then income is stable, which looks very much like Hayek. And despite the formal similarities between this rule and the interest rate parity theorem and their investment theories, it does not look at all like Keynes.

REFERENCES

Fisher, I. (1906), *The Nature of Capital and Income*, New York, Macmillan.

Fisher, I. (1930), *The Theory of Interest*, New York, Macmillan.

Fisher, I. (1933), 'The debt-deflation theory of great depressions,' *Econometrica*, **1**, 337-357.

Keynes, J.M. (1930), *Treatise on Money*, 2 volumes, London, Macmillan.

Keynes, J.M. (1936), *The General Theory of Employment, Interest and Money*, London, Macmillan.

Keynes, J.M. (1973), *The General Theory and After: Part II: Defense and Development*, edited by D. Moggridge, Volume XIV of Keynes' Collected Writings, London, Macmillan.

Kregel, J.A. (1988), 'Irving Fisher, great-grandparent of the *General Theory*: money, rate of return over cost and efficiency of capital,' *Cahiers d'Economie Politique*, **14-15**, 59-68.

Kregel, J.A. (1997), 'The theory of value, expectations and chapter 17 of the *General Theory*' in G.C. Harcourt and P. Riach (eds), *A Second Edition of the General Theory*, London, Routledge, 261-282.

PART SEVEN:
VALUE, PRICES, AND
FINANCIAL ASSETS

14. Irving Fisher's Mathematical Investigations in the Theory of Value and Prices

Ulrich Schwalbe[*]

---

1 INTRODUCTION

The doctoral dissertation *Mathematical Investigations in the Theory of Value and Prices* was Irving Fisher's first contribution to economic theory. It analyzes equilibria in exchange and production economies, and develops many important concepts in consumer and utility theory. First published in 1892, it has been reprinted in 1925 and in 1965, and has been translated into French and Japanese. This interest in Fisher's work indicates that his thesis indeed had a major impact on economic theory. For instance, Samuelson (1967, p. 22) called it the greatest doctoral dissertation ever written. Ragnar Frisch (1947, p. 72) considered it a contribution of monumental importance, and many other eminent economists, including Edgeworth (1893), Schumpeter (1948) and Tobin (1985), praised Fisher's work. In many histories of economic thought Fisher's thesis is regarded as one of his most important books (see e.g. Hutchinson, 1953, p. 271; Ingrao and Israel, 1990, pp. 247-248; Niehans, 1990, p. 270; Spiegel, 1991, pp. 622-623)

Despite these enthusiastic reactions to the *Mathematical Investigations*, the fact that Fisher made substantial contributions to general equilibrium theory has not been fully recognized in the literature, as the perusal of recent textbooks on general equilibrium theory indicates. For instance, the books by B. Ellickson and R. M. Starr don't even mention his name.

The present paper reevaluates Fisher's work. In particular, I discuss his contribution with respect to the problem of equilibria in exchange economies, as well as to utility and consumer theory. The paper is organized as follows: section two gives a short survey of the first part of Fisher's thesis, where he assumes additively separable utility functions. In addition, his models of exchange and production economies are discussed. Section three deals with Fisher's analysis of economies where the agents are characterized by non-separable utility functions. Some remarks are made on the relationship between physics and economics, and on Fisher's interest in the measurement of marginal utility. The fourth section deals with a graphical device introduced by Fisher, which represents an alternative to the famous Edgeworth box. This *net trade diagram* has been used in the literature on quantity rationing, and recently regained interest in textbooks on general equilibrium theory.[1] The fact that this diagram was developed by Fisher has – to the best of my knowledge – hitherto gone unnoticed in the literature.

2   WALRAS SIMPLIFIED?

Fisher's Ph.D. thesis deals with the problem of existence and the comparative statics of equilibria in simple exchange and production economies – the central problems of modern general equilibrium theory. In Fisher's words, it is 'a study by mathematical methods of the determination of value and prices' (Fisher, 1892, p. 3). The *Investigations* are divided into two parts which differ with respect to the assumptions made on the agents' utility functions. In part one, Fisher assumes an agent's utility function to be additively separable, i.e. for each agent the utility of a commodity depends only on the amount of the commodity under consideration and it is independent of the amounts of other goods consumed. In the second part he employs a more general approach and assumes that the utility of a commodity depends on the amount of *all* commodities consumed. The latter assumption is now standard in microeconomic theory.

2.1 Utility and Preferences

Fisher begins with a discussion of the concept of utility. At that time, utility was often thought of as being closely associated with the sensations of pleasure and pain. Fisher wants to free the concept of utility from all those psychological connotations. Therefore, he states the following postulate about the behavior of an economic agent, 'Each individual acts as he desires' (Fisher, 1892, p. 11) – or as it is said today, each agent acts according to his preferences.

In what follows, he presents a rather modern definition of a preference relation and a utility function. First, he assumes that if an agent is indifferent between two commodities, the utility assigned to both commodities is the same (the agent has no desire or preference for the one commodity to the exclusion of the other). Second, if an agent prefers one commodity to the other, the former is associated with a higher utility. These ideas are illustrated with some examples from physics, as e.g., 'two forces are equal if at the same time they alone act on the same particle in opposite directions and no change of motion results' (Fisher, 1892, p. 12).

For introducing the idea of a preference relation and a utility function as a numerical representation of these preferences, Fisher can be considered as a precursor of the modern axiomatic theory of choice. Here, the important economic concept is an agent's preference relation – a utility function is only a derived concept, i.e. a numerical representation of preferences without any intrinsic meaning.

Having defined utility, he employs this concept to analyze the behavior of an agent by introducing the idea of marginal utility. His approach is similar to that of Jevons and Marshall. He shows that in exchanging two commodities, an agent behaves optimally if he consumes quantities such that the ratio of their marginal utilities equals their price ratio. In the following paragraph Fisher makes some remarks about the measurement of marginal utility. He was very much interested in this topic, his pursuit culminating in his 1927 contribution to the *Festschrift* for J.B. Clark, where he suggested a method to use observable data to determine a unique cardinal measure of utility. Fisher's ideas about the measurement of marginal utility will be discussed in section 3.

2.2 Consumer and Producer Behavior

Chapter 2 begins by pointing out analogies and similarities between economics and mechanics: 'Yet so far as I know, no one has undertaken a systematic representation in terms of mechanical interaction of that beautiful and intricate equilibrium which manifests itself on the "exchanges" of a great city but of which the causes and effects lie far outside' (Fisher, 1892, p. 24).

In the following paragraph, he states the assumptions underlying the subsequent analysis. For example, it is assumed that the agents behave as price takers and are completely informed about all relevant variables in the economy; commodities are perfectly divisible and marginal utility is decreasing (marginal disutility is increasing), etc. Fisher points out that these assumptions are essentially those of Auspitz and Lieben (1889, p. 4). Their work was one of the two books on mathematical economics Fisher had read before writing his thesis. Except for the assumption of decreasing marginal utility, these assumptions are very similar to those usually made in modern microeconomics and general equilibrium theory.

To examine an economy with many commodities and agents, Fisher begins his analysis by considering the behavior of one consumer or producer with respect to one commodity, and then shows that a consumer will maximize his utility by consuming such an amount of this commodity that its marginal utility equals its price. A producer will produce an amount of a commodity such that the marginal disutility of this quantity equals its negative price. It should be noticed that Fisher models production strictly analogous to consumption: an individual can produce a commodity by exerting labor and thus incurring negative utility. In his words, '... attention is confined to those features of production which are strictly analogous to consumption' (Fisher, 1892, p. 28). It will later turn out that regarding production as 'negative' consumption is the reason for a production economy being formally equivalent to an exchange economy.

In the next step, Fisher discusses the behavior of many consumers with respect to one commodity and shows that, in an optimum, the marginal utilities for all consumers must be the same since 'there can be but one price, and each individual will make his marginal utility equal to it' (Fisher, 1892, p. 28). To illustrate this situation, Fisher constructs a hydrostatical device consisting of several cisterns connected by tubes. Each cistern represents the marginal utility of a consumer. Since the preferences of the agents might differ, the cisterns are of different shape. If they are filled with water, the liquid will seek its level and thus lead to an equalization of marginal utilities across consumers.

Fisher also gives a mathematical statement of this problem and concludes that the quantities consumed by each consumer as well as the resulting utilities are determinate since the number of unknowns and equations are the same. Of course, the equality of the numbers of equations and unknowns is neither necessary nor sufficient for an equation system to have a unique solution. However, at that time counting equations and unknowns was the normal procedure to make a statement about the existence of a solution.

An equivalent approach is used to characterize the equilibrium of many producers with respect to one commodity. In this case, the marginal disutilities will be equalized across producers. After having considered the behavior of *many* consumers or producers with respect to *one* commodity, chapter III takes a different 'cross-section' through the economy by analyzing the behavior of *one* consumer (or producer) with respect to *many* commodities. He shows that 'a consumer will so arrange his consumption that the marginal utility per dollar's worth of each commodity shall be the same' (Fisher, 1892, p. 32). This result is also illustrated by his mechanical model. The amount of water in the system represents the total income of the consumer which is distributed over the commodities such that marginal rate of substitution between two commodities equals their price ratio. Since production is modeled in a strictly analogous manner to consumption, the equivalent result holds for production. A given amount of expenses has to be distributed over the production of different commodities. An optimum is reached when the marginal rate of technical substitution between two commodities equals their price ratio.

2.3 Equilibrium in an Exchange Economy

After having analyzed these two 'cross-sections' through an economy, Fisher integrates these viewpoints. 'Our discussion is like a tourist's view of a great city, who glances up each east and west street while riding along the same avenue and then takes a "cross town" course and sees each avenue from a single street. We are now to seek a bird's-eye view' (Fisher, 1892, p. 35).

Put differently, he studies the general case with m commodities and n agents. First, he concentrates on the analysis of an exchange economy. In a second step, he combines consumption and production in a general model.

The formal description of an exchange economy and the equilibrium conditions are given – in Fisher's notation – as follows: In a first step, the set of feasible allocations is defined. Let A_i, B_i, C_i etc. denote the amount of commodity A, B, C etc. allocated to agent i. The total amount of commodity A is denoted by K_a. The set of feasible allocations is now given by

$$A_1 + A_2 + \cdots + A_n = K_a$$
$$B_1 + B_2 + \cdots + B_n = K_b$$
$$\cdots\cdots\cdots\cdots\cdots\cdots = \cdots$$
$$M_1 + M_2 + \cdots + M_n = K_m.$$

Let K_i denote the income of agent i. Notice that Fisher assumes the income of each agent to be *given exogenously*. The agents' budget constraints are written as follows:

$$A_1 p_a + B_1 p_b + \cdots + M_1 p_m = K_1$$
$$A_2 p_a + B_2 p_b + \cdots + M_2 p_m = K_2$$
$$\cdots\cdots\cdots\cdots\cdots\cdots\cdots = \cdots$$
$$A_n p_a + B_n p_b + \cdots + M_n p_m = K_n.$$

The agents' marginal utilities $F(\cdot)$ are defined by:

$$\frac{dU}{dA_1} = F(A_1); \frac{dU}{dB_1} = F(B_1); \quad \cdots \quad ; \frac{dU}{dM_1} = F(M_1)$$

$$\frac{dU}{dA_2} = F(A_2); \frac{dU}{dB_2} = F(B_2); \quad \cdots \quad ; \frac{dU}{dM_2} = F(M_2)$$

....

$$\frac{dU}{dA_n} = F(A_1); \frac{dU}{dB_n} = F(B_n); \quad \cdots \quad ; \frac{dU}{dM_n} = F(M_n).$$

Using these concepts, the equilibrium conditions for Fisher's model are given by:

$$\frac{dU}{dA_1} : \frac{dU}{dB_1} : \frac{dU}{dC_1} : \cdots : \frac{dU}{dM_1} = p_a : p_b : p_c : \cdots : p_m$$

$$\frac{dU}{dA_2} : \frac{dU}{dB_2} : \frac{dU}{dC_2} : \cdots : \frac{dU}{dM_2} = p_a : p_b : p_c : \cdots : p_m$$

.... = ...

$$\frac{dU}{dA_n} : \frac{dU}{dB_n} : \frac{dU}{dC_n} : \cdots : \frac{dU}{dM_n} = p_a : p_b : p_c : \cdots : p_m.$$

These are the familiar requirements that in equilibrium the marginal rate of substitution between two commodities is the same for all agents and, further, that it is equal to the ratio of their prices. Thus the economy is in equilibrium if

the marginal utilities of all articles consumed by a given individual are proportional to the marginal utilities of the same series of articles for each other consumer, and this uniform continuous ratio is the scale of prices of those articles (Fisher, 1892, p. 37).

In addition, the following condition has to be satisfied:

The problem which confronts the individual must be figured as to so adjust his consumption of all commodities that the utilities of the last pound, yard, gallon, etc., shall bear the ratio which he finds their prices do, while the market as a whole must cause such prices to emerge as will enable each individual to solve this problem and at the same time just take off the supply' (Fisher, 1892, p. 37).

The 'proof' that an equilibrium exists was carried out, as was usual at that time, by counting equations and unknowns. Since, in his model the number of unknowns is equal to the number of equations, Fisher concludes that an equilibrium exists.

In the preface to the 1892 edition Fisher considers these equations

as an appropriate extension of Jevons' determination of exchange of *two* commodities between *two* trading bodies to the exchange of *any number* of commodities between *any number* of traders (p. 4, emphasis in original).

And further: 'These equations are essentially those of Walras' (Fisher, 1892, p. 4). Schumpeter follows Fisher's remark in stating that these equations, '... do not give the whole of the Walrasian system but do give its core ...' (Schumpeter, 1951, p. 224).

However, there is an important difference between Fisher's system (or the extension of Jevons' model to several agents and commodities) and the Walrasian model of an exchange economy. In the Walrasian model the income of an agent is determined *endogenously* via his initial endowments and the equilibrium price system, whereas Fisher considers the income of agent i as *exogenously* given and thus *independent* of the price system. This income has to be considered as a kind of 'money' to be spent on the other commodities such that markets are cleared. Due to the exogeneity of the income, Fisher's model cannot be considered as a general equilibrium framework in the strict sense of the word. However, it is formally identical to a partial market system, since at least one market is not taken into consideration.

Therefore, Fisher is one step away from the Walrasian general equilibrium system and his model of an exchange economy does not, as Schumpeter (1951, p. 225) claimed, 'simplify and illustrate Walras'. Rather his model has to be considered as an extension of Jevons' partial market model. Nevertheless, with respect to the clarity of exposition, Fisher's ideas are much easier to follow than the model in Walras' *Elements of Political Economy*.

For an exchange economy as described above, Fisher constructed and actually built a hydrostatical model consisting of many cisterns of different shape, representing the agents' marginal utilities. These cisterns are connected by a complex system of tubes and levers to capture all relationships between the variables. This device was used not only to illustrate the working of his system, but also to address questions like: How does the equilibrium of the system change if a parameter, e.g. the agents' income were varied? Stated otherwise, the model could be utilized to derive comparative statics results. As Fisher (1892, p. 51, emphasis in original) put it:

The mechanism just described is the physical analogue of the ideal economic market. The elements which contribute to the determination of prices are represented each with its appropriate role and open to the scrutiny of the eye. We are thus enabled not only to obtain a clear and analytical *picture* of the interdependence of the many elements in the causation of prices, but also to employ the mechanism as an instrument of investigation and by it, study some complicated variations which could scarcely be successfully followed without its aid.

Therefore, Tobin (1985, p. 32) called this device an early analogue computer, making Fisher a precursor of Herbert Scarf in computing solutions for large economic models and of other economists working in computable general equilibrium theory.

To give an example of how Fisher made use of his device, consider a proportional increase in the incomes of all agents as compared to the increase of the income of just one agent. In Fisher's (1892, p. 51) words:

> Depress all income stoppers proportionally, i.e. increase all incomes in the same ratio. Then will all prices increase and the valuation of money decrease exactly in this ratio. There will be no change in the distribution of commodities. There is merely a depreciated standard of money. Formerly, the whole marketed commodity was valued at a given number of dollars, now this number is increased. We have seen ... that an increase in the money income of a single individual without an increase in commodities is a benefit to him, but such an increase when universal is beneficial to no one.

Notice that this kind of comparative statics, e.g. increasing the income of just one agent without changing – via the equilibrium price system – the income of other agents, is in general only possible in a partial equilibrium framework.

2.4 Equilibrium in a Production Economy

In chapter V Fisher integrates consumption and production into a single model. This is an important step, as neither the amounts of the commodities nor the agents' incomes are exogenous any more. Instead, the incomes are determined endogenously, as in a Walrasian general equilibrium model.

As mentioned above, Fisher represents production only in a rather simplistic way. Instead of assuming technologies which allow for the transformation of inputs into outputs, each agent can produce commodities by exerting labor and thereby incurring some disutility. The rudimentary modelling of production has also been pointed out by Tobin (1985, p. 33):

> The supply side of Fisher's model is, as he acknowledges, primitive. Each commodity is produced at increasing marginal cost, but neither factor supplies and prices nor technologies are explicitly modeled.

In contrast to the Walrasian general equilibrium system, the agents in Fisher's model don't have any initial endowments.

As the definition of production is strictly analogous to that of consumption, it does not come as a surprise that the formal description of his model is very similar to an exchange economy. The mathematical structure is summarized as follows:

First, he states the market clearing conditions, i.e. the demand for each commodity has to be equal to it's supply. Or equivalently, the excess demand for each commodity has to be zero:

$$A_{\pi,1} - \ A_{k,1} + A_{\pi,2} - A_{k,2} + \ \cdots \ + A_{\pi,n} - A_{k,n} \ = 0$$

$$B_{\pi,1} - \ B_{k,1} + B_{\pi,,2} - B_{k,2} + \ \cdots \ + B_{\pi,n} - B_{k,n} \ = 0$$

$$\cdots\cdots\cdots\cdots\cdots\cdots\cdots\cdots\cdots\cdots\cdots\cdots\cdots\cdots\cdots = \cdots$$

$$M_{\pi,1} - M_{k,1} \ M_{\pi,2} - M_{k,2} + \ \cdots \ + M_{\pi,n} - M_{k,n} = 0,$$

where the subscripts π and k refer to production and consumption respectively. As opposed to an exchange economy, in an economy with production an agent has no exogenously given income K_i but his wealth is determined endogenously via the price system and the commodities he produces. Therefore, Fisher's model has to be considered as a general equilibrium system in the Walrasian sense.

The budget constraints for each agent are given by:

$$A_{\pi,1}P_a + B_{\pi,1}P_b + \ \cdots \ + M_{\pi,1}P_m \ = A_{k,1}P_a + B_{k,1}P_b + \ \cdots \ + M_{k,1}P_m$$

$$\cdots\cdots\cdots\cdots\cdots\cdots\cdots\cdots\cdots\cdots\cdots\cdots\cdots = \cdots\cdots\cdots\cdots\cdots\cdots\cdots\cdots\cdots\cdots$$

$$A_{\pi,n}P_a + B_{\pi,n}P_b + \ \cdots \ + M_{\pi,n}P_m \ = A_{k,n}P_a + B_{k,n}P_b + \ \cdots \ + M_{k,n}P_m.$$

As in the case of an exchange economy, the marginal utilities (and disutilities) are defined as:

$$\frac{dU}{dA_{\pi,1}} = F(A_{p,1}); \frac{dU}{dB_{\pi,1}} = F(B_{\pi,1}); \ \cdots \ ; \frac{dU}{dM_{\pi,1}} = F(M_{\pi,1})$$

$$\vdots \qquad\qquad \vdots \qquad\qquad \cdots \qquad\qquad \vdots$$

$$\frac{dU}{dA_{k,1}} = F(A_{k,1}); \frac{dU}{dB_{k,1}} = F(B_{k,1}); \ \cdots \ ; \frac{dU}{dM_{k,1}} = F(M_{k,1})$$

$$\vdots \qquad\qquad \vdots \qquad\qquad \cdots \qquad\qquad \vdots$$

$$\frac{dU}{dA_{\pi,n}} = F(A_{\pi,n}); \frac{dU}{dB_{\pi,n}} = F(B_{\pi,n}); \ \cdots \ ; \frac{dU}{dM_{\pi,n}} = F(M_{\pi,n})$$

$$\vdots \qquad\qquad \vdots \qquad\qquad \cdots \qquad\qquad \vdots$$

$$\frac{dU}{dA_{k,n}} = F(A_{k,n}); \frac{dU}{dB_{k,n}} = F(B_{k,n}); \ \cdots \ ; \frac{dU}{dM_{k,n}} = F(M_{k,n}).$$

The first-order condition for an optimum, i.e. equality of the marginal rate of substitution to the price ratio, or as Fisher called it, the 'principle of proportion' is given by:

$$\frac{dU}{dA_{\pi,1}} : \frac{dU}{dB_{\pi,1}} : \cdots \frac{dU}{dM_{\pi,1}} : \frac{dU}{dA_{k,1}} : \frac{dU}{dB_{k,1}} : \cdots : \frac{dU}{dM_{k,1}} =$$

$$\cdots\cdots\cdots\cdots\cdots\cdots\cdots\cdots\cdots\cdots\cdots\cdots\cdots\cdots =$$

$$\frac{dU}{dA_{\pi,,n}} : \frac{dU}{dB_{\pi,n}} : \cdots : \frac{dU}{dM_{\pi,n}} : \frac{dU}{dA_{k,n}} : \frac{dU}{dB_{k,n}} : \cdots : \frac{dU}{dM_{k,n}} =$$

$$- p_{a:} - p_b : \cdots : - p_m : p_a : p_b : \cdots : p_m.$$

In the preface to the 1892 edition of his thesis, Fisher (p. 4) remarks:

> The only fundamental differences [between Fisher and Walras, U.S.] are that I use marginal utility throughout and treat it as a function of the quantities of commodity, whereas Professor Walras makes the quantity of each commodity a function of the prices.

However, this difference is actually not a fundamental one. Walras, in his description of an equilibrium, uses *demand functions*, while Fisher gives the *budget constraints* and the *'principle of proportion'*, i.e. the first-order condition for utility maximization. If the optimization problem is well-behaved, these two sets of equations imply the demand functions. That is, both formulations are in fact equivalent.

Notice that for the determination of an equilibrium, the definition of the marginal utilities (and disutilities) is irrelevant. Only the first-order conditions for utility maximization and the budget constraints are necessary. Since the definition of the marginal utilities adds the same number of equations and unknowns, it does not yield any additional information.

It is important to point out that Fisher (1892, p. 59) was aware that his system of equations was overdetermined: 'There are just one too few equations.' In the second set of equations, there are only $(n-1)$ independent equations instead of n. Stated otherwise: if $(n-1)$ markets are in equilibrium, the nth market has to be in equilibrium as well, which in fact is Walras' law. To overcome this difficulty, Fisher sets $p_a = 1$, i.e. he chooses commodity A as *numéraire* or, as he calls it, the 'standard of value'. This shows that Fisher (re)discovered the important fact that in equilibrium only the price ratios but not the price level is determined. As in the case of an exchange economy, the 'existence proof' for the production economy is by counting equations and unknowns.

Due to the fact that production is modeled only in a rudimentary way, his model is similar to a general equilibrium model of an exchange economy. If e.g. $A_{\pi i}$ is considered not as the amount of commodity A produced by agent i but as agent i's initial endowment, then both models are formally equivalent. Thus, Fisher's contribution is a very modern, concise and clear statement of the mathematical conditions for an equilibrium in an economy, albeit *not* in a production economy.

Fisher's analysis of equilibrium in exchange and production economies as developed in part I of his thesis can be summarized as follows: The model of an exchange economy is in fact not a general equilibrium system, as the agents' incomes are given exogenously. In contrast, his model of a production economy is indeed a general equilibrium model. However, since consumption and production are modeled in the same fashion, it is formally equivalent to an exchange economy, i.e. it is not a production economy as we know it.

3   NON-SEPARABLE UTILITY FUNCTIONS

The second part of his book, entitled 'Utility of One Commodity a Function of the Quantities of all Commodities' considerably generalizes the analysis of the first part. Instead of using additively separable utility functions, as e.g. Jevons and Walras, he assumes that the utility derived from a commodity depends also on the amounts of (all) other commodities consumed, i.e. he introduces general utility functions. The fact that the utility of a commodity cannot be considered independently of other commodities has already been noticed by Edgeworth in his *Mathematical Psychics*. However, while writing his thesis, Fisher was not aware of Edgeworth's work. As he wrote in the preface to his dissertation (Fisher, 1892, p. 4):

> three days after Part II was finished, I received and saw for the first time Prof. Edgeworth *Mathematical Psychics*. I was much interested to find a resemblance between his surface on page 21 and the total utility surfaces described by me. The resemblance, however, extends not far. It consists in the recognition that in an exchange, utility is a function of both commodities (not of only one as assumed by Jevons), the use of the surface referred to as an interpretation thereof and the single phrase (Math. Psych., p. 28) 'and similarly for larger numbers in hyperspace' which connects with part II, chapter II, 5.

Actually, Edgeworth starts with the simplest case of two commodities only, but extends the analysis to three as well as to arbitrary numbers of commodities. As it is clear how to proceed, he closes with the remark quoted by Fisher. So there can be no doubt that Edgeworth was prior to Fisher in introducing the concept of general utility functions in the literature. Being more interested in modeling exchange and contracts between economic agents, Edgeworth didn't develop the idea of general utility functions any further.

However, the fact that the utility of one commodity may also depend on the amounts of other commodities consumed has also been noticed by Auspitz and Lieben, whose book Fisher had read before writing his thesis. Their discussion of interdependent utilities might have lead Fisher to the idea of general utility functions.[2]

3.1 Indifference Curves and Equilibrium

It deserves to be mentioned that Fisher not only used general utility functions to describe the preferences of economic agents, but also employed the concept of indifference curves and budget constraints to illustrate graphically the utility maximizing behavior of a consumer. As Niehans in his *History of Economic Theory* (1990, p. 273) put it:

> The indifference curves were confronted by Fisher with what he called an income line. It represents the combination of goods that can be bought with a given amount of money. For the first time there appears the familiar graph of the convex indifference curves intersected by the budget line, and for the first time a shift in the budget is seen to produce different reactions in 'superior' and 'inferior' goods.

However, it has to be recognized that the idea as well as the name of an indifference curve had already been introduced by Edgeworth in his *Mathematical Psychics*. Edgeworth drew these curves in an 'exchange plane' so that they are positively sloped – one commodity is given away and the other is received. Fisher, however, was the first to draw indifference curves in the form which is still used today.

Being unaware of Edgeworth's work, it has been pointed out by Hutchinson (1953, p. 271-272) that in the construction of indifference curves Fisher had been

> presumably much assisted in his discoveries by Auspitz and Lieben's 'curves of constant satisfaction' and 'satisfaction surfaces', and along with the much wider recognition due to Fisher must go a tribute to the two Austrian business men.

A 'satisfaction surface' shows, for every amount of a commodity *A* and for every expenditure on that commodity, the maximum amount of satisfaction, given that the other commodities have been chosen optimally. The surface over the quantity-expenditure plane shows the maximum amount of satisfaction for every price-quantity combination of this commodity. A 'curve of constant satisfaction' is a horizontal intersection of this 'satisfaction surface' and shows all price-quantity combinations giving the same satisfaction. These 'curves of constant satisfaction' differ from indifference curves in that they are functions of the price and quantity of one commodity, and not of the quantities of two commodities. However, they have in common that they show all those combinations of the variables (price-quantity in the case of a curve of constant satisfaction and quantities of two commodities in the case of indifference curves) which yield the same utility.

Fisher pointed out that there is a relationship between the curvature of an indifference curve and the substitutability of commodities. Substitutes were called 'competing' commodities while complements were referred to as 'completing' commodities since in the latter case only the consumption of both commodities makes the satisfaction complete. As Fisher mentioned in a footnote, these notions for the two types of commodities had been introduced by Auspitz and Lieben.

Fisher (1892, p. 70-71) describes the relationship between the curvature of an indifference curve and the type of commodities as follows: 'For "perfect" substitutes the curves reduce to parallel straight lines whose intercepts on the A and B axes are inversely proportional to the fixed ratio of their marginal utilities'. And in the case of complements (p. 71): 'For perfect completing articles, the whole family of curves reduces to a straight line passing through the origin'. In the first case, a small change in the relative price would produce a large change in the demand for the two commodities, while in the second case, a shift in the relative price would have no or only a small effect on the demand for the commodities.

In his discussion of competing and completing commodities, Fisher used the change in marginal utility of commodity A caused by a change in the amount of commodity B as an alternative criterion to discriminate between these two types of goods. If the marginal utility of A increases with the amount of B, the two commodities are complements, otherwise, they are substitutes.

As shown by Niehans (1990, p. 273), these two criteria, treated as equivalent by Fisher, are actually very different:

> In particular, the signs of the second-order partial derivatives have meaning only for cardinal utility. The curvature of the indifference curves, on the other hand, cannot express the case in which a decline in the price of A, at a given utility level, raises the demand for B, which is a clear case of complementarity. The work of Eugen Slutsky later provided the analytical basis for the modern distinction between substitutes and complements in terms of the income-compensated cross price effects.

As far as general utility functions are concerned, Fisher developed several concepts and ideas which are still used today. He allowed for corner solutions, and discussed the question of superior and inferior commodities. In addition, there are comments about the 'integrability' problem in consumer theory, as it is called in modern terms. This problem can roughly be stated as follows: if demand functions are given, is it always possible to find utility functions such that utility maximization will generate these demand functions?

With respect to the determination and the comparative statics of an equilibrium, either in an exchange or in a production economy, a hydrostatical model could not be constructed. This is because in the case of general utility functions, the following problem arises:

> All the interdependence described in part I exists, but there also exist other connections between the shapes of the cisterns which could not be mechanically exhibited. For any one position of equilibrium the cistern mechanism may represent accurately the quantities, utilities, and prices, but the shape of each cistern is a function of the whole state of equilibrium and differs as soon as that differs (Fisher, 1892, p. 66-67).

However, he stated the conditions for an equilibrium in a very elegant way, using the vector calculus as introduced by his teacher, the physicist J.W. Gibbs. Further, he also developed a graphical device to illustrate an equilibrium, which is known as the 'net trade diagram' to contemporary economists. This diagram, to be discussed in Section 4, can be considered as an alternative to the famous Edgeworth box.

3.2 Ordinal Utility

Fisher's thesis ends with one of his most remarkable contributions to utility theory. His formal and graphical analyses lead Fisher to the conclusion that the very concept of utility might be obsolete. When trying to strip utility 'of all attributes unessential to our purpose of determining objective prices and distribution' (Fisher, 1892, p. 87) he anticipates Pareto in demonstrating that only the direction of the preferences, determined by an arrow perpendicular to an indifference curve, is relevant for the determination of prices. The length of the arrow, i.e. the intensity of the preferences, does not play any role at all in the determination of prices:

> It makes absolutely no difference so far as the objective determination of prices and distribution is concerned what the length of the arrow is at one point compared with another. The ratios of the components at any point are important but these ratios are the same whatever the length of the arrow. Thus we may dispense with the total utility density and conceive the 'economic world' to be filled merely with lines of force or 'maximum directions' (Fisher, 1892, p. 88, emphasis in original).

Summarizing his results, Fisher concludes (1892, p. 89, emphasis in original):

> Thus if we seek only the causation of the *objective facts of prices and commodity distribution* four attributes of utility as a quantity are entirely unessential, (1) that one man's utility can be compared to another's, (2) that for the same individual the

marginal utilities at one consumption-combination can be compared with those at another, or at one time with another, (3) even if they could, total utility and gain might not be integrable, (4) even if they were, there would be no need of determining the constants of integration.

In his unpublished autobiography *My Economic Endeavors*, Fisher states retrospectively his most important contributions in his *Mathematical Investigations*:

1. A concept of utility and marginal utility based on desire and not, as Jevons and others had attempted, on pleasure (gratification of desire) and which leads itself to possible future statistical measurement.
2. Hydrostatic and other mechanical analogies.
3. Distinctive price determining equations.
4. Application to economics of Gibbs' vector concept.
5. Indifference curves.

However, the first of these points puzzled many economists. Why did Fisher try to develop a method to measure marginal utility, a concept which he has already shown to be irrelevant for economic analysis, or even non-existent? As Schumpeter (1951, p. 226) asked:

how was it possible for a man who was able to write part II of *Mathematical Investigations* to conceive of measuring marginal utility as a justifiable goal of econometric research? Did he turn out the concept by one door – as he undoubtedly did in part II – only in order to let it in by another? The answer seems to be this.

To assess Fisher's interest in the measurement of marginal utility, two aspects have to be taken into account: first, his education as mathematician and his close association with thermodynamics, his teacher being the physicist J.W. Gibbs, and secondly, his desire to make economics a 'hard' science like physics.

3.3 Physics and the Measurement of Marginal Utility

The history of general equilibrium theory is characterized by a strong connection between physics and economics.[3] On the one hand, the connection between these two sciences is a personal one, since most of the early general equilibrium theorists and mathematical economists were by education either engineers or mathematicians. For example, Walras, Pareto as well as the German economist Launhard were engineers. Fisher himself was a mathematician, and one of his most influential teachers was J.W. Gibbs, the famous physicist, who worked on problems of thermodynamics. On the other hand, it is a relationship in substance. Walras was inspired to write his *Élements* after reading *Élements du Statique* by L. Poinsot (1803). This might have been the reason why many of the early economists were interested in making economics an exact science, like the natural sciences.

However, nobody has been more explicit in using mechanical or physical analogies with economics than Fisher. There are several instances in his thesis where he refers to physical concepts. In chapter III he explicitly points out analogies between economics and physics by presenting a table the left side of which gives the physical concepts, while the right side shows the corresponding economic analogues (Fisher, 1892, p. 85):

Table 14.1: Analogies between economics and physics

In Mechanics		In Economics
A participle	corresponds to	An Individual.
Space	corresponds to	Commodity.
Force	corresponds to	Marg. ut. or disutility.
Work	corresponds to	Disutility.
Energy	corresponds to	Utility.

To make economics a science comparable to physics, Fisher considered it necessary to define all concepts in a way to make them accessible to measurement.

> So also, while utility has an original 'commonsense' meaning relating to feelings, when economics attempts to be a positive science, it must seek a definition which connects it with objective *commodity* (Fisher, 1892, p. 17).

As Ingrao and Israel pointed out, the problem of measurability of utility is an essential one:

> Measurability was, in any case, essential ... for the leap from qualitative to quantitative science to guarantee sound scientific construction in political economy as in physics (Ingrao and Israel, 1990, p.96).

From the table given above, it follows that Fisher considers utility to be the economic concept corresponding to energy. Since energy is defined as force x space, it follows that utility would be given as marginal utility x commodity. Since a 'commodity' is something objectively given, the measurability of marginal utility would be sufficient to ensure the measurability of utility itself. Similarly for energy; since space can be measured, the measurement of force guarantees the measurability of energy. Both concepts, force and marginal utility, are logically on the same level – Fisher pointed out that both are vectors (force is directed in space and marginal utility is directed in 'commodity space'). Thus, if physics was able to measure energy, it seemed necessary for economics to be able to measure utility or marginal utility.

In a paper Fisher published 35 years after his Ph.D. thesis, he was still interested in the measurement of marginal utility. 'If so-called "marginal utility" of anything ... is a true mathematical quantity, should not that marginal want be measurable?' (Fisher, 1927, p. 158).

He suggested a statistical procedure, based on income and prices to compare the marginal utilities of two families A and B with identical preferences, which have different incomes but face the same prices. To measure the marginal utility of money and commodities like 'food' or 'shelter', he introduces, as a yardstick, a third family with identical preferences but with a different income and – living in another country facing different prices. Fisher showed that the ratio of the marginal utilities of, e.g. income for families A and B is equal to the ratio of the relative prices for 'food' and 'shelter'.

Niehans (1990, p. 271) considered this procedure as

> an ingenious idea, but in view of the stringency of the underlying assumptions, it is not surprising that, except for stimulating Ragnar Frisch, it did not look attractive to econometricians.

Schumpeter (1951, p. 227) agreed that

> a meaningful problem of measurement occurs also within the logic of choice or, to put it differently, that cardinal utility and psychological utility are not as closely wedded as most of us seem still to believe. We may wish to measure heat without wishing – or being able to measure the sensation of heat. I am aware, of course, that the whole idea is under a cloud just now and that hardly anyone is interested in it. But it will come back.

However, Schumpeter's prophecy has not yet come true.

4   THE NET TRADE DIAGRAM

To represent an equilibrium in an exchange economy graphically, the best known diagram is the Edgeworth box, introduced in its modern form by Pareto in 1909 (p. 355). However, an alternative device exists which recently became popular in general equilibrium theory. It has been used in models of quantity rationing, and Ellickson in his 1993 book *Competitive Equilibrium: Theory and Applications* on general equilibrium frequently employs this diagram. 'The net trade diagram is the main device we rely on throughout this book to give the modern, mathematical analysis of competition an intuitive, geometric interpretation' (Ellickson, 1993, p. 18).

The main idea underlying this diagram is as follows: Consider an exchange economy with two commodities, x_1 and x_2. A consumer i has a given endowment of these commodities, denoted by e_{1i} and e_{2i}. It is further assumed that the consumer is a price taker. Usually, an optimum for the consumer would be described by an indifference curve tangent to the budget constraint. However, if the focus were on *transactions* rather than the resulting allocation, the exposition could be changed as follows: To represent the transactions the agent is willing to make for any given prices, his endowment point is shifted to the origin. This amounts to a translation from the 'allocation space' to a 'net trade space'. For given prices, the consumer might be willing to sell some of his endowment of commodity 1 and buy some additional units of commodity 2. In this case, he would choose a point on the price line in the north-western direction. For other prices, he would sell some units of his endowment of commodity 2 and buy some more of commodity 1 instead, thus moving in the south-eastern direction. So this is a simple graphical representation of the transactions a consumer is willing to make at given prices.

Figure 14.1: The net trade diagram

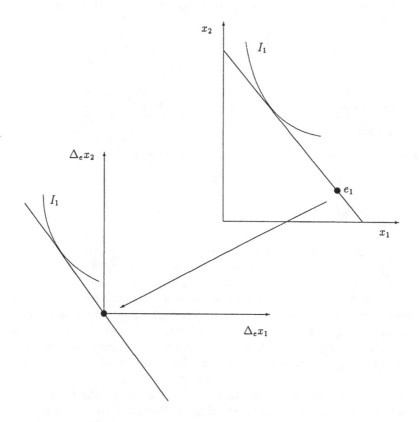

However, the same procedure can be used for another agent j, where the transactions this consumer wants to make can actually be drawn in the same diagram. This is because both consumers face the same prices, i.e. the price line is the same for both agents. Now an equilibrium is reached if the net trades made by the two consumers sum to zero.

So far the net 'trade diagram' seems to be an interesting alternative to the Edgeworth box. However, its main advantage over the latter is that it can be used to analyze equilibria in economies with *more* than two consumers, which is impossible in an Edgeworth box. One only needs to add the net trades of the additional consumers. Figure 14.2 shows a simple example for a three-person economy.

Figure 14.2: A three-person economy

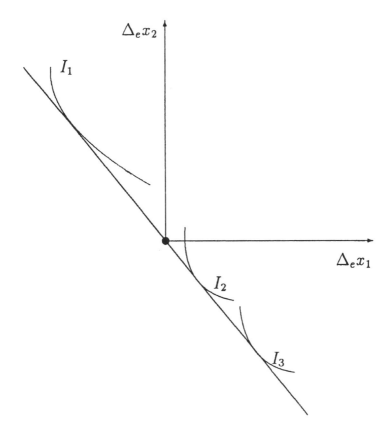

Of course, an equilibrium in this economy is realized if the sum of the net trades over all consumers is equal to zero. In principle, the net trade diagram can easily be extended (though not drawn) to the case of more than two commodities. Here the price line would be a hyperplane through the origin and the indifference curves would be higher-dimensional indifference surfaces.

However, the literature has – to the best of my knowledge – hitherto not noticed that the net trade diagram is due to Fisher. A reproduction of the net trade diagram from Fisher's thesis is given in figure 14.3.

Fisher (1892, p. 78, emphasis in original) describes the diagram as follows:

> If one man should be both a consumer and producer of the same article, the net consumption or production is now to be taken, and the total utility or disutility of this net amount is the density. The planes before referred to as partial income planes may now be called 'total income and expenditure planes,' and they *must each pass through the origin.*

Figure 14.3: Fisher's original diagram

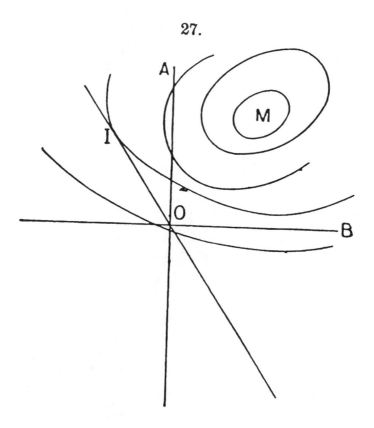

Here, points in the south-east characterize production, whereas points in the north-west describe the consumption of a commodity.

To characterize an equilibrium, Fisher (1892, p. 79, emphasis in original) argues:

> The point in the plane selected by *I* will be that of tangency to an indifference surface for *I*. Likewise for *II*, *III*, etc. Such points could be found whatever the position of the plane. But the plane must assume *such an orientation that the center of gravity of these points shall be the origin.* That is, the algebraic sum of all the A coordinates consumed must equal the sum produced.

Fisher (1892, p. 79) now characterizes an equilibrium as follows:

> (1) All individuals' combinations lie in a common plane through the origin (each individual's sales and purchases cancel).
> (2) Each individual's combination is at the point where this plane is tangent to an indifference surface for that individual (the point of maximum net utility).
> (3) The points in the plane are so distributed as to make the origin the center of gravity (the production and consumption of each commodity balance).

As compared to the diagram used in the modern literature, Fisher's original one differs only in a minor respect: he considers a situation where an agent has no initial endowment, but can produce a commodity by exerting labor. However, due to the fact that production in Fisher's model is equivalent to 'negative' consumption, this difference is one of interpretation but not of economic substance. The equivalence between Fisher's concept and the modern net trade diagram would be complete, if 'consumed' were replaced by 'demanded' and 'produced' by supplied.

5   CONCLUSION

Irving Fisher's Ph.D. thesis added substantially to our understanding of general equilibrium theory, the main contribution being to the theory of exchange economies. However, his model of an exchange economy is not a general equilibrium system, since the agents' incomes are exogenously fixed. In contrast, his production economy is in every respect a model of an economy where all incomes, prices and quantities are determined endogenously. Since Fisher modeled the supply side of the economy in a rather primitive way, i.e. analogously to consumption, he cannot be credited with a memorable contribution to the theory of production economies. His 'economy with production' is formally equivalent to an exchange economy. As compared to the model of Walras, however, his analysis is much clearer, more elegant and easier to follow.

In Fisher's analysis of general utility functions in the second part of his thesis, he introduces various concepts of modern consumer theory: budget lines, indifference curves, changes in consumption due to price variations, etc. In particular, his analysis of the relationship between the curvature of an indifference curve and commodities being substitutes or complements deserves to be mentioned.

Another contribution that has recaptured considerable interest in modern general equilibrium theory is Fisher's net trade diagram. This concept is used in the most contemporary approaches to the theory, albeit without mentioning its being due to Irving Fisher.

NOTES

*   For valuable help and comments I am grateful to Tone Dieckmann.
1   For an example of the net trade diagram in models of quantity rationing see Böhm and Müller (1977). In general equilibrium theory this diagram has been extensively employed by Ellickson (1993).
2   'So wird die Nützlichkeit, die jemand einem bestimmten Jahresquantum, z.B. von Brod, beilegt, eine sehr verschiedene sein, je nachdem nebstbei noch viel oder wenig oder gar kein Fleisch genossen wird, und ebenso wird die Nützlichkeit jedes Nahrungsmittels nicht minder davon beeinflusst, ob der Betreffende durch Kleidung, Wohnung, Beheizung gegen die Unbilden der Witterung mehr oder weniger gut geschützt ist.' (Auspitz and Lieben, 1889, pp. 139-140)
3   See Ingrao and Israel (1990) for a comprehensive discussion of the relationship between economics, especially general equilibrium theory, and physics.

REFERENCES

Auspitz, R. and Lieben, R. (1889), *Untersuchungen über die Theorie des Preises*, Leipzig, Duncker und Humblot.

Böhm, V. und Müller H. (1977), 'Two examples of equilibria under price rigidities and quantity rationing', *Journal of Economics – Zeitschrift für Nationalökonomie*, **37**, 165-173.

Edgeworth, F.Y. (1881), *Mathematical Psychics – An Essay on the Application of Mathematics to the Moral Sciences*, London, C. Kegan Paul.

Edgeworth, F.Y. (1893), 'Review of Irving Fisher's mathematical investigations in the theory of value and prices', *Economic Journal*, **3**, 108-112.

Ellickson, B.C. (1993), *Competitive Equilibrium: Theory and Applications*, Cambridge, Cambridge University Press.

Fisher, I. (1892), *Mathematical Investigations in the Theory of Value and Prices*, in *Transactions of the Connecticut Academy*, **9**, 1-124. Reprinted, New Haven, Yale University Press, 1925. Facsimile reprint, New York, A.M. Kelley, 1961.

Fisher, I. (1927), 'A statistical method for measuring "marginal utility" and testing the justice of a progressive income tax', in J.H. Hollander (ed.), *Economic Essays*

Contributed in Honor of John Bates Clark, New York, Macmillan, 157-193.

Frisch, R. (1947), 'Irving Fisher at eighty', *Econometrica*, **15**, 71-74.

Hutchinson, H.W. (1953), *A Review of Economic Doctrines 1870-1929*, Oxford, Oxford University Press.

Ingrao, I. and Israel, G. (1990*), The Invisible Hand: Economic Equilibrium in the History of Science*, Cambridge, MA, MIT Press.

Jevons, W.S. (1871), *The Theory of Political Economy*, London, Pelican Classics ed., R.D. Collison Black (ed.), Harmondsworth, Penguin Books, 1970.

Miller, J.P. (1967), 'Irving Fisher at Yale', in W. Fellner (ed.), *Ten Economic Studies in the Tradition of Irving Fisher*, New York, J. Wiley and Sons, 1-16.

Niehans, J. (1990), *A History of Economic Theory*, Baltimore, Johns Hopkins University Press..

Pareto, V. (1909), *Manuel d'Economie Politique*, Paris, V. Giard et E. Brière.

Poinsot, L. (1803), *Elements du Statique*, 8th ed., Paris, Bachelier, 1842.

Samuelson, P.A. (1967), 'Irving Fisher and the theory of capital', in W. Fellner (ed.), *Ten Economic Studies in the Tradition of Irving Fisher*, New York, J. Wiley and Sons, 17-38.

Schumpeter, J.A. (1948), 'Irving Fisher's econometrics', *Econometrica,* **6**, 219-231. Reprinted in J.A. Schumpeter, *Ten Great Economists, From Marx to Keynes*, New York, Oxford University Press, 1951, 222-238

Spiegel, H.W. (1991), *The Growth of Economic Thought*, Durham, Duke University Press.

Starr, R.M. (1997), *General Equilibrium Theory: An Introduction*, Cambridge, Cambridge University Press.

Tobin, J. (1985), 'Neoclassical theory in America: J.B. Clark and Irving Fisher', *American Economic Review*, **75**, 28-38.

Walras, L. (1874-77), *Eléments d'Economie Politique Pure ou Théorie de la Richesse Sociale,* Lausanne, L. Corbaz.

Comment on Schwalbe
Irving Fisher's Mathematical Investigations in the Theory of Value and Prices

Norbert Schulz

Suppose you mention, 'Irving Fisher made an essential contribution to the theory of general equilibrium' to a student of this field who started his academic career at the end of the 1960s. The chances are high that you will be met with suspicion and doubt. Indeed, consulting any current textbook – post 1950 – on general equilibrium theory would not reveal Irving Fisher even as a contributor, let alone an important one. Irving Fisher stands as an important contributor to the theory of money, capital and interest but for most students of economics he is by no means considered an essential contributor to general equilibrium theory; when in fact he is!

I was most impressed by his dissertation on general equilibrium theory. In my view his most valuable contribution is his insight that a theory of value and price does not need a concept of utility. What is needed is a concept which we call in modern terms 'preference'. As I know now, this assessment is not new. Paul Samuelson and Joseph Schumpeter for example have perceived his contribution in exactly the same light as I do. Unfortunately their knowledge of Irving Fisher's work has disappeared from the more recent assessment of important early contributors to general equilibrium theory. Fisher's insight is not independent of another accomplishment: a formulation of the conditions of general equilibrium which uses the information of marginal utilities only.

In what follows I would like to comment only on this point, leaving aside his concern with mechanics as a didactical device and his attempts to measure marginal utility. To compare his approach with that of Walras and Edgeworth (Fisher's dissertation appeared earlier than Pareto's related work) I will start by commenting on Fisher's treatment of production. This will lead me to conclude that his model is essentially one of an exchange economy. I will then briefly compare his model and his results with those of Walras and Edgeworth which focus on an exchange economy. Finally, I would like to stress the form of the equations which characterize equilibrium in Fisher's dissertation and compare them with more recent developments which appeared in the 1970s.

1   PRODUCTION IN FISHER'S MODEL

Fisher's model of production exactly parallels his model of consumption. While in consumption a certain amount of income is to be distributed on the purchase of consumption items, in production a set of output levels is selected to achieve a certain income level. To select these quantities his criterion is utility or more precisely disutility. He obviously assumes that a producer suffers from disutility if he produces a certain amount of some commodity. He presumes that the marginal disutility of producing some commodity increases with the amount of the output level. Hence, he assumes a certain kind of diminishing marginal return. If combined with several commodities this assumption is consistent with convex disutility functions which lead in turn to concave indifference curves. Those curves do resemble the usual figure for transformation curves in modern textbooks.

Figure C14.1: Concave indifference curves

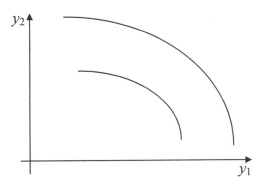

While such indifference curves are consistent with his formally stated assumption, it is no necessary consequence. At a formal level these types of indifference curves have the advantage that they yield interior solutions when disutility is minimized to obtain a certain income level, at least under 'nice' circumstances. This is quite important because with corner solutions he would not be able to use the marginal conditions which are central to his characterizing statements of production decisions. Indeed at that time the differential calculus approach of dealing with corner solutions was not yet available.

In his view on the economic content he seems not to have been happy with his assumption. First of all, he mentions that his assumption of increasing marginal disutility is probably not valid for small levels of output. Therefore the indifference curves should have convex shapes for such small levels of outputs. On a formal level he would then not have been able to deal with this type of case, as corner solutions would be the necessary consequence.

It is interesting to note that Fisher repeatedly stresses the differences between consumption and production. Whenever he does this he points out that in modern times individuals consume more and more types of commodities but produce an ever-decreasing number of commodities. This view is consistent with modeling of consumption to yield 'interior' solutions and production to yield corner solutions. But as has already been said, the technique for dealing with these corner solutions was not available.

When he draws indifference curves in production he does not draw concave types as in the above figure. They are drawn neither completely concave nor completely convex. Near the origin he draws them as concave shapes, in the middle range he draws them concave near the axes and for high levels of disutility he draws them convex. This doesn't fit well with his statement that his assumption of increasing disutility is adequate for high levels of output but not for small ones. It does, however, comply with his view that in more affluent societies production becomes more specialized.

At present of course we know that the assumption of increasing marginal disutility does not imply that the disutility function is convex. Indeed one finds arguments in Fisher's dissertation which maintain that marginal disutility of producing one good increases more if the output level of another commodity is increased. This implies that the total disutility function would not be convex. It may not even be quasi-convex. Therefore while being consistent with concave shapes of indifference curves his assumptions do not necessitate these shapes. It is not clear whether Fisher saw this point. As already noted by Ulrich Schwalbe, Fisher did not argue with second derivatives, which would have been an adequate instrument to bring out these relationships between his assumptions and the form of his indifference curves more clearly. His stated formal assumptions do not in any event fit well with his intentions to describe specialization in production.

In a way Fisher's model of production is more modern than many present-day textbooks, which stress profit maximization as the only objective in production decisions while Fisher's model directly reflects the preferences of the firms' managers, which is in the eyes of some scholars of the theory of the firm the better alternative. On the other hand his view of production neglects the aspects of input markets completely. On these grounds alone the whole economic system studied by him is not the general equilibrium model with production as we know it.

At the end of Part II of his dissertation he effectively dismisses his theory of production. As noted by Ulrich Schwalbe, there he considers net trades. Thereby he subsumes consumption and production in one decision. It is clear from his figures, in particular the net trade diagram, that he assumes that the shapes of the overall indifference curves are those of his consumption model. It therefore seems fair to say that Fisher's main contribution has not been to provide a satisfactory theory of production, but the essence of his final description of an equilibrium fits that of consumption quite well while the relationship to production remains unclear. Stated the other way round: Fisher's characterization of equilibrium is essentially restricted to an exchange economy. Given the state of the art at his time this is a great achievement.

2   WALRAS, EDGEWORTH, FISHER

Comparing Edgeworth, Walras and Fisher is legitimate as they are all essentially considering an exchange economy. As becomes clear from the introduction of Fisher's dissertation, he was not familiar with Walras' *Élements d'Économie politique* (1874) nor was he familiar with Edgeworth's *Mathematical Psychics* (1881) when he started his dissertation. By the end he must have known Walras' work and after his finishing Part II he also knew Edgeworth's. In many respects Walras and Fisher developed independently the same idea of a general equilibrium (many agents, many commodities) in an exchange economy. Comparing Part I of Fisher's dissertation with Walras' book yields minor differences in content. Both start with additively separable utilities. The characterizing statements about general equilibrium use different concepts. While Walras uses demand functions depending on prices, Fisher uses marginal utilities only. Both formulations are equivalent, however.

It is in Part II of his dissertation that Fisher is considerably more general as he drops the assumption of separability of the utility functions. This generalization was quite an achievement which parallels Edgeworth's introduction of utility depending on all commodities simultaneously. As already mentioned above, Fisher did not know Edgeworth's work when he wrote Part II. Edgeworth's main intention was not merely to write down the equations characterizing general equilibrium. He does, however, obtain these conditions almost exactly in the same form as Fisher does (1892, p.42). The only difference being that Edgeworth considers only two commodities explicitly. In this respect Fisher's formulation is more general. As has already been said, Edgeworth was not mainly concerned with these characterizing equations, which are in essence those of Jevons (apart from the more general concept of utility in Edgeworth's work). He was more interested in a theory of multilateral contracts. He essentially gave a sketch of a proof of the relationship between equilibrium allocations and what nowadays are called core allocations. Hence the intentions of both authors were quite different.

Whether these generalizations of aspects of Walras' and Edgeworth's analysis (without being familiar with them at the relevant time) are worth the high praise which Fisher received from many scholars is, of course, partly subject to taste. I think they are indeed great achievements. The best part of Fisher's dissertation, in my view, is his arguments on the irrelevance of cardinal utility. He is very clear on this aspect in chapter IV of Part II. Neither Edgeworth nor Walras realized that the characterizing equations of equilibrium only use the ordinal information of the utility functions. At least they did not mention it.

3   STATING THE EQUILIBRIUM CONDITIONS

Using modern notation Fisher's equilibrium equations are

$$\frac{\operatorname{grad} u_i(z_i)}{\left\| \operatorname{grad} u_i(z_i) \right\|} = \frac{\operatorname{grad} u_j(z_j)}{\left\| \operatorname{grad} u_j(z_j) \right\|} \quad \text{for } i, j,$$

$$\sum_{i=1}^{N} z_i = 0,$$

$$z_i \operatorname{grad} u_i(z_i) = 0, \quad i = 1, \ldots, N.$$

where z_i are net trades. Several aspects of this special form of stating the equilibrium equations are noteworthy. First, the conditions are exclusively expressed in terms of marginal utilities. This means that they are expressed in the primitives of the model and not in terms of a derivative concept like demand. For this reason it is easy to see that the equilibrium allocation only depends on ordinal information of the utility functions. Fisher himself repeatedly stresses that the length of the gradients ('maximum directions') of the utility functions are completely irrelevant. But this is nothing but an alternative formulation of: only ordinal information matters. Thus the form of the equations is particularly well-suited to make this almost immediately apparent.

It is usually stated that checking the equations for consistency (existence of a solution) and determinateness (uniqueness of a solution) consisted in comparing the number of unknowns and the number of equations at the time of Fisher's dissertation. This is what Fisher did. These days we know that this is not a rigorous way of establishing existence or uniqueness. Indeed it took over forty years until Wald suggested the first proof of existence of an equilibrium allocation. By then Walras' formulation of the equilibrium equations had become standard. Therefore the conditions needed for the existence proof were stated in terms of conditions of the demand functions. This is *a fortiori* true for elaborations on the uniqueness of the equilibrium allocation or more generally on the number of equilibrium allocations. It was only in the 1970s that Fisher's characterization was taken up again in the study of existence and uniqueness. It was only then discovered that such a characterization was well-suited to analyze all these questions in a unified framework. In 1974 Stephen Smale uses Fisher's description exactly to show that the number of equilibria is generically finite (and ≥ 1) and locally constant. Hence Fisher's form of description has lent itself to study those questions which at his time had to be left for further study as the necessary tools had not been at hand to do so. Smale's work was conceived as an extension of a theorem of Debreu who had studied the equilibrium correspondence using demand functions. Smale was able to give more general assumptions for Debreu's analysis because he worked with the primitives of the model – preferences – and not with derived concepts like demand.

With Smale's contribution as the very first article appearing in the *Journal of Mathematical Economics* one is tempted to say that Irving Fisher helped to launch this journal by leaving some questions unanswered. By the way, Smale did not refer to Fisher in his contribution.

REFERENCES

Edgeworth, F.Y. (1881), *Mathematical Psychics – An Essay on the Application of Mathematics to the Moral Sciences*, London, C. Kegan Paul.

Fisher, I. (1892), *Mathematical Investigations in the Theory of Value and Prices*, in Transactions of the Connecticut Academy, 9, 1-124. Reprinted New Haven, Yale University Press, 1925. Facsimile reprint, New York, A.M. Kelley, 1961.

Smale, S. (1974), 'Global analysis and economics IIA', *Journal of Mathematical Economics*, **1**, 1-14.

Walras, L. (1874), *Eléments d'Economie Politique Pure ou Théorie de la Richesse Sociale*, Lausanne, L. Corbaz.

15. Real Assets, Financial Assets, and Fisher Separation

Udo Broll and Hellmuth Milde[*]

1 INTRODUCTION

According to the Fisher separation theorem (Fisher, 1930) an individual investor finds his optimal composition of real and financial assets by applying a two-stage decision rule. First, the investor determines the optimal size of the capital budget by maximizing the net present value of all available real investment projects. Second, the decision-maker determines the optimal volume of financial assets by maximizing his utility function, which is defined in terms of current and future consumption. The two sub-decisions are determined by completely different motives. The volume of financial assets is dominated by personal preferences of the investor, the volume of real assets is not. The feature of separation has two important implications: first, the delegation of decision-making authority to professional managers is possible; second, the observable fact of separation of ownership and control in modern corporations has a solid theoretical foundation.

Separation of ownership and control refers to firms in which the people who manage the firm are not the same people who own it. The ownership of the firm is shared among its stockholders. Stockholders delegate the decision-making to managers. Managers are expected to have superior skills at running the firm, acquiring firm-specific information and setting the operating strategy. The advantage of stock ownership is its easy divisibility and transferability. Large corporations may have as many as a million owners with ownership changing almost daily.

The important question is: what are the prerequisites for separation to hold? In this chapter we discuss separation against the background of different economic settings. Assuming uncertainty with respect to commodity prices and interest rates we show and explain that a no-separation solution will emerge. Now we are confronted with the result, that 'everything depends on everything'. In particular, this implies that the capital budgeting decision can no longer be delegated to managers.

How can we escape this dilemma? The answer is: We have to turn our attention to risk-sharing markets. Therefore, hedging activities are taken into consideration. As a matter of fact, this helps to restore separation to a certain degree. Of course, there are several very strong conditions required to end up with a full separation solution. For example, we are going to consider only price uncertainty. We do not discuss quantity uncertainty. Furthermore, we consider only symmetric uncertainty problems. Asymmetry problems are not taken into consideration.

The chapter is organized as follows: in section 2 we review Fisher's separation theorem in a world with certainty. We explain the assumptions that are needed for separation to hold. In section 3 we assume that decision-making takes place in a world with uncertainty. We demonstrate the breakdown of separation in a model without hedging. In the final model we explain why and how corporate hedging can restore the separation property. In section 4 we relate our discussion to some features in Fisher's 'Theory of interest'.

2   DECISION-MAKING UNDER CERTAINTY

2.1 The Model

We consider a two-period model of investment decision-making in a world with certainty. A company's owner and decision-maker is faced with the following alternative. The owner can use a financial market by either borrowing or lending at the one-plus risk-free rate R. Whether a financial market transaction should or should not take place depends both on his consumption plans and on the availability of a superior real investment project. The project is characterized by a transformation function (or intertemporal production function) $G(I)$, with $G'(I) > 0$ and $G''(I) < 0$, where G denotes the future level of output and I the initial input. The input price is given by $Q \equiv 1$ and the output price is denoted by P. Both P and R are given data publicly known to all participants in the marketplace.

Current consumption is denoted by C_0, and future consumption by C_1. Furthermore, Y_0 is defined as the initial wealth of the decision-maker. B is referred to as the volume of risk-free assets in the decision-maker's portfolio, with $B > 0$ indicating lending and $B < 0$ borrowing. Current and future levels of consumption can be written as follows:

$$C_0 = Y_0 - I - B, \tag{15.1}$$

$$C_1 = PG(I) + RB. \tag{15.2}$$

The decision-maker's optimization problem is standard. Taking P, R, Y_0 and technology $G(\cdot)$ as given, the decision-maker chooses I and B to maximize the utility function $U(C_0, C_1)$. The utility function satisfies standard properties. The maximization problem can be written as

$$\max_{I,B} U(C_0, C_1). \tag{15.3}$$

Of course, maximization takes place subject to the constraints (15.1) and (15.2).

2.2 Optimality Conditions

The first-order conditions for the maximization problem (15.3) are:

$$-U_1(C_0^*, C_1^*) + U_2(C_0^*, C_1^*) PG'(I^*) = 0, \tag{15.4}$$

$$-U_1(C_0^*, C_1^*) + U_2(C_0^*, C_1^*) R = 0, \tag{15.5}$$

where U_1, U_2 are marginal utilities of present and future consumption. We denote the optimum for this maximization problem by a star. Equations (15.4) and (15.5) together imply that the decision-maker sets optimal inputs I^* such that

$$PG'(I^*) = R. \tag{15.6}$$

Equation (15.5) can be rewritten as follows:

$$\frac{U_1(C_0^*, C_1^*)}{U_2(C_0^*, C_1^*)} = R. \tag{15.7}$$

The well-known equation (15.7) implies that the optimal composition of intertemporal consumption requires equality of the marginal rate of substitution to the one-plus risk-free rate R. In order to calculate optimal consumption, C_0^*, C_1^*, separately we need an additional equation next to (15.7). This is given by the wealth constraint which is calculated from equations (15.1) and (15.2) by substituting B:

$$Y_0 - I^* + PG(I^*) / R = C_0^* + C_1^* / R \tag{15.8}$$

or alternatively

$$Y_0 + NPV^* = C_0^* + C_1^* / R, \tag{15.9}$$

with

$$NPV^* = -I^* + PG(I^*) / R, \tag{15.10}$$

denoting the net present value of the real investment project by NPV^* in the optimum.

2.3 Discussion

Equations (15.6), (15.7) and (15.8) determine the optimal solutions for investment and consumption: I^*, C_0^*, C_1^*. To be more precise, equation (15.6) exclusively sets I^* while (15.7) and (15.8) simultaneously determine C_0^* and C_1^*. It is easy to see that (15.6) is just the first-order condition to the NPV-function given in (15.10). The decision-maker chooses I to maximize the NPV. This is called the NPV-rule. Following the NPV-rule we find I^*. Given I^* we are in a position to calculate the highest possible NPV^* via equation (15.10).

In equation (15.9) the left-hand side reflects two sources of wealth. The initial wealth Y_0 plus the wealth increase NPV which results from the real investment project. On the right-hand side of equation (15.9) the optimal uses of wealth, C_0^* and C_1^*, are determined. Of course, the C_0, C_1 choice can only be executed by taking (15.7) explicitly into consideration. When making consumption choices we simultaneously determine what amount to borrow or lend. As can be confirmed from (15.1) and (15.2), borrowing, $B < 0$, means more consumption today while lending, $B > 0$, means higher consumption in the future. As we know, borrowing or lending are financial market transactions.

We are now ready to see the different features of investment rules. Via (15.7) investments in financial assets are driven by the decision-maker's personal utility function. Without detailed information about the time preference, no consumption decision and, consequently, no financial market decision is possible. In contrast, the NPV-rule determines the real investment volume completely independently of the decision-maker's personal time preference. The different features of the decision rule is what we call the 'separation' property. Irving Fisher was the first researcher to see both the theoretical concept and the practical implications.

The implications are powerful. It is now possible for different owners of very big firms to delegate decision-making authority to professional managers. The owners or the shareholders only need to tell the managers to follow the NPV-rule. No more information is required. Managers just maximize NPV or shareholders' value. Regardless of their personal preferences or their personal wealth situations, all shareholders will unanimously agree to the choice I^* as determined by the manager. Of course, there is a big problem. What ensures that managers will actually do what is in the best interest of the shareholders? However, this topic is beyond the scope of this paper.

Finally, consider Figure 15.1 which illustrates the results reflected in equations (15.6), (15.7), and (15.8). Figure 15.1 is based on Fisher's famous chart 38 on page 217 of his *Theory of Interest*. Jack Hirshleifer in his publications made the diagram very popular (see Hirshleifer, 1970). There is hardly a textbook on modern financial management that does not show it. To follow Fisher the situation depicted refers to a borrowing case. The consumption point T is located south-east of the production point S. In contrast, a lending case would have located T north-west of S.

Figure 15.1: Certainty situation

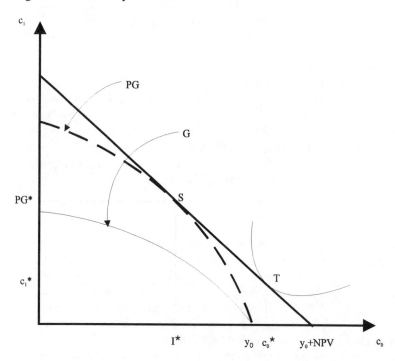

3 DECISION-MAKING UNDER UNCERTAINTY

3.1 The Model

In the discussion above we have assumed that the output price P and the rate of return R were non-stochastic. For the most part, this is not a realistic assumption. Therefore, it is straightforward to extend our discussion to decision-making problems in a world with stochastic prices and stochastic rates of return. In addition, as indicated in the introduction, we take corporate hedging explicitly into consideration. We argue that hedging can increase the company's value not because it lowers the risk borne by the shareholders but because it increases the expected pay-off in the second period.

Generally speaking, hedging refers to activities aimed at reducing the volatility of operating cash flows. To argue that hedging is useful, we must show that shareholder value can be increased. However, there is a problem if investors have low-cost diversification opportunities in existing financial markets. In this case, hedging cannot add value because the company's market value does not depend on the volatility of cash flows. Consequently, hedging is irrelevant. In order to overcome the irrelevance property, market imperfections are introduced. The usual suspects are taxes and distress costs. Because we stick to the symmetric information assumption we do not consider agency costs. Given convex tax schedules or convex distress costs, hedging is in a position to lock in expected cash flows that are bigger than those in a no-hedge alternative. Furthermore the under-investment argument had been developed in more detail recently (see Froot, Scharfstein and Stein, 1993). Following the pecking-order theory external financing is more costly than internal financing. In this situation, hedging is useful because it helps to bridge the gap between supply and demand for investable funds.

In our model we develop a different framework to analyze the under-investment problem. We argue that hedging is helpful in restoring the separation property. As we know separation can avoid under-investment in real assets from taking place. The increase in real assets will eventually generate an increase in future cash flows. That is why shareholders benefit from hedging activities. In this sense, hedging matters.

Comparing the setting of our model in section 3 with the previous section, there are four major changes:

- Both stochastic variables, $\widetilde{P}$ and $\widetilde{R}_A$ follow a joint density function $g(P,R)$. The density function is assumed to be publicly known to all parties in the marketplace.

- The owner is assumed to maximize the expected utility function over present and future consumption, $EU(C_0, \tilde{C}_1)$, with E indicating the mathematical expectations operator. Assuming the standard properties of the utility function (marginal utility is positive and decreasing) this implies that the decision-maker is a risk-averter.
- In addition to the risk-free asset B (yielding the risk-free rate, now denoted by R_B) there exists a risky asset A. The risky asset's rate of return is $\tilde{R}_A$, as already indicated.
- Owners of the firm are engaged in hedging activities in both commodity and financial forward markets. We consider forward contracts as hedging instruments.

Again, we consider a two-period model. Let C_0 denote the consumption volume in the current period. The second period stochastic consumption volume is denoted by $\tilde{C}_1$. We obtain:

$$C_0 = Y_0 - I - A - B, \tag{15.11}$$

$$\tilde{C}_1 = \tilde{P}G(I) + \tilde{R}_A H(A) + R_B B + X(P_f - \tilde{P}) + Z(R_f - \tilde{R}). \tag{15.12}$$

The pay-offs of the risk-free asset and the real investment project are denoted by $R_B B$ and $\tilde{P}G(I)$, respectively.

The risky asset's pay-off is denoted by $\tilde{R}_A H(A)$, with $H'(A) > 0$ and $H''(A) < 0$. The rational for the concavity of the $H(A)$ function is as follows: by definition, risky financial assets are characterized by the existence of default and deadweight costs of financial distress. The frictions and losses are denoted by $L(A)$, with $0 < L'(A) < 1$ and $L''(A) > 0$. Defining the nonstochastic repayment 'quantity' by $H(A) \equiv A - L(A)$, we obtain: $H'(A) = 1 - L'(A) > 0$ and $H''(A) = -L''(A) < 0$. The non-default quantities earn a stochastic rate of return. Consequently, the stochastic pay-off is $\tilde{R}_A H(A)$.

The forward volumes in the output and the financial markets are denoted by X and Z respectively. The forward price and the forward rate are denoted by P_f and R_f respectively. Transactions in forward markets are assumed to involve zero transaction costs. There are no commission payments, no margin requirements, and no capital outlays. The maturity of the forward contract corresponds perfectly with the length of the owner's decision horizon. This is because forward contracts are privately negotiated between the parties involved. The contract terms are tailored according to the case-specific features. As a result, there is no mismatch in the risk exposure and the contract terms. By definition, the basis risk in forward contracting is zero. Note that $\tilde{C}_1$ is a linear function of both $\tilde{P}$ and $\tilde{R}_A$. This feature will have important implications for the optimality of hedging strategies as employed by the owner. Note also that we consider only price risks. There is no production risk taken into consideration.

3.2 The No-Hedging Solution

In order to demonstrate the breakdown of the separation property we briefly consider the special case with no hedging at all: $X \equiv 0$ and $Z \equiv 0$. Without hedging there are only three decision variables left: I, A and B. The owner must choose the volume of real assets, of risky financial assets, and of risk-free financial assets so as to maximize

$$\max_{I,A,B} EU(C_0, \tilde{C}_1), \tag{15.13}$$

subject to the constraints (15.11) and (15.12). We obtain the first-order conditions for the decision problem:

$$EU_2(C_0^*, \tilde{C}_1^*)\tilde{P}G'(I^*) - EU_1(C_0^*, \tilde{C}_1^*) = 0, \tag{15.14}$$

$$EU_2(C_0^*, \tilde{C}_1^*)\tilde{R}_A H'(A^*) - EU_1(C_0^*, \tilde{C}_1^*) = 0, \tag{15.15}$$

$$EU_2(C_0^*, \tilde{C}_1^*)R_B - EU_1(C_0^*, \tilde{C}_1^*) = 0. \tag{15.16}$$

The conditions can be rewritten as follows:

$$\frac{EU_2(C_0^*, \tilde{C}_1^*)\tilde{P}}{EU_2(C_0^*, \tilde{C}_1^*)} G'(I^*) = R_B, \tag{15.17}$$

$$\frac{EU_2(C_0^*, \tilde{C}_1^*)\tilde{R}_A}{EU_2(C_0^*, \tilde{C}_1^*)} H'(A^*) = R_B, \tag{15.18}$$

$$\frac{EU_1(C_0^*, \tilde{C}_1^*)}{EU_2(C_0^*, \tilde{C}_1^*)} = R_B. \tag{15.19}$$

Using the properties:

$$EU_2(C_0^*, \tilde{C}_1^*)\tilde{P} = \text{cov}(U_2(C_0^*, \tilde{C}_1^*), \tilde{P}) + EU_2(C_0^*, \tilde{C}_1^*)E\tilde{P}, \tag{15.20}$$

$$EU_2(C_0^*, \tilde{C}_1^*)\tilde{R}_A = \text{cov}(U_2(C_0^*, \tilde{C}_1^*), \tilde{R}_A) + EU_2(C_0^*, \tilde{C}_1^*)E\tilde{R}_A, \tag{15.21}$$

we are in a position to calculate I^* and A^*. In order to evaluate the results, we compare I^*, A^* with potential certainty equivalent solutions I_c^*, A_c^*. The certainty cases are characterized by $E\tilde{P} = P$, $E\tilde{R}_A = R_A$ and

$$\text{cov}(U_2(C_0^*, \widetilde{C}_1^*), P) = 0, \text{ and } \text{cov}(U_2(C_0^*, \widetilde{C}_1^*), R_A) = 0.$$

We find

Proposition 1: The solutions I^* and A^* are underinvestment cases:

$$I^* < I_c^* \text{ and } A^* < A_c^*.$$

Proof: From the necessary conditions for an optimum in (15.17) and (15.18), we obtain,

$$E\widetilde{P}G'(I^*) > R_B \text{ and } E\widetilde{R}_A H'(A^*) > R_B,$$

since $\text{cov}(U_2(C_0^*, \widetilde{C}_1^*), \widetilde{P}) < 0$ and $\text{cov}(U_2(C_0^*, \widetilde{C}_1^*), \widetilde{R}_A) < 0$. Comparing the certainty equivalent case with the uncertainty case and noting that the maximand in each case is a strictly concave function in I and A, the inequalities of the optimum investment levels are as follows: $I^* < I_c^*$ and $A^* < A_c^*$. □

Proposition 2: The optimal choices of I^*, A^*, and B^*, do depend on the owner's personal utility function and on his probability distribution. As a result, separation no longer exists.

Proof: See equations (15.14), (15.15) and (15.16). □

There is one very important implication. It is no longer possible to delegate the capital budgeting decision to professional managers. The owner has got to solve the problem on his own. His personal preferences and expectations are driving the result. As indicated above the owner is assumed to be a risk-averter. Therefore, he is reluctant to take on excessive risk. By assumption the owner has no hedging alternative to cope with the risk. Consequently, his only choice is, cutting back on I^* and A^*. This explains the under-investment solution.

Increasing the owner's risk aversion will further reduce the optimal solutions for I^* and A^*. On the other hand, reducing the degree of risk aversion will increase the values of I^* and A^*. If the owner's attitude exhibits risk neutrality we will end up in the certainty equivalent solution already mentioned.

Finally, consider Figure 15.2 which reflects equations (15.17) and (15.19). The relevant investment opportunity line is shifted downwards. The new production point is S' and the new consumption point is T', with T' on a lower indifference curve than T. In the next section we shall take hedging into consideration. As a result, the relevant opportunity line is going to shift back to the PG-location, with S and T again the optimal solutions.

Figure 15.2: Uncertainty situation

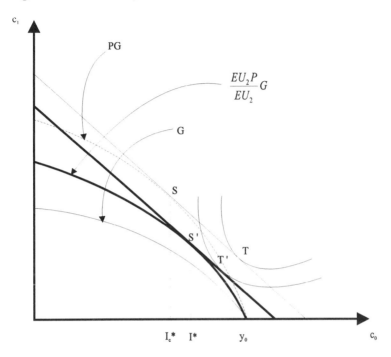

3.3 The Cum-Hedging Solution

3.3.1 The Investment Decision

Our discussion in the previous section was based on the assumptions $X \equiv 0$ and $Z \equiv 0$. As soon as we resume hedging activities the world we consider is very different. With access to hedging opportunities, there are two additional decision variables, i.e., X, Z. Consequently we get two additional first-order conditions. The owner chooses X and Z to maximize the expected utility function (15.13). The resulting first-order conditions are as follows:

$$EU_2(C_0^*, \widetilde{C}_1^*)(P_f - \widetilde{P}) = 0, \tag{15.22}$$

$$EU_2(C_0^*, \widetilde{C}_1^*)(R_f - \widetilde{R}_A) = 0. \tag{15.23}$$

Alternatively, equations (15.22) and (15.23) can be written:

$$EU_2(C_0^*, \widetilde{C}_1^*)\widetilde{P} = P_f EU_2(C_0^*, \widetilde{C}_1^*),$$ (15.24)

$$EU_2(C_0^*, \widetilde{C}_1^*)\widetilde{R}_A = R_f EU_2(C_0^*, \widetilde{C}_1^*).$$ (15.25)

From our previous discussion we know the separation property holds if the capital budgeting decision of the investor is independent of his preferences and independent of the probability distribution of the random variable. Now we prove that the separation property holds in the presence of commodity forward markets. Surprisingly we find that separation holds for risky financial assets as well.

Proposition 3: (Optimal investment in real and risky financial assets)
Assuming that the investor has access to risk-sharing markets, such as forward markets, the firm's optimum real and risky financial investments are determined by

$$P_f G'(I^*) = R_B.$$ (15.26)

$$R_f H'(A^*) = R_B.$$ (15.27)

Hence, the optimum real and risky financial investments do not depend on the preferences, the probability distribution, nor on the initial endowment of the owner. Equations (15.26) and (15.27) exhibit features comparable to (15.6).

Proof: Equations (15.14), (15.16), and (15.24) together imply condition (15.26). Combining (15.15), (15.16), and (15.25) imply that the owner chooses financial investment such that (15.27) holds. □

Eventually, in order to determine the optimal investment in the risk-free asset B^* we find

Proposition 4: (Optimal investment in the risk-free asset) The risk-free financial asset is determined by taking the preferences and probability distribution explicitly into consideration.

Proof: Equation (15.16) can be rewritten as shown in equation (15.19). There is no new decision situation in the hedging case. Furthermore, equations (15.7) and (15.19) are basically identical. Preferences are always relevant. □

The results can be summarized as follows: corporate hedging can restore the separation solution. Separation is beneficial to the shareholder value because it helps to undo under-investment solutions for all forms of risky assets (see also Danthine, 1978; Feder, Just and Schmitz, 1980; Broll and Zilcha, 1994).

3.3.2 Second Thoughts

The last statement opens a link to a different type of separation: the Tobin separation. According to Tobin (1958) there is a two-stage decision rule when it comes to composing the optimal asset portfolio in a world with many risky financial assets plus one risk-free asset. Each stage of the decision process is driven by different features.

In the first place, the composition of a 'market' portfolio containing all risky financial assets is determined. This decision is independent of the decision-maker's personal preferences. In the second place, there is the decision how much to invest in the risky 'market' portfolio and how much to invest in the risk-free asset. The second decision is indeed driven by the investor's personal preferences.

However, there is a substantial difference when comparing Tobin's model and the setting in our paper. Tobin confines his analysis exclusively to informationally efficient financial markets. As a result, no transactions considered in Tobin's scenario are able to create additional value; they are zero *NPV* transactions. The initial wealth in the first period is identical to the wealth in the second period.

According to the scenario in our model, the risky 'market' portfolio contains both real assets I and financial assets A. Because of the $G(I)$ function and the $H(A)$ function both assets are no longer traded in efficient markets by assumption. As a result, changes in the initial wealth take place on a regular basis. Consequently and in contrast to Tobin, the determination of both the composition and the size of the 'market' portfolio is required. As shown in equations (15.26) and (15.27) these two decisions can be executed without taking preferences into consideration. In Tobin's world there is only one degree of freedom in a two-asset case.

The next step is obvious. As discussed in section 2.3 above, it is again possible to delegate the two decisions to professional portfolio managers. The managers decide on two problems. First, what is the optimal size P^* of the 'market' or 'index' portfolio?

$$P^* = I^* + A^*. \tag{15.28}$$

Second, given the size P^*, what is the optimal composition of the portfolio? The decision rule is derived from (15.26) and (15.27)

$$\frac{P_f}{R_f} = \frac{H'(A^*)}{G'(I^*)}. \tag{15.29}$$

Finally, as in Tobin's model there is the decision concerning the risk-free asset B. The solution is given in (15.19). Along the lines of his preferences, the owner determines what amount to borrow or lend at the risk-free rate R_B in order to maximize his expected utility $EU(C_0, \tilde{C}_1)$.

It is important to emphasize the prerequisites for the features discussed in this section one more time. We urgently need hedging instruments in financial and commodity markets, and investment instruments in a risk-free asset. If only one of these instruments is missing the results discussed in this section cannot hold.

3.3.3 The Hedging Decision

In this section we use (15.24) and (15.25) to study the optimal hedging decisions. Due to the existence of risk-sharing markets, real and risky financial investments are independent of utility and expectations. However, the hedging behavior of the owner depends on his attitude towards risk and the distribution of the random variables $\tilde{P}$ and $\tilde{R}_A$. If the risk premium is positive, the owner will hedge less than the exposure. With unbiasedness in both forward markets, the owner is hedging in such a way that there is no more uncertainty left.

Proposition 5: (Optimal hedging)

(a) (Full-double hedge) When both forward markets are unbiased, i.e., $E\tilde{P} = P_f$ and $E\tilde{R}_A = R_f$, then optimal risk-management policy implies a full-double hedge: $X^* = G(I^*)$ and $Z^* = H(A^*)$.

(b) (Biasedness) Let forward markets be biased, i.e., $E\tilde{P} \geq P_f$ and $E\tilde{R}_A \geq R_f$. Then optimal risk-management policy is an underhedge: $X^* \leq G(I^*)$ and $Z^* \leq H(A^*)$. Assume $E\tilde{P} < P_f$ and $E\tilde{R}_A < R_f$, then optimal risk-management policy is an overhedge: $X^* > G(I^*)$ and $Z^* > H(A^*)$.

Proof: (a) First it is shown that

$$(E\tilde{P} - P_f)(G(I^*) - X^*) + (E\tilde{R}_A - R_f)(H(A^*) - Z^*) \geq 0, \tag{15.30}$$

where the equality holds, if and only if, $\tilde{C}_1^*$ is non-random. To prove (15.30) from equations (15.17) and (15.18) it is found that:

$$\operatorname{cov}(U_2(C_0^*, \tilde{C}_1^*), \tilde{C}_1^*) = -EU_2(C_0^*, \tilde{C}_1^*)\{(E\tilde{P} - P_f)(G(I^*) - X^*)$$

$$+ (E\tilde{R}_A - R_f)(H(A^*) - Z^*)\} \leq 0. \tag{15.31}$$

This proves (15.30), since the expected marginal utility of consumption is positive. Now, suppose $E\tilde{P} = P_f$ and $E\tilde{R}_A = R_f$. Then expression (15.31) holds with equality: therefore, $\tilde{C}_1^*$ must be non-stochastic. For consumption,

$\widetilde{C}_1^*$, to be non-stochastic, it must be the case that $X^* = G(I^*)$ (long position) and $Z^* = H(A^*)$ (long position) because according to (15.12)

$$\widetilde{C}_1^* = \widetilde{P}[G(I^*) - X^*] + \widetilde{R}_A[H(A^*) - Z^*] + R_B B^* + P_f X^* + R_f Z^*.$$

This proves the full double-hedge theorem.

(b) The proof of an underhedge (or overhedge) is straightforward from equation (15.31). □

Proposition 5(a) demonstrates that with unbiased forward markets the owner hedges his risk exposure completely. Proposition 5(b) shows that with separately biased forward markets, the owner takes an overhedge or an underhedge position in the commodity and financial forward markets, depending on the sign of the risk premium in these markets (see also Lence, 1995; Broll, 1997).

Note however, that regardless of the hedging outcome, equations (15.26) and (15.27) always hold. As a result, all financial price risks are separated from the underlying business activities. The price risks are transferred to hedging markets. The participants in the hedging markets take care of the optimal risk allocation.

4 CONCLUSION

In our paper we have discussed alternative scenarios to explain, extend, and modify Fisher's separation concept. Not surprisingly, we also came across Tobin's separation idea. For a generation or so Tobin's position has fascinated and influenced finance-related people. In contrast, we think that there is currently a clear renaissance of Fisher's basic ideas.

According to Tobin the risk–return trade-off is the main driving force when it comes to explaining investment decision-making. Furthermore, according to Tobin the implicit view is that asset trading takes places in perfectly functioning financial markets. This idea became very popular after Fama's 1965 paper on efficient markets had been published. The basic idea of the efficient market hypothesis is addressed in the well-known twenty-dollar-bill joke (see Tobin, 1984). Because of the existence of efficient markets people no longer believe that money is lying on the sidewalks. If the observed bill were real money it would already have been picked up. All bargains and treasures are gone. The investors have done their job too well. The implications of efficiency are: asset prices move randomly, consequently, you cannot predict future asset prices by looking at past asset prices.

New empirical findings however, turn the world of finance upside down. Recent evidence (see Fama and French, 1992) shows that returns can indeed be predicted with high levels of accuracy. Surprisingly, for the most part risk variables have very little power in predicting expected rates of return. Even more confusing is the fact that if there is any predicting power of risk variables, then the prediction is in the 'wrong' direction, i.e., low-risk assets have high returns and vice versa. So risk or beta are out. Therefore, the extra returns earned on these assets are not risk premiums any more. Rather, the only interpretation is that the extra returns are based on imperfections and deficiences existing in inefficient financial markets (Haugen, 1996).

Clearly, Tobin's world would not be the appropriate framework to tackle these observations. However, using Fisher's framework we are able to capture the observed features nicely. As presented in this chapter we follow Fisher and assume that financial assets are not traded in efficient markets. Given the fact of financial market inefficiencies it sounds reasonable to go on to assume that companies try to take advantage of these findings. Of course, this has serious consequences for the pricing procedures of assets. That is exactly what the research in the area of 'behavioral' finance is all about.

Unfortunately, we are not in a position to present any research results currently. It is, however, obvious that Irving Fisher's lifetime contributions will provide the main ideas to get the new research program going. From this point of view, Irving Fisher is a most modern economist. He knew all about market frictions, market deficiencies, and market imperfections. We hope to continue our research in his spirit.

ACKNOWLEGEMENTS

* We would like to thank Mark Flannery and Jay Ritter for their helpful comments.

REFERENCES

Broll, U. (1997), 'Cross hedging in currency forward markets: a note', *Journal of Futures Markets,* **17**, 475-482.

Broll, U. and Zilcha, I. (1994), 'Capital markets, the separation property and hedging', *Economics Letters,* **44**, 165-168.

Danthine, J.-P. (1978), Information, futures markets and stabilizing speculation, *Journal of Economic Theory,* **17**, 79-98.

Fama, E.F. (1965), 'Random walks in stock market prices', *Financial Analysts Journal,* 1-15.

Fama, E.F. and French, K.R. (1992), 'The cross-section of expected stock returns', *Journal of Finance*, **47**, 427-465.

Feder, G., Just, R.E. and Schmitz, S. (1980), 'Futures markets and the theory of the firm under price uncertainty', *Quarterly Journal of Economics,* **94**, 317-328.

Fisher, I. (1930), *The theory of interest*, New York, Macmillan.

Froot, K.A., Scharfstein, D.S. and Stein J.C. (1993), 'Risk management: coordinating corporate investment and financing policies', *Journal of Finance*, **48**, 1629-1658.

Haugen, R.A. (1996), 'Finance from a new perspective', *Financial Management,* **25**, 86-97.

Hirshleifer, J. (1970), *Investment, interest, and capital*, Englewood Cliffs, NJ, Prentice Hall.

Lence, S.H. (1995), 'On the optimal hedge under unbiased futures prices', *Economics Letters,* **47**, 385-388.

Tobin, J. (1958), 'Liquidity preference as behavior towards risk', *Review of Economic Studies,* **26**, 65-86.

Tobin, J. (1984), 'On the efficiency of the financial system', *Lloyds Bank Review*, **153**, 1-15.

16. Beyond Fisher's NPV?
Much Ado About Nothing!

Andreas Gintschel[*]

The Principle of Maximum Present Value: Out of all options, that one is selected which has the maximum present value at the market rate of interest. – Irving Fisher (1930)

The net present value criterion (NPV) is the most widely accepted method for choosing between investment opportunities or, more generally, for allocating resources. Derived in its (almost) full glory by Irving Fisher from capital-theory considerations, literally hundreds of textbooks in economics, finance, and accounting devote key chapters to NPV analysis. It is used by most companies in their decision-making process. Government agencies use modified versions of NPV in their attempts at social engineering. Therefore, it is reasonable to claim that Fisher's NPV principle is the most widely applied insight of economics. At the same time, it is probably the most misunderstood and abused.

This chapter analyzes the application of NPV in a world of uncertainty. I show that naive adaptation of NPV to uncertainty can lead to suboptimal decisions.

This does not, however, render NPV obsolete. To the contrary, I argue that NPV is equivalent to any admissible method dealing with investment under uncertainty. In particular, the recently popularized real-options approach is equivalent to NPV analysis and Arrow-Debreu state pricing.

In Section 1, I review Fisher's derivation of NPV. I present a discussion of adapting NPV to uncertainty by adjusting discount rates in Section 2. In Section 3, I demonstrate the equivalency of NPV, state pricing and the real-options approach. Section 4 concludes.

1 LOVE'S LABOUR'S LOST

The idea that resources should be allocated to their best use is an old principle in economics. Resources that yield output only after a certain time span are referred to as investments. It is usually assumed that these resources could be either consumed directly or used to produce (consumable) output. Intuition suggests that (i) delaying consumption requires compensation and (ii) resources should be put to their best use in an intertemporal sense as well.

Either of those statements is sufficient to explain positive prices for loans, i.e., positive interest rates. If appropriate markets exist, agents can evaluate their intertemporal production opportunities by simply comparing benefits and costs in terms of prices. The benefit is the value of tomorrow's output.

The costs are the principal and the foregone interest receipts had the resources been lent to another agent. This notion has been known in economics for a long time. It can be traced back at least to Quesnay (1767) and other physiocrats.

Fisher develops the NPV criterion in an equilibrium model of interest rates. As a first step, he models a deterministic, intertemporal exchange economy with one dated consumption good. Agents either consume their endowment or trade in a competitive market for consumption in later periods. The interest rate is determined by the agents' preferences and the aggregate endowment of dated consumption.

In a second step, Fisher generalizes the model by introducing production opportunities. Agents can shift consumption through time not only via the market but also by means of production. In equilibrium, all agents are indifferent between choosing the market or production as the transformation device. The analysis depends crucially on the agents' choice of investment opportunities. Thus, the equilibrium framework forces Fisher to define the agents' opportunity sets and objective functions in an exact, yet abstract, manner. Using the general equilibrium apparatus developed by Walras and Pareto, Fisher provides a consistent theory of interest rate determination. This is certainly his greatest accomplishment. The formulation of NPV as an investment criterion is a mere byproduct of the modeling approach chosen.

Interestingly, Fisher is not content with defining abstract investment opportunity sets, i.e. collections of vectors, which is all that is required in his model. Rather, he fleshes out his theory by analyzing how the investment opportunity set can be derived from the underlying technology. Unlike most modern financial economists, Fisher interprets his investment opportunity set as more than a collection of cash-flow vectors. Rather, it is a complete characterization of available technology. In particular, he is fully aware of the dynamic structure of the model. Investment is not a static decision but a policy covering the complete planning horizon of the agent. Fisher documents his concern with these dynamic issues in the sections on reallocation of capital, improvement of existing capital stock and the flexibility in allocating labor. Fisher clearly understands that *all possible paths* of investments, improvements, reductions, temporary idleness, etc., together comprise the investment opportunity set.

For the case under uncertainty, Fisher's treatment becomes more tentative and speculative. He argues in favor of adjusting the discount rate to reflect uncertain cash flows. Clearly, he does not envision the analogy of commodities indexed by dates and states that Arrow would draw later. This is why Fisher is unable to present an equilibrium model for stochastic economies. It is interesting, though, that he refuses to formalize his ideas, not even in a partial equilibrium setting for investment decisions. One can only speculate about his reasons. Either he thought a partial model not interesting enough, or he had doubts about his approach.

2   THE COMEDY OF ERRORS

In the seminal analysis of portfolio allocation, Markowitz (1952) shows that risk-averse agents choose well-diversified portfolios of assets. Later, Sharpe (1964) and others use this insight in a one-period stochastic exchange economy to derive the CAPM. In this sense, one of Fisher's problems – how to compute the risk-adjusted discount rate – was resolved. Combining the old NPV principle with the new technique of computing risk-adjusted discount rates became a straightforward exercise as demonstrated by Hirshleifer (1970) and Fama and Miller (1972).

If one makes the appropriate assumptions and interprets the model properly, no harm is done. First, note that the application of the static CAPM to non-financial assets requires a certain degree of market completeness. In other words, it must be possible to generate the cash flows of the non-financial asset by a portfolio of financial assets. In a world of certainty, this is trivially the case since there is only one state of the world. In a stochastic economy, the non-financial asset might yield pay-offs in states of the world where no financial asset generates pay-offs. Second, the CAPM is only a one-period model and gives no predictions for multi-period models. Indeed, as Merton (1973) and Breeden (1979) show, the valuation of assets in a multi-period context depends not only on the correlation between assets' pay-offs, but also on the dynamics of the investment opportunity set. If future investment opportunities yield lower returns, there is less incentive to invest in the present. Therefore, proxies for the shape of the investment opportunity set enter the pricing relation; interest rates in Merton's model and consumption in that of Breeden. Thus, these models adjust for flexibility on the demand side in multiperiod settings.

Denote the per-period risk-adjusted rate of return for asset i as r_i, which is derived from an appropriate CAPM. Denote expected net cash-flows from asset i at date t as $E[CF_{it}]$. The equilibrium price p_i of asset i at date $t = 0$ is

$$p_i = \sum_{t=1}^{T}(1+r_i)^{-t} E[CF_{it}]. \tag{16.1}$$

In any economy with complete financial markets, equation (16.1) is the correct pricing formula for any asset, whether financial or real. The problem is finding the correct values of r_i and $E[CF_{it}]$. If one uses 'wrong' values, equation (16.1) yields the 'wrong' solution.

In applying equation (16.1) in NPV analysis, two related mistakes are common. Consider the typical firm in microeconomic theory. The profit function of the firm has some well-known properties; in particular, it is convex in input and output prices. Usually, the firm has some technological flexibility. The set of feasible technologies is not trivial, i.e. not a singleton. In the case of a non-trivial production set, the profit function is non-concave in prices; in other words, flexibility is valuable. The problem with examples as in Dixit and Pindyck (1994) is not the equation (16.1) itself. Rather, it is neglecting the convexity of the profit function in the NPV analysis that leads to a recommendation inconsistent with the one of the real-options approach. Moreover, the discount rate is sensitive to the cash-flow structure. If the pay-offs are different, the interest rate is different as well. To illustrate these effects, consider the following simple example, which will be used repeatedly in the remainder of this chapter.

Example: The firm can produce a widget at unit cost at date $t = 1$. To start production, the firm has to incur a lump sum payment I at $t = 0$. The competitive price of the widget is known to be $p_0 = 1$ at $t = 0$. There are no storage costs for the widget. At $t = 1$, the price $p \in \{p_l, p_h\}$ with $p_l < 1 < p_h$ is random. The probabilities are $prob(p = p_h) = \pi < 1$ and $prob(p = p_l) = 1 - \pi$. The realization of p is uncorrelated with any existing financial asset in the economy. Therefore, the risk-adjusted expected rate of return on any asset with pay-off p in the second period is the risk-free rate r_f. Once the lump sum is paid, the set of feasible production vectors at $t = 1$ is X. If the technology is inflexible, $X = X_1 = \{1\}$. Alternatively, the technology might exhibit some flexibility, $X = X_2 = \{0,1\}$.

For expositional purposes, I choose the simplest structure possible. Note that, in general, the production set can be indexed by dates and/or states as well. Modeling feasible sets in this fashion captures the dynamics of available production technologies. All results extend easily to more general models.

Alleged counter-examples, e.g. Dixit and Pindyck (1994), to the NPV rule are of the following type. For period $t = 1$, expected profits are inferred as

$$E[\Pi_1] = \pi(p_h - 1) + (1-\pi)(p_l - 1), \tag{16.2}$$

which can take on negative or positive values depending on the probability π. This expected profit function is correct if and only if the adopted technology has no flexibility, $X = X_1 = \{1\}$. If production can be adjusted, profits are no longer linear in prices. Rather, they are non-concave. Consider a technology that allows costless termination of production. The set X of feasible production vectors consists of two elements, $X = X_2 = \{0,1\}$. The correct expected profits are then

$$E[\Pi_2] = \pi(p_h - 1) > 0. \tag{16.3}$$

Of course, if the 'wrong' expected cash-flows (16.2) are used in the valuation formula (16.1) the result is also wrong. In particular, the value of project X_2 is erroneously calculated as

$$NPV_1 = -I + \frac{E[\Pi_1]}{1+r_f}.$$

If the problem is described as in the example, the mistake is rather obvious. In real-world applications, it is less clear. Consider a more realistic example. Suppose, marginal costs are known and constant, but demand is uncertain. It seems quite natural to extrapolate from average historical quantities of goods sold, multiply it by expected future prices, and treat the result as expected sales. This is close to the procedure suggested in practitioners' books on cash flow forecasting (e.g. Loscalzo, 1982). Of course, if technology is flexible, this approach yields misleading results since it ignores optimal adjustment of production to demand.

If, instead, the correct expected cash-flows are used, the valuation formula delivers the correct result. The discount rate r has to be adjusted to reflect the convexity of pay-offs. In other words, the discount rate cannot be inferred from p directly, but rather from a contingent claim on p. To determine the value of the project, using equation (16.1) in a NPV analysis is sufficient.

3   AS YOU LIKE IT

In the following, I outline three equivalent approaches to capital budgeting. Therefore, choosing among them is not a matter of right or wrong, but simply convenience. First, I elaborate on the NPV approach introduced in the preceeding section. In particular, I show how to compute the discount rate. Second, I apply Arrow-Debreu state pricing. Third, I employ the real-options approach. Using the example of the preceeding section, I demonstrate that all three approaches, applied properly, yield the same result.

In this section, assume that the appropriate description of the technology is

$X = X_2$, the flexible technology. After determining the numerator in the valuation formula equation (16.1), one has to determine a discount rate. Clearly, r_f, the discount rate on p, is not appropriate since p has a different pay-off structure. Rather, it is necessary to find, or construct, an asset that mimics the pay-offs of the project. Consider a call option on p with unit strike price that expires at date $t = 1$. Note that the option exactly replicates the pay-offs of the investment project X_2. Using the binomial option pricing model of Cox *et al.* (1979), the option has value

$$c = \frac{\mu(p_h - 1)}{1 + r_f},$$

where $\mu = (1 + r_f - p_l)/(p_h - p_l)$, the risk-neutral probability. The expected rate of return on the option is computed as

$$r_c = \frac{\pi(p_h - 1) - c}{c} = \frac{\pi(1 + r_f)}{\mu} - 1.$$

The NPV of the project is

$$NPV_2 = -I + \frac{E[\Pi_2]}{1 + r_c} = -I + \frac{\mu(p_h - 1)}{1 + r_f}. \tag{16.4}$$

Next, the same investment project is evaluated using Arrow-Debreu state prices. A state price is the $t = 0$ price of one unit of account delivered in exactly one state. The (gross) value of the project is then simply the sum of the pay-offs multiplied by state prices. Since pay-offs in the bad state $p = p_l$ are zero, only the state price for the good state has to be computed. The call option described above almost yields the state price π_h for the good state, except that the option does not yield a unit pay-off, but rather $p_h - 1$. Therefore, instead of using one unit of the option, it must be scaled by $(p_h - 1)^{-1}$. This claim delivers one unit of account in the good state. Of course, the price is simply the option value scaled by $(p_h - 1)^{-1}$. Thus,

$$\pi_h = \mu/(1 + r_f).$$

Computing the net worth of the project using the state price yields equation (16.4), as is easily verified. Lastly, consider the real-options approach. In the language of the real-options literature, the investment project X_2 has an embedded abandonment option at date $t = 1$; the firm operates but can terminate production at no costs. Equivalently, one can think of an embedded expansion option; the firm is idle but can start production at zero cost. The strike price is the unit cost of production. Therefore, the real option is of the form max $\{0, p - 1\}$. This is equivalent to the financial call option described previously, and the same valuation technique applies. The (gross) value of the real option o is then

$$o = \frac{\mu(p_h - 1)}{1 + r_f}.$$

Subtracting the investment outlay yields the net value of the real option, which is identical to the NPV in equation (16.4).

The reason why all three methods yield the same result is the underlying modeling structure. State pricing is, in some sense, the fundamental approach. Arrow (1964) and Debreu (1959) show that all goods can be priced in a dynamic, stochastic economy with no capital market restrictions. Equivalently, a set of state prices exists, which can be used to price any state-indexed commodity. Once state prices are given, simple algebraic manipulations yield the risk-adjusted discount rate and the risk-neutral probabilities of the real-options approach. Imposing no arbitrage is necessary and sufficient to consistently define any concept in terms of another as commodity prices in the economy are the common underlying fundamentals.

As demonstrated, all three approaches lead to the same result. Therefore, no method is inherently inferior to the other. Rather, which approach is preferable depends on the purpose. If the emphasis is on instructiveness – in particular, if flexibility of real investments is to be stressed – the real-options approach might be helpful. For practical purposes, though, which approach to choose depends on data availability. If state prices or price quotes for mimicking assets are readily available, using the real-options approach seems rather circuitous. Usually though, that type of data is not available. In this case, the real-options approach seems computationally easier. Uncertainty can often be linked to input and/or output prices whose process characteristics can be easily estimated. Then, the real-options method seems the most obvious choice. Note that to compute the risk-adjusted discount rate or state prices in the example, the option value has to be determined first. Using the option value immediately in the real-options approach seems a reasonable thing to do.

The real-options method is sometimes criticized on the grounds that it only applies in complete markets. As Schwartz (1994) points out, this is not a valid criticism as, at least within continuous-time models, markets are essentially complete. Almost every pay-off stream can be dynamically replicated (Duffie and Huang, 1985). Therefore, almost every pay-off stream can also be priced correctly in a continuous-time, stochastic economy. Moreover, if incompleteness were indeed a problem, the criticism would be directed against any capital budgeting method. If financial markets are truly incomplete, there is, unless agents have common priors, no unanimity among stockholders about the price process in the economy. Thus, even in a competitive economy, where value maximization is the common goal of shareholders (see Hart, 1979), the capital budgeting decision is the outcome of a bargaining process among owners.

4   ALL'S WELL THAT ENDS WELL

I demonstrate that the apparent inconsistency between NPV and real-option analysis is due to a miscalculation of expected cash-flows. The main problem is ignoring the flexibility inherent to most production technologies. Equivalently, profit functions are erroneously assumed to be linear in future prices. The references from Fisher (1930) show that he was very much aware of the problems arising in multi-period settings or models with dynamic production sets.

The example in Section 3 shows that NPV, state pricing, and real-options approach lead to the same result if properly applied. From a theoretical point of view, there is neither the possibility nor the necessity of a method beyond NPV. For practical purposes, the real-options approach provides an alternative method of estimating the value of an investment project that is more or less convenient than other methods, ultimately depending on the circumstances.

ACKNOWLEDGEMENTS

*   Apologies to an English poet for the obvious.
    Thanks for comments to Kenneth Kotz, Laurence van Lent, Hellmuth Milde, Micah Officer, and Narinder Walia. Financial support from the John M. Olin Foundation is gratefully acknowledged. The usual disclaimer applies.

REFERENCES

Arrow, K.J. (1964), 'The role of securities in the optimal allocation of risk bearing', *Review of Economic Studies*, **31**, 91-96.

Breeden, D.T. (1979), 'An intertemporal asset pricing model with stochastic consumption and investment opportunities', *Journal of Financial Economics*, 7, 265-296

Cox, J.C., Ross, S.A. and Rubinstein, M. (1979), 'Option pricing: a simplified approach', *Journal of Financial Economics*, 7, 229-263.

Debreu, G. (1959), *The Theory of Value*, New York, J. Wiley and Sons.

Dixit, A.K. and Pindyck, R.S. (1994), *Investment under Uncertainty*, Princeton, NJ, Princeton University Press

Duffie, D. and Huang, C. (1985), 'Implementing Arrow-Debreu equilibria by continuous trading of few long-lived securities', *Econometrica*, **53**, 337-356.

Fama, E.F. and Miller, M.M. (1972), *The Theory of Finance*, Hinsdale, IL, Dryden Press.

Fisher, I. (1930), *The Theory of Interest*, New York, Macmillan.

Hart, O.D. (1979), 'On shareholder unanimity in large stock market economies, *Econometrica*, **47**, 1057-1083.

Hirshleifer, J. (1970), *Investment, Interest, and Capital*, Englewood Cliffs, NJ, Prentice Hall.

Loscalzo, W. (1982), *Cash Flow Forecasting*, New York, McGraw-Hill.

Markowitz, H. (1952), 'Portfolio Selection', *Journal of Finance*, **7**, 77-91.

Merton, R.C. (1973), 'An intertemporal capital asset pricing model', *Econometrica*, **41**, 867-887.

Quesnay, F. (1767), *Physiocratie: Discussions et developpemens sur quelques-unes des notions de l'economie politique*, Paris, Merlin.

Schwartz, E. S. (1994), 'Review on investment under uncertainty from Avinash Dixit and Robert Pindyck', *Journal of Finance*, **41**, 1924-1928.

Sharpe, W.F. (1964), 'Capital asset prices: a theory of market equilibrium under conditions of risk, *Journal of Finance*, **19**, 425-442.

Index

Entries in italics refer to the published works of Irving Fisher.